GW00597395

CIM

STUDY TEXT

PROFESSIONAL CERTIFICATE IN MARKETING

PAPER 1

MARKETING FUNDAMENTALS

In this July 2007 edition

- A **user-friendly format** for easy navigation
- Regular **fast forward** summaries emphasising the key points in each chapter
- Recent examples of marketing practice
- Fully revised for recent exams and developments
- A full **index**

FOR EXAMS IN DECEMBER 2007 AND JUNE 2008

BPP
LEARNING MEDIA

Seventh edition July 2007

ISBN 97807517 4167 4
(previous edition 0 7517 2697 4)

British Library Cataloguing-in-Publication Data
A catalogue record for this book
is available from the British Library

Published by:

BPP Learning Media
Aldine House, Aldine Place
London W12 8AA

www.bpp.com/learningmeadia

Printed in Great Britain by
WM Print
45-47 Frederick Street
Walsall
WS2 9NE

All our rights reserved. No part of this publication may
be reproduced, stored in a retrieval system or
transmitted, in any form or by any means, electronic,
mechanical, photocopying, recording or otherwise,
without the prior written permission of BPP Learning
Media.

We are grateful to the Chartered Institute of Marketing
for permission to reproduce in this text the syllabus,
tutor's guidance notes and past examination
questions. We are also grateful to Karen Beamish of
Stone Consulting for preparing the assignment based
assessment learning material, and to Claire Louise
Wright for help in preparing the text.

©
BPP Learning Media
2007

Contents

The BPP Study Text

Aims of this Study Text

To provide you with the knowledge and understanding, skills and application techniques that you need if you are to be successful in your exams

This Study Text has been written around the *Marketing Fundamentals* syllabus.

- It is **comprehensive**. It covers the syllabus content. No more, no less.
- It is targeted to the **exam**. We have taken account of the pilot paper, guidance the examiner has given and the assessment methodology.

To allow you to study in the way that best suits your learning style and the time you have available, by following your personal Study Plan (see below)

You may be studying at home on your own until the date of the exam, or you may be attending a full-time course. You may like to (and have time to) read every word, or you may prefer to (or only have time to) skim-read and devote the remainder of your time to question practice. Wherever you fall in the spectrum, you will find the BPP Study Text meets your needs in designing and following your personal study plan.

To tie in with the other components of the BPP Effective Study Package to ensure you have the best possible chance of passing the exam

BPP LEARNING MEDIA

Recommended period of use	Elements of the BPP Effective Study Package
3-12 months before exam	**Study Text** Acquisition of knowledge, understanding, skills and applied techniques
1-6 months before exam	**Practice & Revision Kit (9/2007)** Tutorial questions and helpful checklists of the key points lead you into each area. There are then numerous examination questions to try, graded by topic area, along with realistic suggested solutions prepared by marketing professionals in the light of the Examiner's Reports.
From three month before the exam until the last minute	**Passcards** Work through these short memorable notes which are focused on what is most likely to come up in the exam you will be sitting.

Settling down to study

By this stage in your career you may be a very experienced learner and taker of exams. But have you ever thought about *how* you learn? Let's have a quick look at the key elements required for effective learning. You can then identify your learning style and go on to design your own approach to how you are going to study this text – your personal study plan.

Key element of learning	Using the BPP Study Text
Motivation	You can rely on the comprehensiveness and technical quality of BPP. You've chosen the right Study Text – so you're in pole position to pass your exam!
Clear objectives and standards	Do you want to be a prizewinner or simply achieve a moderate pass? Decide.
Feedback	Follow through the examples in this text and do the Action Programme and the Quick Quizzes. Evaluate your efforts critically – how are you doing?
Study plan	You need to be honest about your progress to yourself – don't be over-confident, but don't be negative either. Create your Study Plan (see below) and try to stick to it. Focus on the short-term objectives – completing two chapters a night, say – but beware of losing sight of your study objectives.
Practice	Use the Quick Quizzes and Chapter Roundups to refresh your memory regularly after you have completed your initial study of each chapter.

These introductory pages let you see exactly what you are up against. However you study, you should:

- **Read through the syllabus** – this will help you to identify areas you have already covered, perhaps at a lower level of detail, and areas that are totally new to you.

- **Study the examination paper section**, where we show you the format of the exam (how many and what kind of questions etc).

Key study steps

The following steps are, in our experience, the ideal way to study for professional exams. You can of course adapt it for your particular learning style (see below).

Tackle the chapters in the order you find them in the Study Text. Taking into account your individual learning style, follow these key study steps for each chapter.

Key study steps	Activity
Step 1 **Chapter Topic List**	Study the topic list at the start of each chapter. Each numbered topic denotes a **numbered section** within the chapter.
Step 2 **Introduction**	Read through the introduction since it is designed to show you **why the topics in the chapter need to be studied** – how they lead on from previous topics, and how they lead into subsequent ones.
Step 3 **Explanations**	Proceed **methodically** through the chapter, reading each section thoroughly and making sure you understand.
Step 4 **Key Concepts**	**Key concepts** can often earn you **easy marks** if you state them clearly and correctly in an appropriate exam.
Step 5 **Exam Tips**	These give you a good idea of how the examiner tends to examine certain topics – pinpointing **easy marks** and highlighting **pitfalls**.
Step 6 **Note taking**	Take **brief notes** if you wish, whilst avoiding the temptation to copy out too much.
Step 7 **Marketing at Work**	Study each one, and try if you can to add flesh to them from your **own experience** – they are designed to show how the topics you are studying come alive (and often come unstuck) in the **real world**. You can also update yourself on these companies on to the internet.
Step 8 **Action Programme**	Make a very good attempt at all Action Programmes since these are designed to put your **knowledge into practice** in much the same way as you will be required to do in the exam. Check the answer at the end of the chapter in the **Action Programme Review**, and make sure you understand the reasons why yours may be different.
Step 9 **Chapter Roundup**	Check through it very carefully, to make sure you have grasped the **major points** it is highlighting.
Step 10 **Quick Quiz**	When you are happy that you have covered the chapter, use the **Quick Quiz** to check your recall of the topics covered. The answers are in the paragraphs in the chapter that we refer you to.
Step 11 **Illustrative Question(s)**	Either at this point, or later when you are thinking about revising, make a full attempt at the **Illustrative Questions**. You can find these at the end of the Study Text, along with the **Answers** so you can see how you did.

BPP
LEARNING MEDIA

Developing your personal study plan

Preparing a study plan (and sticking closely to it) is one of the key elements in learning success.

First you need to be aware of your style of learning. There are four typical learning styles. Consider yourself in the light of the following descriptions and work out which you fit most closely. You can then plan to follow the key study steps in the sequence suggested.

Learning styles	Characteristics	Sequence of key study steps in the BPP Study Text
Theorist	Seeks to understand principles before applying them in practice	1, 2, 3, 7, 4, 5, 8, 9, 10, 11 (6 continuous)
Reflector	Seeks to observe phenomena, thinks about them and then chooses to act	
Activist	Prefers to deal with practical, active problems; does not have much patience with theory	1, 2, 8 (read through), 7, 4, 5, 9, 3, 8 (full attempt), 10, 11 (6 continuous)
Pragmatist	Prefers to study only if a direct link to practical problems can be seen; not interested in theory for its own sake	8 (read through), 2, 4, 5, 7, 9, 1, 3, 8 (full attempt), 10, 11 (6 continuous)

Next you should complete the following checklist.

Am I motivated? (a) ☐

Do I have an objective and a standard that I want to achieve? (b) ☐

Am I a theorist, a reflector, an activist or a pragmatist? (c) ☐

How much time do I have available per week, given: (d) ☐

- The standard I have set myself

- The time I need to set aside later for work on the Practice and Revision Kit

- The other exam(s) I am sitting, and (of course)

- Practical matters such as work, travel, exercise, sleep and social life?

Now:

- Take the time you have available per week for this Study Text (d), and multiply it by the number of weeks available to give (e)   (e) ☐

- Divide (e) by the number of chapters to give (f)   (f) ☐

- Set about studying each chapter in the time represented by (f), following the key study steps in the order suggested by your particular learning style

This is your personal **study plan**.

Short of time?

Whatever your objectives, standards or style, you may find you simply do not have the time available to follow all the key study steps for each chapter, however you adapt them for your particular learning style. If this is the case, follow the skim study technique below (the icons in the Study Text will help you to do this).

Skim study technique

Study the chapters in the order you find them in the Study Text. For each chapter, follow the key study steps 1–2, and then skim-read through step 3. Jump to step 9, and then go back to steps 4–5. Follow through step 7, and prepare outline Answers to the Action Programme (step 8). Try the Quick Quiz (step 10), following up any items you can't answer, then do a plan for the illustrative question (step 11), comparing it against our answers. You should probably still follow step 6 (note-taking).

Moving on...

However you study, when you are ready to embark on the practice and revision phase of the BPP Effective Study Package, you should still refer back to this Study Text:

- As a source of **reference** (you should find the list of Key Concepts and the Index particularly helpful for this)

- As a **refresher** (the Chapter Roundups and Quick Quizzes help you here)

A note on pronouns

On occasions in this Study Text, 'he' is used for 'he or she', 'him' for 'him or her' and so forth. Whilst we try to avoid this practice it is sometimes necessary for reasons of style. No prejudice or stereotyping accounting to sex is intended or assumed.

BPP
LEARNING MEDIA

Syllabus

Aims and objectives

The *Marketing Fundamentals* module develops a basic knowledge and understanding of marketing, marketing process and the marketing mix. It aims to provide participants with a framework on which to build marketing knowledge and skills through the modules of this stage, through modules at later stages and in the workplace.

Participants will not be expected to have any prior knowledge or experience in a marketing role.

Learning outcomes

Participants will be able to:

- Explain the development of marketing and the ways it can benefit business and organisations.

- Identify the main steps in, and barriers to, achieving a marketing orientation within the organisation.

- Explain the context of, and process for, marketing planning and budgeting including related models.

- Explain the concept of segmentation and the different bases for effective market segmentation.

- Identify and describe the individual elements and tools of the marketing mix.

- Identify the basic differences in application of the marketing mix involved in marketing products and services within different marketing contexts.

Knowledge and skill requirements

Element 1: The development of marketing and market orientation (10%)	
1.1	Explain the development of marketing as an exchange process, a philosophy of business, and a managerial function.
1.2	Recognise the contribution of marketing as a means of creating customer value and as a form of competition.
1.3	Appreciate the importance of a market orientation to organisational performance and identify the factors that promote and impede the adoption of a market orientation.
1.4	Explain the role of marketing in co-ordinating organisational resources both within and outside the marketing function.
1.5	Describe the impacts of marketing actions on society and the need for marketers to act in an ethical and socially responsible manner.
1.6	Examine the significance of buyer-seller relationships in marketing and comprehend the role of relationship marketing in facilitating the retention of customers.

Element 2: Marketing planning and budgeting (20%)	
2.1	Explain the importance of the marketing planning process and where it fits into the corporate or organisational planning framework.
2.2	Explain the models that describe the various stages of the marketing planning process.
2.3	Explain the concept of the marketing audit as an appraisal of the external marketing environment and an organisation's internal marketing operations.
2.4	Describe the role of various analytical tools in the marketing auditing process.
2.5	Explain the value of marketing research and information in developing marketing plans.
2.6	Explain the importance of objectives and the influences on, and processes for setting, objectives.
2.7	Explain the concept of market segmentation and distinguish effective bases for segmenting consumer and business-to-business markets.
2.8	Describe the structure of an outline marketing plan and identify its various components.
2.9	Depict the various management structures available for implementing marketing plans, and understand their advantages and disadvantages.
2.10	Examine the factors that affect the setting of marketing budgets.
2.11	Demonstrate an appreciation of the need to monitor and control marketing activities.

BPP
LEARNING MEDIA

Element 3: The marketing mix and related tools (50%)	
3.1	Describe the essential elements of targeting and positioning, and the creation of an integrated and coherent marketing mix.
3.2	Describe the wide range of tools and techniques available to marketers to satisfy customer requirements and compete effectively.
3.3	Explain the development of the extended marketing mix concept to include additional components in appropriate contextual settings: product, price, place (distribution), promotion (communications), people, processes, physical evidence and customer service.
3.4	Demonstrate awareness of products as bundles of benefits that deliver customer value and have different characteristics, features and levels.
3.5	Explain and illustrate the product life cycle concept and recognise its effects on marketing mix decisions.
3.6	Explain and illustrate the principles of product policy: branding, product lines, packaging and service support.
3.7	Explain the importance of introducing new products, and describe the processes involved in their development and launch.
3.8	Explore the range of internal and external factors that influence pricing decisions.
3.9	Identify and illustrate a range of different pricing policies and tactics that are adopted by organisations as effective means of competition.
3.10	Define channels of distribution, intermediaries and logistics, and understand the contribution they make to the marketing effort.
3.11	State and explain the factors that influence channel decisions and the selection of alternative distribution channel options, including the effects of new information and communications technology.
3.12	Describe the extensive range of tools that comprise the marketing communications mix, and examine the factors that contribute to its development and implementation.
3.13	Explain the importance of people in marketing and in particular the contribution of staff to effective service delivery.
3.14	Explain the importance of service in satisfying customer requirements and identify the factors that contribute to the delivery of service quality.
3.15	Examine the effects of information and communication technology on the development and implementation of the marketing mix.
3.16	Explain the importance of measuring the effectiveness of the selected marketing effort and instituting appropriate changes where necessary.

Element 4: Marketing in context (20%)	
4.1	Explain the importance of contextual setting in influencing the selection of and emphasis given to marketing mix tools.
4.2	Explain differences in the characteristics of various types of marketing context: FMCG, business-to-business (supply chain), large or capital project-based, services, voluntary and not-for-profit, sales support (e.g. SMEs), and their impact on marketing mix decisions.
4.3	Compare and contrast the marketing activities of organisations that operate and compete in different contextual settings.
4.4	Explain the global dimension in affecting the nature of marketing undertaken by organisations in an international environmental context.
4.5	Explain the existing and potential impacts of the virtual marketplace on the pattern of marketing activities in given contexts.

Related skills for marketers

There is only so much that a syllabus can include. The syllabus itself is designed to cover the knowledge and skills highlighted by research as core to professional marketers in organisations. However, marketing is performed in an organisational context so there are other broader business and organisational skills that marketing professionals should also posses. The 'key skills for marketers' are therefore an essential part of armoury of the 'complete marketer' in today's organisations. They have been identified from research carried out in organisations where marketers are working.

'Key skills for marketers' are areas of knowledge and competency common to business professionals. They fall outside the CIM's syllabus, providing underpinning knowledge and skills. As such they will be treated as systemic to all marketing activities, rather than subjects treated independently in their turn. While it is not intended that the key skills are formally taught as part of programmes, it is expected that tutors will encourage participants to demonstrate the application of relevant key skills through activities, assignments and discussions during learning.

Using ICT and the Internet

Planning and using different sources to search for and select information; explore, develop and exchange information and derive new information; and present information including text, numbers and images.

Using financial information and metrics

Planning and interpreting information from different sources; carrying out calculations; and presenting and justifying findings.

Presenting information

Contributing to discussions; making a presentation; reading and synthesising information and writing different types of document.

Improving own learning and performance

Agreeing targets and planning how these will be met; using plans to meet targets; and reviewing progress.

BPP
LEARNING MEDIA

Working with others

Planning work and agreeing objectives, responsibilities and working arrangements; seeking to establish and maintain co-operative working relationships; and reviewing work and agreeing ways of future collaborative work.

Problem solving

Exploring problems, comparing different ways of solving them and selecting options; planning and implementing options; and applying agreed methods for checking problems have been solved.

Applying business law

Identifying, applying and checking compliance with relevant law when undertaking marketing activities.

Assessment

CIM will normally offer two forms of assessment for this module from which centres or participants may choose: written examination and continuous assessment. CIM may also recognise, or make joint awards for, modules at an equivalent level undertaken with other professional marketing bodies and educational institutions.

Marketing journals

In addition to reading core and supplementary textbooks participants will be expected to acquire a knowledge and understanding of developments in contemporary marketing theory, practice and issues. The most appropriate sources of information for this include specialist magazines eg *Marketing*, *Marketing Week*, *Campaign and Revolution*; dedicated CIM publications eg *Marketing Business*; and business magazines and newspapers eg *The Economist*, *Management Today*, *Business Week*, *The Financial Times*, and the business pages and supplements of the quality press. A flavour of developments in academic marketing can be derived from the key marketing journals including:

Admap
European Journal of Marketing
Journal of the Academy of Marketing Science
Journal of Consumer Behaviour: An International Research Review
Journal of Consumer Research
Marketing Intelligence and Planning
Journal of Marketing
Journal of Marketing Management

Websites

The Chartered Institute of Marketing

www.cim.co.uk	CIM website with information and access to learning support for participants.
www.cim.co.uk/learningzone	Direct access to information and support materials for all levels of CIM qualification
www.cim.co.uk/tutors	Access for tutors
www.shapetheagenda.com	Quarterly agenda paper from CIM

Publications online

www.ft.com	Extensive research resources across all industry sectors, with links to more specialist reports. (Charges may apply)
www.thetimes.co.uk	One of the best online versions of a quality newspaper.
www.economist.com	Useful links, and easily-searched archives of articles from back issues of the magazine.
www.mad.co.uk	Marketing Week magazine online.
www.brandrepublic.com	Marketing magazine online.
www.westburn.co.uk	Journal of Marketing Management online, the official Journal of the Academy of Marketing and Marketing Review.
http://smr.mit.edu/smr/	Free abstracts from Sloan Management Review articles
www.hbsp.harvard.edu	Free abstracts from Harvard Business Review articles
www.ecommercetimes.com	Daily enews on the latest ebusiness developments
www.cim.co.uk/knowledgehub	3000 full text journals titles are available to members via the Knowledge Hub – includes the range of titles above - embargoes may apply.
www.cim.co.uk/cuttingedge	Weekly round up of marketing news (available to CIM members) plus list of awards and forthcoming marketing events.

Sources of useful information

www.1to1.com	The Peppers and Rogers One-to-One Marketing site which contains useful information about the tools and techniques of relationship marketing
www.balancetime.com	The Productivity Institute provides free articles, a time management email newsletter, and other resources to improve personal productivity
www.bbc.co.uk	The Learning Zone at BBC Education contains extensive educational resources, including the video, CD Rom, ability to watch TV programmes such as the News online, at your convenience, after they have been screened
www.busreslab.com	Useful specimen online questionnaires to measure customer satisfaction levels and tips on effective Internet marketing research
www.lifelonglearning.co.uk	Encourages and promotes Lifelong Learning through press releases, free articles, useful links and progress reports on the development of the University for Industry (UFI)
www.marketresearch.org.uk	The Market Research Society. Contains useful material on the nature of research, choosing an agency, ethical standards and codes of conduct for research practice
www.nielsen-netratings.com	Details the current levels of banner advertising activity, including the creative content of the ten most popular banners each week (within Top Rankings area)
www.open.ac.uk	Some good Open University videos available for a broad range of subjects
www.direct.gov.uk	Gateway to a wide range of UK government information

BPP LEARNING MEDIA

www.srg.co.uk	The Self Renewal Group – provides useful tips on managing your time, leading others, managing human resources, motivating others etc
www.statistics.gov.uk	Detailed information on a variety of consumer demographics from the Government Statistics Office
www.durlacher.com	The latest research on business use of the Internet, often with extensive free reports
www.cyberatlas.com	Regular updates on the latest Internet developments from a business perspective
http://ecommerce.vanderbilt.edu	eLab is a corporate sponsored research centre at the Owen Graduate School of Management, Vanderbilt University
www.kpmg.co.uk	The major consultancy company websites contain useful research
www.ey.com/uk	reports, often free of charge
www.pwcglobal.com	Pricewaterhouse Coopers
http://web.mit.edu	Massachusetts Institute of Technology site has extensive research resources
www.adassoc.org.uk	Advertising Association
www.dma.org.uk	The Direct Marketing Association
www.theidm.co.uk	Institute of Direct Marketing
www.export.org.uk	Institute of Export
www.bl.uk	The British Library, with one of the most extensive book collections in the world
www.managers.org.uk	Chartered Management Institute
www.cipd.co.uk	Chartered Institute of Personnel and Development
www.emerald-library.com	Article abstracts on a range of business topics (fees apply)
www.w3.org	An organisation responsible for defining worldwide standards for the Internet

Case studies

www.1800flowers.com	Flower and gift delivery service that allows customers to specify key dates when they request the firm to send them a reminder, together with an invitation to send a gift
www.amazon.co.uk	Classic example of how Internet technology can be harnessed to provide innovative customer service
www.broadvision.com	Broadvision specialises in customer 'personalisation' software. The site contains many useful case studies showing how communicating through the Internet allow you to find out more about your customers
www.doubleclick.net	DoubleClick offers advertisers the ability to target their advertisements on the web through sourcing of specific interest groups, ad display only at certain times of the day, or at particular geographic locations, or on certain types of hardware
www.facetime.com	Good example of a site that overcomes the impersonal nature of the Internet by allowing the establishment of real time links with a customer service representative
www.hotcoupons.com	Site visitors can key in their postcode to receive local promotions, and advertisers can post their offers on the site using a specially designed software package
www.superbrands.org	Access to case studies on international brands

The Exam Paper

Format of the paper

Number of marks

Part A: A case study or scenario
Compulsory multi-part question relating to the case study   40
(Answer generally required in report format)

Part B: Three questions from a choice of six (20 marks each)   60
(Answer generally required in essay or report format)
_____
100

Analysis of past papers

The analysis below shows the topics which have been examined since the new syllabus was introduced.

December 2006

Part A (compulsory question worth 40 marks)

1   Gillette is a global market leader in personal grooming, alkaline batteries and oral care brands, due in part to strong new product development.

(a)   Importance of introducing new products
(b)   Stages in developing and launching new products
(c)   New core business, deliver customer value and business success

Part B (three questions, 20 marks each)

2   Marketing communications tools and how selected (B2B market)

3   Principles of segmentation, targeting and positioning; methods of segmentation (TV/audio manufacturer)

4   Channels of distribution; relationships with buyers/suppliers (mobile telecom)

5   Impacts of marketing; influences in international market (food processing)

6   Influences on marketing objectives; use of Ansoff matrix (computer hardware)

7   Extended (7Ps) marketing mix; use of ICT (consumer services)

What the examiner said

- The best answers tended to display a good understanding of marketing frameworks, concepts and models initially by *illustrating* the relevant theoretical point and subsequently by *applying* it using examples from the relevant contextual situation.

- Any models or diagrams must be accurately presented, labelled and cited.

- Application to a given situation or industry helps to explain what, how and why particular types of marketing activity should be undertaken. Candidates must use relevant illustrative examples wherever possible, even if not specifically asked to do so.

- The use of underlined headings, bullet points with explanation, and well-organised structures gives the examiner confidence in the candidate's answer.

- Key weaknesses included failure to identify exactly what the question asked for; failure to link parts (a) and (b) of a question where relevant; and including everything known on a topic, regardless of specific question requirements.

Specific comments are highlighted in the Exam Tips, throughout the Text.

June 2006

Part A (compulsory question worth 40 marks)

1   The Hong Kong and Shanghai Banking Corporation (HSBC) is a leading global financial services brand.

   (a)   Principle of branding and how used by HSBC
   (b)   Five characteristics of services as applied to HSBC
   (c)   Role of people and ICT in meeting customer requirements
   (d)   Five corporate social responsibility issues for HSBC

Part B (three questions, 20 marks each)

2   Structure and content of marketing plan; monitoring/controlling products (fashion clothing) [Briefing paper format]

3   Marketing communication tools; factors in choice (processed foods) [Presentation notes format]

4   Advantages of marketing orientation; factors in marketing budget (government health agency) [Report format]

5   Use of relationship marketing; pricing factors (B2B) [Briefing paper format]

6   Product as 'bundle of benefits'; role of packaging (consumer product format) [Presentation notes format]

7   Use of PLC in marketing audit; marketing mix changes through PLC (digital cameras) [Report format]

What the examiner said

The examiner's comments were identical to those given for the December 2006 sitting, other than for details on specific questions, which will be highlighted in Exam Tips throughout the Text.

December 2005

Part A (compulsory question worth 40 marks)

1   Samsung Electronics has built up a leading market position through new product development, premium pricing and brand communication.

   (a)   Internal/external factors in pricing decisions
   (b)   Stages of new product development (mobile phone)
   (c)   Building relationships with customers

Part B (three questions, 20 marks each)

2   External environment factors (international fast food); how affects mix decisions

3   Benefits of marketing to business organisations, consumers, society, ethical and social responsibility issues

4   Concept and benefits of market segmentation (global automobile manufacturer); criteria for segmentation. [Report format]

5   Promotion mix for customer communication in B2B computer hardware market; how effectiveness of tools can be measured

6   Contribution of people and ICT to customer satisfaction (financial services). Factors in setting marketing objectives. [Report format]

7   Concept of brand (fashion industry); how 4Ps used for brand positioning.

What the examiner said

- Students who have acquired *knowledge* of essential marketing concepts and are able to *explain* them in the *context* of a given situation, or by using other *illustrative* material, have a good chance of passing.

- There is always going to be some effect of examination technique and time management on how students perform. Candidates should give themselves the best chance of doing well by practising past questions and planning answers.

- The best answers make use of practical examples to illustrate how a theoretical point applies in the given situation or a particular industry.

- Candidates *must* comply with the specific requirements of the question – not just write about the main 'subject' of the question, or everything that is known on the topic.

Specific comments are highlighted in the Exam Tips, throughout the Text.

June 2005

Part A (compulsory question worth 40 marks)

1   Levi Strauss, global clothing marketer, is considering launching an extension to its portfolio: men-only retail stores.

(a)   Branding, and how it can be used to develop the new business
(b)   Concept of market segmentation
(c)   Ways of segmenting new retail market
(d)   Components of a marketing plan for the new store.

Part B (three questions, 20 marks each)

2   Channels of distribution (international computer hardware). Factors in channel selection in new international market

3   Market orientation for a charity. Stakeholder communication techniques

4   Characteristics of services, and how they affect extended (7P) marketing mix

5   Product life cycle (TV and Hi-fi) and how affects marketing mix decisions

6   Relationship marketing (consumer services market); role of ICT in building customer relationships

7   Factors in price-setting decisions (household cleaning products). How price could support brand positioning.

What the examiner said

- Good candidates do not just recall information, but focus on demonstrating that they are able to explain exactly what the question requires – avoiding using up precious time in the exam, reproducing material that does not gain marks.

- The examiner appreciates well presented, structured and formatted answers. 'The use of underlining or headings, bullet points (with explanations), and clear structures based on the requirements of the tasks is advisable.'

- There is often a link between parts (a) and (b) within questions: the same context/format requirements must be applied to both, unless otherwise stated.

- Candidates should try to demonstrate knowledge and understanding by including illustrative examples, *particularly* when the question specifically requests this! Examples must be relevant and appropriate to the context.

Specific comments will be highlighted in Exam Tips throughout the Text.

December 2004

Part A (compulsory question worth 40 marks)

1   An international engineering, logistics and industrial equipment company has diversified its product portfolio and is considering moving into children's games.

    (a)   Use of branding to develop the business
    (b)   Outline marketing plan for new board game
    (c)   Use of marketing mix to support the product

Part B (three questions, 20 marks each)

2   Unique characteristics of services affecting marketing. Role of people in providing customer value

3   Benefits of marketing to business organisations, consumers, society. Ethical and social responsibility issues

4   Importance of new products to household cleaning products manufacturer. Stages of new product development process

5   Promotional tools in FMCG market. Factors influencing choice of tools

6   Environmental factors in international soft drinks marketing. Effects on marketing mix

7   Importance of relationship marketing in consumer services. Role of ICT in maintaining long-term relationships.

June 2004

Part A (compulsory question worth 40 marks)

1   An international food company has introduced a new brand of cheese, which has had a short product life cycle, and is vulnerable to price pressure.

    (a)   Market orientation and its importance
    (b)   Adapting marketing mix for decline stage of product life cycle
    (c)   Suggest consumer research methods to explore brand's lack of success

Part B (three questions, 20 marks each)

2   Segmentation, targeting and positioning. Evaluating commercial attractiveness of a market segment

3   SWOT and Ansoff. Uses in marketing planning

4   Marketing planning process. Marketing audit as appraisal of external environment

5   Use of technology in marketing communications. Different tools for B2B and B2C product launch

6   Selecting a market channel for a new FMCG. Advantages/disadvantages of Internet as direct channel

7   Approaching pricing decisions for a car manufacturer. Impact of Internet on price decisions.

December 2003

Part A (compulsory question worth 40 marks)

1   Strongly branded manufacturer of equipment used in the construction industry is planning to move into consumer markets (eg children's toys, heavy duty footwear).

   (a)   Branding
   (b)   Components of marketing plan for children's game
   (c)   Marketing mix and children's games

Part B (three questions, 20 marks each)

2   Services; importance of people

3   Benefits of marketing; social responsibility

4   Importance of new products and stages of development

5   Communication tools for FMCG markets

6   Marketing consumer product internationally

7   Relationship marketing and information and communications technologies

June 2003

Part A (compulsory question worth 40 marks)

1   Dairy company launches new brand of cheese.

(a)   Concept of marketing orientation
(b)   Product life cycle
(c)   Market research methods

Part B (three questions, 20 marks each)

2   Segmentation; targeting; positioning. Evaluating market attractiveness

3   SWOT and Ansoff matrices

4   (a)   Services and relationship marketing and customer care
    (b)   Marketing planning process

5   Communication tools and technology

6   Marketing channels

7   Pricing policies

December 2002

Part A (compulsory question worth 40 marks)

1   World's largest producer of ready-to-eat cereal is developing products for the cereal bar market, including a new 'lifestyle' cereal bar with reduced sugar and fat content.

     (a)   Explain the stages of a marketing plan for this new product, including the marketing audit

     (b)   Adaptation of each element of the marketing mix for the new product; application of the product life cycle for decisions in the introduction and growth stages.

Part B (three questions, 20 marks each)

2   Contribution of accountants and economists to the pricing decision for an Internet company, and the contrast with the marketer's approach

3   Characteristics of services, the resulting problems for marketers, and the steps to take to ensure good customer care and service

4   Use of technology in marketing communications campaigns. Promotions/communications mix to communicate an international sporting event.

5   Marketing research plan for a college. Benefits and limitations of using qualitative data collection techniques.

6   Adding value through customer service, and how it can be used to develop relationships and retain customers in the banking sector

7   New product development process for a new service

Specimen paper

Part A (compulsory question worth 40 marks)

1   Battery firm is launching a new range of rechargeable batteries.

     (a)   Segmentation and its advantages

     (b)   New product development stages

     (c)   Marketing mix for consumer and business market launch

Part B (three questions, 20 marks each)

2   Distribution channels for clothing manufacture. Factors in selection and evaluation

3   Extended marketing mix for services. Role of ICT in adding value for customers

4   Advantages of both consumers and businesses for a car manufacturer. Issues in ethical and socially responsible marketing

5   Outline marketing plan for a Hi-fi manufacturer. Factors in setting budget

6   Marketing mix at different life cycle stages (software market). Internal and external factors in pricing decisions

7   Branding, relationship marketing and customer retention in financial services market.

Guide to the assignment route

- Aims and objectives of this guide
- Introduction
- Assignment route, structure and process
- Preparing for assignments: general guide
- Presentation
- Time management
- Tips for writing assignments
- Writing reports
- Resources to support assignment based assessment

Aims and objectives of this guide to the assignment route

- To understand the scope and structure of the route process
- To consider the benefits of learning through the assignment route
- To assist students in preparation of their assignments
- To consider the range of communication options available to students
- To look at the range of potential assignment areas that assignments may challenge
- To examine the purpose and benefits of reflective practice
- To assist with time-management within the assignment process

Introduction

At time of writing, there are over 80 CIM Approved Study Centres that offer the assignment route option as an alternative to examinations. This change in direction and flexibility in assessment was externally driven by industry, students and tutors alike, all of whom wanted a test of practical skills as well as a knowledge-based approach to learning.

At Stage 1, all modules are available via this assignment route. The assignment route is however optional, and examinations are still available. This will of course depend upon the nature of delivery within your chosen Study Centre.

Clearly, all of the Stage 1 subject areas lend themselves to assignment-based learning, due to their practical nature. The assignments that you will undertake provide you with an opportunity to be **creative in approach and in presentation.** They enable you to give a true demonstration of your marketing ability in a way that perhaps might be inhibited in a traditional examination situation.

The assignment route offers you considerable scope to produce work that provides existing and future **employers** with **evidence** of your **ability.** It offers you a **portfolio** of evidence which demonstrates your abilities and your willingness to develop continually your knowledge and skills. It will also, ultimately, help you frame your continuing professional development in the future.

It does not matter what type of organisation you are from, large or small, as you will find substantial benefit in this approach to learning. In some cases, students have made their own organisation central to their assessment and produced work to support their organisation's activities, resulting in subsequent recognition and promotion: a success story for this approach.

So, using your own organisation can be beneficial (especially if your employer sponsors you). However, it is equally valid to use a different organisation, as long as you are familiar enough with it to base your assignments on it. This is particularly useful if you are between jobs, taking time out, returning to employment or studying at university or college.

To take the assignment route option, you are required to register with a CIM Accredited Study Centre (ie a college, university, or distance learning provider). **Currently you would be unable to take the assignment route option as an independent learner**. If in doubt you should contact the CIM Education Division, the awarding body, who will provide you with a list of local Accredited Centres offering the Assignment Route.

Structure and process

The **assignments** that you will undertake during your studies are normally set **by CIM centrally** and not usually by the study centre. All assignments are validated to ensure a structured, consistent, approach. This standardised approach to assessment enables external organisations to interpret the results on a consistent basis.

Each module at Stage 1 has one assignment, with four separate elements within it. This is broken down as follows.

- The **Core Section** is compulsory and worth 40% of your total mark.

- The **Elective Section** has four options, from which you must complete **two**. Each of these options is worth 25% of your total mark. Please note here that it is likely that in some Study Centres the option may be chosen for you. This is common practice and is done in order to maximise resources and support provided to students.

- The **Reflective Statement** is also compulsory. It is worth 10%. It should reflect what you feel about your learning experience during the module and how that learning has helped you in your career both now and in the future.

The purpose of each assignment is to enable you to demonstrate your ability to research, analyse and problem-solve in a range of different situations. You will be expected to approach your assignment work from a professional marketer's perspective, addressing the assignment brief directly, and undertaking the tasks required. Each assignment will relate directly to the syllabus module and will be applied against the content of the syllabus.

All of the assignments clearly indicate the links with the syllabus and the assignment weighting (ie the contribution each assignment makes to your overall marks).

Once your assignments have been completed, they will be marked by your accredited centre, and then **moderated** by a CIM External Moderator. When all the assignments have been marked, they are sent to CIM for further moderation. After this, all marks are forwarded to you by CIM (not your centre) in the form of an examination result. Your **centre** will be able to you provide you with some written feedback on overall performance, but **will not** provide you with any detailed mark breakdown.

Preparing for assignments: general guide

The whole purpose of this guide is to assist you in presenting your assessment professionally, both in terms of presentation skills and overall content. In many of the assignments, marks are awarded for presentation and coherence. It might therefore be helpful to consider how best to present your assignment. Here you should consider issues of detail, protocol and the range of communications that could be called upon within the assignment.

Presentation of the assignment

You should always ensure that you prepare two copies of your assignment, keeping a soft copy on disc. On occasions assignments go missing, or second copies are required by CIM.

- Each assignment should be clearly marked up with your name, your study centre, your CIM Student registration number and ultimately at the end of the assignment a word count. The assignment should also be word-processed.

- The assignment presentation format should directly meet the requirements of the assignment brief, (ie reports and presentations are the most called for communication formats). You **must** ensure that you assignment does not appear to be an extended essay. If it does, you will lose marks.

- The word limit will be included in the assignment brief. These are specified by CIM and must be adhered to.

- Appendices should clearly link to the assignment and can be attached as supporting documentation at the end of the report. However failure to reference them by number (eg Appendix 1) within the report and also marked up on the Appendix itself will lose you marks. Only use an Appendix if it is essential and clearly adds value to the overall assignment. The Appendix is not a waste bin for all the materials you have come across in your research, or a way of making your assignment seem somewhat heavier and more impressive than it is.

Time management for assignments

One of the biggest challenges we all seem to face day-to-day is that of managing time. When studying, that challenge seems to grow increasingly difficult, requiring a balance between work, home, family, social life and study life. It is therefore of pivotal importance to your own success for you to plan wisely the limited amount of time you have available.

Step 1   Find out how much time you have

Ensure that you are fully aware of how long your module lasts, and the final deadline. If you are studying a module from September to December, it is likely that you will have only 10-12 weeks in which to complete your assignments. This means that you will be preparing assignment work continuously throughout the course.

Step 2   Plan your time

Essentially you need to **work backwards** from the final deadline, submission date, and schedule your work around the possible time lines. Clearly if you have only 10-12 weeks available to complete three assignments, you will need to allocate a block of hours in the final stages of the module to ensure that all of your assignments are in on time. This will be critical as all assignments will be sent to CIM by a set day. Late submissions will not be accepted and no extensions will be awarded. Students who do not submit will be treated as a 'no show' and will have to resubmit for the next period and undertake an alternative assignment.

Step 3   Set priorities

You should set priorities on a daily and weekly basis (not just for study, but for your life). There is no doubt that this mode of study needs commitment (and some sacrifices in the short term). When your achievements are recognised by colleagues, peers, friends and family, it will all feel worthwhile.

BPP
LEARNING MEDIA

Step 4   **Analyse activities and allocate time to them**

Consider the **range** of activities that you will need to undertake in order to complete the assignment and the **time** each might take. Remember, too, there will be a delay in asking for information and receiving it.

- Preparing terms of reference for the assignment, to include the following.

    1   A short title

    2   A brief outline of the assignment purpose and outcome

    3   Methodology – what methods you intend to use to carry out the required tasks

    4   Indication of any difficulties that have arisen in the duration of the assignment

    5   Time schedule

    6   Confidentiality – if the assignment includes confidential information ensure that this is clearly marked up and indicated on the assignment

    7   Literature and desk research undertaken

This should be achieved in one side of A4 paper.

- A literature search in order to undertake the necessary background reading and underpinning information that might support your assignment

- Writing letters and memos asking for information either internally or externally

- Designing questionnaires

- Undertaking surveys

- Analysis of data from questionnaires

- Secondary data search

- Preparation of first draft report

Always build in time to spare, to deal with the unexpected. This may reduce the pressure that you are faced with in meeting significant deadlines.

Warning!

The same principles apply to a student with 30 weeks to do the work. However, a word of warning is needed. Do not fall into the trap of leaving all of your work to the last minute. If you miss out important information or fail to reflect upon your work adequately or successfully you will be penalised for both. Therefore, time management is important whatever the duration of the course.

Tips for writing assignments

Everybody has a personal style, flair and tone when it comes to writing. However, no matter what your approach, you must ensure your assignment meets the **requirements of the brief** and so is comprehensible, coherent and cohesive in approach.

Think of preparing an assignment as preparing for an examination. Ultimately, the work you are undertaking results in an examination grade. Successful achievement of all four modules in a level results in a qualification.

There are a number of positive steps that you can undertake in order to ensure that you make the best of your assignment presentation in order to maximise the marks available.

Step 1   Work to the brief

Ensure that you identify exactly what the assignment asks you to do.

- If it asks you to be a marketing manager, then immediately assume that role.

- If it asks you to prepare a report, then present a report, not an essay or a letter.

- Furthermore, if it asks for 2,500 words, then do not present 1,000 or 4,000 unless it is clearly justified, agreed with your tutor and a valid piece of work.

Identify whether the report should be **formal or informal**; who it should be **addressed to**; its **overall purpose** and its **potential use** and outcome. Understanding this will ensure that your assignment meets fully the requirements of the brief and addresses the key issues included within it.

Step 2   Addressing the tasks

It is of pivotal importance that you address **each** of the tasks within the assignment. **Many students fail to do this** and often overlook one of the tasks or indeed part of the tasks.

Many of the assignments will have two or three tasks, some will have even more. You should establish quite early on, which of the tasks:

- Require you to collect information
- Provides you with the framework of the assignment, i.e. the communication method.

Possible tasks will include the following.

- *Compare and contrast.* Take two different organisations and compare them side by side and consider the differences ie the **contrasts** between the two.

- *Carry out primary or secondary research.* Collect information to support your assignment and your subsequent decisions

- *Prepare a plan.* Some assignments will ask you to prepare a plan for an event or for a marketing activity – if so provide a step-by-step approach, a rationale, a time-line, make sure it is measurable and achievable. Make sure your actions are very specific and clearly explained. (Make sure your plan is SMART.)

- *Analyse a situation.* This will require you to collect information, consider its content and present an overall understanding of the situation as it exists. This might include looking at internal and external factors and how the current situation evolved.

- *Make recommendations.* The more advanced your get in your studies, the more likely it is that you will be required to make recommendations. Firstly **considering and evaluating your options** and then making justifiable **recommendations**, based on them.

- *Justify decisions.* You may be required to justify your decision or recommendations. This will require you to explain fully how you have arrived at as a result and to show why, supported by relevant information. In other words, you should not make decisions in a vacuum; as a marketer your decisions should always be informed by context.

- *Prepare a presentation.* This speaks for itself. If you are required to prepare a presentation, ensure that you do so, preparing clearly defined PowerPoint or

BPP LEARNING MEDIA

overhead slides that are not too crowded and that clearly express the points you are required to make.

- *Evaluate performance*. It is very likely that you will be asked to evaluate a campaign, a plan or even an event. You will therefore need to consider its strengths and weaknesses, why it succeeded or failed, the issues that have affected it, what can you learn from it and, importantly, how can you improve performance or sustain it in the future.

All of these points are likely requests included within a task. Ensure that you identify them clearly and address them as required.

Step 3   Information search

Many students fail to realise the importance of collecting information to **support** and **underpin** their assignment work. However, it is vital that you demonstrate to your centre and to the CIM your ability to **establish information needs**, obtain **relevant information** and **utilise it sensibly** in order to arrive at appropriate decisions.

You should establish the nature of the information required, follow up possible sources, time involved in obtaining the information, gaps in information and the need for information.

Consider these factors very carefully. CIM are very keen that students are **seen** to collect information, **expand** their mind and consider the **breadth** and **depth** of the situation. In your *Personal Development Portfolio*, you have the opportunity to complete a **Resource Log**, to illustrate how you have expanded your knowledge to aid your personal development. You can record your additional reading and research in that log, and show how it has helped you with your portfolio and assignment work.

Step 4   Develop an assignment plan

Your **assignment** needs to be structured and coherent, addressing the brief and presenting the facts as required by the tasks. The only way you can successfully achieve this is by **planning the structure** of your assignment in advance.

Earlier on in this unit, we looked at identifying your tasks and, working backwards from the release date, in order to manage time successfully. The structure and coherence of your assignment needs to be planned with similar signs.

In planning out the assignment, you should plan to include **all the relevant information as requested** and also you should plan for the use of models, diagrams and appendices where necessary.

Your plan should cover your:

- Introduction
- Content
- Main body of the assignment
- Summary
- Conclusions and recommendations where appropriate

Step 5   Prepare draft assignment

It is good practice to always produce a **first draft** of a report. You should use it to ensure that you have met the aims and objectives, assignment brief and tasks related to the actual assignment. A draft document provides you with scope for improvements, and enables you to check for accuracy, spelling, punctuation and use of English.

Step 6   Prepare final document

In the section headed 'Presentation of the Assignment' in this unit, there are a number of components that should always be in place at the beginning of the assignment documentation, including **labelling** of the assignment, **word counts**, **appendices** numbering and presentation method. Ensure that you **adhere to the guidelines presented**, or alternatively those suggested by your Study Centre.

Writing reports

Students often ask 'what do they mean by a report?' or 'what should the report format include?'.

There are a number of approaches to reports, formal or informal: some report formats are company specific and designed for internal use, rather than external reporting.

For continuous assessment process, you should stay with traditional formats.

Below is a suggested layout of a Management Report Document that might assist you when presenting your assignments. (Further guidance is given in Chapter 12 of this Text.)

- *A Title page* includes the title of the report, the author of the report and the receiver of the report

- *Acknowledgements* – this should highlight any help, support, or external information received and any extraordinary co-operation of individuals or organisations

- *Contents page* provides a clearly structured pathway of the contents of the report – page by page.

- *Executive summary* – a brief insight into purpose, nature and outcome of the report, in order that the outcome of the report can be quickly established

- *Main body of the report divided into sections, which are clearly labelled.* Suggested labelling would be on a numbered basis eg:

    - 1.0   Introduction
    - 1.1   Situation analysis
    - 1.1.1 External analysis
    - 1.1.2 Internal analysis

- *Conclusions* – draw the report to a conclusion, highlighting key points of importance, that will impact upon any recommendations that might be made

- *Recommendations* – clearly outline potential options and then recommendations. Where appropriate justify recommendations in order to substantiate your decision

- *Appendices* – ensure that you only use appendices that add value to the report. Ensure that they are numbered and referenced on a numbered basis within the text. If you are not going to reference it within the text, then it should not be there

- *Bibliography* – while in a business environment a bibliography might not be necessary, for an **assignment-based report it is vital**. It provides an indication of the level of research, reading and collecting of relevant information that has taken place in order to fulfil the requirements of the assignment task. Where possible, and where relevant, you could provide academic references within the text, which should of course then provide the basis of your bibliography. References should realistically be listed alphabetically and in the following sequence

    - Author's name and edition of the text
    - Date of publication
    - Title and sub-title (where relevant)
    - Edition 1st, 2nd etc

- Place of publication
- Publisher
- Series and individual volume number where appropriate.

Resources to support assignment based assessment

The aim of this guidance is to present you with a range of questions and issues that you should consider, based upon the assignment themes. The detail to support the questions can be found within your BPP Study Text and the 'Core Reading' recommended by CIM.

Additionally you will find useful support information within the CIM Student website www.cim.co.uk -: www.cimvirtualinstitute.com, where you can access a wide range of marketing information and case studies. You can also build your own workspace within the website so that you can quickly and easily access information specific to your professional study requirements. Other websites you might find useful for some of your assignment work include www.wnim.com - (What's New in Marketing) and also www.connectedinmarketing.com - another CIM website.

Other websites include:

www.mad.com	– Marketing Week
www.ft.com	– Financial Times
www.thetimes.com	– The Times newspaper
www.theeconomist.com	– The Economist magazine
www.marketing.haynet.com	– Marketing magazine
www.ecommercetimes.com	– Daily news on e-business developments
www.open.gov.uk	– Gateway to a wide range of UK government information
www.adassoc.org.uk	– The Advertising Association
www.marketresearch.org.uk	– The Marketing Research Society
www.amazon.com	– Online Book Shop
www.1800flowers.com	– Flower and delivery gift service
www.childreninneed.com	– Charitable organisation
www.comicrelief.com	– Charitable organisation
www.samaritans.org.uk	– Charitable organisation

Part A
The development of marketing orientation

PART A   THE DEVELOPMENT OF MARKETING ORIENTATION

Marketing and market orientation

Syllabus content

- Explain the development of marketing as an exchange process, a philosophy of business, and a managerial function (1.1)
- Recognise the contribution of marketing as a means of creating customer value and as a form of competition (1.2)
- Appreciate the importance of a market orientation to organisational performance and identify the factors that promote and impede the adoption of a market orientation (1.3)
- Explain the role of marketing in co-ordinating organisational resources both within and outside the marketing function (1.4)
- Describe the impacts of marketing actions on society and the need for marketers to act in an ethical and socially responsible manner (1.5)
- Examine the significance of buyer-seller relationships in marketing and comprehend the role of relationship marketing in facilitating the retention of customers (1.6)

Introduction

'Market'-ing, quite obviously, is to do with **markets**. Originally a market was a physical place, where buyers and sellers met up and **exchanged** things, so that they both got what they needed: a sheep in exchange for three bags of corn, say.

A market today is not really much different, except that buyers and sellers do not necessarily need to meet in person (or even live on the same continent), and it is easier to carry money around than bags of corn or sheep.

However, this simple chore of going to market to satisfy basic needs and exchange wares has evolved into a **marketing concept** that (many would argue) dictates all the actions of a modern business organisation.

In this chapter we are going to look at the development of marketing as an exchange process, a managerial function and a philosophy of business. We'll also take a broad look at the place of marketing in society and its impact on society.

1 The development of marketing

1.1 Definitions

FAST FORWARD

'**Marketing** is the management process responsible for identifying, anticipating and satisfying customer requirements profitably.' (CIM: www.cim.co.uk)

To begin, here are some formal definitions of modern marketing.

Key concepts

'**Marketing** is the management process responsible for identifying, anticipating and satisfying customer requirements profitably.' (CIM: www.cim.co.uk)

'**Marketing** is the process of planning and executing the conception, pricing, promotion, and distribution of ideas, goods, and services to create exchanges that satisfy individual and organisational objectives.' (AMA: www.marketingpower.com)

'**Marketing** is to establish, maintain and enhance long-term customer relationships at a profit, so that the objectives of the parties involved are met. This is done by mutual exchange and fulfilment of promises.' (*C Gronroos*, 1990)

These definitions have several key points in common.

- They all make it clear that there has to be some motivation for the selling organisation such as **'profit'** or, more broadly, satisfied **'organisational objectives'**.
- They all stress the importance of **customer satisfaction**, making marketing a **'mutual exchange'** between buyer and seller.
- They all see marketing as a process that is **planned and managed**.

There are also some subtle differences, most notably the reference to 'enhancing long-term customer relationships' in the third definition: this is of great importance in the latest ideas about relationship marketing.

BPP LEARNING MEDIA

1.2 The development of marketing

FAST FORWARD

Marketing has its origins in **exchange processes**. It has become increasingly important due to factors such as geographical separation of buyers and sellers, communications and transportation technologies, and global competition.

Marketing grew out of **exchange** (in other words, 'markets').

- In early societies trade is by **barter**: exchanging goods for other goods.

- When a society becomes capable of producing more than is necessary for individual survival (a **surplus**), the extra can be **traded** for other goods and services.

- And as societies develop, trade takes place using an agreed medium of exchange, usually **money**.

The production of goods before the industrial revolution was usually small-scale and aimed at local customers. Buyers and sellers had **direct contact**, which made it easy for sellers to find their buyers' needs and wants. There was no real need for marketing in the modern sense.

This began to change due to a number of factors: Figure 1.1.

Figure 1.1: Factors in the growth of marketing

During the **industrial revolution** (18th and 19th century), production became organised into larger units. As towns grew bigger, producers and the people they sold to began to be geographically separated. But right up until the early 20th century it was still most important to **produce enough** of a product to satisfy strong demand. Thinking about 'customer needs' was secondary.

Mass production techniques have increased the volume and range of goods on the market. For most products and services the ability now exists to produce much more than is demanded. Meanwhile developments in transportation and communications have made it possible to reach buyers in any part of the world.

Simple **mass marketing techniques** were first used in the 1950s for fast-moving consumer goods (FMCG) such as washing powder and groceries. The focus switched from 'how to produce and supply enough' to 'how to increase demand'. Marketing techniques, and marketing as a **managerial function**, grew out of this switch.

Marketing techniques – and marketing departments – have grown in importance as **competition** (that is, consumer choice) and **geographical separation** have increased, especially since the 1980s. From concentrating on advertising and sales, marketing methods have become wide-ranging, complex and scientific.

Modern marketing is about **identifying ever-changing customer needs** in a global market and continually creating products that **satisfy those needs**. And many organisations have adopted this as the philosophy that drives all of their business functions.

Exam tip

> It's unlikely that you'll be asked directly about the historical development of marketing, but it is important to understand that marketing is still, fundamentally, about **exchanges** between buyers and sellers. Modern marketing is based on the perception of **mutual benefit**: the organisation prospers when its customers (and other stakeholders) are satisfied.

1.3 The nature of exchange

For a **profit-making organisation**, the exchange of mutual benefits will be an exchange of products/services (supplied to customers) for money (supplied by customers in payment) and other resources (such as customer feedback information). *G Lancaster & F Witney* (2005) emphasise, however, that this is not the only type of exchange. Government units, charities, churches and other **voluntary/not-for-profit** organisations are also now seen as engaging in marketing. In such organisations, the nature of the exchange is different. Services, advocacy, membership, information (and so on) are supplied to a variety of 'customers' (or **stakeholders**) in exchange for a range of returns: allegiance, volunteer labour, donations, information and so on.

We shall look at these different marketing contexts later in the Text.

2 The contribution of marketing

FAST FORWARD

> Marketing creates **value** for customers and helps organisations **compete** through judicious use of the **marketing mix** variables: Product, Price, Place, Promotion.

2.1 Creating customer value

Marketing aims to make sure that the customer **values** an organisation and what it has to offer. How does it do this? It makes sure that the customer knows that the organisation produces the products or services the customer wants to buy, at a price they are prepared to pay, in a place that is mutually convenient.

Marketing also **adds value** to the customer's **experience** of the organisation's offering: giving them products that satisfy their needs better; enhancing sales and after-sales service; helping them make better buying decisions; making purchasing easier and more enjoyable – and so on.

2.1.1 The four Ps

Key concept

> **Marketing mix variables** are traditionally expressed in a highly memorable form called **'the Four Ps'**: Product, Price, Place and Promotion.

These four variables are at the heart of all aspects of marketing. They have been supplemented by three extra **service marketing variables**: People, Process and Physical Evidence.

The complete marketing mix can be illustrated as follows: Figure 1.2

Figure 1.2: The extended marketing mix

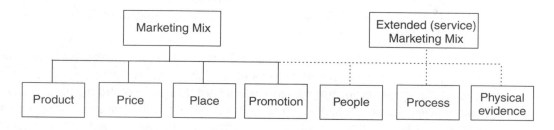

Exam tip

> CIM examiners often complain that students fail to distinguish accurately between the marketing mix (4Ps), the service marketing mix (extra 3Ps), the full or extended marketing mix (7Ps) – and other variations such as the promotional mix (different promotion tools). The examiner for this paper has helpfully started specifying the number of 'Ps' in questions – but make sure you know the difference and read the terms carefully. (Don't waste time in an exam writing 20 marks' worth of answer to a question that was never asked!)

The ways in which marketing **adds value** – both for the **marketing organisation** and for the **customer** – through the 4Ps can be summarised as follows.

4 Ps	How marketing creates value
Product	Marketing undertakes various kinds of product and market research about customers' needs and wants. This generates ideas for **product improvements** and **new products**, either extending the existing product range, or meeting a previously unrecognised need. This adds value to the *business* (by enhancing its offering) and adds value for *customers* (by meeting their needs and preferences).
Price	Some products are valued because they are cheap (low-cost phone calls), some because they are expensive (designer-label clothes). Marketing adds value for the *business* by researching how buyers **perceive prices** for different goods and enabling the organisation to **target** its goods or services appropriately. Price decisions add value for *customers* by offering value for money, rewards for bulk or repeat purchases, esteem value and so on.
Place	More usually called **distribution** or **logistics** in modern management-speak. Marketing adds value for the *business* by getting goods and services to market reliably and efficiently. It adds value for *customers* by creating a comfortable and convenient place to buy, in the case of a supermarket or restaurant. Or it invents new ways of displaying goods and getting them into people's homes, in the case of e-commerce sites such as Amazon.com.
Promotion	Also called **marketing communications**, this includes a vast array of techniques, from media advertising to personal selling (the sales force) to direct mail to public relations. Promotion adds value to the *business* by securing demand for its offering, building customer loyalty, promoting a positive image (for its brands and for the organisation as an employer). It adds value for *customers* by making sure that they can make well-informed **buying decisions**, are rewarded for their loyalty and are able to feel good about their purchases.

Why do you think the term 'mix' is used, when talking about these 'marketing mix variables'?

Exam tip

A question in the December 2003, 2004 and 2005 exams asked you to outline the **benefits** of marketing for the business, consumers and society as a whole. This is a rather different way of looking at the 'social responsibility' of marketing organisations – which often focuses on controlling the potential for negative impacts: manipulation, exploitation and so on (the December 2006 exam asked for both positive and negative impacts). The table in Paragraph 2.1.1 above is just a starting point for thinking about this. As you proceed through the Text, ask yourself – in relation to each approach or tool discussed – 'How does this add value for the **customer/consumer**?', 'How does this contribute to business success or competitive? ' 'How might this add value for other **stakeholders**?'. (The December 2006 case study also asked you to analyse how the scenario organisation contributed to *customer value* and *business success* in each of its core product areas, again, the table above is a good starting point.)

2.2 Marketing as a form of competition

Marketing must also aim to make sure that customers value an organisation and what it has to offer *more highly* than they value other similar organisations. This means 'doing your Ps' better than anyone else!

4 Ps	Marketing as a form of competition
Product	Marketing keeps a close eye on the products of competitors, finds out why customers prefer (or do not prefer) competitors' products, and aims to produce better quality, better targeted or more highly differentiated products.
Price	The competitive element is highly important in setting price. If your product is regarded as the same in all respects as a competitor's but is cheaper, then the chances are yours will be preferred – in theory! However, you may also compete on the basis of perceived *quality*, in which case your offering may be (in the words of one brand campaign) 'reassuringly expensive'.
Place	An organisation may aim to deliver goods faster than its competitors or give a cast-iron guarantee to deliver within a specific time, or deliver in a more convenient way (eg purchase online or by phone), or in a more pleasant environment. Competition can actually be a *determinant* of place. For instance, you will often find that several different car dealers set up showrooms in the same street, because that means that customers are more likely to come to that street to look at cars in the first place.
Promotion	Marketing communications have a key role in *informing* customers about the competitive features of products and services. They also compete themselves: more effective advertisements, more highly skilled sales people, more attractive free gifts, better press coverage, more effective website, sponsorship of a more prominent sports event – and so on.

3 Market orientation: a philosophy

We saw earlier that the historical trend has been for organisations to move from a focus on producing as much as possible to a focus on producing what the market *wants*. In other words, organisations have become increasingly **market oriented**.

BPP LEARNING MEDIA

But it is not only a matter of history. In the recent past many brilliant production engineers have made the mistake of starting up their own business to manufacture their astounding new invention … only to find that there are no customers who are actually prepared to buy their astounding new invention. Many excellent graphic designers have spent weeks or months creating fabulous websites displaying their talents … but they still have no customers!

3.1 Different ways of doing business

FAST FORWARD

> The **marketing concept** holds that the starting place of all organisational activity is the needs and wants of its target markets. It aims for profitability through customer satisfaction, rather than sales volume (selling concept), efficiency (production concept) or quality (product concept).

Key concept

> The **marketing concept** holds that 'achieving organisational goals depends on determining the needs and wants of target markets and delivering the desired satisfactions more effectively and efficiently than competitors' (*P Kotler*, 2002).

This concept can be contrasted with other concepts or orientations by which organisations conceive, conduct and co-ordinate their marketing activities.

Concept	Focus	Means	Aims
Marketing concept	Customer needs and wants; long-term customer relationships	Integrated marketing activities	Profitability through customer satisfaction
Selling concept	Existing products made by the firm; creating sales transactions	Energetic selling and promoting	Profitability through sales volume
Production concept	Assumed customer demand for product availability and affordability	Improving production and distribution efficiency	Profitability through efficiency
Product concept	Assumed customer demand for product quality, performance and features	Continuous product improvements	Profitability through product quality

The marketing concept can be stated in various ways. *P Drucker* (1995) defined it as 'Marketing is the whole business seen from the point of view of its final result, that is from the customer's point of view.' *H McDonald* (2002) puts it even more succinctly: 'marketing means finding out what people want and giving it to them'.

The activities and philosophy of **market oriented** companies contrast sharply with **production oriented** and **sales oriented** organisations: Figure 1.3.

Figure 1.3: Market orientation compared to other orientations

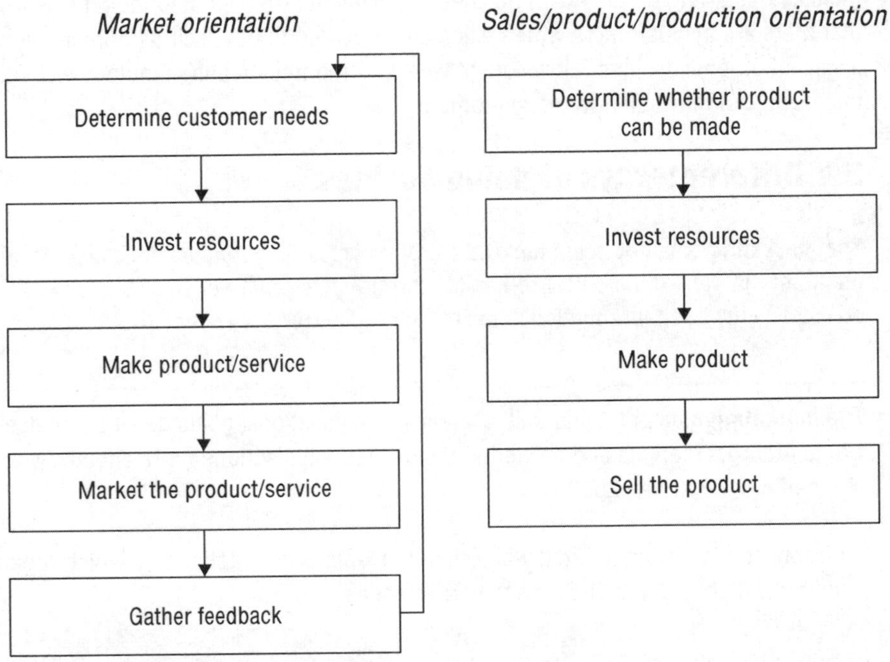

Exam tip

> The difference between marketing and selling featured in an old syllabus question. One way of tackling this answer is to talk not only about the different jobs that marketers and sales people do, but about the different orientations outlined above.

3.1.1 Production orientation

The production orientation is epitomised by the famous comment attributed to Henry Ford about his Model T car, which customers could buy in 'any colour, so long as it's black'. In order to keep the production process as fast as possible, all cars needed to be the same colour – and black was the fastest-drying paint.

Whether or not Ford really made the comment, the point remains that it was inconvenient for his company's production process to make cars in colours other than black. The customer's wishes were unimportant because there was no competition and the customers had no choice.

Of course, at any particular point in time all organisations still offer their customers only what they are capable of producing (at a profit). But in the modern world, if Organisation A cannot quickly learn to produce the equivalent of a Model T in pink (because that is what customers want to buy) then Organisation B will come along, with better knowledge and/or better technology, and take their place.

3.1.2 Product orientation

There are also still many companies that have a product orientation, based on the illusion that because an idea looks good to the producer it will satisfy the customer. To an extent this is understandable. The producers are usually people who have a deep love of the product and an in-depth understanding of its qualities, and the effort it takes to make it: who better, in theory, to judge?

It is all too easy, however, to become blinkered by the beauty of your own product. Most people who buy electric drills do not really want an electric drill at all: what they want is holes! If there were some easier, safer way of making holes than by using an electric drill, the electric drill market would disappear.

T Levitt (1986) argues that any organisation that defines its business or purpose purely in terms of its products/services is being short-sighted, or suffering from **'marketing myopia'**.

BPP LEARNING MEDIA

Action Programme 2

Did you buy this book because you wanted something to read? Or was it because you want to pass your *Marketing Fundamentals* exam? Or would you rather not do the exam at all? What is it that you really, really want?

And before you pick on this book too much, try applying this argument to your own organisation's products or services! It's a good habit to get into.

Marketing at Work

Product orientation *is not dead, and not likely to die. This is a genuine case, but we have disguised the company name.*

WideWorld was a company set up in the mid 1990s to provide web hosting services. Web hosting companies own and maintain the complex computer hardware and software and telecommunications links needed to keep a website constantly accessible on the Internet. They rent out their hard disk space and provide services to website owners.

WideWorld was run by highly talented experts, and for a time WideWorld topped the charts of 'best web hosts' in both the UK and the US.

Meanwhile, between the mid and late 1990s, Microsoft developed its own web platform. This allowed other web hosts to offer all sorts of user-friendly bells and whistles to website owners, who were able to administer their own sites without needing in-depth technical expertise.

WideWorld had always been able to offer at least the same level of service, but users always had to ask an expert member of WideWorld's staff to set it up for them.

Towards the end, WideWorld started to send its customers highly technical e-mails about 'the very low incidence of outages', the need to 'reboot hubs ', the problem of 'mail backing up on the tertiary MX servers' and so on, which probably meant little to the vast majority of new-style users.

WideWorld – a classic product-oriented company – went into liquidation in 2001.

3.1.3 Sales orientation

Sales oriented organisations make the product first, and then try to sell it. Underlying this philosophy is a belief that a good sales force can sell just about anything to anybody.

If you think product-oriented or production-oriented organisations are arrogant and uncaring, you will probably think that sales-oriented organisations are downright manipulative.

Marketing at Work

The **sales orientation** is far from dead, as you will know if you have ever been the victim of cold calling by companies selling double-glazing, kitchen replacements and the like. You are called because you happen to have a particular post code or telephone dialling code, not because there is anything wrong with your windows.

The classic example of the problems with a sales orientation in the UK is the insurance companies' attempts to sell personal pensions in the late1980s and early 1990s. Many people were incorrectly advised to opt out of company pension schemes by agents tied to pushing particular insurance company products.

When it came to light that people had been sold a product that actually left them worse off than they would otherwise have been the insurance companies faced heavy financial penalties, a stricter regulatory regime and compulsory training for staff.

Partly adapted from Marketing, 11 January 2001

T Levitt (1986) distinguishes between sales and marketing orientations as follows.

> 'Selling focuses on the needs of the seller; marketing on the needs of the buyer. Selling is preoccupied with the seller's need to convert his product into cash; marketing with the idea of satisfying the needs of the customer by means of the product and the whole cluster of things associated with creating, delivering and finally consuming it.'

If new products are developed without regard for customer requirements, an expensive selling effort will be needed to persuade customers that they should purchase something that probably does not quite fit their needs. Repeat purchase is also less likely.

P Drucker (1955) suggests that **'the aim of marketing is to make selling superfluous'**. If the organisation gets its marketing right, it will produce products and services that meet customers' requirements at a price that customers accept. The selling function will require fewer resources, as customers will be receptive to the product.

Exam tip

> Questions in both June and December 2004 and June 2006 asked you to outline the **benefits** to an organisation (as well as consumers) of having a marketing orientation. The June 2006 question was set in the context of a public sector organisation (a government health promotion agency): don't forget that public sector organisations have 'customers' too.

3.2 Market orientation

FAST FORWARD

> **A market-oriented organisation** is fundamental to the continuation and competitiveness of the organisation, as an approach to attracting and retaining customers.

A market oriented organisation avoids the problems of short-term sales-focused relationships with potentially indifferent or resistant customers.

- It **focuses** on meeting the needs of customers, which have been clearly identified and fully understood.

- Its **structure** and **processes** are designed to meet the needs of customers.

- All activities are **co-ordinated** around the needs of the customer.

Underlying all of this is the belief that a market orientation is fundamental to the **continuation** and **competitiveness** of the organisation. When customers' needs change, as they surely will, or whenever better solutions emerge that more closely meet customers' needs, the organisation **adapts and responds**. Otherwise the organisation does not survive.

The marketing concept, as the basic philosophy that underpins modern corporate strategy, is now widely accepted. How far it is actually put into practice in different organisations still depends very much on the power and interests of different stakeholders in the organisation.

BPP
LEARNING MEDIA

Action Programme 3

Quality Goods makes a variety of widgets. Its Chairman, in the annual report, boasts of the firm's 'passion for the customer'. 'The customer wants quality goods, and if they don't get them they'll complain, won't they?'

Is this a marketing oriented firm?

3.3 Measuring market orientation

Marketing orientation is not confined to the marketing department: it is a **culture** or way of thinking that needs to permeate the whole organisation. How can you tell if (or how far) this is happening?

An organisation wishing to **assess its market orientation** might look at:

- Self-appraisal or feedback from managers and employees in different organisational functions

- Formal attitude surveys of managers and staff

- Evidence in the organisation's business definition, mission statement, value statements and strategies

- Formal marketing audit results (specifically asking questions about the customer focus of different structures and processes)

- Evidence in the extent of organisation-wide communication on customer needs; willingness to gather and use customer feedback; co-ordination between functions in the interest of meeting customer needs; and so on

- Customer feedback and research: are customer needs in fact being met (regardless of perceived 'orientation')?

3.4 Fostering market orientation

For a product or selling oriented organisation to *become* market oriented represents a major, possibly transformational change. It may require a **programme of change** including the following measures.

- Review and change of the **organisation structure**:

    - To remove 'vertical' barriers (between different functions) which get in the way of people co-operating to meet customer needs. *T Peters* (1994) advocates 'horizontal' structures (such as customer account or product teams), which match customers' essentially horizontal experiences of the organisation (needing to flow smoothly from sales information to transaction processing to after-sales service, say – without needing to know that these are three different departments!)

    - To enhance the influence of the marketing function (as discussed later in the chapter), in order to set a customer focused strategic direction

- Review and alignment of **business processes**. 'Process alignment' refers to the exercise of ensuring that all business systems and processes (work and information flows) contribute to the satisfaction of customer needs. As Levitt's comment (quoted in paragraph 3.1.2 above) shows, customer needs are satisfied not just by the product, but by all the processes associated with designing, creating, delivering and consuming it.

- Engage in **internal marketing**. The marketing function, supported by senior management, needs to promote the business needs for marketing orientation and the values associated with it. An extensive programme of employee education and communication may be necessary to introduce customer focus.

- Implement relevant customer research, customer care, quality and service **policies** and programmes. (This area is covered in detail in the *Customer Communications* module.)

- Create and reinforce **cultural values** based on customer focus. This may be done by:

    (a)   Expression and modelling of the desired values by management (from the top down)

    (b)   Expression of values in corporate mottos, slogans, team-building and so on

    (c)   Use of customer service values as recruitment and selection criteria

    (d)   Reinforcing values through other HR systems: education, training, coaching and employee development programmes; incentives, pay and bonuses (or non-financial awards such as 'employee of the month' schemes); performance appraisal and management; and so on

    (e)   Management style: celebrating and praising customer focused behaviour; encouraging initiative and learning in the interests of customer service etc.

- **Benchmarking** the organisation's processes and performance against best practice or best competitor practice.

Exam tip

> Think about why a marketing orientation is important, and how it could be achieved, in different organisational contexts. The June 2005 exam, for example, focused on the benefits of a market orientation for a **charity** of your choice. Who are its 'customers'? What will be gained by satisfying them?

3.5 Problems in introducing a market orientation

FAST FORWARD

> When a sales or product oriented organisation decides to become market oriented, there are a number of issues that need to be addressed.

The organisation should understand what a market orientation actually means, and that major **organisational**, **structural** and **cultural changes** will be required.

Exam tip

> The December 2002 paper contained a Part B question on the introduction of customer care systems. This would involve issues such as:
>
> - Defining customer needs and expectations
> - Gaining top management commitment
> - Setting and monitoring minimum service levels
> - Investment in information systems
> - Adaptation of internal structures
>
> All of the above reflect a marketing orientation. **Customer care** is now part of the *Customer Communications* syllabus, but be ready to use your learning to illustrate marketing orientation as a customer-focused philosophy and culture.

The organisation will have to consider **the four Ps** with the customers' needs as the priority consideration.

Problems may arise within the **structure** of the company. Sales and product oriented firms do not require the same degree of 'working together' as a marketing oriented company.

When progressing to marketing orientation, **effective communication** is vital to prevent confusion and provide reassurance.

Problems will arise if managers do not adopt a marketing philosophy and build it into their **culture**. Commitment from management will feed down to other staff. Without total **organisation-wide** dedication – and reinforcement by the staff recruitment, training, appraisal and reward systems – changing to a market oriented organisation is not possible.

Without care, a marketing orientation itself can have **adverse consequences**.

- Organisations may develop a **bias** that favours marketing activities at the expense of production and technical improvements which could offer a more appealing product.

- Focusing new product development on satisfying immediate customer perceptions of what is needed can **stifle innovation.** Organisations should devote at least some of their expertise to *future* customer requirements.

It is worth noting, too, that the total marketing concept itself may or may not represent a real shift in philosophy.

- Perhaps it simply reflects the fact that the **business environment** is now much more sophisticated. For instance, it just makes sense to use advanced information management techniques and technologies in advertising and market research. Those techniques weren't used before simply because they weren't available.

- Perhaps today's **consumers** are more sophisticated, with more information, better education and greater expectations of influence. So-called 'modern marketing techniques' are really just the same old process of persuasion, more cleverly disguised.

Action Programme 4

A customer contacts your company and asks whether it can make a completely silent washing machine. This is not possible with current technology. What is your reaction?

4 Marketing as a managerial function

This section examines how marketing fits in with the **management structure** of the organisation as a whole.

Market-orientated companies need proper **co-ordination** between market needs, production decisions and financial well-being. That requires good **communication** between the marketing function and people responsible for development, design and manufacturing, and finance.

However, that does not mean that the marketing department can impose their will on all other departments. Relationships with other departments should be developed and managed to ensure all departments are working towards the **same overall goal**.

4.1 The scope of marketing activities

FAST FORWARD

While the **marketing function** typically has responsibility for a range of marketing mix decisions, it should be remembered that all functions are part of the **customer value chain**.

The table below shows the types of decision typically taken by a marketing department. However, bear in mind that in the truly market-oriented organisation, marketing is not an activity that can be pigeon-holed as the responsibility of the marketing department. *All* of the company's activities must be co-ordinated around the needs of the customer.

Marketing decision	Policies and procedures relating to:
Product planning	Product lines to be offered – qualities, design, detailed contents
	Markets - to whom, where, when and how much
	New product policy – research and development programme
Branding	Selection of trade marks and names
	Brand policy – individual or family brand
	Sale under private brand or unbranded
Pricing	The level of premiums to adopt
	The margins to adopt – for the trade, for direct sales
Channels of distribution	The channels to use between company and consumer
	The degree of selectivity amongst intermediaries
	Efforts to gain co-operation of the trade
Selling	The burden to be placed on personal selling
	The methods to be employed (1) within the organisation and (2) in selling to intermediaries and the final consumer
Marketing communications (promotions)	The amount to spend – the burden to be placed on advertising
	The platform to adopt – product image, corporate image
	The mix of tools used – to the trade, to consumers
Servicing and customer relationships	Providing after-sales service to intermediaries and to final consumers (such as direct mail offers)
	Creating points of contact with customers in an integrated way

4.2 Relationship with other departments

FAST FORWARD

The marketing department is well-placed to be the **co-ordinator** of all organisational resources in a market oriented company.

Although every organisation is different, common patterns appear in the structure of organisations.

- Marketing departments have often **evolved from sales departments**. In traditional sales or production orientated organisations, marketplace issues were the responsibility of a **sales director** reporting to senior management.

- When the need for a market orientated approach became apparent, a **marketing director** appeared in parallel to the sales director, but each had **separate functional departments**.

- With fuller recognition of the marketing approach to business, sales and marketing may become a **single department**, with **sales as a sub-group** within marketing (as opposed to marketing being a sub-group within sales).

Marketing managers have to take responsibility for planning, resource allocation, monitoring and controlling the marketing effort, but it can also be claimed (and often is, by marketing managers!) that marketing involves every facet of the organisation's operations. If the philosophy of a market orientation is regarded as a prerequisite for success, the marketing department naturally becomes the main **co-ordinator**.

4.2.1 Conflicts with other departments

Nevertheless, care should be taken not to understate the role of finance, production, personnel and other business functions, as this may cause resentment and lack of co-operation. To reduce the potential for conflict, senior management should ensure that departmental heads have clear instructions as to the organisation's priorities.

Action Programme 5

Conflict is often reported between the marketing and research and development (R&D) departments. What possible causes of conflict exist between R&D and marketing? Why is it essential, in a marketing orientated organisation, for R&D and marketing to have a close relationship?

[Key Skill for Marketers: Working with others]

The following table illustrates areas of business that need to be co-ordinated to ensure that some compromise acceptable to both parties is found.

Other departments	Their emphasis	Emphasis of marketing
Engineering	Long design lead time	Short design lead time
	Functional features	Sales features
	Few models with standard components	Many models with custom components
Purchasing	Standard parts	Non-standard parts
	Price of material	Quality of material
	Economic lot sizes	Large lot sizes to avoid stockouts
	Purchasing at infrequent intervals	Immediate purchasing for customer needs
Production	Long order lead times and inflexible production schedules	Short order lead times and flexible schedules to meet emergency orders
	Long runs with few models	Short runs with many models
	No model changes	Frequent model changes
	Standard orders	Custom orders
	Ease of fabrication	Aesthetic appearance
	Average quality control	Tight quality control
Inventory management	Narrow product line	Broad product line
	Economic levels of stock	Large levels of stock
Finance	Strict rationales for spending	Intuitive arguments for spending
	Hard and fast budgets	Flexible budgets to meet changing needs
	Pricing to cover costs	Pricing to further market development
Accounting	Standard transactions	Special terms and discounts
	Few reports	Many reports

Other departments	Their emphasis	Emphasis of marketing
Credit	Full financial disclosures by customers	Minimum credit examination of customers
	Lower credit risks	Medium credit risks
	Tough credit terms	Easy credit terms
	Tough collection procedures	Easy collection procedures

Source: Kotler (1965)

5 Marketing and society

5.1 Societal marketing and social responsibility

FAST FORWARD

Marketing should aim to maximise **business performance** through **customer satisfaction**, but within the constraints that all firms have a responsibility to **society** as a whole and to the **environment**.

Critics of the marketing concept suggest that marketing is so powerful that it can make people want things they don't really need, or worse, create a desire for products and services that are against the long-term interests of consumers and of society as a whole. Current examples include cigarettes; non-nutritious 'junk' or convenience food products; and gambling products like instant-win scratch cards which appeal most to the poorest members of society.

A number of writers have suggested that a **societal marketing concept** should replace the marketing concept as a philosophy for the future.

Key concepts

The **societal marketing concept** is a management orientation that holds that the key task of the organisation is to determine the needs and wants of target markets and to adapt the organisation to delivering the desired satisfactions more effectively and efficiently than its competitors *in a way that preserves or enhances the consumers' and society's well-being.*

Exam tip

Social responsibility is accepting ethical responsibilities to the various publics of an organisation which go beyond contractual or legal requirements. It recognises that organisational activities may have adverse impacts on external stakeholders, and that these should be minimised.

Marketing should aim to maximise **business performance** through **customer satisfaction**, but within the constraints that all firms have a responsibility to **society** as a whole and to the **environment**. For example:

(a)   Some products which consume energy (eg motor cars) should perhaps make more efficient use of the energy they consume.

(b)   It may be possible to extend the useful life of certain products, rather than encouraging obsolescence for repeat or updating purchases.

(c)   Other products might be made smaller, so that they make use of fewer materials (eg products made using microtechnology).

(d)   The organisation should exercise fair safe and sustainable business and employment practices. (This is currently a major issue for firms employing off-shore low cost labour for manufacturing.)

(e)   The organisation should arguably resist the temptation to persuade people to consume excessively (creating debt, disposal issues etc).

BPP LEARNING MEDIA

(f)   The organisation may seek to 'put something back' into the communities or societies on which it depends.

Action Programme 6

Does your own organisation do anything that indicates to you that it takes a responsible attitude towards society and the environment? Think through each of the 4Ps as a framework for your answer: how might an organisation be responsible in each of the four areas.

Marketing at Work

Surf's still up for DHL

'DHL has announced it will extend its **relationship** with Surf Life Saving Australia (SLSA) for another three years, continuing to provide funds for training, uniforms and rescue gear to 304 surf clubs around Australia.

As a result of the partnership, DHL's distinctive yellow and red logo will continue to be visible on all beaches throughout Australia, appearing on surf lifesaving patrol uniforms nationally and on lifesaving equipment in key locations.

The partnership between the two companies dates back to September 2003. DHL also has a relationship with surf lifesaving organisations in New Zealand and Japan.'

B&T 12 May 2006

5.2 Why be socially responsible?

FAST FORWARD

Although **social responsibility** may sometimes conflict with business objectives there is a growing body of opinion that accepts that it is in the organisation's own best interests.

Institutions like hospitals and schools exist because health care and education are seen to be *desirable* **social objectives** by government and the public at large. Where does this leave *businesses*? How far is it reasonable, or even appropriate, for businesses to exercise 'social responsibility' by giving to charities, voluntarily imposing strict environmental objectives on themselves, offering the same conditions of work to all workers, and so on?

Exam tip

Social responsibility and the related topic of business ethics often feature in exam questions, so be clear about their meaning and the arguments for and against. You also need to be able to identify specific ethical and social responsibility issues facing a given organisation (as in the June 2006 scenario), or more generally facing marketers in recent times – and within your own national culture and the global marketplace. (This was set as a question in the December 2004 and 2005 exams, for example.) Asking the 'added value' question of any given marketing decision should highlight areas in which the organisation's interests potentially conflict with those of other stakeholders in its activity … Think through the news headlines: what corporate social responsibility issues have faced Nike, McDonalds, Oxfam?

Marketing at Work

The following index from Nestlé's website indicates the range of issues that may be considered part of **corporate social responsibility**.

Africa Report
Nestlé demonstrates its commitment to Africa - see how. ▸

Environment
Addressing the needs of today while safeguarding our environment for future generations. ▸

UN Global Compact
Integrating a concern for global issues in our everyday operations. ▸

Infant Formula
Responsible improvement, promotion and distribution of Infant Formula products. ▸

Gene Technology
Supporting the safe, responsible and regulated use of Gene technology. ▸

Sustainability
Ensuring Nestlé's future through innovation, renovation and operational efficiency. ▸

Quality
Discover how our quest for quality is a daily pursuit and the axis of our operations. ▸

Nestlé in the Community
At Nestlé we believe in making a long-term commitment to the health and well being of people in every country in the scope of our operations. ▸

Nestlé Donations
Our ongoing commitment to education, social responsibility and helping those in need. ▸

Water
Water – essential for life; a scarce and renewable resource that we treat with respect in manufacture of all our products. ▸

(www.nestle.com, 05/04/2005)

Managers need to take into account the effect of organisational outputs into the market and the wider **social community**, for several reasons.

(a) The modern **marketing concept** says that in order to survive and succeed, organisations must satisfy the needs, wants and values of customers and potential customers. Communication and education have made people much more aware of issues such as the environment, the exploitation of workers, product safety and consumer rights. Therefore an organisation may have to be seen to be responsible in these areas in order to retain public support for its products.

(b) There are skill shortages in the labour pool and employers must compete to attract and retain high quality employees. If the organisation holds a reputation as a socially responsible employer it will find it easier to do this, than if it has a poor **'employer brand'**.

(c) Organisations **rely** on the society and local community of which they are a part, for access to facilities, business relationships, media coverage, labour, supplies, customers and so on. Organisations which acknowledge their responsibilities as part of the community may find that many areas of their operation are facilitated.

(d) Law, regulation and Codes of Practice **impose** certain social responsibilities on organisations, in areas such as employment protection, equal opportunities, environmental care, health and safety, product labelling and consumer rights. There are financial and operational **penalties** for organisations which fail to comply.

Economist *Milton Friedman*, however, argued that the social responsibility of business is **profit maximisation**. The responsibility of a business organisation – as opposed to a public sector one – is to maximise wealth for its owners and investors. This does not mean that the business will not be socially responsible, but it will be so out of 'enlightened self interest': protecting its corporate image, ability to retain staff and so on.

H Mintzberg (1983) argues that:

- A business's relationship with society is not only economic, because a business is an open system with many other non-economic impacts: employees, image, information, environmental effects

- Social responsibility helps to create a social climate in which the business can prosper in the long term

5.3 Responsibilities to customers

FAST FORWARD

> Responsibilities towards **customers** are mainly those of providing a product or service of a quality that customers expect, and of dealing honestly and fairly with customers.

To some extent these responsibilities coincide with the organisation's marketing objectives.

The importance of customer care has been acknowledged as a result of the growth of **consumerism**. In the UK, a number of consumer rights have been recognised in law.

(a) The right to be **informed of the true facts** of the buyer-seller relationship (eg truth in advertising) and the content of products (eg in food labelling).

(b) The right to be **protected** from unfair exploitation or invasion of privacy (eg in the use of personal information or the sale of mailing lists).

(c) The right to **safety and health protection**: safe products, health warnings, product labelling and so on.

Key concept

> **Consumerism** is a term used to describe the increased importance and power of consumers. It includes the increasingly organised consumer groups, and the recognition by producers that consumer satisfaction is the key to long-term profitability.

Marketers are increasingly responsive to consumer pressures to maintain a responsible image and reputation. This may deter aggressive marketing tactics, as the need to consider the best interests of customers should be paramount in a marketing strategy. This approach should bring long-term benefits, rather than attempting to maximise short-term profits.

5.4 Responsibilities towards the community

A business only succeeds because it is part of a wider community. It should be responsible for:

(a) Upholding the social and ethical **values** of the community

(b) Contributing towards the **well-being** of the community, eg by sponsoring local events and charities, or providing facilities for the community to use (eg sports fields), or (more fundamentally) by producing safe products, pricing essential products for affordability and maintaining a local employment market

(c) Responding constructively to **complaints** from local residents or politicians (eg about problems for local traffic caused by the organisation's delivery vehicles)

(d) Maintaining a **sustainable** presence in the community, in terms of the exploitation of labour and business relationships, impacts on the environment and use of resources.

Artistic sponsorships, charitable donations and the like are, of course, also a useful medium of **public relations** and can reflect well on the business.

Marketing at Work

'Studies all over the world repeatedly tell us people have lost faith in the corporate world and the media. Trust of these institutions is at an all time low. Grey Worldwide's annual study 'Eye on Australia' places Australian advertising agencies very low on the **trust rating scale**. It is intriguing that much of the advertising industry is prepared to accept this situation. This complacency is concerning because the consumer is in need of things that have a soul and are authentic and genuine – things you can really believe in and trust – the precise opposite of conventional advertising …'

RATING OF TRUST

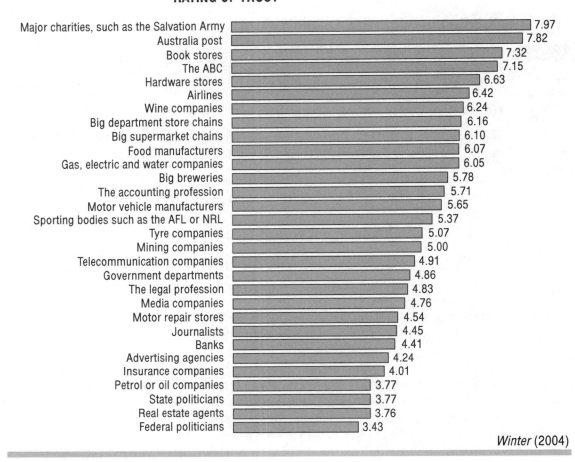

Major charities, such as the Salvation Army	7.97
Australia post	7.82
Book stores	7.32
The ABC	7.15
Hardware stores	6.63
Airlines	6.42
Wine companies	6.24
Big department store chains	6.16
Big supermarket chains	6.10
Food manufacturers	6.07
Gas, electric and water companies	6.05
Big breweries	5.78
The accounting profession	5.71
Motor vehicle manufacturers	5.65
Sporting bodies such as the AFL or NRL	5.37
Tyre companies	5.07
Mining companies	5.00
Telecommunication companies	4.91
Government departments	4.86
The legal profession	4.83
Media companies	4.76
Motor repair stores	4.54
Journalists	4.45
Banks	4.41
Advertising agencies	4.24
Insurance companies	4.01
Petrol or oil companies	3.77
State politicians	3.77
Real estate agents	3.76
Federal politicians	3.43

Winter (2004)

5.5 Responsibilities to employees

FAST FORWARD

Employees are major stakeholders in (and contributors to) the organisation: responsible employment practices are a key part of the organisation's 'employer brand'.

Responsible policies should address matters such as:

- Fair pay and conditions

- Safe and healthy working conditions

- Learning/development opportunities: consultation and participation in decisions which affect the workforce

- Commitment to equal opportunity, non-discrimination and wider diversity

- Fair and humane management of disciplinary situations, dismissals and redundancies and so on

- Support for employee welfare (benefits, counselling and so on, where required)

 Marketing at Work

Sports shoe manufacturers Nike (www.nike.com) have in the past been fiercely attacked over their alleged **mistreatment of workers** in third world countries, where most of their shoes are actually made.

Reebok's shoes are also made mainly in third world countries and the company has gone to considerable lengths over the years to stave off criticism.

'More than a decade ago, it set up the Reebok Human Rights Foundation (www.reebok.com/Reebok/US/HumanRights), which gives financial aid to human rights groups such as Human Rights Watch, the Commission for Refugee Women and Children, and The Carter Center.

'The company also became the sponsor of the Reebok Human Rights Award, which provides grants of $50,000 to human-rights activists under the age of 30 "who have made significant contributions to the field of human rights strictly through non-violent means". Since the awards were introduced in 1988, more than 60 recipients from over 35 countries have received the award.'

Adapted from *PR Week* (USA edition) 5 August 2002

5.6 Responsibilities to suppliers and competitors

The responsibilities of an organisation towards its **suppliers** come down mainly to maintaining trading relationships.

(a) The organisation's size could give it considerable **buying power**. It should not use its power unscrupulously (eg to force the supplier to lower his prices under threat of withdrawing business).

(b) The organisation should not delay **payments** to suppliers beyond the agreed credit period. Suppliers (especially small businesses) might rely on getting prompt payment in accordance with the terms of trade negotiated with its customers.

(c) All **information** obtained from suppliers and potential suppliers should be kept confidential, particularly where competing tenders or offers are being considered.

(d) All suppliers should be **treated fairly**, including:

   (i) Giving potential new suppliers a chance to win some business
   (ii) Maintaining long-standing relationships that have been built up over the years.

Some responsibilities should also exist towards **competitors**. Responsibilities regarding competitors are by no means solely directed by social conscience or ethics, however: there is also a great deal of law surrounding the conduct of fair trading, monopolies, mergers, anti-competitive practices, abuses of a dominant market position and restrictive trade practices. Companies may compete aggressively (as in the case of Coke and Pepsi), but they may not compete unfairly (as, for example, Microsoft have been accused of doing).

5.7 Business ethics

FAST FORWARD **Business ethics** are the values underlying what an organisation understands by socially responsible behaviour.

An organisation may have **values** covering non-discrimination, fairness and integrity. It is very important that managers understand:

- The importance of **ethical behaviour**, and
- The differences in what is considered ethical behaviour in **different cultures**

E Sternberg (2000) suggests that two ethical values are particularly pertinent for business, because without them business could not operate at all. These are:

(a) **Ordinary decency.** This includes respect for property rights (eg copyright and patents) honesty, fairness and legality.

(b) **Distributive justice.** This means that organisational rewards should be proportional to the contributions people make to organisational ends. The supply and demand for labour will influence how much a person is actually paid, but if that person is worth employing and the job worth doing, then the contribution will justify the expense.

Business ethics in a **global market place** are, however, far from clear cut. If you are working outside the UK, you will need to develop – in line with whatever policies your organisation may have in place – a kind of 'situational' ethic to cover various issues.

(a) **Gifts** may be construed as bribes in Western business circles, but are indispensable in others.

(b) Attitudes to **women** in business vary according to ethic traditions and religious values.

(c) The use of **cheap labour** in very poor countries may be perceived as 'development' – or as 'exploitation'.

(d) The expression and nature of **agreements** varies according to cultural norms.

Assuming a firm wishes to act ethically, it can embed ethical values in its decision processes in the following ways.

- Include **value statements** in corporate culture, policy and codes of practice

- Ensure that **incentive systems** are designed to support ethical behaviour

- Identify ethical objectives in the **mission statement**, as a public declaration of what the organisation stands for

- Encourage **communication** about ethical dilemmas and issues (eg in employee forums, ethics committees)

5.7.1 The CIM and ethics

The CIM published a Code of Professional Standards, Ethics and Disciplinary Procedures in 1997. Here are the main points.

 Marketing at Work

1   A member shall at all times conduct himself with **integrity** in such a way as to bring credit to the profession of marketing and The Chartered Institute of Marketing.

2   A member shall not by **unfair** or **unprofessional practice** injure the business, reputation or interest of any other member of the Institute.

3   Members shall, at all times, **act honestly** in their professional dealings with customers and clients (actual and potential), employers and employees.

BPP LEARNING MEDIA

4   A member shall not, knowingly or recklessly, disseminate any **false** or **misleading information**, either on his own behalf or on behalf of anyone else.

5   A member shall keep abreast of **current marketing practice** and act competently and diligently and be encouraged to register for the Institute's scheme of Continuing Professional Development.

6   A member shall, at all times, seek to **avoid conflicts of interest** and shall make prior voluntary and full disclosure to all parties concerned of all matters that may arise during any such conflict. Where a conflict arises a member must withdraw prior to the work commencing.

7   A member shall keep business information **confidential** except: from those persons entitled to receive it, where it breaches this code and where it is illegal to do so.

8   A member shall promote and seek business in a **professional** and **ethical manner**.

9   A member shall **observe** the **requirements** of all other codes of practice which may from time to time have any relevance to the practice of marketing insofar as such requirements do not conflict with any provisions of this code, or the Institute's Royal Charter and Bye-laws; a list of such codes being obtainable from the Institute's head office.

10   Members shall not hold themselves out as having the Institute's endorsement in connection with an activity unless the Institute's **prior written approval** has been obtained first.

11   A member shall not use any **funds** derived from the Institute for any purpose which does not fall within the powers and obligations contained in the Branch or Group handbook, and which does not fully comply with this code.

12   A member shall have due regard for, and comply with, all the relevant **laws** of the country in which they are operating.

13   A member who knowingly causes or permits any other person or organisation to be in substantial breach of this code or who is a party to such a breach shall himself be guilty of such breach.

14   A member shall observe this Code of Professional Standards as it may be expanded and annotated and published from time to time by the Ethics Committee in the manner provided for.

 Action Programme 7

Obtain a copy of the CIM code and read the Code in full. You can download a copy from the CIM website, www.cim.co.uk.

[Key Skill for Marketers: Using ICT and the Internet]

6 Relationship marketing

FAST FORWARD

Relationship marketing is the process of creating, building up and managing long-term relationships with customers, distributors and suppliers. It aims to change the focus from getting customers to keeping customers.

Since the mid–1990s the concept of relationship marketing has been gaining steady ground.

Key–concept

Relationship marketing is the process of creating, building up and managing long-term relationships with customers, distributors and suppliers. It aims to change the focus from getting customers to keeping customers.

6.1 Types and levels of relationship

FAST FORWARD There has been a general shift from transaction (one-way, short-term) to relationship (two-way, on-going) marketing.

The type of relationship between a buyer and a seller may be of two types.

(a) In a **transaction**, a supplier gives the customer a good or service in exchange for money. The marketer, in offering the good or service, is looking for a response. Transaction-based marketing is based on individual transactions and little else, such as when you buy a bar of chocolate.

(b) In a **relationship approach**, a sale is not the end of a process but the start of an organisation's relationship with a customer.

So building up customer relationships requires a change of focus from the transaction-based approach to the relationship approach. The contrast is summarised in the table below.

TRANSACTION MARKETING	RELATIONSHIP MARKETING
(*mainly one-way communication*)	(*mainly two-way communication*)
• Focus on single sale	• Focus on customer retention
• Orientation on product features	• Orientation on product benefits
• Short timescale	• Long timescale
• Little customer service	• High customer service
• Limited customer commitment	• High customer commitment
• Moderate customer contact	• High customer contact
• Quality is the concern of production	• Quality is the concern of all

There are five different levels of customer relationship.

(a) **Basic**

The organisation sells the product/service without initiating or inviting any further contact with the customer.

(b) **Reactive**

The customer is invited to contact the organisation if there are any problems.

(c) **Accountable**

The organisation follows up the sale, contacting the customer to see if there are any problems and inviting feedback for future improvements.

(d) **Proactive**

The organisation contacts the customer on a regular basis, for a range of purposes (additional offerings, incentives, updates, loyalty rewards, feedback seeking).

(e) **Partnership**

Organisation and customer exchange information and work together to achieve customer savings and added value. Commercial buyers often work closely with a supplier to ensure that all aspects of the deal suit the needs of both parties, not just for *this* deal, but those that can be expected in the future.

BPP
LEARNING MEDIA

Broadly speaking, the greater the number of customers and the smaller the profit per unit sold, the greater the likelihood that the type of marketing will be basic. At the other extreme, where a firm has few customers, but where profits are high, the partnership approach is most likely. Many firms, however, have begun to move towards proactive relationships – even in consumer markets – in order to build customers' loyalty to the brand, open feedback channels, cross-sell related products and so on.

 Marketing at Work

'The Flying Dutchman' programme

'Customer rewards are essential to the success of an airline and one of 2004's most innovative schemes was from the Dutch airline KLM which created a 'customer lifetime experience' through a personalised customer loyalty program that was strategically different from those being offered by its competitors ...

'KLM vice-president of marketing and services, Simone Wickenhagne, says good and clear **communication** of the benefits and services to the customer is essential.

'A major part of KLM's strategy has been integrating the program **online as well as offline** and **improving the online proposition** to make it the more attractive service channel for customers to use. This has been done by giving a discount on award tickets ordered online or by giving extra miles when using a service online, such as Internet check-in.

' "The aim is to offer certain services exclusively online, not offering these services via the offline channels any more. The goal is to make things easier and more convenient for the client and less costly for KLM."

'As a result of the scheme, **benchmarking research** has shown that KLM's customer loyalty program scores position KLM above its competitors for those in the scheme and online members are now responsible for approximately 40% of KLM passenger revenues.'

(Professional Marketing, February 2005)

6.2 Benefits of relationship marketing

FAST FORWARD

The key **benefit of relationship marketing** is in retaining and deepening customer loyalty to the brand, for greater marketing efficiency, sales volume and word-of-mouth promotion.

Kotler (2002) identifies the lifetime value of a customer to a company, in terms of revenue and profits. This is known as **lifetime customer value**. Existing, loyal customers are valuable because:

- They do not have to be acquired, or cost less to acquire
- They buy a broader range of products
- They cost less to service as they are familiar with the company's ways of doing business
- They become less sensitive to price over time
- They can recommend by word of mouth to others

The process of retaining customers for a lifetime is an important one – and one in which **integrated marketing communication**s have an important role to play. Instead of one-way communication aimed solely at gaining a sale, it is necessary to develop an effective two-way communication process to turn a prospect into a lifetime advocate. This is shown in the **ladder of customer loyalty**: Figure 1.4.

Figure 1.4: Ladder of customer loyalty

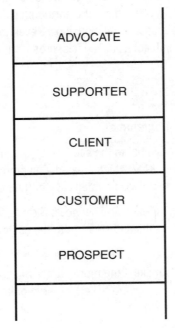

The main justification for relationship marketing comes from the need to **retain customers**. It has been estimated that the cost of attracting a new customer may be five times the cost of keeping a current customer happy.

In terms of competitive forces, relationship marketing attempts to make it harder, or less desirable, for a buyer to **switch** to another seller. It raises switching costs (emotional, if not financial).

Relationship marketing also opens **channels of communication** for marketers to **cross-sell** related products, solicit **feedback** for further marketing planning, make special offers (to boost sales or increase customer loyalty) and so on.

6.3 Characteristics of relationship marketing

FAST FORWARD

Key **features of relationship marketing** include: customer/supplier collaboration; personalisation of service; and a continually deepening dialogue through multiple points of contact.

Relationship marketing tends to operate in three main ways.

(a) Borrow the idea of **customer/supplier partnerships** from industry. By sharing information and supporting each other's shared objectives, marketers and their customers can create real mutual benefits.

(b) Recreate the **personal feel** that characterised the old-fashioned corner store. Make customers feel **recognised and valued as individuals** and demonstrate that their **individual needs** are being recognised and catered for. (This is particularly easy to do with new technologies such as the Internet, databases and computer-integrated telephone systems.)

(c) **Continually deepen and improve** the relationship. Make sure that every customer experience satisfies – and even **delights** – through reliable product quality, customer care and value-adding contacts.

The distinguishing characteristics of relationship marketing are as follows.

(a) A focus on **customer retention** rather than attraction

(b) The development of an **on-going relationship** as opposed to a one-off transaction

(c)   Emphasis upon the **benefits** of the product or service to the customer

(d)   A **long timescale** rather than short timescale

(e)   **Direct and regular** customer contact rather than impersonal, discrete sales

(f)   **Multiple employee/customer contacts,** hence the increased importance of all-staff customer care awareness

(g)   Quality and customer satisfaction being the concern of **all employees** rather than just those who work in the marketing department

(h)   Emphasis on **key account** relationship management, **service quality** and buyer (partner) behaviour rather than the marketing mix

(i)   Importance of **trust** and **keeping promises** rather than making the sale: to have an ongoing relationship, both parties need to trust each other and keep the promises they make. (Marketing moves from one-off potentially manipulative exchanges towards co-operative relationships built on financial, social and structural benefits.)

(j)   Multiple exchanges with a number of parties: **network relationships**, rather than a single focus on customers. Customer relationships are important, but so too are the relationships with other **stakeholders** such as suppliers, distributors, professional bodies, banks, trade associations etc.

Exam tip

> Exam questions have asked you to suggest how relationship marketing could be used to attract and retain customers by an automobile manufacturer (December 2004), a consumer service of your choice (June 2006) and a B2B global microchip manufacturer (June 2006).
>
> In December 2005, the compulsory question asked how building relationships with customers could help the case study organisation grow its business. In December 2006, you were asked how a mobile phone producer could develop and maintain relationships with buyers (customers) and suppliers: the examiner regarded this as a clear relationship marketing question. This is a core topic, so make sure you've got to grips with the principles – and look out for examples!

Some firms are therefore trying to convert a 'basic' transaction based approach into relationship marketing. Many car dealerships, for example, seek to generate additional profits by servicing the cars they sell, and by keeping in touch with their customers so that they can earn repeat business. Other strategies for relationship marketing include **loyalty schemes** such as club cards, and **special privileges** such as hospitality at sporting events.

 Marketing at Work

'Marketing, used to be a relatively straightforward profession that centred around sales and promotion activities, brand building and the four Ps (product, price, place and promotion).

'But now Marketing is about the four Ps plus 1 R and 1 T. The R stands for **Relationships** and the T stands for **Technology**.

'R for Relationships: you probably recognise this letter from today's leading buzzword 'CRM' [Customer Relationship Management]. Sometime last year, CRM overtook 'e-business' as the buzzword of the new millennium. Much like 'e-business', CRM is a transitional term, something to call a collection of activities while it's relatively new, until these activities become a natural part of how we conduct business.

'Creating **long-term profitable relationships** with your key customers is all the rage today, everyone is talking about it, but few are doing it very well. The fundamental problem with the R in CRM is the way companies define the term relationship.

'Many marketers believe they have a relationship with you because they have your name, phone number, email address and profession. What a bunch of rubbish. Relationships cannot be defined by how the company views them; instead they must be defined by how the customer defines them. If you fool yourself into believing you have an enduring relationship with a customer, when you really do not, you will find this out very quickly the next time your competitor offers a similar product or service for 10 per cent less. Relationships are the new battlefield that companies will fight each other on and the traditional metric of market share will take a back seat.

'Why? For the simple reason that it typically costs between five and 10 times more to attract a new customer than to keep an existing one.'

Extracted from: 'Relationships are the new battlefield for brands in Asia', *Media Asia,* 5 April 2002.

6.4 Customer relationship management (CRM)

FAST FORWARD

Customer relationship management (CRM) describes the methodologies and ICT systems that help an enterprise manage customer relationships.

Key concept

Customer relationship management (CRM) describes the methodologies and ICT systems that help an enterprise manage customer relationships.

CRM consists of systems which:

(a) Help an enterprise to identify and target their **most profitable customers** and generate quality leads

(b) Assist the organisation to improve telesales, account, and sales management by optimising **information sharing**, and **streamlining** existing processes (for example, taking orders using mobile devices)

(c) Provide employees with **information** to **integrate all communications** with customers: facilitating 'recognition' of customers; consistent and up-to-date account/product/ delivery information and so on.

Each time a customer contacts a company with an effective CRM system – whether by telephone, in a retail outlet or online – the customer should be recognised and should receive appropriate information and attention. CRM software provides advanced personalisation and customised solutions to customer demands, giving customer care staff a range of key information about each customer which can be applied to the transaction.

Basically, CRM involves a single **comprehensive database** that can be accessed from any of the points of contact with the customer. Traditional 'vertical' organisation structures have tended to create stand-alone systems developed for distinct functions or departments, which were responsible for the four main types of interaction with the customer: marketing, sales, fulfilment and after-sales. These systems need to be integrated into (or replaced by) a central customer database, with facilities for data to be **accessed from** and **fed into** the central system from other departments and applications (including the Website), so that all customer information can be kept up-to-date and shared.

Action Programme 8

Can you think of other ways in which information and communications technology (ICT) can be used to develop and maintain long-term customer relationships?

(This was worth 10 marks in a question in the December 2003 and June 2005 exams. If you can't think of a number of applications, give careful attention to our Action Programme Review.)

[Key Skill for Marketers: Using ICT and the Internet]

6.5 Issues in relationship marketing

FAST FORWARD

Permission and **privacy considerations** are key constraints on unsolicited marketing contacts.

You should note that not all customers *want* multiple, multi-source communications from organisations – even those from whom they have purchased products or services in the past!

(a) **Permission marketing** is an important concept, based on the belief that people should be given the choice of whether to receive further marketing communications or not – and that customers are likely to respond more positively to contacts that they have requested (or given permission for), than to unsolicited approaches. This was a major issue for 'junk mail' promotions, and is equally important in regard to Internet/email marketing: spam (unsolicited online direct mailings) are a major source of resistance to e-marketing.

(b) Many countries have **legislated** against unsolicited and intrusive marketing, and the sharing of personal data given to one organisation with other organisations. For some years, organisations have clearly stated their privacy polices and offered 'opt out' clauses ('if you do not wish to receive other offers, tick this box'). Many countries are now legislating for 'opt in' clauses ('If you wish to receive other offers, tick this box').

  • The UK **Data Protection Act 1998** requires data users to be registered with the Data Protection Registrar; to limit their use of personal data to registered users; and not to disclose data to third parties (even as email addresses sent in a 'cc' reference) without permission.

  • The UK **Privacy & Electronic Communications Regulations 2003** update existing UK legislation covering unsolicited email, phone calls, faxes and the Internet. It covers matters such as: explaining to customers the purpose of cookies (programs which personalise customer contacts with the website) and describing how to block them; obtaining permission for email/SMS/txt advertising to individuals; telephone marketing subject to 'opt out' ('Do not call') requests; and fax marketing to individuals by 'opt in' (request) only.

Chapter Roundup

- 'Marketing is the management process responsible for identifying, anticipating and satisfying customer requirements profitably.' (CIM: www.cim.co.uk)

- Marketing has its origins in **exchange processes**. It has become increasingly important due to factors such as geographical separation of buyers and sellers, communications and transportation technologies, and global competition.

- Marketing creates **value** for customers and helps organisations compete through judicious use of the **marketing mix variables**: Product, Price, Place, Promotion.

- The **marketing concept** holds that the starting place of all organisational activity is the needs and wants of its target markets. It aims for profitability through customer satisfaction, rather than sales volume (selling concept), efficiency (production concept) or quality (product concept).

- A **market-oriented organisation** is fundamental to the continuation and competitiveness of the organisation, as an approach to attracting and retaining customers.

- When a sales or product oriented organisation decides to become market oriented, there are a number of issues that need to be addressed.

- While the **marketing function** typically has responsibility for a range of marketing mix decisions, it should be remembered that all functions are part of the customer value chain.

- The marketing department is well-placed to be the **co-ordinator** of all organisational resources in a market oriented company.

- Marketing should aim to maximise **business performance** through **customer satisfaction**, but within the constraints that all firms have a responsibility to **society** as a whole and to the **environment**.

- Although **social responsibility** may sometimes conflict with business objectives there is a growing body of opinion that accepts that it is in the organisation's own best interests.

- Responsibilities towards **customers** are mainly those of providing a **product or service** of a **quality** that customers expect, and of **dealing honestly** and **fairly** with customers.

- **Employees** are major stakeholders in (and contributors to) the organisation: responsible employment practices are a key part of the organisation's 'employer brand'.

- **Business ethics** are the values underlying what an organisation understands by socially responsible behaviour.

- **Relationship marketing** is the process of creating, building up and managing long-term relationships with customers, distributors and suppliers. It aims to change the focus from getting customers to keeping customers.

- There has been a general shift from transaction (one-way, short-term) to relationship (two-way, on-going) marketing.

- The key **benefit of relationship marketing** is in retaining and deepening customer loyalty to the brand, for greater marketing efficiency, sales volume and word-of-mouth promotion.

- Key **features of relationship marketing** include: customer/supplier collaboration; personalisation of service; and a continually deepening dialogue through multiple points of contact.

- **Customer relationship management (CRM)** describes the methodologies and ICT systems that help an enterprise manage customer relationships.

- **Permission** and **privacy considerations** are key constraints on unsolicited marketing contacts.

Quick Quiz

1   Give a definition of marketing that takes into account relationship marketing.

2   Which of the following is true about the marketing mix variable Place?

    A   It only really applies to shops
    B   It is more accurately described as distribution or logistics
    C   Other marketing mix variables try to make it unimportant
    D   It is determined by competition

3   There are no organisations these days that have a production or sales orientation.

    True   ☐

    False ☐

4   Give three characteristics of a market oriented organisation.

5   Fill in the blanks in the statements below, using the words in the box.

Market oriented companies need proper (1)............................. . This requires good (2) .... between departments.

Production departments favour (3)...................... while marketing departments prefer (4) ....

Marketing departments favour (5) .... while credit controllers prefer (6) ....

No model changes	Tough credit terms	Communication
Easy credit terms	Co-ordination	Frequent model changes

6   Name three consumer rights that have been recognised in law.

7   Marketers have no responsibility towards competitors, except in the business sense that they should try to 'beat' the competition.

    True   ☐

    False ☐

8   There are five different levels of customer relationship. You could remember these using the acronym BRAPP. What does BRAPP stand for?

9   Customer relationship management describes the (1)....................... and (2)...................... systems that help an enterprise manage customer relationships.

Answers to Quick Quiz

1   'Marketing is to establish, maintain and enhance long-term customer relationships at a profit, so that the objectives of the parties involved are met. This is done by mutual exchange and fulfilment of promises.' (Gronroos)

2   B (although D is partly true)

3   False. There are many.

4   • It focuses on meeting the needs of customers, which have been clearly identified and fully understood.

• Its entire structure and all of its processes are designed to meet the needs of customers.

• All activities are co-ordinated around the needs of the customer.

5   (1) Co-ordination (2) Communication (3) No model changes (4) Frequent model changes (5) Easy credit terms (6) Tough credit terms.

6   • The right to be informed of the true facts
     • The right to be protected from unfair exploitation
     • The right to a particular quality of life

7   False. Whatever the marketer's personal view, there are many legal restrictions controlling actions with regard to competitors.

8   Basic, Reactive, Accountable, Proactive, Partnership.

9   (1) Methodologies (2) ICT.

Action Programme Review

1   The clue is in the question. The four Ps are 'variables' because they are of varying importance to the marketing effort as a whole, depending what it is you are marketing and what you are trying to achieve. They can be 'mixed' together in a huge number of different ways (and sometimes you have to add in other ingredients), just like flour, water and eggs may make pasta or they may make a Victoria sponge. The marketer's job is to find the right mix.

2   Perhaps what you want is promotion, or a new job, or a larger salary, none of which you will get simply by possessing this book. Hopefully, though, you also want more knowledge: read on!

3   No. A mere absence of complaints is not the same as the identification of customer needs. The firm, if anything, has a product orientation.

4   Firstly, establish the demand for completely silent washing machines. If demand is sufficiently widespread it is worth trying to address the problem. However, you must find out, by talking to customers, what the real problem is – perhaps that the sound travels to other rooms and wakes the baby or annoys the neighbours. There may well be product modifications, or add-on products, that can minimise this problem.

5   Part of the problem might be cultural. To the marketing department, the R&D department is filled with scatty boffins; to the R&D department, the marketing department is full of intellectually vacuous wideboys. Furthermore the R&D department may have an 'academic' or university atmosphere, not a commercial one.

Part of the problem is organisational. If R&D consumes substantial resources, it would seem quite logical to exploit economies of scale by having it centralised.

Marketing work and R&D work differ in many important respects. R&D work is likely to be more open-ended than marketing work.

Two good reasons why R&D should be more closely co-ordinated with marketing.

- With the marketing concept, the 'identification of customer needs' should be a vital input to new product developments.

- The R&D department might identify changes to product specifications, so that a variety of marketing mixes can be applied.

6   There may be policies about recycling toner cartridges or other office waste, special deals for disadvantaged groups, a favourite charity, a payroll giving scheme, and so on. Find out, if you don't know what your organisation does: it may well boast about it in its published accounts.

7   You should ensure you do this and relate it to your own career.

8   ICT applications in relationship marketing and maintenance include:

- The use of **databases**, to improve marketing planning, personalisation of customer contacts and provision of 'real-time' account/product/delivery details to customers (in conjunction with systems such as computer-telephony integration and sales force automation).

- The use of **multiple communication channels** for contact, including e-mail, website, mobile phone SMS messaging and so on.

- The use of **websites** to increase voluntary contact by customers: providing value-adding features (eg communities, database searches, special offers) and changing content to stimulate repeat 'visits'.

- The use of database, web and computer technology to **personalise customer contacts**: from personally addressed letters and postcards (using basic word processing 'merging' of databased details) to customer 'recognition' by customer service staff (using computer-telephony integration) to customised web experience (using cookies to 'remember' user preferences).

- The use of ICT to improve the **quality of customer contacts** and service: e-mail speeding up responses to queries; FAQs on websites allowing 'self-service' information; automated voice systems allowing telephone self-service (eg for routing of calls, bill payments by credit card, cinema ticket bookings and so on); e-commerce empowering customers (online shopping, Internet banking and so on).

- The use of online **monitoring and feedback** forms to gather customer preference data, enabling further contacts and offerings to be better tailored to customer needs.

- **Creative applications** aimed at customer 'delight' – eg sending birthday cards/e-mails to loyal customers.

- Using ICT tools for **loyalty schemes**: swipe card points systems, online vouchers and so on.

- Creating **customer communities**, as an incentive to identify with the organisation or brand (eg 'membership clubs', or online discussion boards).

Now try Question 1 at the end of the Study Text

Part B
Marketing planning and budgeting

Planning and budgeting

2

Syllabus content

- Explain the importance of the marketing planning process and where it fits into the corporate or organisational planning framework (2.1)
- Explain the models that describe the various stages of the marketing planning process (2.2)
- Explain the importance of objectives and the influences on, and processes for setting, objectives (2.6)
- Describe the structure of an outline marketing plan and identify its various components (2.8)
- Depict the various management structures available for implementing marketing plans, and understand their advantages and disadvantages (2.9)
- Examine the factors that affect the setting of marketing budgets (2.10)
- Demonstrate an appreciation of the need to monitor and control marketing activities (2.11)

Introduction

In this chapter, we look at aspects of marketing planning.

(a) We start with the role of the **marketing plan** within the corporate planning framework.

(b) We then look at a range of **models** for analysing the marketing situation (both external and internal) and for plotting competitive and growth strategies. (We pursue this further in Chapter 3, where we examine marketing research and audit.)

(c) Finally, we look at the setting of marketing **budgets** (as financial expressions of the marketing plan) and at how budgetary control and other methods can be used to monitor and control marketing activities.

1 A marketing plan

A **plan** is a way of achieving something. The shopping list you take to the supermarket is a simple example: it aims to achieve a well-stocked fridge and larder.

But imagine you are writing a shopping list so that another family member can do your food shopping for you. That's much closer to planning in an organisational sense.

- You'll need to spell out some things, eg where the most convenient supermarket is for your house, and what brands you prefer.

- You'll have to be flexible, giving the other person options if, for example, the brand specified on your list is out of stock.

- You'll have to make sure that doing the shopping fits in with the person's other plans.

- You'll need to set a limit on how much to spend.

A marketing plan is similar: as **detailed** as it needs to be; **adaptable** if necessary; **compatible** with the organisation's overall plan; properly **budgeted** and **controlled**.

1.1 An outline marketing plan

FAST FORWARD

The **marketing plan** should include situation analysis, objectives, strategy, action programmes, budget and controls.

Both in your CIM studies and in your career, you may be asked to prepare a marketing plan. Below is a suggested **outline** of a comprehensive plan. You may not understand some of the terms yet, but don't worry: all will be explained in this chapter and the next.

Exam tip

The December 2002, 2003 and 2004 and June 2005 and 2006 exams included questions on the stages or components of a marketing plan! (In 2005, it was part of the compulsory Part A question.) In other words, you must learn the material! This is, in any case, a helpful **framework** for thinking through marketing strategies.

BPP LEARNING MEDIA

Marketing Plan

1	**Executive summary**	A short high-level summary of the major points of the plan to orient the reader, if the plan is a lengthy report
2	**Mission statement and corporate objectives**	The internal context of the plan: where the organisation is trying to get to, and what its key guiding values are
3	**Situation analysis/marketing audit**	
	• Macro environment audit	Eg PEST factor analysis
	• Micro environment audit	Eg Internal systems/culture/skills audit
		Competitor analysis
		Customer analysis
		Market/product/price research
		[including product life cycle analysis, market share analysis etc]
4	**SWOT analysis**	Appraisal of internal strengths and weaknesses, and external opportunities and threats
5	**Marketing objectives**	What the marketing plan is intended to achieve (in the light of elements 2-4)
6	**Marketing strategies**	How marketing objectives will be achieved
	• Matching or conversion?	Suggested by SWOT analysis
	• Competitive strategies?	Suggested by competitor/market/product analysis
	• Growth strategies?	Suggested by product/market analysis [eg Ansoff matrix]
	• Market segmentation /targeting?	Identifying targetable sub-sections of the market or customer population
	• Product/brand positioning?	Determining how product/brand should be perceived by the relevant target market/segment
7	**Marketing tactics**	Action plans for each of the elements of the (extended) marketing mix, to implement marketing strategies
	• Product plans	
	• Pricing plans	
	• Distribution plans	
	• Promotion plans	
8	**Marketing budget**	Quantified monetary plans: sales/revenue forecasts, costs/expenditure budgets, forecast profit and loss statement
9	**Timetable**	Detailed timescales for implementation of plans
10	**Monitoring and control**	How progress and results will be monitored, reviewed and measured against objectives/budget
11	**Summary/conclusion**	If required. There may also be an appendix (or appendices) with supporting documents and figures which are too detailed to include in the body of the plan.

Note that a comprehensive plan provides for:

- **Analysis** of the situation/market/SWOT
- **Planning**: objective setting and strategy formulation
- **Implementation**: action plans and budgets to guide implementation
- **Control**: measuring progress/results against the plan

Note also that this is only an **outline** – and only an **example**. Depending on the context, and the information available, some of the steps may change, or change priority. If you are working with a very constrained or pre-set budget, for example, the budget item may need to be stated early in the plan. The models used to determine strategy will depend on the marketing audit and SWOT analysis (as we will see later).

There is a US company called Mplans that sells templates for marketing plans and you can look at some samples free if you visit the website: www.mplans.com. The CIM Learning Zone also contains an online marketing planning tool: www.cim.co.uk.

2 Corporate strategy and marketing planning

FAST FORWARD

Planning enables organisations to be effective, not just efficient. Information is gathered and used to develop a corporate plan which acts as a framework within which specific functions such as marketing can develop their own objectives and plans.

Take good note of the following terms: you will encounter them whenever you are reading about any aspect of marketing or business as a whole.

Key concepts

Planning involves:

- setting objectives, quantifying targets for achievement and communicating these targets to others
- selecting strategies, tactics, policies, programmes and procedures for achieving the objective

Goals: what you are trying to achieve; the intention behind any action.

Objectives: a goal which can be quantified. *Example:* increase profits by 30% over the next 12 months.

Aims: goals which cannot be expressed in quantifiable terms. *Example:* customer satisfaction or loyalty.

Strategy: the method chosen to achieve goals or objectives. *Example:* we will achieve our objective of increasing profits by growing market share in existing markets.

Tactics: how resources are deployed in an agreed strategy. *Example:* we will set up a new telephone call centre and target new customers.

Action Programme 1

Explain your CIM studies using the key concepts listed above.

2.1 Marketing planning in context

An organisation's overall development is guided by **corporate strategic plans**.

Marketing plans and strategies will be developed within that framework and will be very closely linked with plans for other functions of the organisation. This approach ensures that marketing efforts are consistent with organisational goals and that the resources available within the organisation are used as effectively as possible.

This can be depicted as follows: Figure 2.1.

Figure 2.1: The hierarchy of planning

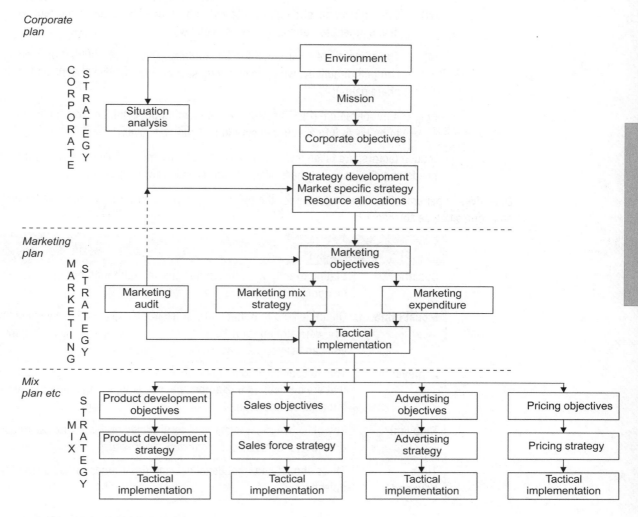

2.2 Setting objectives

FAST FORWARD

Objectives should be **SMART**: Specific, Measurable, Achievable, Relevant and Time-bounded.

Objectives should set out clearly what the organisation is aiming to achieve. Objectives enter into the planning process both at the corporate level and at the marketing level.

(a) **Corporate objectives** define specific goals for the organisation as a whole. These may be expressed in terms of profitability, returns on investment, growth of asset base, earnings per share and so on. They may also reflect non-financial goals: innovation, market share, corporate social responsibility, leading employer brand etc.

(b) Corporate objectives need to be translated into market-specific **marketing objectives**. These may involve targets for the size of the customer base, growth in the usage of certain facilities, gains in market share for a particular product type etc. Marketing objectives will be influenced by a range of factors including:

(i)   The strategic objectives of the business as a whole (eg growth, innovation);

(ii)   The resources (skills, competences, finance, relationships) available;

(iii)   Marketing strategy decisions, eg cost leadership or differentiation (Porter's generic strategies); product/market strategies (Ansoff matrix);

(iv)   Other functional strategies that need to be aligned with marketing (eg HR development to support marketing activity);

(v)   The competitive environment in the industry (Five Forces model) or specific competitor activity; which may dictate specific competitive objectives (eg market share gains);

(vi)   Environmental (PEST) factors (eg presenting opportunities to exploit or constraints to be taken into account in setting realistic objectives).

If such factors, are taken into account, objectives are more likely to be relevant (to the needs and challenges of the business) and realistic (given its constraints).

Objectives in general should be evaluated for the following criteria, in order to be effective for directing and controlling performance.

SMART	In what sense is an objective SMART?
Specific	Stating exactly what has to be achieved (although not how the job should be done).
Measurable	Quantified, so that that you can tell if the objective has been achieved. If you were aiming for a 10% market share and gained a 15% market share you can tell you have achieved your objective.
Achievable	The objective has to be realistic in the circumstances, given the resources that are available: for example, people, equipment, materials, money, information and time.
Relevant	The objective must relate both to the roles of those who are to achieve the objective and to the wider objectives of the organisation.
Time bounded	There should be target deadlines and timeframes for achieving the objective

2.3 Summary: the marketing planning process

The planning process can be expressed as shown in Figure 2.2. The process is continual and the plan could be reviewed and 'restarted' at any stage.

BPP LEARNING MEDIA

Figure 2.2: The marketing planning process

3 Planning models

FAST FORWARD

A variety of **models** can be used in the marketing planning process, including: PEST analysis, SWOT analysis, Porter's five competitive forces, and Ansoff's growth matrix.

Key concept

A **model** is a representation of a 'real-world' situation. There are physical models (like product prototypes or architectural models) and also visual or verbal or mathematical descriptions of things that happen in the real world.

3.1 Situation analysis

FAST FORWARD

Situation analysis is used to provide the context for marketing planning.

Situation analysis requires a thorough study of the broad trends within the economy and society, as well as a detailed analysis of markets, consumers and competitors.

- **PEST factor analysis** (see below) may be used to describe relevant factors and trends in the external environment.

- **Marketing research** (including market research, product research and customer research) provides information on the external environment.

- An **audit** of the organisation's marketing activities provides information on the internal environment.

- Various models such as **SWOT analysis** (see below) may be used to organise and present the results of a situation analysis.

Marketing research and marketing audit are discussed in Chapter 3. We will look briefly at PEST and SWOT here.

3.2 PEST factors

FAST FORWARD

PEST analysis looks at Political/legal, Environmental, Social/cultural, and Technological factors affecting the organisation.

An organisation exists within society as a whole: changes in the **external environment** will form the basis for drawing up marketing plans, identifying profitable products and determining the best routes to reach consumers. Careful monitoring of the external environment will help an organisation to identify opportunities and threats and be proactive rather than reactive in the face of change. (This will be discussed further in your studies for the *Marketing Environment* module.)

The external environment can be described in terms of four key components: Political/legal, Economic, Social/cultural, and Technological (**PEST factors**). A more complete version of this model is STEEPLE: Socio-cultural, Technological, Economic, Ecological, Political, Legal and Ethical factors. Figure 2.3 below shows these factors.

Figure 2.3: The total environment

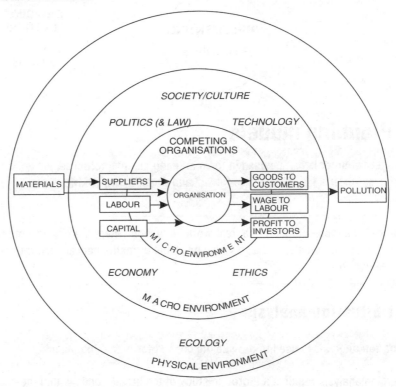

3.2.1 The political/legal environment

This involves the interaction between organisations and **government** or regulatory bodies. It includes **legal restrictions** imposed to regulate businesses and less formal aspects of government relations with businesses, such as nationwide initiatives to encourage skills training. International developments, including formalised **trade agreements** (eg the European Union), are becoming increasingly important.

3.2.2 The economic environment

Developments within **the economy** – which are likely to have an impact on businesses either directly, or as a result of their impact on consumer spending – are critical to business. Key aspects of the economic environment include inflation, unemployment, economic growth, consumer income, interest rates and currency fluctuations (in international trade).

BPP
LEARNING MEDIA

3.2.3 The social/cultural environment

This includes **demographic change** and changing **attitudes and perceptions**. Many developed countries have an ageing population, which has many implications for marketers and recruiters. The changing role of women may also affect the marketer. The focus on 'green'/ environmental and ethical issues has had an increasing influence over the last few years. Cultural values and norms also influence buyer behaviour and tastes in different national/ethnic contexts, creating particular challenges for international marketing.

3.2.4 The technological environment

The nature and rate of change in technology affects the way an organisation undertakes its business. **Technological change** has been ever greater and ever faster in recent years, most notably in computing and telecommunications (or ICT), but also in the biological sciences. This creates new product potential – as well as new marketing tools.

Action Programme 2

How might each of the PEST factors impact on decisions about the 4Ps of the marketing mix? Give one example of possible impacts of each PEST factor on each 'P'.

Exam tip

> The impact of environmental factors on the marketing mix was set as a question in December 2003, 2004 and 2005. The questions all specified an **international** context. Tip 1: learn to notice key words like this in exam questions! Tip 2: if asked to discuss PEST or environmental factors, don't forget that the relevant environment is, these days, quite *likely* to be international or even global. Tip 3: PEST is sometimes referred to as SLEPT (Social, Legal, Economic, Political, Technological) or PESTLE (Political, Economic, Social, Technological, Legal, Ecological) or even STEEPLE (Social, Technological, Economic, Ecological, Political, Legal, Ethical): don't panic! Tip 4: don't forget the industry/market context. (PEST factors relevant to a computer manufacturer may be different to those affecting a fast food retailer and a global aid/charity organisation … Think how.)

3.3 SWOT analysis

FAST FORWARD

> **SWOT analysis** enables an organisation to plan how to match its strengths to available opportunities and/or to convert its weaknesses into strengths or its threats into opportunities.

This technique provides a method for organising information to identify strategic direction. The basic principle is that any internal feature of an organisation can be classified as a potential Strength or Weakness, and any feature of its external environment can be classified as a potential Opportunity or Threat.

Classification	Comment
Strength	A particular skill or distinctive competence which the organisation possesses, which will aid it in achieving its stated objectives.
Weakness	Any aspect of the company which may hinder the achievement of specific objectives.
Opportunity	Any feature of (or change in) the external environment which creates conditions potentially advantageous to the firm in relation to specific objectives.
Threat	Any feature of (or change in) the external environment which present problems or hinder the achievement of organisational objectives.

This information would typically be presented as a **matrix**: Figure 2.4. Effective SWOT analysis does not simply categorise information: it also requires some evaluation of the relative importance of the various factors.

Figure 2.4: SWOT matrix

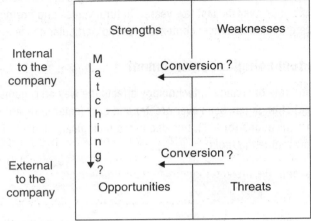

Two major **strategic options** arise from a SWOT analysis

(a) **Matching** the strengths of the organisation to the opportunities presented by the market: the strengths should allow the organisation to capitalise on the opportunity.

(b) **Conversion** of weaknesses into strengths in order to take advantage of some particular opportunity, or of threats into opportunities which can then be matched by existing strengths. This may require the organisation to recruit or develop new competences, improve its systems, invest in new technology, develop or improve products and so on.

Marketing at Work

As just one example of how environmental threats can be turned into strategic opportunity ...

'GlaxoSmithKline (GSK), Britain's largest drugs company, is in talks with the World Health Organisation (WHO) about a proposal for a subsidised mass vaccination programme against avian flu for developing countries.

'GSK's chief executive, will meet the WHO's director-general to discuss proposals to provide low-cost vaccines against the H5N1 virus to countries such as Indonesia, which has suffered the highest number of deaths from avian flu so far.

'The negotiations come after concern that poorer countries, particularly in the Far East, are likely to be at the forefront of any human outbreak of pandemic flu but could be unable to afford to buy the vaccines being developed by big Western drug companies.

'The governments of Switzerland and the United States have already begun to stockpile a prepandemic H5N1 flu vaccine developed by GSK. The company is also in talks with the governments of Britain, France and other countries.'

Times Online, April 2, 2007

Action Programme 3

Think about the issues involved in SWOT analysis in relation to the company you work for, or the organisation you study with.

3.4 Competitive strategies

FAST FORWARD

Competitive strategies (Porter) involve deciding

- whether to compete across the whole market or only in certain segments (competitive scope)
- whether to compete through low costs/prices or by offering a differentiated product range (competitive advantage)

Management must decide how it will compete with other organisations and what it perceives as the basis of its competitive advantage.

3.4.1 Five competitive forces

The American strategist *Michael Porter* (1998) categorises **five competitive forces** in the environment of a firm. These can be used to determine the overall potential profitability of an industry for an existing or potential player in the market. Industry potential depends on:

- The threat of **new entrants** to the industry, and the existence of **barriers to entry** which might *deter* new entrants

- The threat of **substitute products** or services

- The bargaining power of **customers**

- The bargaining power of **suppliers**
- The rivalry amongst **current competitors** in the industry

Force	Example
The threat of new entrants	Australian airline Qantas faced with the entry of Virgin Blue into the Australasian market.
The threat of substitute products or services	Traditional mail services being overtaken by email and mobile text messaging.
The bargaining power of customers	Supermarket chains (as customers) can dictate to suppliers over packaging and pricing.
The bargaining power of suppliers	Software. Once time has been invested using a package it is often not practical to change suppliers.
The rivalry amongst current competitors	Mobile phone companies, MP3 players.

3.4.2 Generic competitive strategies

Organisations must decide whether to compete across the entire market or only in certain segments (**competitive scope**), and whether to compete through low costs and prices or through offering a differentiated product range (**competitive advantage**).

These competitive strategy options can be expressed as four possible **generic strategies**.

- Cost leadership
- Cost focus
- Differentiation leadership
- Differentiation focus

The strategies can be shown as a matrix: Figure 2.5.

Figure 2.5: Competitive strategy matrix

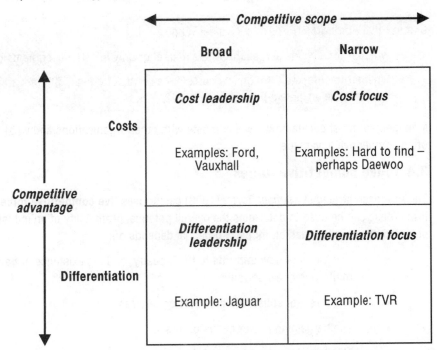

(a) **Cost leadership** attempts to control a broad market through being the low cost producer. This would be appropriate if an organisation has a costing advantage over competitors, due to factors such as economies of scale, superior working practices or a technological advantage.

(b) **Differentiation leadership** aims to offer products which are recognised as unique in areas which are highly valued by the consumer. It is the products' uniqueness and the associated customer loyalty that protects the firm from competition. However, the price premium received must outweigh the costs of supplying the differentiated product and the customer must feel that the extra features more than compensate for the price premium.

(c) **Focus** strategies use either **costs** or **differentiation** within particularly attractive market segments or **niches**.

- In **cost focus** a firm seeks a cost advantage in its target segment.
- In **differentiation focus** a firm seeks differentiation in its target segment.

Differentiation focus is the most common form of focus strategy and implies producing highly customised products for very specific consumer groups.

It is important to avoid being 'stuck in the middle' – trying to be all things to all consumers. The firm trying to perform well on costs *and* on differentiation is likely to lose out to firms concentrating on either one strategy or the other.

3.5 Growth strategies

FAST FORWARD

The **Ansoff Product/Market matrix** is used to classify growth strategies. It produces four strategies: market penetration or development, product development and diversification.

Ansoff's Product/Market matrix (Figure 2.6) suggests that an organisation's attempts to grow its business depends on whether it markets new or existing products in new or existing markets. This produces four possible options.

BPP LEARNING MEDIA

Figure 2.6: Ansoff's growth strategies

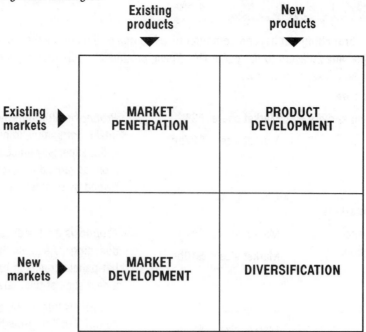

(a) **Market penetration**

This involves selling more of the existing products in existing markets. Possible options are persuading existing users to use more; persuading non-users to use; or attracting consumers from competitors. This is only a viable strategy if the market is not already saturated with suppliers.

(b) **Market development**

This involves expanding into new markets with existing products. These may be new markets geographically, new market segments or new uses for products. For example, a lawyer based in the north of a country may start to offer an online legal advice service, thereby opening up a much larger market nationwide, or even worldwide.

(c) **Product development**

This approach requires the organisation to develop new products to appeal to existing markets. This may be done by tailoring the products more specifically to the needs of existing consumers, or by developing related products which will appeal to the customer base. An example might be a supermarket that extends its opening hours to 24 hours a day, and starts selling petrol or financial services on site.

(d) **Diversification**

Diversification – new products into new markets – is a more risky strategy because the organisation is moving into areas in which it has little or no experience. Instances of pure diversification are rare and usually occur only when there are no other possible routes for growth available. Virgin is one example of a company that has diversified very successfully.

Exam tip

The December 2006 exam asked you to explain the factors influencing a firm's marketing objectives, and how Ansoff's matrix could be used to develop marketing strategies to meet these objectives. Most candidates were able to discuss the matrix – but you needed (a) to apply it to the context (a computer hardware manufacturer) and (b) show how the most appropriate strategy could be selected, based on the organisation's marketing objectives. You must learn to read all parts of a question in order to interpret the examiner's requirements correctly.

Marketing at Work

Intel is **branching out** beyond computer chips to make semiconductors for a host of new products, from portable video players to flat-panel TVs. These products, in turn, are expected to boost Intel's core PC and server business. Here's how:

At the core

PCs and servers	Market share	83%	*Prognosis* Although rival AMD is coming on strong, Intel's dominance in microprocessors seems rock-solid, especially since it has five factories with the most advanced technology to every one factory owned by competitors.
	Market size	$27bn	

New markets

Flat-panel televisions	Market share	0%	*Prognosis* Intel is developing processors for decoding TV signals that could cut the cost of some flat-panel screens in half this year. That could win it a neat slice of the market.
	Market size	$10bn	
Handhelds	Market share	50%	*Prognosis* Intel's chips power half of all handheld computers, but growth prospects are dim. The market contracted 18% last year.
	Market size	$2bn	
Personal media players	Market share	0%	*Prognosis* Intel is positioned to become a leading maker of processors and memory chips for these portable video players, but the demand is still tiny.
	Market size	$50m	
Cellular phones	Market share	20%	*Prognosis* Intel's memory-chip sales have been relatively strong, but its bid in digital signal processors and other phone chips has been a flop so far
	Market size	$9bn	
Entertainment PCs	Market share	90%	*Prognosis* Intel-powered PCs designed to play movies or music in the living room are flying off the shelves. New designs due later this year could boost sales further.
	Market size	$120m	

Business Week (Asia) March 8, 2004

4 Marketing management structure

FAST FORWARD

There are a variety of ways in which the **marketing function** can be **organised** to implement marketing plans most effectively: by function, by geography, by product market or some other kind of matrix structure.

4.1 Functional organisation

The department organised by function (Figure 2.7) is typically headed by a marketing director who is responsible for the overall co-ordination of the marketing effort. A number of **functional specialists**, such as a market research manager and a public relations manager, will be found in the second tier of management and they take responsibility for all activities in their specialist discipline across all products and markets.

This approach also allows individuals to develop their particular specialisms while the marketing director co-ordinates their plans and budgets to ensure the development of a coherent marketing mix for elements of the product range.

Figure 2.7: Functional organisation

For a limited range of products, the burden on the marketing director is unlikely to be severe. As the organisation's range of products and markets expands, however, this arrangement will tend to be less efficient. There is always the danger that a particular product or market may be neglected because it is only one of a great variety being handled by a specific functional manager.

4.2 Geographical organisation

A simple geographical organisation for a marketing department (Figure 2.8) is an extension of the functional organisation in which responsibility for some or all functional activities is devolved to a **regional level**.

This type of organisation would be suitable for firms operating **internationally**, where the various functional activities would be required for each national market or group of national markets.

The structure also tends to be adopted by larger companies where there are strong **regional differences**. An FMCG manufacturing company, for example, may supply multiple grocery chains that are organised regionally and therefore develop regional sales/sales promotions managers to link up with customers and regional store managers.

Figure 2.8: Geographical organisation

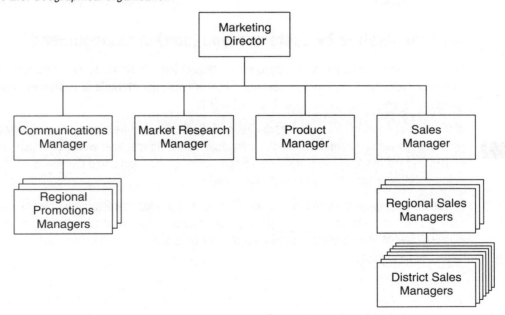

4.3 Product-based organisation

This involves adding an additional tier of management which supplements the activities of functional managers. Product managers take responsibility for specific products or groups of products. This type of approach is likely to be particularly appropriate for organisations with either very diverse products or with a large range of products, possibly even different brands that compete against one another: Figure 2.9.

Figure 2.9: Product management

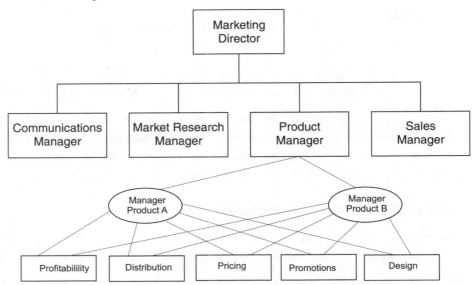

The individual product manager is responsible for developing plans to suit specific products and ensures that products remain competitive, drawing on the experience and guidance of functional managers. This allows the individual product managers to build up considerable experience and understanding of particular product groups, which is invaluable within a rapidly changing competitive environment. Very often the title **brand manager** rather than product manager will be used.

The product-based approach is becoming increasingly popular, because the benefits of managers having accountability and expertise for specific product groups outweigh the costs associated with a loss of functional specialisation.

4.4 Organisation by customer type (market management)

In a variant on the product-based approach, instead of individual managers taking responsibility for particular products, they may take responsibility for particular **markets** or **customer segments**: in banking, for example, corporate, personal or high-net-worth.

In the case of services, for instance, market management would be a useful way of developing closer relationships with customers, since the individual marketing manager would be much better able to understand the range of needs displayed by particular groups and could then draw on the organisation's product range as appropriate to meet those needs.

Where the buying motives and the buying behaviour of groups of customers differ radically from those of other groups, there is a case for organising marketing by customer type - often to the extent that each type will have its own dedicated marketing mix, its own dedicated marketing team and sometimes even a dedicated sales force.

BPP LEARNING MEDIA

Action Programme 4

What would be the characteristics of a market-based approach to organising marketing departments in a banking environment?

4.5 Matrix management

Product and market management are forms of **matrix structure**, where people report *both* to:

(a)   their managers in functional departments *and*

(b)   a product/brand/market manager who co-ordinates the activities of staff across functional boundaries, in order to achieve shared objectives.

Project management (which might be used to put together a product 'pitch' to a client, say) is another example of multi-disciplinary team working under the authority of a co-ordinating manager.

Tom *Peters* (1994) called this a form of **horizontal structure**, which facilitates the flow of work across department/function boundaries, overlaid on the **vertical structure** of organisational authority (down the chain of line management). Horizontal structures (such as multi-disciplinary or project teams) are important in customer service, Peters argues, because the experience of a customer is horizontal, moving from one function to another (marketing, sales, accounts, after-sales service).

Action Programme 5

What do you think are the advantages of adopting a matrix structure?

While this system may seem the ideal approach to resolving the dilemma about the most appropriate form of organisation for a marketing department, it presents certain **problems**.

- **Cost** is likely to be significant because there are more managers.

- There are also possible sources of **conflict** between functional and product/market/ project managers.

- Managers' concerns about their own **status** may make a matrix structure, and the culture of co-operation that it fosters, difficult to accept.

4.6 Divisional marketing organisation

Within many organisations larger product groups have developed into separate divisions. **Divisions** have a high degree of control over their own affairs, but are ultimately responsible to head office.

Marketing activity here will often be devolved to divisional level. Some marketing activities will be the responsibility of corporate headquarters, but the extent of corporate involvement can vary greatly.

5 Marketing budgets

FAST FORWARD

A marketing budget shows **how much the organisation intends to spend** carrying out the marketing plan.

5.1 Setting marketing budgets

FAST FORWARD

Marketing budgets may be set using a number of methods, of which the objective and task method is the most scientific. Budgeting may be tricky if expenditure is very dependent on the level of sales, because that is hard to predict.

There are a number of ways of setting marketing budgets.

(a) **Percentage of sales**. Research in the UK has shown that some marketing budgets are fixed by some rule-of-thumb, non-scientific methods, for example.

  (i) A percentage of the **previous year's sales**
  (ii) A percentage of the **budgeted annual sales**
  (iii) A percentage of the **previous year's profit**

  There is no reason, however, why marketing costs should relate directly to either total turnover or profits. Given that large amounts of expenditure may be incurred on advertising, these arbitrary guesswork systems reveal an alarming lack of proper financial control.

(b) **Competitive parity**, ie fixing marketing expenditure in relation to the expenditure incurred by competitors. (This is unsatisfactory because it presupposes that the competitor's decision must be a good one.)

(c) **All-you-can-afford**. Crude and unscientific, but commonly used. The firm simply takes a view on what it thinks it can afford to spend on marketing.

(d) **The objective and task method**. The marketing objectives are set and then the tasks needed to accomplish them are identified. The budget is set by estimating the cost of these tasks. This is the most scientific method, but obviously it is much more difficult and time-consuming to prepare such a budget.

Exam tip

> The June 2006 exam asked for four factors that should be considered when setting a marketing budget. You could use the methods above as a framework. However, as this particular question concerned a government department, the 'affordability' factor might also have raised issues of centrally-set budgets and budgetary constraints. *Always* think about the context!

The example below shows a typical marketing budget.

Marketing budget

	£m
Salaries and wages of marketing staff	X,000
Advertising expenses	X,000
Travelling and distribution costs	X,000
Market research activities	X,000
Promotional activities	X,000
Selling and agency commission	X,000
	X,000

Cost items such as salaries are **fixed** costs (being allocated regardless of the amount of activity or sales), although there will be some **variable** costs, such as sales commission (which will vary according to the volume of sales). Some of the marketing budget will have to be prepared in conjunction with the **sales budget**, since different levels of sales require different levels of marketing support. The balance of the budget may well be determined by the activity anticipated from new products which may be launched during the year, and which will need extra promotional support.

5.2 Advertising costs

Advertising is an important feature of the marketing budget. It operates on the theory of **diminishing returns**. For every extra £1 of advertising spent, the company will earn an extra £x of profit, but the marginal return £x typically diminishes until it is less than the amount spent in achieving it: further expenditure cannot be justified past this point. Unfortunately, the marginal return from additional advertising cannot usually be measured easily in practice.

(a) Advertising is only **one aspect** of the overall marketing mix.

(b) Advertising has a **long-term effect**, which goes beyond the limits of a measurable accounting period.

The US merchant John Wanamaker is supposed to have said: 'I know that 50 per cent of my advertising is wasted, but I don't know which 50 per cent'.

Recommended practice for fixing advertising cost budgets would include the use of the following.

(a) **Empirical testing** (eg with direct response advertising, web advertising or in retail sales). It may be possible to measure the effect of advertising on sales by direct observation.

(b) **Mathematical models** using data about media and consumer characteristics, desired market share, and using records of past results.

6 Monitoring and control

FAST FORWARD

Marketing plans should be **monitored** (using the full range of available management information) to make sure they are progressing as intended. **Control action** should be taken if things start to go wrong.

Once the marketing plan is implemented, the task of management is to monitor and control what happens. Monitoring means **checking** that everything is going to plan. Control means taking **corrective action** as early as possible if things are not going to plan.

Monitoring and control is accomplished in, the following ways.

- Regular comparison of actual sales and marketing costs against **budget**

- Analysis of the **performance** of individual products, individual distribution outlets, individual sales people, etc. Information collected by the accounting system and other management systems can be used to calculate a huge variety of financial and non-financial performance measures, as regularly as is felt necessary.

- Collection of **feedback** from customers and other stakeholders

- Analysis of **media coverage**, for instance reviews of new products in the trade press

- Continual observation of the **environment**. Have competitors unexpectedly launched a new product? Is the economy going into recession? And so on.

We will be talking in more detail about the kind of monitoring and control information you can get from a modern **marketing information system** in the next chapter, as part of our discussion of marketing audit.

Meanwhile, remember a point that we made at the very beginning of this chapter (when we were sending your family member shopping). A marketing plan is not set in stone: it needs to be **flexible**. If market conditions have changed quite unpredictably, as they did for many businesses on September 11 2001, or with the SARS or bird flu outbreaks there is no point in agonising over not meeting the original targets. It is time to draw up a new plan.

Chapter Roundup

- The marketing plan should include **situation analysis**, **objectives**, **strategy**, **action programmes**, **budget** and **controls**.

- **Planning** enables organisations to be effective, not just efficient. Information is gathered and used to develop a corporate plan which acts as a framework within which specific functions such as marketing can develop their own objectives and plans.

- Objectives should be **SMART**: Specific, Measurable, Achievable, Relevant and Time-bounded.

- A variety of **models** can be used in the marketing planning process, including: PEST analysis, SWOT analysis, Porter's five competitive forces, and Ansoff's growth matrix.

- **Situation analysis** is used to provide the context for marketing planning.

- **PEST analysis** looks at Political/legal, Environmental, Social/cultural, and Technological factors affecting the organisation.

- **SWOT analysis** enables an organisation to choose whether to match its strengths to available opportunities, or to convert its weaknesses into strengths or its threats into opportunities.

- **Competitive strategies** (Porter) involve deciding

  - whether to compete across the whole market or only in certain segments (competitive scope)
  - whether to compete through low costs/prices or by offering a differentiated product range (competitive advantage)

- The **Ansoff Product/Market matrix** is used to classify growth strategies. It produces four strategies: market penetration or development, product development and diversification.

- There are a variety of ways in which the **marketing function can be organised** to implement marketing plans most effectively: by function, by geography, by product market or some other kind of matrix structure.

- **Marketing budgets** may be set using a number of methods, of which the objective and task method is the most scientific. Budgeting may be tricky if expenditure is very dependent on the level of sales, because that is hard to predict.

- Marketing plans should be **monitored** (using the full range of available management information) to make sure they are progressing as intended. **Control action** should be taken if things start to go wrong.

BPP
LEARNING MEDIA

Quick Quiz

1 What are the six stages in the marketing planning cycle?

2 Why should objectives be Measurable and Time-bounded?

3 You should be able to fill in this grid easily.

The letter stands for:	And its opposite is:
S....................	....
T....................	....
O....................	....
W....................	....

4 Give one example of each of the PEST factors.

Factor	Example
Political/legal	
Economic	
Social/cultural	
Technological	

5 The five competitive forces are:

(1) N............ E....................

(2) S....................... P........................

(3) C.............................. B................................. P.................................

(4) S.............................. B................................. P.................................

(5) C..............................

6 'Differentiation leadership' and 'Differentiation focus' – what's the difference?

7 Fill in the grid with the word 'Existing' or 'Modified' or 'New', as appropriate.

Growth strategy	Products	Market
Diversification		
Product development		
Market penetration		
Market development		

8 Draw an organisation chart showing a marketing department organised on a geographical basis.

9 What are four common ways of setting a marketing budget? Which is the best, in theory?

10 Monitoring and control can be done in a large variety of ways including (1)................. of (2) .... against (3) ...., collection of (4) ...., measuring of (5) .... and (6) .... of the environment.

Feedback	Performance	Budget
Comparison	Actual figures	Observation

Answers to Quick Quiz

1   Marketing audit, deciding objectives, deciding strategy, deciding objectives, implementation and control.

2   They should be measurable so you can tell whether or not you have achieved them. They should be time-bound because after a certain time it will be too late to achieve them.

3   We jumbled them up to make you think a bit harder.

The letter stands for:	And its opposite is:
Strengths	Weaknesses
Threats	Opportunities
Opportunities	Threats
Weaknesses	Strengths

4

Factor	Example
Political/legal	Legislation against unsolicited marketing, age discrimination (coming up in 2006) etc
Economic	Inflation, putting pressure on prices
Social/cultural	Attitudes (for example the role of junk fund in child obesity) Fashions (for example, i-pods)
Technological	Genetically modified crops; e-commerce and m-commerce options

5   (1)   New Entrants
    (2)   Substitute Products
    (3)   Customers' Bargaining Power
    (4)   Suppliers' Bargaining Power
    (5)   Competitors

6   Differentiation leadership: the organisation aims to offer products which are recognised as unique in areas which are highly valued by consumers. Differentiation focus: a firm seeks differentiation leadership, but in its target segment only.

7

Growth strategy	Products	Market
Diversification	New	New
Product development	Modified	Existing
Market penetration	Existing	Existing
Market development	Existing	New

8

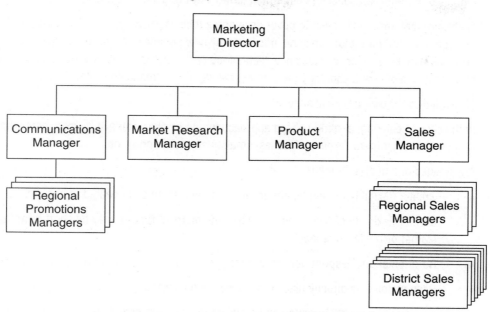

Geographical organisation

9   Percentage of sales: Competitive parity: All-you-can-afford; The objective and task method. The objective and task method is the best in theory, though the most time-consuming and difficult to implement (although with modern information systems this is a poor excuse).

10   (1) Comparison; (2) Actual figures; (3) Budget; (4) Feedback; (5) Performance; (6) Observation. If you had (2) and (3) the other way round that is OK, provided you don't think the budget is more important than what happened in real life.

Action Programme Review

1   **Aim**   Be successful in your career

     Strategy   Study for the CIM qualification

     Goals   Pass the exams

     Objectives   Pass the December 2007 or June 2008 exams

     Tactics   Study for 2 hours a night

     Planning   What you've been doing if you answered this question seriously!

2   **Political/legal**: government policy may affect **price** through the imposition of tariffs; **place** decisions may be influenced by government grants for development in specific areas; legal restrictions may influence **product** packaging and safety; legislation also constrains **promotional** messages and methods (eg truth in advertising).

     Economic: **price** may be affected by exchange rates and the disposable income of a society; **place** decisions may be affected by viability of markets and the need for low-cost distribution; **products** will be influenced by the level of demand within an economy; and **promotion** will need to be tailored to consumer perceptions of affluence or economic hardship.

     Social/cultural: **price** may be affected by cultural values about frugality or quality; **place** may be affected by social norms about shopping (eg preferences for markets, e-commerce take-up, preference for personal service); **products** will respond to consumer trends and fashions, demographic factors (different needs of youth and 'grey'/aged markets); **promotion** will likewise respond to cultural values and attitudes (eg use of humour, influence of children on family buying, gender buying roles).

Technological: **price** may need to cover development costs, or pass on cost savings (eg lower sales costs through e-commerce); **place** may be influenced by new channels of distribution (eg Internet purchasing); **products** may be developed to use new technology (eg digital cameras or e-learning services); **promotions** may make use of new technology (eg Internet selling, e-mail marketing, SMS marketing).

3   This will be your own personal answer.

4   In the case of banking, a market based approach would be characterised by managers with responsibility for personal customers, large businesses, small businesses and so on.

5   Advantages of a matrix structure

- Greater flexibility of people. Employees and departments are geared to change.

- Greater flexibility of tasks and structure. The matrix structure may be short term (as with project teams) or readily amended.

- Re-orientation. Responsiveness to customer needs is closer to pure market-orientation.

- Responsibility is directly placed on individual managers.

- Interdisciplinary co-operation and a mixing of skills and expertise.

- Arguably, motivation of employees by providing them with greater participation in planning and control decisions.

Now try Questions 2 and 3 at the end of the Study Text

Marketing research, market segmentation and marketing audit

3

Syllabus content

- Explain the concept of the marketing audit as an appraisal of the external marketing environment and an organisation's internal marketing operations (2.3)
- Describe the role of various analytical tools in the marketing auditing process (2.4)
- Explain the value of marketing research and information in developing marketing plans (2.5)
- Explain the concept of market segmentation and distinguish effective bases for segmenting consumer and business-to-business markets (2.7)

Introduction

In this chapter we will have an in-depth look at some of the 'situational analysis' stages of the marketing planning process.

A **market orientation** is about identifying and satisfying customer needs better than competitors. This requires **research**: gathering information about customers, competitors, products etc.

The organisation may wish to tailor its marketing efforts more closely to the needs of potential customers. **Market segmentation** recognises that, although buyers have diverse needs, sets of needs may be grouped together and a different marketing approach may be used for each group. This also requires information about the external environment, in order to identify targetable sections of the customer population and their characteristics.

A **marketing audit** is an internal review of the organisation's recent past performance and current capabilities, but it is also the launchpad for the next marketing plan: how can we do it better next time? What is our potential for growth and change?

We are still talking about marketing planning, but the topics discussed here are so fundamental to good marketing practice that they deserve a separate chapter to themselves.

1 Marketing research

FAST FORWARD

Marketing research is the gathering, recording and analysing of data about problems relating to the marketing of goods and services.

Key concept

Marketing research is 'the systematic gathering, recording and analysing of data about problems relating to the marketing of goods and services' (*The American Marketing Association*).

Within this definition, there are a few points to note.

(a)   Marketing research should provide a **regular** information system to aid planning and control decisions by marketing and senior management.

(b)   Marketing research is concerned with **all types of customer** and user (industrial, government and resellers) not just the household consumer.

(c)   Marketing research provides information which enables managers to make **decisions about the marketing mix**: product, place, price and promotion. It is not simply 'market' research.

Marketing plans are made under conditions of uncertainty and risk. Marketing research aims to reduce risk by providing information about the factors involved and possible outcomes of particular actions.

1.1 Information for marketing

FAST FORWARD

Market research has a narrower focus. It involves gathering information about the market for a particular product or service (typically, consumer attitudes, existing product usage etc). Other forms of research include product, price, sales promotion and distribution research – covering the full range of marketing mix variables.

A wide variety of information may be relevant to marketing decisions.

(a) **Market research** involves the gathering of information about the market for a particular produce or service : consumer attitudes, environmental influences on supply and demand, competition, product usage and so on.

- Analysis of the market potential for existing products
- Forecasting likely demand for new products
- Sales forecasting for all products
- Study of market trends
- Study of the characteristics of the market
- Analysis of market share and competitor activity

(b) **Product research** is concerned with the product – whether in development, new, improved or already on the market – and how customers might respond to it.

- Customer acceptance of proposed new products
- Comparative studies between competitive products
- Studies into packaging and design
- Forecasting new uses for existing products
- Test marketing
- Research into the development of a product line (range)

(c) **Price research**

- Analysis of the market's sensitivity to price (or price changes)
- Analysis of costs and contribution or profit margins
- The effect of changes in credit policy on demand
- Customer perceptions of price (and quality)

(d) **Sales promotion research**

- Motivation research for advertising and sales promotion effectiveness
- Analysing the effectiveness of advertising (or individual media and techniques) on sales demand
- Analysing the effectiveness of the sales force
- Analysing the effectiveness of other promotion methods and tools
- Comparison of competitors' promotion 'mix'

(e) **Distribution research**

- The location and design of distribution centres
- The analysis of packaging for ease of transportation and shelving
- Dealer supply requirements
- Dealer advertising requirements
- The cost of different methods of transportation and warehousing
- Comparison of channel performance

Action Programme 1

What kind of information might emerge from research into a product's packaging?

Exam tip

Please note that **market research** is only one component of **marketing research**. (If in doubt, remember that 'marketing' is the longer word!) This is a classic exam pitfall!

1.2 The research procedure

Marketing research involves the following stages: Figure 3.1.

Figure 3.1: Stages of marketing research

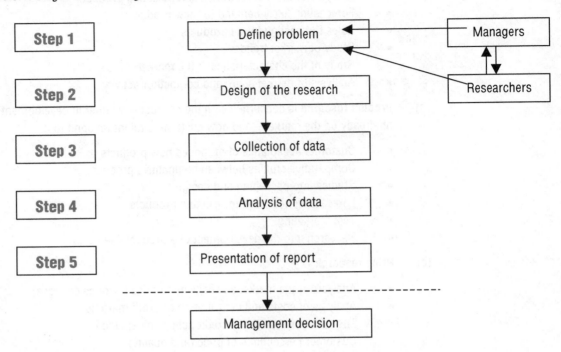

One way of classifying research approaches is by the nature of the sources of data they use. Marketing research information is composed of primary data and secondary data.

Key concepts

> **Primary data** are data collected especially for a particular purpose, directly from the relevant source.
>
> **Secondary data** are data which have already been gathered and assembled for other purposes or general reference.

1.3 Primary research techniques

FAST FORWARD

> **Primary data** are data collected especially for a particular purpose, directly from the relevant source.

The collection of primary data is sometimes known as **field research**. It is typified by the researcher in the street with a clip-board talking to consumers. We'll mention a few of the many primary research techniques in the paragraphs that follow.

1.3.1 Observation

Observation may involve machines, fieldworkers or technology used to monitor hits on (and traffic through) websites. It may involve simply recording behaviour, or require the fieldworker to interpret behaviour, or even interact with subjects ('participant observation').

BPP LEARNING MEDIA

Marketing at Work

The collection of research data by **physical observation** is widespread.

For example, it is common to see researchers logging details of traffic passing along a particular road at certain times of day. This enables local authorities to improve services (by introducing traffic lights, constructing roundabouts or putting in speed control humps).

Users of public transport will often see researchers counting the number of passengers passing through, say a railway station at a particular time, again with a view to assessing and possibly improving service levels.

1.3.2 Questionnaires

Questionnaires are structured sets of questions. They can be administered in a number of ways.

Method	Comment
Telephone interviews	These offer a speedy response and can cover a wide geographical area fairly cheaply. The drawback is that interviews must be fairly short and cannot use visual methods.
Personal interviews	Allow greater interaction and more detailed questioning, but are slow and expensive in relation to other methods.
Replies by mail (or e-mail)	Fairly cheap, and avoids interviewer interference, but there is no control over the completion of the questionnaire. Low response rates, often below 5%, might make the sample data unrepresentative.
Internet forms	Questionnaires on websites (or in HTML formatted e-mail) offer a good deal more control over the responses that are allowed. They can be tedious to complete if they are too long or badly designed, however. This method is becoming more and more common. The potential for visual and even animated display is much greater than with other methods, adding incentive to participate.
Self-completion	The disadvantage of this form of survey is that respondents may not understand questions properly (as with postal surveys) and don't have the opportunity to seek clarification. The questionnaire should be short to encourage completion.

Postal surveys tend to attract a relatively low response rate and unrepresentative respondents, with unsolicited questionnaires often obtaining only a 2% or 3% return. Under these circumstances great care should be taken interpreting results. Follow-up letters may improve responses. Better results from postal surveys have been achieved when directed at specialist populations (eg enthusiasts) and when inducements are offered (such as entry in a prize draw).

Action Programme 2

Think of some simple techniques which might improve the response rate to a postal survey.

1.3.3 Consumer panels

Consumer panels consist of a representative cross-section of consumers who have agreed to give information about their attitudes or buying habits. Consumer panels with personal visits are called **home audit panels** and panels which send data by post or by computer are called **diary panels**.

Problems experienced with consumer panels include recruitment and representativeness. Willing participants may not be the 'typical consumer', and may represent only a limited section of the population in question.

1.3.4 Trade audits or retail audits

Trade audits are carried out among panels of wholesalers and retailers, and **retail audits** among panels of retailers only. A research firm sends auditors to selected outlets at regular intervals to count stock and deliveries, thus enabling an estimate of sales volume to be made.

Action Programme 3

How can the data from a retail audit be of any value to a manufacturer who is not making retail sales?

Marketing at Work

The best-known examples of **retail audit** are the Retail Measurement Services provided by ACNielsen (www.acnielsen.com).

'ACNielsen SCANTRACK Services are the recognized industry standard for scanner-based marketing and sales information, gathered weekly from a sample of more than 4,800 stores representing more than 800 retailers in 50 major markets. Providing basic tracking information at multiple levels ranging from category-level total U.S. all-outlet sales volume to single item performance in one market, SCANTRACK establishes the common language needed to facilitate product business reviews, sales meetings and market analyses. ACNielsen provides customers with the ability to monitor performance trends and evaluate price and promotion effectiveness by tracking and forecasting non-promoted as well as promotional product movement.

'ACNielsen SCANTRACK Services comprise the following:

- SCANTRACK Basic Services, providing detailed product movement and merchandising information for food stores and food/drug combos

- Procision, adding the breadth of drug stores and mass merchandisers to SCANTRACK food store information

- C-Store Plus, giving even more market intelligence by adding convenience store sales and causal information to the SCANTRACK Portfolio

'SCANTRACK provides insight into:

- Which markets represent the greatest sales growth opportunities for my brand?
- What was the sales impact of the last TPR that I took?
- How much lift does a display generate versus an ad?
- How successful is my merchandising strategy?'

Source: www.acneilsen.com website

1.3.5 Pre-testing

The effect of a particular **promotional campaign** is hard to isolate, and therefore hard to measure. Other influences in the market place, such as price cuts and sales promotions by competitors, will also have an effect.

Measurement of the **communication effect** is more reliable than attempts to measure the **sales effect** attributable to a particular advertising campaign. Much research therefore focuses on the effectiveness of the campaign in communicating with its target audience, which can be estimated by measuring **awareness levels** before and after the campaign.

Pre-testing may take a number of forms.

(a) **Motivational research** is carried out to pre-test advertising material. Subjects are invited to watch a film show which includes new TV advertising, and a measure of the shift in their brand awareness is taken after the show. **Copy research** might involve showing members of the public a number of press advertisements and then asking questions about them (in order to measure the recall and impact of different slogans or headlines).

(b) **Laboratory tests**, recording the physiological reactions of people watching advertisements (eg heart beat, blood pressure, dilation of the pupil of the eye, perspiration), measure the arousal or attention-drawing power of an advertisement.

(c) **Ratings tests** involve asking a panel of target consumers to look at alternative advertisements and to give them ratings (marks out of ten) for attention-drawing power, clarity, emotional appeal and stimulus to buy.

(d) **Test marketing** aims to obtain information about how consumers react to a product - will they buy it, how frequently, etc? A test market involves testing a new product in selected areas which are thought to be representative of the total market. This avoids the costs of a full-scale launch, while permitting the collection of market data. The firm will distribute the product through the same types of sales outlets it plans to use in the full market launch, and use the promotion plans it intends to use in the full market. This enables the company to 'test the water' before launching the product nationally. Data obtained helps develop sales forecasts, and can also be used to identify flaws in the marketing plans.

(e) **Simulated store technique** (or laboratory test markets) involves a group of shoppers watching a selection of advertisements for a number of products, including an advertisement for the new product. They are then given money and invited to spend it in a supermarket or shopping area. Their purchases are recorded and they are asked to explain their decisions. Some weeks later they are contacted again and asked about their product attitudes and repurchase intentions. These tests provide a quick, simple way to assess advertising effectiveness *and* product satisfaction, as a guide to forecasting sales volumes.

(f) **Controlled test marketing**. A panel of stores carries the new product for a given length of time. Shelf locations, point-of-sale displays and pricing etc are varied; the sales results are then monitored. This test (also known as 'minimarket testing') helps to provide an assessment of 'in-store' factors in achieving sales.

1.3.6 Post-testing

Post-testing concentrates on the **communication effect** of advertisements.

(a) **Recall tests** ask the interviewee to remember advertisements which have been viewed previously.

(b) **Recognition tests** involve giving the interviewee some reminder of an advertisement, and testing his/her recognition of it.

1.4 Secondary research techniques

FAST FORWARD

Secondary data are data which have already been gathered and assembled for other purposes or general reference.

Desk research involves collecting data from internal and external sources. The sources of secondary data for marketing will vary according to the needs of the organisation.

(a) Records **inside the firm**, gathered by another department or section for its own purposes.

- Data about sales volumes, analysed by sales area, salesman, quantity, price, profitability, distribution outlet, customer etc

- Customer database interrogation

- Data about marketing itself, such as promotion and brand data

- All cost and management accounting data

- Marketing Information Systems, which model and analyse marketing data to support decisions

(b) **Published information** from external sources

- Publications of market research agencies, such as the ACNielsen
- Government statistics
- Publications of trade associations
- Professional journals

(c) The **government**: a major source of information about industry, population and social trends. See the website of the Office for National Statistics (www.statistic.gov.uk) where you can feely view and download a wealth of economic and social data. For national equivalents (outside the UK), go to: www.wto.org.

(d) **Non-government sources**, including:

- The **national press** (*Financial Times* etc) and financial and professional magazines and journals (and their websites)

- Companies and other organisations specialising in the provision of **business information** (eg Reuters, LexisNexis) on a subscription basis, and **specialist research** organisations who analyse certain markets and publish and sell the results (eg Mintel, Euromonitor)

- **Professional institutions** (eg Chartered Institute of Marketing, Chartered Management Institute, Institute of Practitioners in Advertising)

- **Trade sources** such as the Association of British Insurers (ABI), or the Society of Motor Manufacturers and Trades (SMMT)

Action Programme 4

Make a list of all the secondary data sources you would use to research the industry/company you work in.

BPP LEARNING MEDIA

1.5 Quantitative and qualitative research

FAST FORWARD

Marketing data will be both **quantitative** (statistically valid, numerically measurable) and **qualitative** (focusing on values, attributes and perceptions).

Another way of classifying research approaches is according to the type of data gathered.

Key concepts

Quantitative research gathers statistically valid, numerically measurable data, usually via a survey.

Qualitative research focuses on values, attitudes, opinions, beliefs and motivations.

Both types of data may be gathered from primary and/or secondary sources.

(a) Quantitative research answers questions such as: How many? What percentage? How often? How many times? How much? Where? This is essentially **demographic**, statistical information, telling the marketer who buys what, and where, in what quantities and at what price.

(b) While quantitative data may show that 75% of men aged 18-35 drive a car, qualitative data might reveal how they go about choosing a car, how they feel about their car, what would make them change cars and so on. This is essentially **psychographic** information.

The main methods of qualitative research are the open-ended interview, whether this be a **depth interview** (one-to-one) or a **group discussion** (focus group), and **projective techniques**. The key to qualitative research is to allow the respondents to say what they feel and think in response to flexible, 'prompting' questioning, rather than to give their responses to set questions and often set answers in a questionnaire.

The advantages and disadvantages of group discussions and depth interviews are as follows.

Group discussions	
Advantages	**Disadvantages**
• Less intimidating • Easily observed • Range of attitudes can be measured • Social aspect reflects real world • Dynamic and creative • Cheaper	• Participants may not express what they really think – they may be inhibited or they may be showing off • Views may be unrealistic – meaningful in a group context but not for the individual

Depth interviews	
Advantages	**Disadvantages**
• Decision making processes can be analysed • Majority and minority opinion can be captured • Sensitive topics more easily discussed • Unusual behaviour can be discussed	• Time consuming • Less creative • More expensive

Action Programme 5

Give examples of qualitative and/or quantitative data that might be gathered in the following circumstances.

(a)   The sales of a product appeared to be declining in a particular region
(b)   You wanted to know whether customers would support night-time opening
(c)   You were about to schedule TV advertising

2 Market segmentation

2.1 What is market segmentation?

FAST FORWARD

Market segmentation recognises that, although buyers have diverse needs, sets of needs may be grouped together and a different marketing approach may be used for each group.

Research into the customer population in a given market will show that markets are not homogeneous. Customers differ according to age, sex, income, geographical area, buying attitudes, buying habits and so on. Each of these differences can be used to divide a market into **segments**.

Exam tip

Market segmentation may be set directly in the exam, as in June 2004 (how a company could segment its markets); December 2004 (customer characteristics of an international airline that could be used for segmentation); June 2005 (concept of segmentation and bases which could be used for segmentation by a men's fashion retailer); December 2005 (a similar question set in the context of a global car manufacturer); and December 2006 (a similar question in the context of TV/audio products).

Remember to consider segmentation, however, as part of any targeting or positioning strategy you recommend, ie as part of a 'How can the marketing mix be used ...?' question.

Key concept

Market segmentation involves: 'the subdividing of a market into distinct and increasingly homogeneous subgroups of customers, where any subgroup can conceivably be selected as a target to be met with a distinct marketing mix.'

(*T Cannon*, 1980)

Market segmentation recognises that, although buyers have diverse needs, sets of needs may be grouped together and a different marketing approach may be used for each group: Figure 3.2.

BPP
LEARNING MEDIA

Figure 3.2: Segmented market

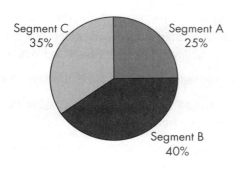

Market for Product X

- Each segment is made up of buyers with common needs and preferences, who may react to 'market stimuli' in much the same way

- Each segment can become a target market with a suitably tailored marketing mix

A total market may occasionally be **100% homogeneous** (all customers are alike) but this is rare. A segmentation approach to marketing succeeds when there are identifiable 'clusters' of consumer wants in the market.

Action Programme 6

Suggest how the market for umbrellas might be segmented.

Marketing at Work

One of the reasons for the growth in fast food has been the rise in the number of **small and single person** households. Chicken Tonight, the UK's most popular brand of cooking sauces, saw major growth in the cooking sauce market following the launch of different sized jars, and the addition of new recipes to its range.

The reason for this change was the growing number of one and two person households, which already account for 62% of UK dwellings, and the belief that these will offer the key to continued growth in the cooking sauce market. The brand launched a range of 'serves-two' jars to maximise the potential offered by the 1.8 million smaller households which did not currently buy cooking sauces. Why was this a profitable marketing move?

Firstly, because the new jars were ideally suited to the consumer profile of independent retailers and forecourts, as well as major multiples. Many of the small household buyers obtain foods from these sources. Retailers were encouraged to stock these products using introductory discounts and the brand was supported by intensive advertising, which also made it attractive to these retailers.

Secondly, this was an untapped market and this size of jar was intended to stimulate a trial of the product at minimum outlay. Recipes also reflected the growing popularity of flavours found in the takeaway food market, such as garlic and curry.

The product provided an opportunity for small households to buy the product at locations where it would previously have been unavailable, and also allowed larger households to try the new flavours, which were also available in the family size jars. This new product launch, achieved a number of marketing objectives very effectively within the same product concept.

2.2 Benefits of market segmentation

Benefits of market segmentation may be as follows (if it is done right …).

- Improved contribution to **profits**

- Better position to identify and capitalise on **marketing opportunities**, due to a better understanding of customer needs: possibility of customer delight and loyalty

- **Specialist** expertise focused on key segments (eg banks' small business counsellors)

- **Optimal return on investment**: total marketing budget is allocated taking into account the needs of each segment and the likely return from each segment

- **Competitive advantage**, through serving and dominating a segment (differentiation or price focus)

2.3 The bases for segmentation

FAST FORWARD

There are many possible **bases for segmentation**, notably behavioural, demographic and psychographic data.

There are many different bases for segmentation. One basis will not be appropriate in every market, and sometimes two or more bases might be required at the same time.

Typical bases for segmentation include the following.

(a) **Geographical area**. For example, the needs and behaviour of potential customers in Poland may differ from those in Latvia and Estonia.

(b) **End use**. For example, paper used in an office may vary in quality depending on whether it is used for formal letters (letter quality) or for internal memos (draft quality). 'Use' in the consumer market might refer to leisure or work use. This might also include **'occasion segmentation'**, referring to the context in which a product is used. As an example, consider Kodak's range of disposable cameras, marketed for holidays, weddings and so on (according to photographic conditions).

(c) **Buyer behaviour**. Some segments of a market (such as older consumers) may have a preference for face-to-face transactions, for example, while others (younger consumers) may prefer web-based transactions, mobile phone text message advertising and so on. Other behavioural bases for segmentation may include **user status** (non-user, ex-user, potential user, regular user) or **usage rate** (light, medium or heavy user).

(d) **Demographic segmentation**. Here the market is divided on the basis of age, gender, socio-economic group, housing, family characteristics or family life cycle stage. Demographic segmentation covers a wide range of possibilities, discussed further below.

(e) **Psychographic segmentation**, by lifestyle, opinions and interests (also discussed below).

(f) **Benefit segmentation**: dividing a market into sub-groups, according to the particular benefits they look for or will value in the product. A classic example is the toothpaste user market, which may be segmented according to whether the key benefit is perceived as taste, medicinal value, cosmetic benefit or price comparison.

BPP
LEARNING MEDIA

Exam tip

Remember the full range of bases – and choose the one(s) most relevant to the context given in an exam question (or your own organisation). The June 2005 exam asked for segmentation bases for a new men-only retail outlet: you didn't have the option of male/female segmentation! The examiner was disappointed that key retail factors (lifestyle, attitudes to fashion, shopping habits) were ignored in favour of mass demographics.

2.4 Demographic segmentation

FAST FORWARD

Demographic segmentation uses population factors such as age, gender, family or socio-economic characteristics.

'Demographics' is the study of population and population changes. Demographic data (provided by government censuses and statistics and research reports) are widely used in market segmentation.

(a)   Segmentation by **age**. For example, High Street banks attempt to attract 18-year olds as customers, especially new students in the higher education sector.

(b)   Products targeted by **gender** include cosmetics, clothing, alcohol, cars and even financial services.

(c)   Segmentation based on the **family type**: the size and constitution of the family unit. There have been changes in the characteristics of the family unit in the last few decades (eg the increase in single parent families) and 'convenience' products and non-stereotyped marketing messages cater to their needs.

(d)   Specific **social groupings** may also be targeted, since they often correlate to disposable income and buying patterns.

2.4.1 The NRS scale

The National Readership Survey (formerly JICNARS) scale is used by the UK market research industry to provide standardised social groupings (see www.nrs.co.uk). These are based entirely on occupation of the head of the household.

Socio-economic groups in the UK

Social grade	Description of occupations	Example
A	Higher managerial and professional	Company director
B	Intermediate managerial and supervisory	Middle manager
C1	Non-manual	Bank clerk
C2	Skilled manual	Electrician
D	Semi-skilled and unskilled manual	Labourer
E	Those receiving no income from employment/casual workers	Unemployed

Similar scales, such the National Readership Survey published by the Indian Market Research Bureau (www.imrbint.com), are used elsewhere.

Socio-economic groups are a useful way of segmenting markets

- You can make reliable inferences about **consumer behaviour** within each group

- There are clear **differences in purchase and consumption patterns** (even where the total disposable income between two groups may be similar)

- The categories are **stable and enduring**, and can be compared across time

- Each group tends to have **identifiable attitudinal and behavioural patterns.** For instance ABC1 groups tend to be more 'future orientated' than C2DE groups, which are more 'present orientated'. That might be significant for a company trying to market long-term savings products or private education.

2.4.2 ACORN

Because of criticisms of the JICNARS classification, more sophisticated measures of socio-economic and group membership have been devised. **Housing type and ownership** is a particularly important method of segmentation for many types of good.

In Great Britain the use of this method is made much easier by the major categorisation scheme for all housing types, known as ACORN: A Classification of Residential Neighbourhoods, a product of market analysis company CACI Limited.

Group	Type	% of GB population
Group 1 **Wealthy Achievers, Suburban Areas**	Type 1 Wealthy Suburbs, Large Detached Houses	3.0%
	Type 2 Villages with Wealthy Commuters	2.7%
	Type 3 Mature Affluent Home Owning Areas	2.8%
	Type 4 Affluent Suburbs, Older Families	3.8%
	Type 5 Mature, Well-Off Suburbs	2.7%

Other work has cross-referenced ACORN with postcodes, making specific identification of customer types more flexible.

ACORN is updated regularly. The latest version can be downloaded from the Brochures section of the CACI website (www.caci.co.uk).

2.4.3 Family life cycle

The **family life cycle (FLC)** looks at the effects of age, marital status, career status (income) and the presence or absence of children and identifies the various stages through which households progress.

The table below shows a fairly traditional life cycle. Particular products and services can be target-marketed at specific stages in the life cycle of families.

Stage	Description	Consumer interests
Bachelor	Independent. Young. Early stage of career and earnings	Clothing. Car. Travel. Café. Entertainment
Newly Married	Two incomes. Relative independence. Present and future oriented	Furnishing. Travel. Clothing. Durables. Appeal to togetherness
Full Nest 1	Youngest child under 6 years. One / One and a half incomes. Limited independence. Future oriented	Goods and services geared to child. Family oriented items. Practicality of items and appeal to economy
Full Nest 2	Youngest child under 6 years. One and a half to two incomes. Dependent. Future oriented	Savings, Home, Education. Children oriented items. Family vacations. Appeal to comfort and luxuries
Full Nest 3	Youngest child at home but independent. High income level. Independent. Thoughts of retirement	Education. Expensive durables for children. Replacement and improvement of parents' durables. Appeal to comfort and luxuries
Empty Nest 1	No children at home. Independent. Good income. Thoughts of retirement and self	Retirement home. Travel. Entertainment. Luxuries. Appeal to self gratification

BPP LEARNING MEDIA

Stage	Description	Consumer interests
Empty Nest 2	Retirement. Limited income. Present oriented	Travel , Recreation, Health related items. Little interest in luxury. Appeal to comfort
Sole Survivor 1	Only one spouse alive. Good income. Employed. Present oriented	Immersion in jobs and friends. Travel. Entertainment. Clothing. Health
Sole Survivor 2	Only one spouse alive. Limited income. Retired.	Travel. Entertainment. Health related items. Appeal to economy and social activity

You may not recognise yourself in any of these traditional categories. Important **social trends** in the UK include later marriage and childbearing; dual income households; more single parent and blended families. New **niche markets** in these areas are likely to grow, whilst traditional markets may be declining.

2.5 Psychographic segmentation

FAST FORWARD

Psychographics or *lifestyle segmentation* seeks to classify people according to their values, opinions, personality characteristics and interests.

Lifestyle segmentation deals with the person as opposed to the product, and attempts to discover the lifestyle patterns shared by groups of customers. This offers an insight into their preferences for various products and services. Marketers can assign and target products and promotion at particular target lifestyle groups. Typical lifestyle variables are shown on the table below.

Lifestyle dimensions

Activities	Interests	Opinions
Work	Family	Themselves
Hobbies	Home	Social issues
Social events	Job	Politics
Vacation	Community	Business
Entertainment	Recreation	Economics
Club membership	Fashion	Education
Community	Food	Products
Shopping	Media	Future
Sports	Achievements	Culture

(*J Plummer*, 1974)

Marketing at Work

For examples of how major brands **segment and target** their markets, check out the websites of Nestlé (www.nestle.com/Our-Brands) or Kellogg's (www.kelloggs.com). Note that there are consumer, B2B, media and community areas.

Kellogg's 'Food Away From Home' (B2B) segments/channels are an excellent example of segmentation and targeting according to usage context and benefit, distinguishing snack food used in: lodgings; restaurants; business settings; colleges and universities; K-12 schools; hospitals; convenience stores; and vending machines.

Lifestyle data can be used to place consumers in various lifestyle categories which can be targeted appropriately. The following is just one example of such a classification.

Category	Comment
Upwardly mobile, ambitious	Seeking a better and more affluent lifestyle, principally through better paid and more interesting work, and a higher material standard of living. A customer with such a lifestyle will be prepared to try new products.
Traditional and sociable	Compliance and conformity to group norms bring social approval and reassurance to the individual. Purchasing patterns will therefore be 'conformist'.
Security and status seeking	Stressing 'safety' and 'ego-defensive' needs. This lifestyle links status, income and security. It encourages the purchase of strong and well known products and brands, and emphasises those products and services which confer status and make life as secure and predictable as possible. These would include insurance, membership of the AA or RAC etc. Products that are well established and familiar inspire more confidence than new products, which will be resisted.
Hedonistic preference	Places emphasis on 'enjoying life now' and the immediate satisfaction of wants and needs. Little thought is given to the future.

It is possible to gain further insights into **lifestyle behaviour** by cross-referring demographic variables to observed behaviour which indicates lifestyle types: for example, x% of those aged 15-24 use certain media and consumer certain products and so on. Various markets (eg leisure, social and travel facilities) can be profiled according to the sex, age and social grade of users. This type of analysis has become easier and cheaper to obtain in the last few years, due to advances in the power and efficiency of computer systems.

 Marketing at Work

'In the evolution of adjectives describing the **25-plus male market**, we have seen snags (sensitive, new-age) being replaced by metrosexuals (in-touch with their feminine side), progressing to uber-sexuals (politically aware and passionate) and now, reports *Sunday Life* magazine, emerges the ladult.

'According to a report in the UK's *Observer* the ladult is single, self-assured, solvent and secure in his new-found masculinity. He spends a lot of money on gadgets and DVDs, and enjoys poker, online gambling and even fly fishing. He irons his own shirts and can cook simple meals. He has no problem with the notion that women are his equals, but secretly thinks they are "different" .....'

B&T 28 April 2006

2.6 Database segmentation

FAST FORWARD

Databased information on customer/contact preferences and characteristics increasingly makes it possible to narrow the 'segment' concept and target individual customers (**one to one marketing**).

All large organisations now hold extensive data on their own customers. The data is stored in a **database** and can be used for a variety of purposes. For instance, mailing lists of potential customers for a new product can be created simply by running a search specifying the required combination of variables: for example, you may wish to mailshot all customers aged 18-24 with incomes over £25,000 pa who live in ACORN type 16 housing.

BPP LEARNING MEDIA

The use of internally-generated information such as this will become more and more widespread as more and more companies develop e-commerce and make it worthwhile for customers to register online.

P Postma (1999) argues that electronic database technology should in fact eliminate market 'segments' and enable organisations to target the buying preferences and behaviours of **individual customers**. *D Peppers and M Rogers* (1993) call this 'one to one' marketing.

2.7 Requirements for effective market segmentation

FAST FORWARD

The **suitability** of a market for segmentation depends on measurability, accessibility and substantiality.

The decision of whether to target market segments may be summarised as follows: Figure 3.3.

Figure 3.3: The segmentation decision

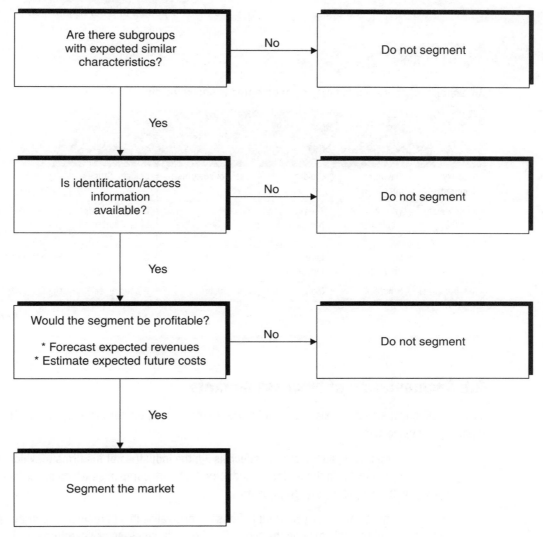

(a) **Measurability**

Can information relating to the factor that the market is to be segmented on be obtained and measured cost effectively? (How would you go about obtaining information on the personality traits of buyers?)

(b) **Accessibility**

The degree to which the organisation can focus effectively on the chosen segments using marketing methods. (Educational establishments can be identified and reached easily, while individuals with income over £30,000 per annum might be more difficult to isolate effectively.)

(c)   **Substantiality**

Is the segment large enough to be worth considering as a separate market? Mounting marketing campaigns is expensive, and so a minimum size for a segment is required for profitability.

Action Programme 7

A previous advertising campaign by McDonalds (before the "I'm lovin' it" re-branding) was aimed at the older generation. Why?

Marketing at Work

An example of how a market may be **segmented** is shown below.

Segmentation of the toothpaste market						
Segment name	**Principal benefit sought**	**Demographic strengths**	**Special behavioural characteristics**	**Brands favoured**	**Personality characteristics**	**Lifestyle characteristics**
Sensory segment	Flavour, appearance	Children	Users of spearmint flavour	Colgate, Stripe	High self-involvement	Hedonistic
Sociables	Whiteness of teeth, breath freshness	Teens, young people	Smokers	Macleans, Ultra Brite, Thera-med	High sociability	Active
Worriers	Decay prevention	Large families	Heavy users	Crest	Hypochondriacs	Conservative
Independents	Price	Men	Heavy users	Brands on sale	High autonomy	Value- oriented

Kotler et al (1999)

2.8 Segmentation of business markets

Segmentation can also be applied to an **industrial market** based on, for instance, the nature of the customer's business.

- Components manufacturers specialise in the industries of the firms to which they supply components. In the motor car industry, there are companies which specialise in the manufacture of car components.

- Accountants or lawyers might choose to specialise in a particular type of business. For an accountant this may be the accounts of retail businesses or tax returns. A firm of solicitors may specialise in conveyancing.

A useful starting point in identifying possible industrial market segments is the **Census of Production**. This is an annual government-produced book providing production data by company for each industry in the United Kingdom.

BPP LEARNING MEDIA

Exam tip

The information within this chapter generally applies to **business to business** (B2B) as well as **consumer** markets. Remember to use the theory provided, but relate it to the question asked, ie if the scenario is set in a B2B, service or international market.

2.9 Segmentation, targeting and positioning (STP)

Segmentation is often related to targeting and positioning: two strategies by which the marketer can tailor the marketing mix to the specific needs and characteristics of a market segment. We have covered market segmentation here, as it is founded on the gathering of research information about market. We cover targeting and positioning as part of our exploration of marketing mix decisions, in Chapter 4.

3 The marketing audit

FAST FORWARD

A **marketing audit** is an examination to determine problem areas and opportunities and recommend ways of improving marketing performance.

Marketing operations need regular reviews and overhauls, and this is the purpose of an internal **marketing audit**.

Key concept

'A **marketing audit** is a systematic, independent and periodic examination of a company's – or business unit's – marketing environment, objectives, strategies and activities with a view of determining problem areas and opportunities and recommending a plan of action to improve the company's marketing performance.'   (P Kotler, W T Gregor & W H Rodgers, 1989)

Unlike financial audits, marketing audits are not required by law and it is up to the individual organisation how extensive its marketing audits are. In theory, though, a marketing audit should:

- Be conducted regularly (probably annually)
- Take a comprehensive look at every product, market, distribution channel, ingredient in the marketing mix
- Be carried out according to a set of predetermined, specified procedures
- Be systematic
- Be done by someone independent of the people who actually carry out the activities being scrutinised (either a third party firm of marketing auditors or a separate department of the organisation)

3.1 Components of the marketing audit

FAST FORWARD

A marketing audit will evaluate six aspects of marketing: the environment, strategy, organisation, systems, productivity and functions.

Kotler et al identify six components of a full marketing audit: the environment, strategy, organisation, systems, productivity and functions.

The marketing audit should look at both the **macro environment** (PEST factors, as discussed in the previous chapter) and also the organisation's **micro environment**.

The micro environment comprises the **market environment** (all aspects of a market which affect the company's relationship with its customers and the patterns of competition) and also includes **internal** operations and aspects of the organisation (such as corporate culture), which may influence the development of a marketing strategy. Figure 3.4 illustrates this.

Figure 3.4: The micro environment

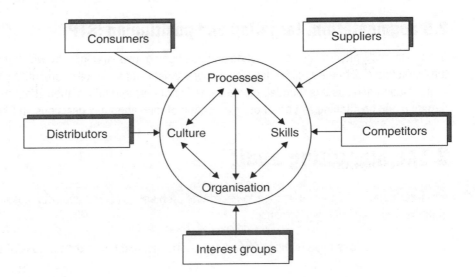

 Marketing at Work

'How are we doing?'

The following 2005 'research facts and figures' are posted on the Virgin website (www.virgin.com).

- 100% brand awareness in UK: 96% in Australia; 56% in USA
- No 1 brand to represent Britain in the future
- No 1 most respected brand amongst men
- 2nd most 'responsible' brand (after Body Shop)
- Forbes' 4th best marketed brand in the world (after Dell, Sony, Harley Davidson)
- More trusted than the Bank of England

The **micro environment** and **internal audit** would therefore cover the following.

Micro environment	Audit issues
Suppliers	The availability of resources, selling policies
Distribution	Main distribution channels, their efficiency levels and potential for growth.
Markets	Developments in major markets, market growth, and changes in turnover and profits. Performance of different market segments.
Customers	Customer views on price quality and service given by organisation and its competitors. Decision processes of different types of customer.
Competitors	Objectives and strategies, market share, and strengths and weaknesses. Developments in future competition.
Stakeholders/publics	Important groups and how they have been dealt with

Internal environment	Audit issues
Marketing strategy	What are the organisation's marketing objectives and how do they relate to overall objectives? Are they reasonable?
	Are enough (or too many) resources being committed to marketing to enable the objectives to be achieved; is the division of costs between products, areas etc satisfactory?
Marketing organisation	Does the organisation have the structural capability to implement the plan? How effective is the structure of the marketing department? How effectively does it interact with other departments?
Marketing systems	What are the procedures for gathering information, formulating marketing plans and exercising control over these plans? Are they satisfactory?
Marketing productivity	How profitable and cost effective is the marketing programme?
Marketing functions	A review of the effectiveness of each element of the mix should be carried out, evaluating:
	• Price levels (effects on demand, customer attitudes).
	• Products (and their market 'health') and the product mix as a whole, using the product life cycle (PLC) and/or BCG matrix as a framework for analysis. (These techniques are discussed in Chapter 5.)
	• Distribution channels
	• The promotion mix: personal selling, advertising, promotions and so on.

 Action Programme 8

What questions might a marketing auditor want answered about the sales force?

Exam tip

Marketing audit has repeatedly been set in these exams, including a 20-mark question in June 2004. The examiner was disappointed that candidates confused 'marketing audit' with a 'marketing plan': don't make this basic mistake! (And read questions carefully ...)

3.2 Analytical tools

FAST FORWARD

Marketing information systems and specialised marketing software offer many analytical tools that can assist with the marketing audit and marketing management in general.

Any of the tools and techniques described in this chapter and the last (**SWOT** analysis, **Ansoff's matrix** etc) could be used by an auditor, but above all (*Kotler et al*, 1989) **information technology** now makes it exceptionally easy to manipulate company data.

Many companies now have tools that can be used in auditing embedded within their information systems. Systems that are widely used in large companies, such as **SAP R3** and **Oracle**, have specific marketing modules. There are also companies like Objexis (www.objexis.com) who provide 'enterprise marketing management' software.

The extracts from SAP's brochure below will give you an excellent idea of what is now possible.

Marketing at Work

SAP'S ANALYTICAL CRM: AN INTEGRATED SUITE OF ANALYTICAL APPLICATIONS

Analytical CRM in mySAP CRM is an integrated suite of analytical applications that help you transform your customer data into strategic information so you can measure and optimize your customer relationships. These analytical applications consist of more than just prepackaged, ready-to-run reporting applications … . Whereas such analyses often deal with the past, analytical methods frequently need to concern the future and predict purchasing behaviour or customer lifetime value. In this way, they can contribute much toward gaining insights for current decision-making.

360° Customer Knowledge Base. The customer knowledge base combines all relevant information about your customers and … integrates the data from the following sources:

- Customer interactions across all channels and touchpoints
- Internal systems (CRM, SCM, back office, and so on)
- External sources (market data, competitor data, Web surveys, and so on)
- Analytical results

Customer Analytics. Customer analytics offers a variety of methods to analyse and mine your customer knowledge base to derive insights from your data. Depending on the business problem, the SAP solution offers an extensive suite of methods, ranging from generic procedures to ready-to-run business solutions. Customer analytics provides comprehensive answers for customer behaviour modelling, customer value assessment, and customer portfolio analysis to create an accurate understanding of your customers.

Marketing Analytics. Marketing analytics offers a variety of analytical applications:

- **Market and competitor research** helps you discover new market opportunities and understand their potential. Marketing planning and optimisation tools help executives and marketing management measure and plan marketing performance by time, territory, distribution channel, and so forth. Campaign planning and optimisation tools extend across planning campaigns, simulating their outcome, and monitoring their success once carried out. You can measure this using response rates, contribution margins per campaign, conversion rates, campaign ROI, and so on.

- **Product and brand analysis** functions deliver a full range of product-related planning and analysis tasks that enable you to control and optimize performance with individual products or product groups.

Sales Analytics. Sales analytics provides answers to numerous business questions:

- **Sales planning** tools provide a comprehensive environment to plan, predict, and simulate your sales volumes and profits.

- **Sales pipeline analysis** helps you analyse and predict the pipeline of opportunity, quotes, and contracts in order to better manage anticipated selling opportunities.

- **Sales cycle analysis** helps you gain insights into all aspects of your sales process across the overall sales cycle, starting with the leads, then the opportunities, and right through to sales order processing.

- **Team performance analysis** helps you discover how your sales organization, sales channels, and sales territories are performing as well as understand the ROI of your sales activities and promotions.

Service Analytics. Service analytics delivers a whole spectrum of answers to all questions related to service, ranging from customer satisfaction, product quality, and trends related to complaints, right through to key figures like resolution quotes and workload in your service organization. Detailed analysis of service revenues and costs helps you optimize the performance of your service organization.

BPP
LEARNING MEDIA

Channel Analytics. Channel analytics supports you with analytical capabilities that are tailored to the needs of specific channels, like the Web or your customer interaction center. Related information on customer interactions is equally integrated into the customer knowledge base. **Web analytics** includes Web traffic and performance analysis, which reveals what happens on your Web site and indicates what areas of your Web site met with customer interest. More importantly, it also includes e-commerce analysis, which enables you to understand the buying behaviour of your Web customers and provides you with different metrics, such as conversion rates, number of unique visitors, and Website frequency. **Customer interaction center analytics** helps you gain a clear picture of the performance and workload of your customer interaction center.

Chapter Roundup

- **Marketing research** is the gathering, recording and analysing of data about problems relating to the marketing of goods and services.

- **Market research** has a narrower focus. It involves gathering information about the market for a particular product or service (typically, consumer attitudes, existing product usage etc). Other forms of research include product, price, sales promotion and distribution research – covering the full range of marketing mix variables.

- **Primary data** are data collected especially for a particular purpose, directly from the relevant source.

- **Secondary data** are data which have already been gathered and assembled for other purposes or general reference.

- Marketing data will be both **quantitative** (statistically valid, numerically measurable) and **qualitative** (focusing on values, attributes and perceptions).

- **Market segmentation** recognises that, although buyers have diverse needs, sets of needs may be grouped together and a different marketing approach may be used for each group.

- There are many possible **bases for segmentation**, notably behavioural, demographic and psychographic data.

- **Demographic segmentation** uses population factors such as age, gender, family or socio-economic characteristics.

- **Psychographics** or *lifestyle segmentation* seeks to classify people according to their values, opinions, personality characteristics and interests.

- Databased information on customer/contact preferences and characteristics increasingly makes it possible to narrow the 'segment' concept and target individual customers (**one to one marketing**).

- The **suitability** of a market for segmentation depends on measurability, accessibility and substantiality.

- A **marketing audit** is an examination to determine problem areas and opportunities and recommend ways of improving marketing performance.

- A **marketing audit** will evaluate six aspects of marketing: the environment, strategy, organisation, systems, productivity and functions.

- **Marketing information systems** and specialised marketing software offer many analytical tools that can assist with the marketing audit and marketing management in general.

Quick Quiz

1   List five types of marketing research.

2   Primary data is more important than secondary data.

    True   ☐

    False   ☐

    (Explain your answer.)

3   Which one of the following statements is correct?

    A   When test marketing an organisation will use sales outlets that it never uses in practice, in case customers don't like the product

    B   Simulated store technique is a way of testing whether consumers like the layout and design of supermarkets

    C   Recall tests are carried out if nobody buys a new product and the products are all sent back to (or recalled by) the manufacturer

    D   Laboratory tests record the heart beat and pupil dilation of people watching advertisements

4   Pick the correct three words from the six options given.

    ACORN is based on (1) .... The National Readership Survey is based on (2)................. Psychographic segmentation is based on (3)....................

Lifestyle	Age and marital status	Type of housing
Income	Newspaper readership	Geographical area

5   There are three criteria for effective market segmentation. What are they?

6   Business markets cannot be effectively segmented because businesses do not get married or have attitudes.

    True   ☐

    Partly true   ☐

    False   ☐

7   Draw a diagram of an organisation's micro environment.

8   Which of the six components of the marketing audit might investigate things like how many sick days the marketing staff take and how long marketing staff spend at lunch?

9   Analytical tools can only tell you what happened in the past so they are not much use for planning.

    True   ☐

    False   ☐

Answers to Quick Quiz

1 Market, product, price, promotion, distribution

2 False. Primary data is gathered from research you undertake yourself, whereas secondary data is gathered from data published by others. Secondary data may well be superior to information you are able to gather yourself, especially if it is produced by a specialist with greater research resources.

3 D

4 (1) Type of housing; (2) Income; (3) Lifestyle

5 Measurability, Accessibility and Substantiality. Make sure you know what this means by looking back at the relevant pages in this book: don't just cheat!

6 Partially true although business markets can be segmented to some extent. It is true that businesses don't get married, and it is true that it is far more difficult to measure attitudes when you are dealing with a group of people. But many business buying decisions are ultimately the responsibility of a specific person: this is why personal selling is more important in the business-to-business market. In addition, businesses have different levels of income and go through different stages of development and are located in different places, so there is plenty of scope for segmentation.

7

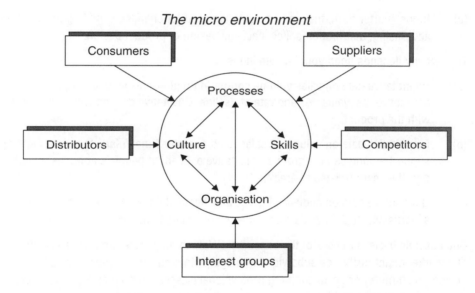

The micro environment

8 The marketing function audit might look into these matters if there was any reason for concern. (We were trying to tempt you to say 'productivity', of course.)

9 False. Sophisticated software tools will be able to take all the variables in the past data and use a variety of mathematical techniques to predict what might happen in the future. Even something as simple as a spreadsheet can be used to see what the outcome would have been if certain factors were changed ('what-if' analysis). Analysis of past data is especially important if things went wrong, because it will help you avoid making the same mistakes again.

Action Programme Review

1   Packaging serves a number of functions. For instance, your research could discover that the existing packaging did not protect the product adequately, or that the product was not recognised as being one made by your organisation, or that its look put customers off buying the product, or that it was an inconvenient size to fit on supermarket shelves, or it made the product hard to carry. You may have had other ideas.

2   Measures could include sending to named individuals and taking care that information, such as job titles, is up to date. (This can be difficult if the sample is being drawn from a trade directory. It takes up to one year to update such directories, and the current year's edition will be on average six months old when reference is made.) It also helps to send a covering letter and to stress confidentiality and anonymity for the respondent. Finally, the inclusion of a stamped and addressed envelope for the reply helps, particularly if a stamp rather than a prepaid envelope is used.

3   Because they provide continuous monitoring of retail activity, retail audits may be of value to such a firm for the following reasons.

(a)   Problems in retail sales provide an early warning of problems the manufacturer may soon have to expect in ex-factory sales.

(b)   They indicate long-term trends in the market place, thus providing helpful information for strategic marketing planning.

(c)   In the shorter term, they may indicate the need for changes in pricing policy, sales promotion or advertising, distribution policy, package design or product design.

4   This activity depends upon your chosen industry.

5   (a)   Quantitative data on sales volume comparing region-on-region and year-on-year to establish amount (units, value, %) and rate of decline. Qualitative data on why consumers are less happy with the product.

(b)   Quantitative data on volume of sales in comparable times/markets during night hours, percentage support among sample groups. Qualitative data about people's attitudes to night shopping, possible fears (related to area?).

(c)   Quantitative data on audience figures at scheduled times, demographics of audience, cost of advertising. Qualitative data on audience response to the ad.

6   One possible basis is the sex of the consumer. Women may prefer umbrellas of different size and weight. The market might further be subdivided into age (with some age groups buying few umbrellas and others buying much more) or occupation (eg professional classes, commuters, golfers). Each subdivision of the market (each subsegment) will show increasingly common traits. Golfers, for example, appear to buy large multi-coloured umbrellas.

7   Apart from the fact that the ads were humorous enough to have general appeal the most obvious reason is to imply to the older generation that it is OK to eat at McDonalds. An important additional point, however, is that older people are likely to have grandchildren who may see a visit to McDonalds as a treat. Older people have more disposable income than the children's parents and are more likely to indulge the children.

8   Here are the suggestions made by Kotler *et al.*

(a)   What are the organisation's salesforce objectives?

(b)   Is the salesforce large enough to accomplish the company's objectives?

(c)   Is the salesforce organised along the proper principle(s) of specialisation (territory, market, product?)

BPP
LEARNING MEDIA

(d)   Does the salesforce show high morale, ability, and effort? Are they sufficiently trained and motivated?

(e)   Are the procedures adequate for setting quotas and evaluating performance?

(f)   How is the company's salesforce perceived in relation to competitors' salesforces?

Now try Questions 4 and 5 at the end of the Study Text

Part C
The marketing mix and related tools

4

Managing the marketing mix

Syllabus content

- Describe the essential elements of targeting and positioning, and the creation of an integrated and coherent marketing mix (3.1)

- Describe the wide range of tools and techniques available to marketers to satisfy customer requirements and compete effectively (3.2)

- Explain the development of the extended marketing mix concept to include additional components in appropriate contextual settings: product, price, place (distribution), promotion (communications), people, processes, physical evidence and customer service (3.3)

- Explain the importance of people in marketing and in particular the contribution of staff to effective service delivery (3.13)

- Explain the importance of service in satisfying customer requirements and identify the factors that contribute to the delivery of service quality (3.14)

- Examine the effects of information and communication technology on the development and implementation of the marketing mix (3.15)

- Explain the importance of measuring the effectiveness of the selected marketing effort and instituting appropriate changes where necessary (3.16)

Introduction

We introduced the 4 Ps in Chapter 1 because it is difficult to say anything at all about marketing without referring to them. In Part C of this book we are going to have a much more detailed look.

This chapter covers a number of general marketing mix issues that apply equally to each of the Ps.

We'll start out by reminding you what the Ps are and then extend the concept to take account of other Ps that are increasingly important in a modern marketing-orientated company. In particular we'll look at quality of **service**, one of the key reasons why customers buy your products and come back for more … or, if it is bad, why they do not!

Then we'll think about how the marketing mix can be managed for **targeting** and **positioning**: how you help buyers in your chosen segment(s) of the market to get hold of your product, and how you distinguish it from the mass of competing products.

The next section talks generally about the **impact of ICT** on marketing, a topic we've touched on already, and which we will return to, in context, in later chapters.

Finally, we have a few general words to say about **measuring the effectiveness** of the marketing effort, another topic that will be mentioned in more specific contexts in later chapters.

1 The marketing mix

1.1 The four Ps

FAST FORWARD

The **marketing mix** concept concentrates on the variables under the organisation's control. The **4 Ps** are highly interactive: decisions regarding one affects all the others.

The current, most common, definition of the marketing mix concentrates on the variables under the firm's control. Marketing managers manipulate these variables in an attempt to achieve tactical marketing objectives. The four Ps of the marketing mix are often described as **'the controllables'**, to distinguish elements that an organisation can influence from those that are beyond its control. **'Uncontrollables'** include competitor's actions, government policy, general economic conditions and so on.

Exam tip

The exam may require you directly to recommend the appropriate marketing mix for a particular product, including suggestions for its price, product features, distribution and promotion, and their appropriateness for the chosen marketing strategy. Get used to thinking how each of the 4Ps could be used to market any product or service you come across!

The 4Ps would, however, also make a good *framework to structure answers* on questions such as: 'How can an organisation market …?', 'How do PEST/environment factors affect the marketing of …?'. When you see the phrase 'marketing', consider whether the 4Ps would be a helpful structuring device. However, you need to watch out: if the question refers to the 'full marketing mix', you may need to address the 'extended' marketing mix: an additional 3Ps discussed in Section 2 of this chapter.

- The **product** can be a service such as an insurance policy as well as a physical thing. Products have tangible benefits which can be measured, such as the top speed of a car, and intangible benefits that cannot be measured, such as the enjoyment the customer will get from owning and using the product. Marketing organisations need to put together a 'bundle' of the benefits that will be most valued by customers.

- **Price** is obviously very important. If it is set too high, target customers may not be able to afford it; if it is set too low, customers may think there is something wrong with the product and they will get better quality if they pay more. More fundamentally, if the price is set too low, the company will not cover its costs and may go out of business! There are many different pricing strategies that companies can use to decide on a price, as we will see.

- **Place** is more accurately called **distribution**. This is partly determined by the nature of the product (you wouldn't try to sell a cement mixer in a supermarket), but there are a wide variety of choices: selling direct to the customer, selling through a retailer or wholesaler, delivery over the Internet and so on.

- **Promotion** is more accurately called **marketing communications**. There is no point in making a product, setting a price and putting the product on shelves unless you tell people you've done so! Promotion is used to inform people about the benefits of a product and persuade them to purchase it. Promotional methods include: advertising, public relations, direct selling, sales promotions (eg free gifts) and many other communication tools. The suite of tools chosen by the organisation is called the 'promotional mix' (*not* to be confused with the *marketing mix*).

Each element will be covered in much greater depth in Chapters 5 to 8.

Marketing mix variables are highly interactive. A decision relating to one variable is very likely to have an effect on other elements of the mix. A highly co-ordinated approach is needed if the company is to arrive at the most effective blend of factors.

Action Programme 1

How would you take account of the uncontrollables in your marketing planning?

1.2 Four Cs

FAST FORWARD

The Four Ps can be balanced by **customer-focused equivalents**: Choice, Cost, Convenience and Communication.

At some time in your marketing studies you will probably start thinking that the 4 Ps are rather old hat. That may be true – and two of them don't really begin with P anyway! – but we will stick with it in this book, not least because it will help you find your way around any other marketing book you read, as your studies progress.

Other formulations of the marketing mix have been proposed by various writers. *C Ace* (2001) argues that the 'Ps' of the extended marketing mix have a producer or service provider focus. She suggests four **customer-focused** 'C' equivalents.

Producer/provider focused activity	Customer/consumer focused activity
Product Plan product/service mix	**Choice** Consider how customers make choices: differentiate and inform to support the purchase decision
Price Consider all elements of the price mix	**Cost** Consider how customers perceive value for money

Producer/provider focused activity	Customer/consumer focused activity
Place Manage distribution channels	**Convenience** Consider what customers find convenient: they may not like the channels (for example Internet) that are most 'efficient'
Promotion Persuade customers that the product meets their needs	**Communication** Enter into dialogue with customers; inform and support their decision-making: they are increasingly aware that promotion is being used to persuade or manipulate

Action Programme 2

To get yourself into the habit, think of three things that you have bought fairly recently and describe them in terms of the 4 Ps or the 4 Cs. Take one grocery product (food, make-up, say), one service (a train journey, say), and your most recent large-ish purchase (a TV, a business suit, say).

2 The extended marketing mix

FAST FORWARD ▶

Some argue that 4 Ps are not enough, especially where **services** are concerned, and add three additional Ps: people, process, and physical evidence. The 7Ps are known as the **extended marketing mix**.

Whatever letter they begin with, it is often argued, especially when discussing the marketing of services (transport, insurance, and so on), that four ingredients are not enough to describe the marketing mix.

This applies particularly to services, because a service does not primarily involve a **physical** product. If you go on a train journey the ticket itself does not magically transport you to your destination and you don't get to keep the train (and in fact you usually have to give the ticket back, too, at the end of the journey!).

Most products have some element of service in them, too. If you buy a product over the telephone your purchase may be enhanced by delightfully friendly and helpful service from the telesales assistant. So where do **people** feature in the 4 Ps?

And the telesales assistants may be able to offer that help because the ordering **process** is managed by a sophisticated customer and product database and a customer relationship management system.

It has therefore been suggested that another 3 Ps should be added to make an **extended marketing mix**.

- People
- Process
- Physical evidence

2.1 People

FAST FORWARD ▶

Service quality can be defined as the difference between what the customer expects and what he or she perceives him/herself to be receiving. Improved service quality leads to higher profits and is a key task for service marketers.

The higher the level of customer contact involved in the delivery of a product or service, the more crucial is the role of people. In many cases the delivery and the physical presence of personnel involved are completely inseparable.

In some cases, the physical presence of people actually performing the job is often a vital aspect of **customer satisfaction**. Think of counter staff in a bank, or waiters and waitresses in a restaurant, or builders who leave your house tidier than they found it. The people involved are performing or 'producing' the service, selling the service and also liaising with the customer to promote the service, gather information and respond to customer needs.

Organisations therefore need to take measures to institute a **customer orientation** in all sectors of activity. People issues will include the following.

- Appearance
- Attitude
- Commitment (including quality/customer)
- Behaviour

- Professionalism
- Skills/competence
- Discretion/confidentiality
- Integrity/ethics

Managers must promote values of customer service in order to create a **culture of customer service**. This may entail any or all of the following.

- Job design to give people the authority they need to meet customer needs flexibly

- Careful policies of recruitment and selection

- Programmes of training and development to ensure that staff have service values/competences, both in technical competences and people skills

- Standardised operational rules and practices, to ensure consistent basic levels of service

- Effective programmes of staff motivation and reward, creating commitment to the organisation, quality and customers

- Effective communication of quality, service and customer care values

 Action Programme 3

Is domestic central heating a product or a service? What are the implications?

Exam tip

> You may be asked to explain the extended (7Ps) services marketing mix (December 2006) or to explain how any element of the mix can be used to add value for customers. In December 2005 and in the 2006 case study, you were asked 'how people and ICT contribute to satisfying customer requirements' (in the financial services industry). You might have interpreted these questions in a general sense – but the word 'people' should alert you to the need to identify staff/service as part of the extended marketing mix.
>
> Read all questions carefully, though. A question may ask you to apply the service marking mix (7Ps) to a product – or the marketing mix (4Ps) to a service organisation! Don't confuse the two – and define your terms, concisely, in your answer.

2.1.1 Why care about service quality?

Quality of service is an important issue for marketers because it is one of the most significant ways in which customers differentiate between competing products and services.

An organisation can give better service through any of the seven Ps – make a better product, do a special deal on price, open for longer hours, give more information in the brochure, buy a new carpet, process orders more quickly, and so on. But the main way is through the P of people.

> **Service quality** is the totality of features and characteristics of that service which bears on its ability to meet stated or implied needs.

There are essentially two ways organisations can gain from improving their quality of service to customers.

(a)   **Higher sales revenues** and **improved marketing effectiveness** may come through improved customer retention, positive word-of-mouth recommendations and the ability to increase prices.

(b)   Better quality **improves productivity** and **reduces costs** because there is less rework, higher employee morale and lower employee turnover.

2.1.2 What is 'service quality'?

Quality is a difficult concept to define in a few words and has been defined in a number of ways. A market-led definition of quality is based on the idea that quality can only be defined by customers and occurs where a firm supplies products to a specification that satisfies their needs. Customer expectations serve as standards, so when the service they receive falls short of expectations, dissatisfaction occurs.

Service quality has a number of dimensions.

(a)   **Technical quality** of the service encounter (ie what is received by the customer). Was the meal edible? Was the train on time? Were the shelves fully stocked? Problems of this sort must be addressed by improving the processes of production and delivery.

(b)   **Functional quality** of the service encounter (ie how the service is provided). This relates to the psychological interaction between the buyer and seller and is typically perceived in a very subjective way.

   (i)   **Relationships between employees**. For instance, do these relationships appear to be professional? Do they chat to each other whilst serving the customer? Does each appear to know their role in the team and the function of their colleagues? Do they know who to refer the customer to if there is a need for more specialist advice? Are they positive about their colleagues or unduly critical?

   (ii)   **Appearance and personality of service personnel**. For instance, do they seem interested in the customer and the customer's needs? Are they smartly presented? Do they convey an attractive and positive image? Do they reflect the organisation or brand (eg through uniform/livery)?

   (iii)   **Service-mindedness of the personnel**. For instance, do they appear to understand and identify with the needs of the customer? Do they convey competence? Do they show willingness to help?

   (iv)   **Accessibility of the service to the customer**. For instance, do the service personnel explain the service in language which the customer can understand?

   (v)   **Approachability of service personnel**. For instance, do the service personnel appear alert, interested or welcoming? Or are they day-dreaming, yawning or looking at their watches?

R Overton (2002) identifies the following key elements in customer service.

Tangibles	The quality of the service area, products and information must be consistent with the desired image.
Reliability	Getting it right first time is very important, not only to ensure repeat business, but as a matter of ethics, if the customer is buying a future benefit (as in financial services).
Responsiveness	Staff must be willing to deal with customer queries and problems, responding flexibly to needs.
Communication	Staff should provide appropriate information to customers in language they can understand.
Credibility	The organisation should be perceived as honest, expert and trustworthy, acting in the best interests of customers.
Security	The customer needs to feel that transactions are safe, and where necessary, private and confidential.
Competence	Service staff need to develop competence in meeting the needs of the customers and using systems efficiently.
Courtesy	Customers should experience service staff as polite, respectful and friendly.
Understanding customers' needs	Service staff need to listen to and meet customer needs rather than try to sell products. This is a subtle but important difference.
Access	Minimising queues, having a fair queuing system and speedy service are all factors in customer satisfaction.

2.1.3 Improving service quality and customer care

An organisation can use a number of methods to try to improve its quality of service and customer care.

(a)   Development of customer-orientated **mission statement** and **customer care policy**, with clear **senior management support** for quality improvement initiatives.

(b)   **Customer satisfaction research**, both formal (eg customer surveys, customer panels, analysis of complaints data) and informal (eg tuning in to customer feedback at the point of sale/service).

(c)   **Monitoring and control**: feedback should be communicated, and standards constantly reviewed.

(d)   Customer **complaints and feedback** systems, with incentives to *encourage* customers to complain!

(e)   **Employee involvement**: eg through the use of quality circles, project teams and other forms of internal communication on quality/service issues. This is a cornerstone of a Total Quality Management approach (TQM), which you will encounter in your studies for *Customer Communications*.

(f)   Customer care **training and development**.

(g)   **Rewarding** excellent service

Action Programme 4

What evidence do you see of firms implementing quality programmes and continually improving service quality? How does your company, or one you have worked for in the past, measure service quality?

2.2 Process

FAST FORWARD Efficient **processes** can become a marketing advantage in their own right.

Process involves the ways in which marketing tasks are achieved. They include all administrative, ordering and customer service features.

- Procedures
- Policies
- Automation of processes
  (eg online or by automated telephony)

- Information flow to service units/customers
- Capacity levels, for continuous performance
- Speed/timing of service
- Queuing/accessibility arrangements

Efficient processes can become a marketing advantage in their own right. For example, computer company Dell's success is due as much to the remarkable efficiency of its ordering and customer information system as it is to the quality and manufacturing efficiency of its production system. The company's marketing line is 'Easy as Dell', which refers to the process and sums up Dell's competitive advantage in a nutshell. Take a look, even if you don't want to buy a computer: www.dell.com.

The level and quality of service which is available to the customer is especially sensitive. (Think of the train which is always late and overcrowded.) Process issues include the following.

(a) **Capacity utilisation**, matching resource/staff utilisation to anticipated demand, to avoid delays, bottlenecks and waste.

(b) **Managing customer contacts and expectations**: keeping people realistically informed and empowering staff to respond to changing needs.

2.2.1 Automation for process efficiency?

Customer handling is increasingly automated in order to increase process efficiency. Examples include web-based transactions and information provision; voice mail systems (for recording customer telephone queries); and automated call handling (ACH) and interactive voice response (IVR) systems, which allow customers to select menu options (eg for call routing, product ordering or information requests) using telephone keypad or verbal responses. You may have used such a system for telephone bill payments or taxi bookings, say.

The automation of customer-handling operations can have a **positive impact** for the customer and supplier alike.

(a) The organisation is **available for contact** 24 hours, 7 days.

(b) **Ordering** can be conducted 'instantly' and at any time to suit the customer.

(c) Frequently asked questions (FAQs) and e-mail contacts can **reduce waiting time** for answers to customer queries.

(d) Customer information is made available to **personalise** the transaction and build **customer relationships**. This includes recognition of customer telephone numbers, for example, so that call centre staff can address customers by name and do not have to ask repeatedly for address and other details. On a fully automated level, it includes the personalisation of the customer's interface with a web page.

(e) Automation creates significant **cost savings** for the company: reducing the number of customer-service staff required, and enabling other to work from home or in (in-house or outsourced) call centres.

(f) Fewer 'missed' calls and better **customer service** supports customer attraction, retention and loyalty.

Automated **Customer Relationship Management** systems (CRM) can be used to empower customers to control the purchase and service process. *C Allen et al* (2001) suggest that 'Many Web users have found that a well-constructed website provides better on-demand services than they usually receive through a company's human-based contacts. The website lets customers easily obtain product and service information that helps them investigate product features, make purchases and solve problems without help from the more costly sales and support staff.'

Negative impacts of automation, however, include the following.

- Customers (particularly in certain age or cultural groups) may simply want to talk to a human being.

- Automation leads to the loss of customer service jobs.

- Automated call management systems can frustrate the customer by creating a lengthy 'loop' of menus.

2.3 Physical evidence

FAST FORWARD

Physical evidence is an important remedy for the intangibility of many services.

You receive monthly bank statements – but all they are, really, is reassurance in tangible form that the bank still has your money.

The following are other examples of items of physical evidence that the marketer can use in the marketing mix.

Environment of service delivery	Facilities	Tangible evidence of purchase
• Colours	• Vans/vehicles/aeroplanes	• Labels and other printed information
• Layout	• Equipment/tools	
• Staff uniforms		• Tickets, vouchers and purchase confirmations
• Noise levels		• Logos and other visible evidence of brand identity
• Smells		
• Ambience		• Packaging
• Website design		

The layout, décor and 'branding' of a bank or travel agency, for example, are likely to be an important part of the customer's experience of receiving services which are otherwise 'virtual'/ intangible. Likewise, the appearance, user-friendliness and branding of a company's website gives a visible, interactive face to a virtual entity.

A service can be presented in tangible (and promotional) physical form: consider how travel tickets are presented in branded envelopes (or more sophisticated document wallets), with vouchers for added services, information leaflets and other added value elements – despite the fact that all the customer has purchased is the promise of a future benefit.

Note that physical evidences can be used as a **marketing communications** tool: staff livery uniforms, logos and corporate identity features, and promotional messages printed on vouchers/ envelopes/receipts are all promotional opportunities.

 Action Programme 5

See if you can think of three customer-focused 'C' equivalents to People, Processes and Physical evidence – in line with Section 1.2 earlier. What might these 3Ps look like from the customer's point of view?

3 Targeting

FAST FORWARD

Targeting involves selecting one or more customer groups (segments) and satisfying them with a tailored marketing mix.

We discussed **segmentation** in Chapter 3. Targeting is one way of using the marketing mix to capitalise on the potential of market segments.

Key concept

> **Targeting** is 'the use of market segmentation to select and address a key group of potential purchasers' (CIM).

3.1 Targeting strategies

FAST FORWARD

Marketing may be undifferentiated, concentrated or differentiated, according to the degree of targeting used.

An organisation has several targeting options to choose from (or a combination of each).

Option	Comment
Undifferentiated	Produce a single product and hope to get as many customers as possible to buy it; that is, ignore segmentation entirely. (Not very common now. An early example was the Ford Model T car.)
Concentrated	Attempt to produce the ideal product for a *single* segment of the market (eg Rolls Royce cars, Mothercare mother and baby shops).
Differentiated	The company attempts to introduce several product versions, each aimed at a different market segment (for example, one company producing several different brands of washing powder or cereal).

These can be illustrated as follows: Figure 4.1.

Figure 4.1: Targeting strategies

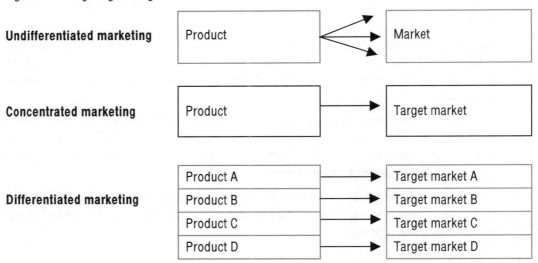

Targeting is not restricted to consumer markets: there is an opportunity for business-to-business targeting as well (for example, Rolls Royce aero engines targeting quality aircraft manufacturers).

The major disadvantage of **concentrated marketing** is reliance on a single segment of a single market, eg Barings Bank specialising in futures trading. On the other hand, specialisation in a particular market segment can give a firm a profitable, although sometimes temporary, competitive edge over rival firms, eg Rolls Royce cars at the premium end of the car market.

The major disadvantage of **differentiated marketing** is the additional cost of marketing and production (more product design and development costs, the loss of economies of scale in production and storage, additional promotion costs and administrative costs, etc). When the costs of further differentiation of the market exceed the benefits from further segmentation and target marketing, a firm is said to have 'overdifferentiated'. Some firms have tried to overcome this problem by selling the same product to two market segments. An example of differential marketing is the recent split of washing powers into general, colour, non-biological, etc. Or think about toothpaste, breakfast cereals, holidays – or McDonald's outlets (McCafe, Drive-through only etc).

3.2 Choice of targeting strategy

As we discussed in relation to market segmentation, targeting is not always the appropriate approach.

(a)   Is the product and/or the market homogeneous? Mass marketing may be 'sufficient' if the market is largely homogeneous (eg safety matches).

(b)   Will the company's resources be overextended by differentiated marketing? Small firms may succeed better by concentrating on one segment only (eg Stain Devils cleaning products).

(c)   Is the product sufficiently advanced in its 'life cycle' to have attracted a substantial total market? If not, segmentation and target marketing is unlikely to be profitable, because each segment would be too small in size.

Action Programme 6

You will encounter the idea of the product 'life cycle' in the next chapter. Without looking ahead, what do you think it means?

3.3 Benefits of segmentation and target marketing

FAST FORWARD

Market targeting, on the basis of **segmentation**, should result in increased total sales and profits because products/services will be more likely to appeal to the target segments and pricing policy can be more sophisticated.

Some key benefits of targeting marketing can be summarised as follows.

(a)   **Product differentiation**: a feature of a particular product might appeal to one segment of the market in such a way that the product is thought better than its rivals.

(b)   The seller will be more **aware** of how product design and development may stimulate further demand in a particular area of the market.

(c)   The **resources** of the business will be used more effectively, because the organisation should be more able to make products which the customer wants and will pay for.

Marketing at Work

Kleenex is repackaging its women's tissues in a square box to make it more suitable for a dressing table, and changing the design to feature images of close-ups of female faces in warm muted shades. The revamp aims to extend the use of the product beyond everyday tissues into the cosmetics and toiletries market, targeting women under 30.

Marketing, 22 August 2002

Dyson UK recently launched its '2-drums allergy' washing machine, specifically targeted to the needs of customers with allergic sensitivities. The product features include:

- An allergy duvet cycle, designed to kill dustmites and allergens
- A sensitive stain rinse, to remove all traces of detergent
- A self-clean cycle, to avoid build-up of germs and bacteria
- An automatic water saving device
- The first and only 'Seal of Approval' granted by the British Allergy Foundation.

(www.dyson.co.uk, 2005)

Good examples of targeting based on **benefit segmentation**!

4 Positioning

FAST FORWARD

> **Product/brand positioning** refers to the market's perception of the characteristics of a brand in relation to other brands.

Key concept

> **Positioning** is how a product appears (how it is perceived by the market) in relation to other products in the market.

The 'positioning' of a product or brand in relation to its competitors is defined in terms of how consumers/customers perceive key characteristics of the product.

Possible **positioning characteristics** (*Y Wind*, 1981) include:

- Specific product features, eg price, speed, ease of use, softness/strength (in the case of toilet tissue)
- Benefits, problems, solutions, or needs
- Specific usage occasions
- User category, eg age, gender
- Against another product, eg comparison with a market leader
- Product class disassociation ('stand-out' features from the general mass of products), eg organic food, lead-free petrol, hypo-allergenic cosmetics
- Hybrid basis: a combination of any of the above (eg positioning a brand of toilet tissue according to perceptions of softness and strength, by female/male users, compared to competing brands)

Action Programme 7

Give an example for each of Wind's list of key characteristics.'

LEARNING MEDIA

4.1 Product maps

FAST FORWARD

Market perceptions can be plotted on **product maps**, to suggest marketing opportunities, brand perception and competitive position.

A useful tool for positioning is to 'map' the product/brand on a simple matrix. The following basic **perceptual map** is used to plot brands in perceived price and perceived quality terms: Figure 4.2.

Figure 4.2: Price/quality matrix

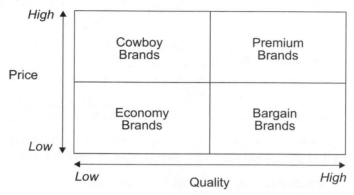

Most consumers will not see price and quality as independent variables. A 'high' price will usually be associated with high quality and equally low price with low quality.

Action Programme 8

Select a product brand and place it where you think appropriate in the quality/price map?

Exam tip

In a June 2004 question on how price can be used to support brand positioning, the examiner noted that a perceptual map would have been welcomed as an illustration. A similar question was set in June 2005, and the examiner was disappointed that the concept of brand positioning was poorly understood. Get to grips with this now!

4.2 Identifying a gap in the market

Market research can determine where customers perceive competitive brands in relation to *each other*, in relation to *target characteristics,* and this can also be shown on a perceptual map: Figure 4.3.

Figure 4.3: Perceptual map for restaurant brand

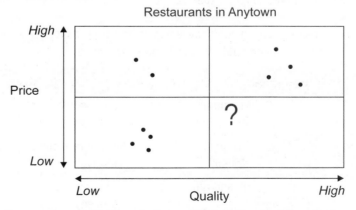

In the model above, there appears to be a gap in the market for a moderately priced, reasonable quality eating place.

Perceptual maps can also plot how customers perceive competitive brands performing on key product user benefits. *Kotler* (2002) gives hypothetical examples from the US breakfast market: Figures 4.4 and 4.5.

Figure 4.4: Product-positioning map: Breakfast market

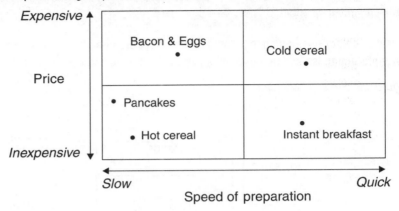

Within this market, a producer might be interested in entering the instant breakfast market. It would then be advisable to plot the position of the various instant breakfast brands.

Figure 4.5: Brand-positioning map: Instant breakfast market

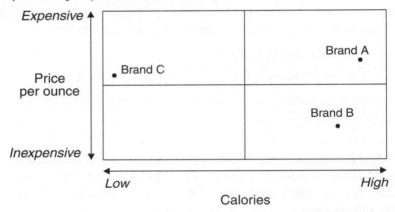

The above analysis now shows an apparent gap for a modest priced slimmers' brand. Once again, it would be necessary to establish whether or not there is sufficient demand for such a product.

4.3 Competitive positioning

Key concept

> **Competitive positioning** concerns 'a general idea of what kind of offer to make to the target market in relation to competitors' offers' (*Kotler*, 2002).

Important considerations in competitive positioning are product quality and price. *Kotler* identifies a 3 × 3 matrix of nine different **competitive positioning strategies**.

Product	High price	Medium price	Low price
High	Premium strategy	Penetration strategy	Superbargain strategy
Medium	Overpricing strategy	Average quality strategy	Bargain strategy
Low	Hit and run strategy	Shoddy goods strategy	Cheap goods strategy

BPP LEARNING MEDIA

Marketing at Work

For an example of a brand with a very strong **self-identity and positioning**, check out the website of the Virgin group: www.virgin.com

Virgin defines its brand values as follows (05/04/2005).

Value for Money
Simple, honest and transparent pricing – not necessarily the cheapest on the market.
eg Virgin Express and Virgin Blue Australia – low cost airlines with transparent pricing – you only pay for the basics.

Good Quality
High standards, attention to detail, being honest and delivering on promises.
eg Virgin Atlantic Upper Class Suite – limousine service, lounge, large flat bed on board, freedom menu etc.

Brilliant Customer Service
Challenging convention with big and little product/service ideas; innovative, modern and stylish design.
eg Virgin Trains new pendolino – fast tilting train with shop, radio, digital seat reservations and new sleek design ... rolling out across the network now.

Competitively Challenging
Sticking two fingers up to the establishment and fighting the big boys – usually with a bit of humour.
eg Virgin Atlantic successfully captured the public spirit by taking on BA's dirty tricks openly – and winning. Later, advertising messages such as BA Don't Give a Shiatsu both mocked BA and delivered a positive message about the airline's service.

Fun
Every company in the world takes itself seriously so we think it's important that we provide the public and our customers with a bit of entertainment – as well as making Virgin a nice place for our people to work.
eg VAA erected a sign over the BA-sponsored, late finishing London Eye saying: BA Can't Get It Up.

5 ICT and the marketing mix

FAST FORWARD

Technological developments, especially the Internet, have had, and will continue to have, a significant influence on all aspects of the marketing mix and marketing management.

ICT stands for Information and Communication Technology. We have already mentioned the impact of ICT on marketing in a number of places in this book, for example when discussing customer relationship management (CRM), marketing research and the analytical tools available in marketing management software. We will mention ICT again in appropriate places, notably in Chapters 7 and 10.

In this section we will make some general comments about the impact of ICT on the marketing mix.

5.1 ICT and product

ICT is itself a product.

(a) **Technology components, tools and services** are sold in both consumer and B2B markets: think of PCs, mobile phones, digital cameras, i-Pods (and their accessories) Internet services, web page design services, database and other software packages, ICT consultancy and so on.

(b)   ICT enables **information** to be sold as a product/service: think of subscriptions to on-line databases, publications and news services; business consulting via the Internet and so on.

(c)   ICT enables **service** provision: think of online banking, telephone banking, online travel reservations, online education/learning provision, dating/friendship communities and so on.

ICT is now used to add value to conventional products and services. For example, if you send a parcel by international courier, you can track its progress online. If you study by distance education, you can use TV, video, CD-ROM and online (e-learning) methods to enhance the interest, interactivity and demonstration aspects of the curriculum. Even a tin of baked beans is enhanced – as a total package of benefits – by its packing being electronically bar-coded: providing information to the retailer and supplier (or sales value/frequency etc) and to the consumer (recording special offers, use-by-dates and so on).

 Marketing at Work

An ingenious British student may have prevented the oft-cited **Internet Toaster** going the same way as the Flying Car.

Robin Southgate, a final year Industrial Design student at Brunel University has designed a unit that grabs the weather forecast, and burns it onto a piece of bread. Mark One doesn't reproduce the full glory of weather maps – such as isobars and cold fronts – on your toast just yet, and instead displays an appropriate symbol: a cloud, sun or raindrop. But it's seamless and doesn't take any longer than a regular, or dare we say 'legacy' toaster.

Source: www.theregister.co.uk 30 March 2002

A company in Cheshire is designing a **futuristic toilet** which can monitor human waste and spot health problems.

At the first sign of a medical condition, the Versatile Interactive Pan (VIP) would contact a GP via the Internet. The VIP concept has been produced by the bathroom manufacturers Twyford.

With a voice-activated seat, automatic flush and the ability to detect health problems, the company says it is a "major breakthrough" in toilet technology.

Although the model is not yet in production, Twyford predicts it could be on the market within the next five years.

Spokesman Terry Wooliscroft said: "We also want to link to the local supermarket.

"If, for example, a person is short on roughage one day, an order of beans or pulses will be sent from the VIP to the supermarket and delivered that same day."

He said it would not be long before the VIP would be ready for production.

Source: www.bbc.co.uk, 11 July 2001

5.2 ICT and price

ICT gives the marketer more sophisticated tools for **analysing costs**. This may otherwise be a very complex task for a product that uses a great many components.

It also allows the marketer to **analyse customer response to price changes** in much more depth than was previously possible.

Customers and competitors have greater **access to price information** too. You could view the many online price comparison sites as a threat, especially if your product or your retail outlet comes out as the most expensive!

BPP LEARNING MEDIA

Marketing at Work

One of many examples of a **price comparison site** is **DealTime** (www.dealtime.co.uk) where you can check the prices of dozens of products. Categories include Appliances (Fridges, Vacuum Cleaners, Washing Machines, etc), Books, Cars (Motor Insurance, Car Loans), Used Cars, Computers, Electronics (Digital Cameras, DVD Players, Televisions, etc), Finance (Loans, Life Insurance, Insurance, etc), Flowers & Wine, Health & Beauty (Women's Fragrance, Face Makeup, Skin Care, etc), Home & Garden, Jewellery, Lingerie , Mobile Phones, Software, Toys & Games, Travel Insurance, Hotels, Car Hire, Video Games.

Several **online catalogues** use price in a way that has not been so easily available before. For instance, if you need to buy a gift for someone and have no bright ideas you can visit the website of, say, Argos, click on Gifts, and specify the price you want to pay and the sort of person you're buying for (toddler, teenager, 'for him', for her', etc) and be presented with lots of ideas.

Also relevant here is the growth of **online auctions**, a topic we will return to in the final part of this book when we are talking about the virtual marketplace. Effectively this means that the customer decides the price (s)he is willing to go pay.

The use of ICT may also enable suppliers to **reduce prices** (especially for products/services sold online), because of the reduction in sales and administration costs enabled by 'self-service' marketing by e-commerce, m-commerce (using mobile phones), telephone ordering and so on. There are often special discounts available if customers order online, for example.

5.3 ICT and place

ICT has enabled **direct marketing** of products and services to consumers/business users, cutting short distribution channels, by:

(a) **Facilitating conventional direct sales**: offering sales force information linked to central databases, allowing personalised direct mail and online mail order catalogues and so on.

(b) **Empowering customers to purchase direct** from 'virtual' stores and auctions. E-commerce and its B2B equivalent (e-purchasing) via the Internet has exploded in many sectors over recent years, especially in markets such as music and books, apparel, travel products, banking services, groceries and niche goods (arts and crafts).

(c) **Facilitating home delivery of goods**, eg by allowing remote ordering, payment and tracking – and 'virtual' supply (eg by downloading information, software, books or music direct from the Internet).

Increasingly, the online shopping experience is simulating 'place', with familiar **processes** (eg 'shopping carts' and 'checkouts'), access to **people** (eg e-mail contact or voice/phone options) and **physical evidence** (eg downloadable/printable order confirmations, vouchers and brochures) and so on.

Marketing at Work

'**TriSenx** is planning to take [**virtual shopping**] one step further, by allowing users to not only download scents, but to print out flavours that can be tasted. The Savannah, Ga., based company has developed a patented technology that allows users to print smells onto thick fibre paper sheets and taste specific flavours by licking the paper coated with the smell.

'Just as advertisers used scratch and sniff technology a couple of decades ago, they will likely use the novelty of digital scents to peddle their products now. Coca-Cola could embed their cola smell into banner ads, which could be triggered by a user scrolling over the ad. Suddenly, you're thirsty for a Coke. Sounds like pretty effective advertising.

'Consumers may also benefit from this aromatic technology. With online spending on the rise, shoppers will now be able to sample some of the goods that they buy, including flowers, candy, coffee and other food products. Soon, you'll be able to stop and smell the roses without leaving your workstation.'

Source: www.howstuffworks.com

5.4 ICT and promotion

ICT can add impact, speed, interactivity and fun to the full range of **promotional methods and tools**, including:

(a) **Advertising**: eg using direct response advertising, web-advertising, CD-ROM and video packages, and mobile phone advertisements.

(b) **Direct marketing**: eg using e-mail or mobile text messages instead of conventional mail shots.

(c) **Sales promotion**: eg online vouchers, discounts, loyalty schemes, 'SMS to win', competitions.

(d) **Public and media relations**: eg corporate image on the website, posting of online press releases, special areas of the website for trade/press/client publics.

(e) **Point of sale display**: eg at online shopping sites.

(f) **Personal selling**: eg connecting mobile sales forces to customer/product databases and sales tools (eg video or computer modelling on the sales person's laptop, demonstrating product use or performance).

(g) **Relationship marketing**: eg generating multiple contacts via website, e-mail, phone 'remembering' customer details and preferences; allowing customer service staff to 'recognise' callers with relevant data; and so on.

ICT has also offered significant new **media** for promotional purposes. This includes not just the Internet, but (*F Brassington & S Pettitt*, 2003):

- **E-mail marketing**: used to target customers with regular and relevant contact via their e-mail, and so build up a relationship.

- **Wireless marketing** (also known as mobile marketing): uses mobile telephones and text messaging, or SMS, to send short 'reminder' messages to target customers. This is getting increasingly sophisticated, with '3G' (third-generation) mobile phone technology.

- **Interactive television (iTV) marketing**: provides the opportunity for two-way communication between marketers and an individual via the television set (for example, to request further information about a product).

It is important for marketers to be aware of what ICT – especially the Internet – *can't* do. It may be able to deliver some products/services in 'real time', or very fast: information, music and images, educational material, banking transactions and so on.

However, many products will still have to be physically delivered. What's more, because the Internet is global in its reach, products may have to be delivered *internationally* – and this takes resources, logistics, infrastructure (road, rail) and time!

BPP LEARNING MEDIA

Because of the promotional strengths of the Internet, there is great potential for customer disappointment if the product does not live up to the sophistication of the promises – or if it cannot be delivered in a reasonable condition or within a reasonable period of time.

Exam tip

> A question in December 2004 asked you to examine the role of ICT in providing additional value to customers: it is worth being realistic in any claims you make!

6 Measuring effectiveness

FAST FORWARD

> Overall **marketing effectiveness** can be difficult to measure. Some writers recommend a subjective approach. Others prefer audits, financial measures, targets and information gathering such as customer feedback.

Marketing effectiveness is not always easy to measure precisely, especially as marketing 'assets' are hard to measure and value. We will discuss the measurement of specific aspects of the marketing mix, such as the effectiveness of a sales promotion, in the appropriate chapters. The remarks that follow apply generally.

6.1 Rating tool

Marketing guru Philip *Kotler* (2002) has developed the thinking on marketing effectiveness into a general purpose rating tool based upon fifteen key questions. The questions are arranged under five headings with three questions under each.

- Customer philosophy
- Marketing organisation
- Marketing information
- The strategic perspective
- Operational efficiency

We won't take you through all the questions (you'll learn more in your later studies) but an example, under the Marketing Information heading is:

> *How frequently does the company conduct market research studies of customers, channels and competitors?*

Each question has three possible answers – to no extent, to some extent or to a very high extent – and these are awarded a score of 0, 1 or 2. The scores are then added up and the overall measure of marketing effectiveness can then be assessed against the following scale.

0 – 5	= None	
6 – 10	= Poor	Firm's survival in doubt
11 - 15	= Fair	
16 - 20	= Good	Opportunity to improve
21 - 25	= Very good	
26 - 30	= Superior	Beware complacency

6.2 Other ways of reviewing marketing effectiveness

Other systematic ways of reviewing marketing effectiveness include:

(a)   Monitoring the product's **market share**.

(b)   Customer, competitor and internal **marketing audits**, as discussed in Chapters 2 and 3.

(c)   **Planning and control systems**. There may be **annual targets** (sales, budgets, expenditure budgets etc) against which performance can be measured.

- **Moving standards** (such as monthly sales targets) allow the same performance measurement on an on-going control basis.

- **Diagnostic standards** monitor how the market is responding to the marketing activity, to give continuous performance feedback (eg via electronic point of sale information or market research).

  Monitoring output against the marketing plan
  Measuring volume and/or growth of sales
  Comparing marketing activities (and/or sales) this year against last year
  Monitoring market share, and any year-on-year changes
  Monitoring customer complaints, returns or repeat sales and recommendations
  Gathering research on customer satisfaction, awareness, response to marketing
  Measuring the accuracy of budgets and schedules
  Comparing sales figures (and/or enquiries, size of contacts base and so on)
  Measuring direct responses (coupons returned, calls to response lines)

One final possibility is to **let others judge**.

- The CIM and *Marketing Week* run **Marketing Effectiveness Awards**. Look at the Marketing Week website: www.mad.co.uk/mw/.

- The Institute of Practitioners in Advertising (IPA) run a bi-annual **Advertising Effectiveness Awards** competition and encourage entries from companies of all sorts and sizes. See the IPA website (www.ipa.co.uk) which gives details of the judging criteria. Registration is free.

- The Medinge Group, an international think-tank on branding and business, launched an annual **'Top Brands with a Conscience'** list in 2004. The 2005 list featured companies like Dilmah Tea (for its community work), Semco (for its democratic management approach), and the John Lewis Partnership. (To see the 2006 list, go to www.medinge.com).

Action Programme 9

Read the material below about Guardian Unlimited. How useful do you think this information is in judging the marketing effectiveness of the Guardian and its website?

BPP
LEARNING MEDIA

Marketing at Work

British Press Awards 2002

Website of the Year

"A stylish, pace-setting and necessary destination for journalists and news junkies"

Against strong competition, Guardian Unlimited won because it had kept ahead of the pack. Judges felt that it was a stylish and pace-setting site with a distinctive character and a sense of humour. For many it was a "must-visit" site, full of tremendous journalism. One judge remarked that it was "what a print newspaper should look like online – it talks directly to its readers and delivers so much more than a newspaper alone can".

Finalists for the award included BBC News Online, FT.com, telegraph.co.uk, Ananova and Femail.

PPAi Interactive Publishing Awards

Guardian Unlimited dominated the PPAi awards in 2001, winning every category nominated.

Best Consumer Product or Service

Best Integration of Media

Best Online Publisher

The judges said: "The clarity of navigation, speed, immediacy and interactivity all add up to an enjoyable experience." The statement praised the breadth of information, saying the site was a "real challenge to the newspaper".

Source: www.guardian.co.uk

Chapter Roundup

- **The marketing mix** concept concentrates on the variables under the organisation's control. The **4 Ps** are highly interactive: decisions regarding one affects all the others.

- The 4 Ps can be balanced by **customer-focused equivalents**: Choice, Cost, Convenience and Communication.

- Some argue that 4 Ps are not enough, especially where **services** are concerned and add three additional Ps: people, process, and physical evidence. The 7Ps are known as the **extended marketing mix**.

- **Service quality** can be defined as the difference between what the customer expects and what he or she perceives him/herself to be receiving. Improved service quality leads to higher profits and is a key task for service marketers.

- Efficient **processes** can become a marketing advantage in their own right.

- **Physical evidence** is an important remedy for the intangibility of many services.

- **Targeting** involves selecting one or more customer groups (segments) and satisfying them with a tailored marketing mix.

- Marketing may be undifferentiated, concentrated or differentiated, according to the degree of targeting used.

- Market targeting, on the basis of segmentation, should result in increased total sales and profits because products/services will be more likely to appeal to the target segments and pricing policy can be more sophisticated.

- **Product/brand positioning** refers to the market's perception of the characteristics of a brand in relation to other brands.

- Market perceptions can be plotted on **product maps**, to suggest marketing opportunities, brand perception and competitive position.

- **Technological developments**, especially the Internet, have had, and will continue to have, a significant influence on all aspects of the marketing mix and marketing management.

- Overall **marketing effectiveness** can be difficult to measure. Some writers recommend a subjective approach. Others prefer audits, financial measures, targets and information gathering such as customer feedback.

BPP LEARNING MEDIA

Quick Quiz

1   Give alternatives beginning with C for the following marketing mix variables.

Price	
Place	
Promotion	
Product	

2   List five ways in which an organisation can create a culture of customer service.

3   Who defines quality?

   A   The Product Manager
   B   The Board of Directors
   C   The Customer
   D   The Marketing Manager

4   Minimising queues and maintaining security are aspects of which extended marketing mix variable(s)?

   A   People
   B   Process
   C   Physical Evidence

5   What is the difference between segmentation and targeting?

6   Three targeting options are (1) to produce a single product; (2) to produce several products; (3) to produce the ideal product. What are the names given to these approaches?

   (1)   …………………………..

   (2)   …………………………..

   (3)   …………………………..

7   Draw a basic perceptual map.

8   This table showing different competitive strategies has been jumbled up. Rearrange it into the proper order. You will probably find it easiest to redraw it from scratch.

	High quality	Low quality	Medium quality
Medium price	Superbargain strategy	Cheap goods strategy	Penetration strategy
High price	Hit and run strategy	Premium strategy	Overpricing strategy
Low price	Average quality strategy	Bargain strategy	Shoddy goods strategy

9   Which of the following is true of a business website?

   A   Long download times are acceptable if the resulting graphics are beautiful
   B   It makes other forms of promotion unnecessary
   C   It can be updated dynamically and be tailored for the specific person who is looking at it
   D   It makes it harder for customers to compare prices because there are no legal requirements

10   List five ways of measuring marketing effectiveness.

Answers to Quick Quiz

1

Price	Cost to the customer
Place	Convenience
Promotion	Communication
Product	Customer value

2
- Job design
- Policies of selection
- Training and development
- Operational rules and practices
- Motivational and reward programmes

3   C

4   Both people and process, and possibly all three.

5   Segmentation is a way of analysing customers. Targeting is a way of using a marketing mix to satisfy a segment.

6   (1)   Undifferentiated
        (2)   Differentiated
        (3)   Concentrated

7

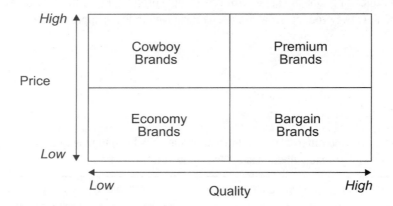

8

	High quality	Medium quality	Low quality
High price	Premium strategy	Overpricing strategy	Hit and run strategy
Medium price	Penetration strategy	Average quality strategy	Shoddy goods strategy
Low price	Superbargain strategy	Bargain strategy	Cheap goods strategy

9   C

10   There are lots of possibilities. Check your answer against Section 6.

BPP LEARNING MEDIA

Action Programme Review

1   You would do this as part of your marketing planning using PEST analysis, competitor analysis and so on. This question is just to check that you have not forgotten what you have read so far.

2   We don't know what you bought, obviously. Your answer should explain what benefit you got from the products, whether you perceived their price to be 'right', how easy it was to get the products, and what persuaded you to buy what you chose rather than another brand.

3   You could buy all the pipes, radiators, thermostats, boilers and install the system yourself, in which case you would no doubt think of it as a product. Most people would employ a company such as Glowarm to supply all the equipment and install it, in which case it is very much a mixture of product and service, and the skills and attitude and behaviour of people – the installation engineers – is vitally important. Central heating perhaps remains a product as long as it is working properly but becomes a service when it goes wrong!

4   You are likely to be seeing lots of evidence. Quality programmes have become a major industry – partly because companies that were certified under the old version of the international quality systems standard, ISO 9000 (1994), have been working to get themselves certified under the much-changed revision, ISO 9000:2000.

5   *Ace* (2001) suggests the following.

People	Care
Select, train and manage staff in service delivery	Communicate and implement customer care values
Processes	**Corporate Competence**
Organise, plan and control systems and operations	Understand customer expectations and convey commitment to deliver: customers don't need to know how things are done (much less how difficult they are to do...)
Physical evidence	**Consistency**
Manage all physical factors (premises, logos etc)	Ensure that customer contacts and experiences are alike, to establish recognition and positive associations.

6   The product life cycle describes how a product changes between its introduction to the market, its growth perhaps into a market leader and (in some, but not all, cases) its eventual decline. The marketing implications of each stage can be very different. For instance the marketing mix for the recently launched 'Internet Fridge', described later in this chapter, is very different to that for an ordinary fridge.

7   (a)   *Positioning by specific product features.* Most car advertisements stress the combination of product features available and may also stress what good value for money this represents.

    (b)   *Positioning by benefits, problems, solutions, or needs.* Pharmaceutical companies position their products to doctors by stressing effectiveness and side effects. Other examples include Crest, which positions its toothpaste as a cavity fighter, and DHL, which uses its worldwide network of offices as a basis for its positioning.

    (c)   *Positioning for specific usage occasions.* Johnson's Baby Shampoo is positioned as a product to use if you shampoo your hair every day, and Hennessy Cognac is for special occasions.

    (d)   *Positioning for user category.* Age has been used as a basis for positioning by many breakfast cereal producers (compare the target markets for Kellogg's Rice Krispies and Special K) and by beauty care products for women over a certain age.

(e) *Positioning against another product.* Confused.com implies that other all other car insurers' products are too complicated. Mobile phone retailers have done likewise in the past.

(f) *Product class disassociation.* Alpen (cereal) attempts to distinguish itself as a luxury more than a breakfast product for the very health-conscious.

(g) *Hybrid basis.* The Porsche positioning, for example, is based on the product benefits as well as on a certain type of user.

8 As our example, furniture manufacturer MFI would probably claim to be in the 'bargain' quadrant. Many potential customers think that they are at the lower end of the economy segment. MFI's practice of frequent sales and discounts has the effect of overcoming at least some of the difficulties resulting from individuals using price as a surrogate for assessment of quality. Thus the price label shows the higher pre-discounted price and the low sale price. The assumption is that customers will use the pre-sale price to confirm promotional claims about quality.

9 The criteria for judging are mostly highly subjective ('stylish', 'distinctive character') with the exception, perhaps of 'speed' and 'clarity of navigation'. For the sake of Guardian Unlimited we can only hope that the judges were genuinely representative of the intended market. It is interesting that the site boasts that it offers 'more than a newspaper alone can', that it is 'a real challenge to the newspaper'. Is this the *Guardian* (newspaper) shooting itself in the foot? Or has it learned that the website is no real challenge to newspaper sales?

Now try Questions 6 and 7 at the end of the Study Text

BPP LEARNING MEDIA

5

Products and services

Syllabus content

- Describe the wide range of tools and techniques available to marketers to satisfy customer requirements and compete effectively (3.2)
- Demonstrate awareness of products as bundles of benefits that deliver customer value and have different characteristics, features and levels (3.4)
- Explain and illustrate the product life cycle concept and recognise its effects on marketing mix decisions (3.5)
- Explain and illustrate the principles of product policy: branding, product lines, packaging and service support (3.6)
- Explain the importance of introducing new products, and describe the processes involved in their development and launch (3.7)

Introduction

In this chapter we'll start off by thinking about the essential characteristics of a product and the main **types of product**.

Next we'll think about the **'life' of a product**. As you can probably appreciate, the marketing implications for a product that has just been introduced to the market are different to the implications for a product that consumers already know and love – or one that has 'had its day' and been supplanted by the 'Next Big Thing'.

We'll think about **product development**: where do ideas for new products come from, and how do they get onto the market?

Finally, we'll consider **services** – things you pay for but can't touch, like banking or education or cleaning. How do you market something when you can't show it to customers or give them something for their money that they can feel good about or show off to their friends?

Action Programme 1

Before you read on, think of one or two products you own that you really like. Get a sheet of paper and write down keywords or phrases explaining what it is you like about them, how they enhance your life. Or just talk enthusiastically about them to a friend or colleague, if they will listen.

1 Bundles of benefits

Those unfamiliar with marketing probably think of a 'product' as a physical object. However, in marketing the term must be understood in a broader sense.

1.1 What is a product?

FAST FORWARD

> **Products** are bundles of benefits that the customer values. Benefits may be tangible, such as good design and functionality, or intangible, for example image.

Key concept

> A **product** is a bundle of benefits which satisfy a set of wants that customers have.

A product is a 'thing' with 'features', which offer a total package of benefits. Products have:

- A **physical aspect**, which relates to the components, materials and specifications (colour, size etc) of the product: for example, a size 12 pullover made of 100% pure wool in a natural colour.

- A **functional aspect**, which describes how a product performs and for what purpose it is likely to be bought: for example, a pullover which gives warmth and comfort and lasts well through washing.

- A **symbolic aspect**, which represents the qualities the product suggests to, or offers, the buyer: the '100% pure wool' label may represent quality, status or eco-friendliness.

BPP LEARNING MEDIA

1.1.1 Product attributes

For the marketer, the total benefit package will include:

(a) **Tangible attributes**

- Availability and delivery
- Performance (usefulness, effectiveness, efficiency)
- Price
- Design (appearance, feel etc)
- Packaging (durability, convenient size, information given)
- The range of complementary products in a 'line'
- The availability of accessories and suppliers for product use or maintenance

(b) **Intangible attributes**

- Image
- Perceived value

These features are interlinked. A product has a tangible **price**, but you obtain the **value** that you perceive the product to have. The suitability of the product for its purposes (ease of use, convenient storage, low maintenance) may be important to you. So may its aesthetic qualities (looks good, your favourite colour, says 'modern'). So may its 'esteem' value (rare, high quality, trendy, impressive to friends, sentimental value). Whether or not you perceive the product as offering 'value for money' depends not only on how much you pay for it – but what value you get from it.

Exam tip

Ten marks were available in December 2004 and again in June 2006 for explaining the 'bundle of benefits' concept. Get used to thinking about the full range of product attributes. What, for example, really accounts for the phenomenal success of the i-Pod, and its resistance to competition from other MP3 player brands?

1.1.2 Product levels

Lancaster & Witney (2005) suggest that it is useful for marketers to think of a product, and its attributes, at different levels: Figure 5.1

Figure 5.1: Levels of product

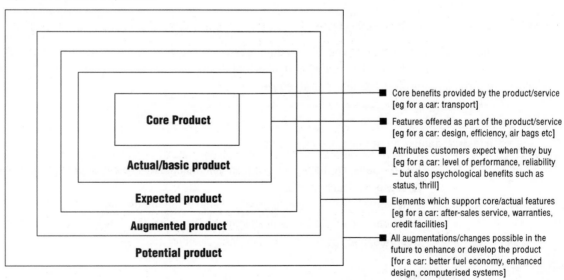

Many products are marketed at the **augmented product** level – as you might expect from our discussion of the extended marketing mix: the total package of the customer's experience of purchasing and consuming the product/service is relevant.

The **expected product** level is also important, because of the potential for customers to be dissatisfied (by disappointed expectations) or delighted (by exceeding expectations).

The **potential product** is important in providing the marketing organisation with future avenues to develop the product (and marketing message) in order to stay competitive and 'fresh' in the market.

1.2 Product classification

FAST FORWARD

Products can be classified as **consumer goods** or **industrial goods**.

Consumer goods are sold directly to the person who will ultimately use them. **Industrial goods** are used in the production of other products.

Key concept

FMCG stands for **Fast Moving Consumer Goods** – items such as packaged food, beverages, toiletries, and tobacco.

Consumer goods can be classified as follows.

Convenience goods	The weekly groceries are a typical example. There is a further distinction between **staple goods** (eg bread and potatoes) and **impulse buys**, like the bar of chocolate that you find at the supermarket checkout. **Brand awareness** is extremely important in this sector. Advertising tries to make sure that when people put 'beans' on their list they have in mind *Heinz* beans.
Shopping goods	These are the more durable items that you buy, like furniture or washing machines. This sort of purchase is usually only made after a good deal of advance planning and shopping around.
Speciality goods	These are items like jewellery or the more expensive items of clothing.
Unsought goods	These are goods that you did not realise you needed! Typical examples are new sometimes 'gimmicky' products, such as 'wardrobe organisers', or fire resistant car polish!

 Action Programme 2

Think of three products that you have bought recently, one low-priced, one medium-priced, and one expensive item. Identify the product attributes that made you buy each of these items and categorise them according to the classifications shown above.

Industrial goods can be classified as follows.

- **Installations**, eg major items of plant and machinery like a factory assembly line
- **Accessories**, such as PCs
- **Raw materials**, for example plastic, metal, wood, foodstuffs and chemicals
- **Components**, eg the Lucas headlights on Ford cars, the Intel microchip in most PCs
- **Supplies**, such as office stationery and cleaning materials

1.3 Branding

Key concept

A **brand** is a name, term, sign, symbol or design intended to identify the product of a seller and to differentiate it from those of competitors.

Branding might be discussed under any of the four Ps. For instance, part of the branding of a Rolls Royce is the unmistakeable design of the Product; or you might buy a 'cheaper brand' of washing-up liquid if you are concerned about price. However, as the definition above suggests, most brands are created and maintained by **marketing communications** such as advertising and promotions. So although we use the term 'brand' frequently in this chapter, we discuss branding in detail in Chapter 8 on Promotion.

2 The product life cycle

2.1 What is the product life cycle?

FAST FORWARD

The **product life cycle** can be demonstrated best by reference to the standard diagram, showing the PLC 'curve'.

Key concept

The **product life cycle** uses a 'biological' analogy to suggest that products are born (or introduced), grow to reach maturity and then enter old age and decline.

The profitability and sales position of a product can be expected to change over time. The 'product life cycle' is an attempt to recognise **distinct stages in a product's sales history**. Here is the classic representation of the life cycle: Figure 5.2.

Figure 5.2: The product life cycle

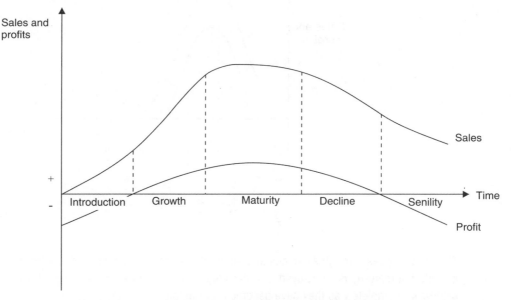

(a) **Introduction**. A new product takes time to find acceptance by consumers and there is slow growth in sales. Only a few firms sell the product, unit costs are high due to low output and there may be early teething troubles with production technology. Prices may be high to cover production costs and sales promotion expenditure. For example, pocket calculators, video cassette recorders and mobile telephones were all very expensive when launched. The product, initially, is a loss maker.

(b) **Growth**. If the new product gains market acceptance, sales will rise more sharply and the product will start to make profits. New customers buy the product and, as production rises, unit costs fall. Since demand is strong, prices tend to remain fairly static for a time. However, the prospect of cheap mass production and a strong market will attract competitors, so that the number of producers increases. With increased competition, manufacturers must spend a lot of money on product improvement, sales promotion and distribution to obtain a dominant or strong market position.

(c)   **Maturity**. The rate of sales growth slows down and the product reaches a period of maturity, which is probably the longest period of a successful product's life. Most products on the market are at the mature stage of their life. Eventually sales will begin to decline so that there is overcapacity of production. Severe competition occurs, profits fall and some producers leave the market. The remaining producers seek means of prolonging the product life by modifying it and searching for new market segments.

(d)   **Decline**. Most products reach a stage of decline, which may be slow or fast. Many producers are reluctant to leave the market, although some inevitably do because of falling profits. If a product remains on the market too long, it will become unprofitable and the decline stage in its life cycle then gives way to a 'senility' stage.

2.1.1 Non-classic PLC

Figure 5.2 shows the classic product life cycle. This is a good starting point when thinking about any product, even though very few products will follow the cycle exactly. For example, the life cycle of a fad product such as the 'cyber pet', or fast changing information technology products, would look like this: Figure 5.3.

Figure 5.3: Short PLC

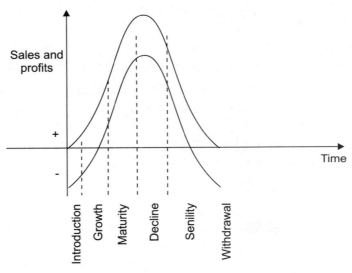

The product goes through all stages at a rapid rate. A short introduction phase leads to extreme sales growth, but maturity is short-lived, and decline is just as rapid as growth was. Often products are withdrawn completely as they have become unprofitable.

Fad products may be relaunched in a modified form, to repeat the process, eg the scooter.

Exam tip

> Be ready to advocate specific mix strategies to address any or all of the stages of the PLC. In June 2003, a challenging question asked you to suggest mix factors in the decline stage of a product (a brand of cheese) that had enjoyed only short-lived success: you were also asked how you would investigate the reasons for this short life-cycle. (This is a useful pointer to how the PLC can be used in marketing planning.) In June 2005, you were asked how the PLC could assist a manufacturer of TV/hi-fi products to manage its products – and how the marketing mix might change through the PLC for any one product example. June 2006 focused on use of the PLC in a marketing audit – and how the mix might change through the PLC of a digital camera. The examiner is repeatedly disappointed by poorly labelled and inaccurate/incomplete PLC diagrams, and failure to link PLC stages with relevant mix decisions.

Action Programme 3

Can you think of any products that have disappeared in your lifetime or are currently in decline?

2.1.2 International PLC

Evidence seems to suggest (*Lancaster*) that there is another lifecycle overlaid on the PLC for products sold in international markets. This comes about because as a product reaches maturity and decline in one market, it may be exported to other countries in order to maintain sales: the product re-enters the growth phase, internationally. At maturity, however, domestic products compete with the imported product – and may even export *back* to the original market, in an on-going see-saw cycle.

2.2 How are life cycles assessed?

The life cycle stage of a given product can be assessed in various ways.

(a)   There ought to be a regular **review of the sales performance** of existing products, as a part of marketing management responsibilities. This should identify upward and downward trends.

(b)   Information should be obtained about the **likely future** of each product.

- An analysis of past trends
- The history of other products
- Market research
- An analysis of competitors

The future of each product should be estimated in terms of both sales revenue and profits.

(c)   Estimates of future life and profitability should be discussed with **experts**: R & D staff in regard to product obsolescence, management accountants re costs, marketing staff re prices and demand.

The following (Figure 5.4) suggests where some products are in their PLC (although, note that particular **brands** of each product may be differently positioned).

Figure 5.4: Products at different PLC stages

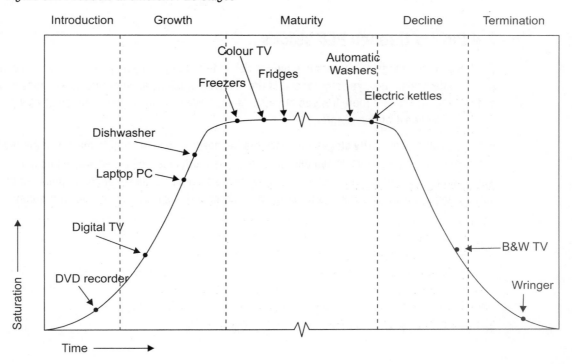

Action Programme 4

Where do you consider the following products or services to be in their product life cycle?

(a) Digital cameras
(b) Baked beans
(c) MP3 players
(d) Cigarettes
(e) Carbon paper
(f) Mortgages
(g) Writing implements
(h) Car alarms
(i) Organically grown fruit and vegetables

2.3 Mix implications of the product life cycle

FAST FORWARD

Marketing can **prolong the life** of some products, perhaps indefinitely, through manipulation of the marketing mix.

When assessments are made, decisions must be taken about what to do with each product.

(a) **Continue** selling the product, with no foreseeable intention of stopping production.

(b) **Initiate action to prolong a product's life**: for example, advertise more, try to cut costs or raise prices, improve distribution packaging or sales promotion methods, or put more effort into direct selling. We will discuss the marketing mix implications of this below.

(c) **Plan to stop producing** the product and either replace it with new ones in the same line or diversify into new product-market areas.

The implications of the product life cycle for marketing mix decisions can be summarised as in the table on the following page.

2.4 Buyers through PLC stages

The **introductory stage** represents the highest risk in terms of purchasing a new, as yet untested product. Buyers reflect this. They typically consist of the relatively wealthy, to whom the risk of loss is quite small, and the young, who are more likely to buy risky items. (We will look at the adoption of new products further in Section 4 of this chapter.)

In the **growth and maturity stages** the mass market needs to be attracted to maximise the product's potential to generate profits. When **decline** sets in the product is well tested with all its faults 'ironed' out. At this stage enter the most risk-averse buyers, termed laggards. These are the opposite of those who participated in the introductory stage, being the poorer and older sections of the community.

BPP LEARNING MEDIA

	Introduction	Growth	Maturity	Decline
PRODUCT	• Initially poor quality • Product design and development key to success • No standard product: frequent design changes	• Competing products have marked quality/technical differences • Quality improves • Product reliability becomes important	• Products become more standardised and differences between competing products less distinct • Product modification may extend maturity stage	• Products even less differentiated • Quality becomes more variable • Perception of 'out of date-ness' • Difficulty getting replacement parts etc
PRICE (and profits)	• High prices possible (because of product impact and few competitors) • High fixed costs (production, promotion) • May require pricing at a loss to stimulate demand	• High contribution, profit margins as costs fall • May reduce initial high prices to drive demand, as competitors enter the market	• Reaching mass market saturation: may need price reduction to extend stage • Competition at its peak: prices falling • Profit margins preserved by high sales volumes • Market segmentation may allow price differentiation	• Prices low – and profits falling with sales volume • Cost savings on reduced promotion • May increase prices at late stage, to 'milk' final sales, especially as competitors dropping out
PLACE	• Few distribution channels available • May require trade promotion/ incentives	• Need to expand distribution channels to meet demand • Distribution channels beginning to flourish	• Fully developed distribution network • Less successful channels can be cut	• Intermediaries dropping out due to low demand • Focus on low-cost distribution
PROMOTION	• High launch (advertising, trade/consumer promotion) costs • Focus on creating awareness • Focus on inducing early trial • Focus on selling in to distributors • Promotion mix: advertising, PR, sales promotion, personal selling	• Percentage of promotion costs falling • Fewer incentives required, as demand strengthens • Promotion mix: maintain advertising/PR; reduce sales promotion?	• Mass market saturation approaching • Focus on repeat purchase (customer loyalty incentives) • Focus on brand image (to maintain profile of known product) • Focus on market segmentation/ targeting (to maximise competitive differentiation) • Promotion mix: less aggressive advertising/PR (perhaps sponsorship?), targeted messages, maintain sales promotion to maximise sales	• Promotion costs reduced to maintain profitability • Focus on securing last available sales • Promotion mix: reduce all activity; use sales promotion to induce repeat/multiple purchase

2.5 Criticisms of the product life cycle model

FAST FORWARD Although it is widely used, the PLC remains controversial.

Dhalla and Yuspeh attempt to expose what they term the 'myth' of the PLC. They point out that:

> 'in the absence of technological breakthroughs, many product classes appear to be almost impervious to normal life cycle pressures, provided they satisfy some basic need, be it transportation, entertainment, health, nourishment or the desire to be attractive.'

While accepting the possibility of a **product** life cycle, Dhalla and Yuspeh reject the existence of **brand** life cycles. They assert that any underlying PLC is determined by marketing actions. In other words, if a brand appears to be in decline, this is not happening as a result of market changes, but because of either reduced or inappropriate marketing by the producer, or better marketing by competitors.

Criticisms of the practical value of the PLC include the following.

(a)   The stages cannot be easily defined.

(b)   The traditional bell-shaped curve of a product life cycle does not always occur in practice. Some products have no maturity phase and go straight from growth to decline. Others have a second growth period after an initial decline. Some have virtually no introductory period and go straight into a rapid growth phase.

(c)   Strategic decisions can change a product's life cycle: for example, by repositioning a product in the market, its life can be extended. If strategic planners 'decide' what a product's life is going to be, opportunities to extend the life cycle might be ignored.

(d)   Competition varies in different industries and the strategic implications of the product life cycle will vary according to the nature of the competition. The 'traditional' life cycle presupposes increasing competition and falling prices during the growth phase of the market and also the gradual elimination of competitors in the decline phase. This pattern of events is not always true.

 Action Programme 5

There must be many products that have been around for as long as you can remember. Companies like Cadbury's have argued that they spend so much on brand maintenance that they should be able to show a value for their brands as an asset in their accounts (though accountants find this hard to accept).

Think of some examples of brands or products that go on and on from your own experience, and try to identify what it is about them that makes them so enduring.

3 Product portfolio planning

3.1 The product mix

FAST FORWARD **Product portfolio planning** aims to balance cash-generating and cash-using products in the product mix.

Key concept

> A company's **product portfolio** (or product assortment or mix) is all the product lines and items that the company offers for sale.

A company's **product mix** can be described in the following terms.

Characteristic	Defined by:
Width	Number of product lines: eg cosmetics, haircare, toiletries and health products.
Depth	Average number of items per product line: eg cosmetics including moisturiser, cleanser, toner, lipstick, eyeshadow etc.
Consistency	Closeness of relationships in product range eg end users, production, distribution.

3.2 Managing the product portfolio

FAST FORWARD

> There are benefits to be gained from using a systematic approach to the management of the product range.

The product mix/portfolio can be **reduced** (eg by discontinuing a product) or **extended** by:

- Introducing variations in models or style (eg a paint manufacturer introducing different colours, types and pot sizes)

- Differentiating the quality of products offered at different price levels (eg 'premium' paints and 'value' paints)

- Developing associated items (eg a paint roller and brushes, paint trays, colour charts etc)

- Developing new products with little technical or marketing relationship to the existing range (eg wallpaper and DIY accessories – or something completely different)

Managing the product portfolio also raises broad issues such as:

- What role a product should play in the portfolio. ('Flagship' brand? Profit provider? Niche filler? New market tester/developer? Old faithful, retaining customer loyalty?) The roles of products in the mix should create a balanced portfolio, with sufficient **cash-generating** products to support **cash-using** (declining or new/market-developing) products

- How resources should be allocated between products

- What should be expected from each product

- How far products should be integrated within the brand image: complementary, recognisable as part of the brand family and so on

Marketing is not an exact science and there is no definitive approach or technique which can determine how resources should be shared across the product range. There are, however, techniques which can aid decision making. Ultimately the burden of the decision is a management responsibility and requires judgement, but tools such as **product-market matrices** and the **product life cycle** can help the decision making process.

3.3 The BCG matrix

FAST FORWARD

> The **BCG matrix** divides products into four categories: Problem Child, Star, Cash Cow, Dog. These relate to a product's market share and the rate of growth in the market for that product.

The **BCG matrix** (Figure 5.5) classifies products or brands on the basis of their **market share** and according to the **rate of growth in the market** as a whole, as a way of assessing their role in the product portfolio.

Figure 5.5: The BCG matrix

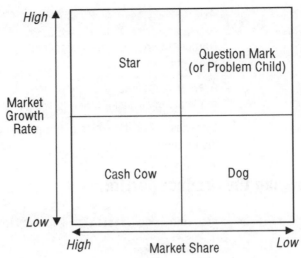

On the basis of this classification, each product may fall into one of four broad categories.

(a)   **Problem Child (or question mark)**: A small market share in a high growth industry. The generic product is clearly popular, but customer support for the particular brand is limited. A small market share implies that competitors are in a strong position and that if the product is to be successful it will require substantial funds, and a new marketing mix. If the market looks good and the product is viable, then the company should consider a **'build'** strategy to increase market share: increasing the resources available for that product to permit more active marketing. If the future looks less promising, then the company should consider withdrawing the product. What strategy is decided will depend on the strength of competitors, availability of funding and other relevant factors.

(b)   **Star**: A high market share in a high growth industry. The star has potential for generating significant earnings, currently and in the future. At this stage it may still require substantial marketing expenditure as part of a **'maintain'** strategy, but this is probably regarded as a good investment for the future.

(c)   **Cash Cow**: A high market share in a mature slow-growth market. Typically, a well established product with a high degree of consumer loyalty. Product development costs are typically low and the marketing campaign is well established. The cash cow will normally make a substantial contribution to overall profitability. The appropriate strategy will vary according to the precise position of the cash cow. If market growth is reasonably strong then a **'holding'** strategy will be appropriate, but if growth and/or share are weakening, then a **'harvesting'** strategy may be more sensible: cut back on marketing expenditure and maximise short-term profit.

(d)   **Dog**: A low market share in a low-growth market. Again, typically a well established product, but one which is apparently losing consumer support and may have cost disadvantages. The usual strategy would be to consider **divestment**, unless the cash flow position is strong, in which case the product would be **harvested** in the short term, prior to deletion from the product range.

3.3.1 BCG and PLC

You may have spotted a relationship between the BCG matrix and the classic **product life cycle**. The typical new product is likely to appear in the 'problem child' category to begin with (introduction). If it looks promising, and with effective marketing, it might be expected to become a 'star' (growth). Then, as markets mature, a 'cash cow' (maturity) and finally a 'dog' (decline). The suggestion that most products will move through these stages does not weaken the role played by marketing. Poor marketing may mean that a product moves from being a problem child to a dog without making any substantial contribution to profitability. Good marketing may enable the firm to prolong the 'star' and 'cash cow' phases, maximising cash flow from the product.

3.3.2 Benefits of using BCG analysis

The framework provided by the matrix can offer guidance in terms of developing appropriate strategies for products and in maintaining a **balanced product portfolio**, ensuring that there are enough cash-generating products to match the cash-using products.

3.3.3 Criticisms of BCG

Like any model, the matrix should be used with caution.

(a) It **oversimplifies product analysis**. It concentrates only on two dimensions of product markets, size and market share, and therefore may encourage marketing management to pay too little attention to other market features.

(b) **'Relative market share' and 'rate of market growth'** are not always relevant. Not all companies or products will be designed for market leadership. So describing performance in terms of relative market share may be of limited relevance. Many firms undertaking this approach have found that all their products were technically 'dogs' and yet were still very profitable, with no need to divest. Firms following a nicheing strategy will commonly find their markets are (intentionally) small.

(c) **The matrix assumes a relationship between profitability and market share**. There is empirical evidence for this in many but not all industries, particularly where there is demand for more customised products.

4 New product development

Questions in December 2003, June 2004, December 2005 and December 2006 (compulsory question) were devoted to the new product development (NPD) process, including (a) **why** a company would wish to introduce new products and (b) the stages of the product development **sequence**. Do not forget that NPD can apply to a new service. Think about the stages that are involved – and be sure to **apply** them (as required) to the specific product or market cited by the exam question.

4.1 Why develop new product?

FAST FORWARD

New product development is important for: maintaining customer satisfaction through change; refreshing or extending the product portfolio; and adapting to environmental opportunities and threats.

There are a number of reasons why a company may consider extending its product mix with the introduction of new products.

(a) To meet the **changing needs/wants of customers**: a new product may meet a new need (eg for environmentally friendly alternatives) or meet an existing need more effectively (eg digital cameras).

(b) To **pace (or outpace) competitors**: responding to innovations and market trends before or shortly after competitors, so as not to miss marketing opportunities.

(c) To respond to **environmental threats and opportunities**: capitalising on opportunities presented by new technology, say (digital cameras), or other products (accessories and supplies for digital cameras); minimising the effects of threats such as environmental impacts (developing 'green' alternatives) or safety concerns (developing new safety features).

(d) To **extend the product/brand portfolio** as part of a product development or diversification growth strategy. (See Chapter 2 if this doesn't ring a bell.) New products can bring new customers to the brand, enable cross-selling of products in the mix and so on.

(e) To **extend the 'maturity' stage of the PLC for a product**, by modifying it to maintain interest, simulate re-purchase (because it is 'new and improved') and/or target as yet unreached market segments.

(f) To **refresh the product portfolio**, as products go into the decline stage of their life cycle. Some products may become obsolete and need updating. Others will simply be deleted, and the company will need to replace them in the product mix in order to maintain brand presence and profitability.

4.2 New products

FAST FORWARD

New products may be genuinely innovative, but may also be adapted, repackaged or introduced in a new market.

What is a new product?

- One that opens up an entirely new market
- One that replaces an existing product
- One that broadens significantly the market for an existing product

An old product can be new if:

- It is introduced to a new market
- It is packaged in a different way
- A different marketing approach is used
- A mix variable is changed

Action Programme 6

Can you think of examples of new products and 'new' old products to fit into each of the above categories?

Marketing at Work

Procter & Gamble has engineered a *business turnaround* in recent years, under new CEO A G Lafley.

- *Core brands* were re-positioned and re-vamped. The Crest toothpaste brand went into whitening products – and doubled its size in the four years to 2004. The Pringles chip range added single-serve packages and chips imprinted with trivia questions – boosting market share by 14%.

- *New products* have been introduced, including joining forces with other brands (Glad Press'n'Seal plastic wrap, joint ventured with Clorox) and licensing new products (like the Swiffer Duster and Mr Clean Magic Eraser).

Business 2.0, Jan/Feb 2005

There are also **degrees of 'newness'**!

(a) **The unquestionably new product**, such as such as products for the treatment of AIDS and cancer using nanotechnology and fullerenes (in other words, things that have only just been discovered or become possible: see www.csixty.com). Marks of such a new product are: technical innovation – high price – initial performance problems – limited availability.

(b) **The partially new product**, such as the DVD player. The main marks of such a product is that it performs better than the equivalent old product.

(c) **Major product change**, such as the digital camera. Marks of such a product: radical technological change altering the accepted concept of the order of things (no need to get your films developed: print them out at home or show them round by e-mail).

(d) **Minor product change**, such as styling changes. Marks of such a product: extras which give a boost to a product. The motor industry does this all the time.

4.3 Sources of new products

New products may arise from a number of sources.

- Licensing (eg Formica, Monopoly)

- Acquisition (buy the organisation making it)

- Internal product development (your own Research and Development team)

- Customers (listen to and observe them, analyse and research) and sales people that have contact with them

- External freelance inventors

- Competition (eg Dyson's bag-less vacuum cleaners, or Apple's i-Pod MP3 player, now copied by other manufacturers)

- Patent agents

- Academic institutions (eg the pharmaceutical industry funds higher education research)

- PEST factor changes, presenting new opportunities and threats

 Marketing at Work

'Get ready for one of the most **aggressive marketing battles** yet seen in the Australian home entertainment industry. The computing and information technology giant Hewlett-Packard (HP) is about to take on the biggest brands in the TV, DVD and CD market as part of its most ambitious **new-product push** so far. HP wants to convince consumers that it is not only a leader in home computing, but that its new range of home entertainment products is second to none. With competitors such as Sony to contend with, HP's task is enormous.

'Worldwide, the company is spending US $300 million this year on marketing its entry into home entertainment, which is new territory for HP. And as if that were not enough, the company also wants to revolutionise the way consumers manage their audio and viewing entertainment by providing a new hardware and software concept it is calling the media hub.

'HP has already taken on the digital photography market. Vice-president for imaging and printing, Vyomesh Joshi ... says: "We offer a complete system of digital photography – the camera, the printer, the PC. So what we have come up with is not a **product value proposition** but an **experience proposition**, allowing consumers to create a rewarding experience from taking digital photos, printing them and putting them on the computer. That is a very different proposition from the Kodaks and Fujis, which are just offering cameras."

'That is also what the company wants to offer in the video and audio market. ...

'For any company, an initiative of this size relies heavily on strong distribution. That presents no problem for HP. It already has 3,000 retail outlets in Australia, and 10% of all shelf space in the imaging, printing and PC category. The main task is education, and Joshi says the company's investment in **educating retailers** is "one of the most important parts" of the project.'

S Lloyd (2004)

4.4 New product development (NPD) process

FAST FORWARD

The **NPD sequence** typically includes: conception; screening of ideas; business analysis; product development and marketing mix planning; market testing; and launch.

New products should only be taken to advanced development if there is evidence of:

- Adequate demand
- Compatibility with existing marketing ability
- Compatibility with existing production ability

The stages of new product (or service) development are as follows: Figure 5.6.

Figure 5.6: NPD

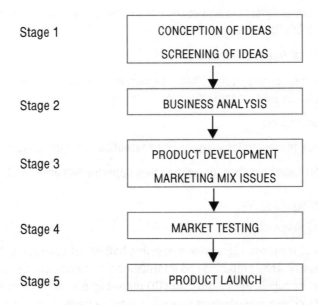

The mortality rate of new products is very high. To reduce the risk of failure new product ideas must be screened. Only the best will make it to the next development stage.

4.4.1 Initial assessment

The **concept** for the new product could be **tested on potential customers** to obtain their reactions, with caution.

(a)   When innovative new designs are tested on potential customers it is often found that they are conditioned by traditional designs and are dismissive of new design ideas.

(b)   However, testers may say they like the new concept at the testing stage, but when the new product is launched it is not successful because people continue to buy old favourites.

4.4.2 Business analysis

A thorough business analysis is required for each product idea, projecting future sales and revenues, giving a description of the product so as to provide costs of production, providing estimates of sales promotion and advertising costs, the resources required, profits and return on investment. Other factors such as the product life cycle, legal restrictions, competitors' reactions etc, must also be evaluated. Products which pass the business evaluation will be developed. A timetable and a budget of resources required and of cost must be prepared, so that management control can be applied to the development project.

4.4.3 Development

Money is invested to produce a working **prototype** of the product, which can be tried by customers. This stage ensures that the product can be produced in sufficient quantities at the right price. The form which the product **test** takes will depend very much on the type of product concerned. The test should replicate reality as closely as possible.

(a) If the product is used in the home, a sample of respondents should be given the product to use at home.

(b) If the product is chosen from amongst competitors in a retail outlet (as with chocolate bars), then the product test needs to rate response against competitive products.

(c) If inherent product quality is an important attribute of the product, then a 'blind' test could be used.

(d) An industrial product could be used for a trial period by a customer in a realistic setting.

The marketing mix for the product will need to be planned at this stage.

4.4.4 Market testing

The purpose of **market testing** is to obtain information about how consumers react to the product. Will they buy it, and if so, will they buy it again? With this information an estimate of total market demand for the product can be made.

A market test involves implementing marketing plans in selected areas which are thought to be 'representative' of the total market. In the selected areas, the firm will attempt to distribute the product through the same types of sales outlets it plans to use in the full market launch, and also to use the intended advertising and promotion plans. (This was discussed in Chapter 2.)

4.4.5 Commercialisation

Finally the product is developed for **full launch**. This involves ensuring that the product is in the right place at the right time, and that customers know about it.

4.5 The diffusion of innovation

FAST FORWARD

The **'diffusion'** of the new product refers to the spread of information about the product in the market place. **Adoption** is the process by which consumers incorporate the product into their buying patterns.

The classification of adopters is shown in Figure 5.7.

Figure 5.7: Adoption of new product

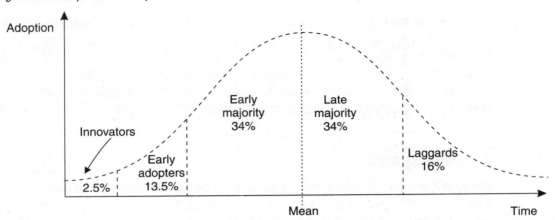

Early adopters and **innovators** are thought to operate as 'opinion leaders' and are therefore targeted by companies in order to influence the adoption of a product by their friends.

The main problem with this model is that the categories appear to add up to 100% of the target market. This does not reflect marketers' experience. Some potential consumers do not adopt/purchase at all. It has consequently been suggested that an additional category is needed: **non-adopters, or non-consumers**.

 Marketing at Work

'**Innovation**' features highly in the marketing press, and in companies' self image.

- **Blackwood Distillers** recently launched a new range of white spirits in Australia, featuring a unique recipe of Shetland spring water and indigenous botanicals. The company aims to position itself – not just on the drinks – but on innovation. To decide on which countries to launch the white spirits, Blackwood looked at those which were receptive to innovation, using measures such as the uptake of iPods and the Internet.

- **Wendy's Supa Sundaes** won a 2004 marketing award for developing and launching the first ice cream enriched with anti-oxidants – the latest 'food craze'. The group was looking for a point of difference to low-fat ice-creams.

- Engineering company **Dyson** (innovators in vacuum cleaners and washing machines – and the subject of the June 2004 exam case study) pride themselves on innovation, R&D and quality. Their website (www.dyson.co.uk) features advice for inventors, information on the product testing/ development process and so on.

5 Packaging

5.1 Functions of packaging

FAST FORWARD

Product packaging serves a number of functions, including product protection, user convenience, and product promotion.

Product packaging fulfils a number of functions.

- **Protection of contents** from damage or deterioration

- **Distribution**, helping to transfer products from the manufacturer to the customer (eg bulk storage packs)

- **Selling**, as the design and labelling provide information and convey an image

- **User convenience**, as an aid to storage and carrying (eg aerosol cans and handy packs)

- **Compliance** with government regulations eg providing a list of ingredients and contents by weight, as in food packaging

- **Promotion**, as packs can be used to print sales promotion information

- **Management information**, as bar codes can be used to track sales

Exam tip

> You might think this is 'common sense' or marginal material – but 10 marks were available for discussing the role of packaging for a consumer product. Could you have come up with 10 marks' worth on 'common sense' alone?

5.2 The qualities required of a pack

A number of different criteria may be used to plan and evaluate packaging.

(a) In industries where **distribution** is a large part of total costs, packaging should include the following.

- Protect, preserve and convey the product to its destination in the desired condition
- Use vehicle space cost effectively
- Fit into the practices of mechanised handling and storage systems
- Be space efficient, but also attractively display items
- Convey product information to shoppers effectively
- Preserve the products' condition

(b) Packaging is an important **aid to selling**. Where a product cannot be differentiated by design techniques, the packaging takes over the design selling function. This is particularly so for basic commodities such as flour.

- Help to promote the advertising/brand image
- Shape, colour and size relate to customer motivation (for 'value' or 'quantity')
- Appropriate size for the expected user of the product (eg family size packets)
- Promote impulse buying (eg new FMCG products, snack foods, etc)
- Convenience pack (tubes, aerosols) where this is important
- Maintain product quality standards
- Attract attention of potential customers in-store

Packaging must appeal not only to consumers, but also to distributors. A sales outlet wants a package design which helps to sell the product, but also minimises the likelihood of breakage, or extends the product's shelf life, or makes more economic use of shelf space.

The **packaging of industrial goods** is primarily a matter of maintaining good condition to the point of use. In itself this is a selling aid in future dealings with the customer. Large, expensive and/or fragile pieces of equipment must be well packaged.

6 Services and service marketing

FAST FORWARD

> **Services** are increasingly important in developed economies. A service has five distinguishing characteristics: intangibility, inseparability, heterogeneity, perishability, and ownership. Each of these has marketing implications.

'Products' is a generic term and can, in many case, include 'services' for the practical purpose of marketing. There are very few pure products or services. Most products have some service attributes (the extended marketing mix) and many services are in some way attached to products.

Key concepts

> **Services** include:
>
> '... those separately **identifiable but intangible activities that provide want-satisfaction**, and that are not, of necessity, tied to, or inextricable from, the sale of a product or another service. To produce a service may or may not require the use of tangible goods or assets. However, where such use is required, there is no transfer of title (permanent ownership) to these tangible goods.'
>
> *(Cowell*, 1995*)*
>
> '... any **activity of benefit** that one party can offer to another that is essentially **intangible** and does not result in the ownership of anything. Its production may or may not be tied to a physical product.'
>
> *(Kotler et al*, 2002*)*

The marketing of services presents a number of distinct problems. As a consequence, particular marketing practices must be developed. There are many service industries which are highly market-oriented (for instance, in retailing, transport hire, cleaning and hotel groups), but there are many which remain relatively unaffected by marketing ideas and practices, or which have only just begun to adopt them (for example, public sector and legal services). Marketing ideas are likely to become much more important as competition within the service sector intensifies.

Action Programme 7

What evidence have you seen that legal services (for example) have begun to adopt marketing ideas and practices?

6.1 The rise of the service economy

In terms of employment, more people now work in the service sector than in all other sectors of the economy. In terms of output, the major contributors to national output are the public and private service sectors. The extension of the service sector and the application of 'market principles' across what were previously publicly-owned utilities has made a large number of service providers much more marketing conscious.

The service sector extends across the **public sector** in the legal, medical, educational, military, employment, credit, communications, transportation, leisure and information fields. Some are 'not-for-profit', but increasingly there are profits involved as services are run as businesses.

The **private sector** includes areas such as arts, leisure, charities, religious organisations and educational institutions, as well as business and professional services involved in travel, finance, insurance, management, the law, building, commerce, and entertainment.

6.2 Marketing characteristics of services

The following characteristics of services distinguish them from goods: Figure 5.8.

- **Intangibility**: services cannot be touched or tasted
- **Inseparability**: services cannot be separated from the provider
- **Heterogeneity** (or lack of 'sameness'): the standard of service will vary with each delivery
- **Perishability**: services cannot be stored for provision 'later'
- **Ownership**: service purchase does not transfer ownership of property

Figure 5.8: Distinguishing characteristics of services

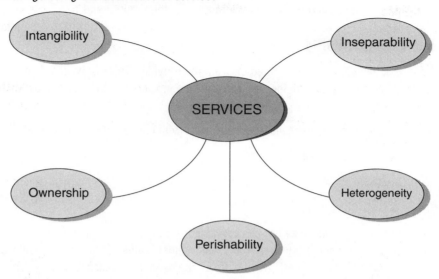

We will look at each characteristic in detail, along with its marketing implications.

Exam tip

> Questions have been set in December 2003, June 2005 and June 2006 (as part of the compulsory case study) asking you to illustrate how the unique characteristics of services affect an organisation's extended marketing mix. The examiner was disappointed that weaker candidates could not cite the characteristics of service – and that the 'extended marketing mix' (where specified) was linked only to the extra 3Ps, rather than the full 7Ps (you have been warned!).

6.2.1 Intangibility

'Intangibility' refers to the lack of substance which is involved with service delivery. Unlike goods, there are no substantial material or physical aspects to a service: no taste, feel, visible presence and so on. Clearly this creates difficulties and can inhibit the desire to consume a service, since customers are not sure what they will receive.

> 'Ultimately the customer may have no prior experience of a service in which he or she is interested, nor any conception of how it would satisfy the requirements of the purchase context for which it was intended.'
> (*A Morden*, 1993)

Marketers and consumers need to try to overcome this problem. The consumer needs information to avoid making a mistake, to obtain some grounds for forming a judgement and to cut down risk. The marketer wishes to make the choice of the product 'safer' and make the consumer feel more comfortable about paying for something they do not then own and which has no physical form.

Dealing with intangibility may involve the following.

(a) **Increasing the level of tangibility**. Use physical or conceptual representations/illustrations to make the customer feel more confident as to what it is that the service is delivering: the 'physical evidences' component of the extended marketing mix.

(b) **Focusing the attention of the customer on the principal benefits of consumption**. Communicating the benefits of purchasing the service so that the customer visualises its use. Promotion and sales material could provide images or records of previous customers' experience.

(c) **Differentiating the service and reputation-building**. Enhancing perceptions of customer service and customer value by offering excellence in the delivery of the service. This reputation can be attached to brands, which must then be managed to secure and enhance their market position. (For example, the Virgin brand.)

6.2.2 Inseparability

Services often cannot be separated off from the provider. Think of having dental treatment or taking a journey. Neither exists until they are actually being experienced/consumed by the person who has bought them.

The 'creation' of many services is simultaneous with consumption, where the service is

- Made available
- Produced   } all at the same time
- Sold
- Consumed

Provision of the service may not be separable from the person or personality of the seller. Consequently, increasing importance is attached to the need to instil values of quality, reliability and to generate a service ethic in customer-facing staff. This points up the need for excellence and customer orientation and the need to invest in high quality people and high quality training: the 'people' component of the extended marketing mix.

6.2.3 Heterogeneity (lack of 'sameness' or consistency)

Many services face the problem of maintaining consistency in the standard of output. Variability of quality in delivery occurs because of the large number of variables involved. The quality of the service may depend heavily on who it is that delivers the service, or exactly when it takes place. Booking a holiday using standard procedures may well be quite different on a quiet winter's afternoon then on a hectic spring weekend, and may well vary according to the person dealing with your case.

It may also be impossible to obtain influence or control over customers' perceptions of what is good or bad service. From the customer's perspective it is, of course, very difficult to obtain an idea of the quality of service in advance of purchase/consumption.

In terms of marketing policy, heterogeneity highlights the need to develop and maintain processes for:

- Consistency of **quality control**, with clear and objective quality measures

- Consistency of **customer service** and customer care, standardising as far as possible

- Effective staff selection, training and motivation in customer care

- Adopting the Pareto principle and so identifying and responding most closely to potential **'troublespots'**. (The Pareto principle states that 80% of the difficulties arise from 20% of events surrounding the service provision)

- **Monitoring** service levels and customer perceptions of service delivery

These measures correspond to both the 'processes' and 'people' elements of the extended marketing mix.

6.2.4 Perishability

Services cannot be stored: they are innately perishable. Seats on a bus or the services of a doctor exist only for periods of time. If they are not consumed, they 'perish'. They cannot be used later. They cannot be 'produced' in advance, to allow for peaks in demand.

This presents specific marketing problems. Meeting customer needs depends on staff being available as and when they are needed. This must be balanced against the need for a firm to minimise unnecessary expenditure on staff wages. **Anticipating and responding to levels of demand** is, therefore, a key planning priority, in order to avoid:

- Inadequate level of demand accompanied by substantial variable and fixed costs
- Excess demand resulting in lost custom through inadequate service provision

Policies must seek to **smooth out fluctuations** in the supply/demand relationship, or allow for **contingencies**. Examples include:

- Using price variations to encourage off-peak demand (eg on travel services)
- Using promotions to stimulate off-peak demand (eg free mobile calls between certain hours)
- Using flexible staffing methods to cover fluctuations in demand (eg part-time and temporary working, outsourcing to call centres)

6.2.5 Ownership

Services do not result in the transfer of property. The purchase of a service only gives the customer access to or the right to use a facility, not ownership. This may lessen the perceived customer value of a service – particularly if the benefit does not accrue until some time in the future (like a pension, or a voucher for future use).

There are two basic approaches to addressing this problem.

- **Promote the advantages of non-ownership**. This can be done by emphasising the benefits of paid-for maintenance, or a periodic upgrading of the product. Radio Rentals have used this as a major selling point with great success.

- **Make available a tangible symbol or representation of ownership** such as a certificate, voucher, merchandise item or simple receipt. This can come to embody the benefits enjoyed.

Action Programme 8

A national charity wants to send out a mailshot to attract donations. Describe in detail what you would suggest that receivers should find in the envelope. (Note: The charity faces the same problems as a typical service provider. The key is to overcome the lack of a physical product.)

Chapter Roundup

- **Products** are bundles of benefits that the customer values. Benefits may be tangible, such as good design and functionality, or intangible, for example image.

- Products can be classified as **consumer goods** or **industrial goods**.

- The **product life cycle** can be demonstrated best by reference to the standard diagram, showing the PLC 'curve'.

- Marketing can **prolong the life** of some products, perhaps indefinitely, through manipulation of the marketing mix.

- Although it is widely used, the PLC remains controversial.

- **Product portfolio planning** aims to balance cash-generating and cash-using products in the product mix.

- There are benefits to be gained from using a systematic approach to the management of the product range.

- The **BCG matrix** divides products into four categories: Problem Child, Star, Cash Cow, Dog. These relate to a product's market share and the rate of growth in the market for that product.

- **New product development** is important for: maintaining customer satisfaction through change; refreshing or extending the product portfolio; and adapting to environmental opportunities and threats.

- New products may be genuinely innovative, but may also be adapted, repackaged or introduced in a new market.

- The **NPD sequence** typically includes: conception; screening of ideas; business analysis; product development and marketing mix planning; market testing; and launch.

- The **'diffusion'** of the new product refers to the spread of information about the product in the market place. **Adoption** is the process by which consumers incorporate the product into their buying patterns.

- **Product packaging** serves a number of functions, including product protection, user convenience, and product promotion.

- **Services** are increasingly important in developed economies. A service has five distinguishing characteristics: intangibility, inseparability, heterogeneity, perishability, and ownership. Each of these has marketing implications.

BPP
LEARNING MEDIA

Quick Quiz

1   CUSS is an acronym for four types of consumer goods (and is also what you may do after you buy one of the categories, when you come to your senses). SCARI is an acronym for industrial goods. What do CUSS and SCARI stand for?

2   According to the PLC, what happens towards the end of a product's maturity?

3   Draw a diagram of the PLC for the Tamagotchi, i-Dog or other virtual reality pet.

4   The ten items in the first table below are in no particular order, but each belongs in one of the four columns – Introduction, Growth, Maturity or Decline – in the second table. Your job is to fill in the columns correctly: you can just fill in the numbers if you like. We've done one for you.

(1) Differences between competing products less distinct.	(2) Quality variable.	(3) Poor quality.	(4) Products even less differentiated.	(5) Competitor's products have marked quality and technical differences.
(6) Product design and development are a key to success.	(7) No standard product and frequent design changes.	(8) Products become more standardised.	(9) Product reliability may be important.	(10) Quality improves.

	Introduction	Growth	Maturity	Decline
Product	(7)			

5   (a)   High or low? A cash cow has a .... market share in a .... growth market.
     (b)   What animal or symbol is diagonally opposite a cash cow?

6   You need to collect three pieces of evidence before you take a new product to advanced development. What are they?

7   Packaging:

A   Forces resellers to extend their shelves
B   Is an important aid to selling basic commodities
C   Is not important for industrial goods
D   Should come in as many ranges and sizes as possible to appeal to different segments of the market

8   What are the marketing implications of the 'inseparability' of some services?

9   What does heterogeneity mean? Give an example.

10   Self-service in petrol stations and restaurants and so on is a way of counteracting service marketing problems such as inseparability and perishability.

True ☐

False ☐

Answers to Quick Quiz

1   CUSS stands for Convenience goods, Unsought goods, Shopping goods, and Speciality goods. The unsought goods are ones most likely to make you swear. SCARI: Supplies, Components, Accessories, Raw materials, Installations.

2   Sales begin to decline so that there is overcapacity of production. Severe competition occurs, profits fall and some producers leave the market. The remaining producers seek means of prolonging the product life by modifying it and searching for new market segments.

3

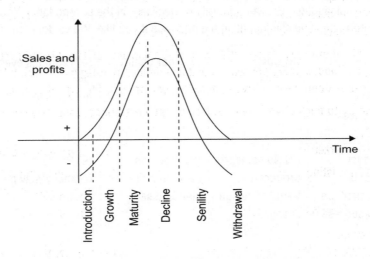

4

	Introduction	Growth	Maturity	Decline
Product	(3), (6),(7)	(5), (10), (9)	(8), (1)	(4), (2)

5   (a)   A cash cow has a high market share in a low growth market.
    (b)   A problem child (or question mark).

6   Evidence of adequate demand, evidence that you can market the product, and evidence that you can produce it.

7   B

8   Services often cannot be separated off from the provider, so it is important to generate a customer service ethic in the staff who deliver the service.

9   It means lack of sameness or consistency (lack of 'homogeneity'). A good example is a train journey. You may catch the same train to work every day, but it will not always arrive at the same time. Or a telephone sales person may be pleasant and polite one day and grumpy the next. There are countless other examples.

10   False. It is a way of employing fewer people.

BPP LEARNING MEDIA

Action Programme Review

1   The outcome of this activity depends upon the products that you have chosen. It should have set you up well for your study of this chapter.

2   Again, this depends upon the products you have chosen. The table in Paragraph 1.2 should have helped if you were stuck for inspiration.

3   Some ideas to start you off are manual typewriters and vinyl records. Also, almost anything subject to fads or fashions.

4   You could perhaps pin down some of these items, but most are open to discussion, especially if you take an international perspective. For many you may consider that the PLC is not valid, and you will not be alone, as the discussion within the chapter has shown.

5   There are lots of examples to consider. Many products are such an integral part of everyday life (cars, chocolate, pet food, laundry powder...) that it is difficult to imagine life without them. Any selection will always depends upon the country / culture that you are considering, of course.

6   You should try to think of your own examples, but these suggestions may help.

New product

Entirely new market	Web 'browsers', National Lottery
Replacing an existing product	Centrino replacing Celeron processors; digital cameras replacing film, MP3 replacing CD
Broadening the market	Cable for satellite, TV and telephones

'New' old product

In a new market	German confectionery (in the UK)
New packaging	Anything
New marketing	French wine competing with Australian wine

7   The most obvious example (in the UK, at least) is the proliferation of companies offering to help out if you have an accident at work. It is very difficult to avoid their TV ads. For instance Claims Direct was launched in 1996 by a former London cabbie called Tony Sullman, and has since grown to become the largest direct-response advertiser in the market. The "personal injury compensation specialist" has a panel of more than 300 solicitors and claims that over 75 per cent of cases are successful. In 2000, Claims Direct became the 69th-biggest-spending advertiser in the UK, investing more than British Airways, Lloyds TSB and Nissan.

8   You may well have received such a mailshot yourself. One received by the editor from the National Society for the Prevention of Cruelty to Children (NSPCC) contained five items in an envelope printed with black and white photo of a sad and neglected little girl. The five items were as follows.

(a)   An A3 sheet folded to make a four A4 page letter printed in two colours and with more black and white photos of neglected children on paper with a recycled feel. The letter tells the story of Ellie, the child shown on the envelope, and in emotive language, asks for £15 and describes what good can be done with that money by the NSPCC.

(b)   An A5 size donation form printed on both sides. You can tick a box saying '£15' or fill in your own amount. You can give your credit card details. You can opt *not* to receive further mailings. On the other side, Ellie's story and NSPCC action is described again in a sort of brief 'photo-story'.

(c)   An envelope addressed to the Director of the NSPCC at a FREEPOST address (but suggesting that if you use a stamp it will save the NSPCC the postage).

(d)   A 'Thank You' card with a picture of Ellie smiling on the front, a further plea from the Director of the NSPCC, and a thank you message in a 'hand-written' typeface.

(e)   A car sticker saying 'Support the NSPCC'.

Now try Questions 8 and 9 at the end of the Study Text

6

Price

Syllabus content

- Describe the wide range of tools and techniques available to marketers to satisfy customer requirements and compete effectively (3.2)
- Explore the range of internal and external factors that influence pricing decisions (3.8)
- Identify and illustrate a range of different pricing policies and tactics that are adopted by organisations as effective means of competition (3.9)

Introduction

In this chapter, we introduce basic concepts in pricing strategy and decisions.

(a) We explore a range of **internal and external factors** which influence pricing decisions, focusing on the key factors of: objectives, costs, competition and demand.

(b) We look at some of the dynamics by which price affects consumer buying decisions, and suggest a range of **pricing policies and tasks** that an organisation might adopt to achieve its market objectives.

1 The role of price in the marketing mix

FAST FORWARD

Pricing decisions are important to the firm, as they are the basis of profits. Pricing is also the only element of the marketing mix which generates revenue rather than creating costs.

All profit organisations and many non-profit organisations face the task of pricing their products or services. Price can go by many names: fares, fees, rent, assessments and so on.

Price was once the single most important decision made by the sales department. In those production-oriented times, price was viewed as the major factor in satisfying customer needs, and a price change was the usual reaction to competitor activity.

Today, though, marketing managers view price as just one of the factors involved in customer satisfaction. In fact it is sometimes suggested that marketing aims to make price relatively unimportant to the consumers' decision making process. There is certainly some truth in this view. The other elements of the marketing mix are concerned with adding value to the product and tailoring it to the consumers' needs, to ensure that the choice between two products is not simply based on their different prices.

However, the **role of price** in the marketing mix is still significant, and should not be underestimated.

- Pricing is the only element of the mix which generates revenue rather than creating costs.

- It also has an important role as a competitive tool to differentiate a product and organisation, and thereby exploit market opportunities.

- Pricing must also be consistent with other elements of the marketing mix, since it contributes to the overall image created for the product.

Key concept

Price can be defined as a measure of the value exchanged by the buyer for the value offered by the seller.

It might be expected that the price would reflect the costs to the seller of producing the product and the benefit to the buyer of consuming it. This simplistic view is not always accurate.

 Action Programme 1

In what circumstances would you expect price to be the main factor influencing a consumer's choice?

A price aims to produce the desired level of sales in order to meet the objectives of the business. Pricing must take into account the internal needs of, and the external constraints on, the organisation.

C Jasper (2005) offers the following essential *tips for pricing.*

- Don't base pricing on cost recovery. Use the three Cs – cost, competitors and customer value.
- Differentiate your product or service to maximise your pricing options.
- Pricing is the strongest driver of business profitability.
- Don't discount just because your competitors have cut prices – think through all the options first.
- Pricing strategies should be viewed as an ongoing, work-in-progress.

2 Influences on pricing decisions

FAST FORWARD

Pricing decisions are effected by a range of factors, both **internal** (to the organisation) and **external** (in the competitive environment).

These factors can be summarised as follows. (Note that they may have a strategic – as well as a purely tactical – influence on marketing decisions.)

Internal factors	External factors
• **Marketing objectives**: profit maximisation; market share leadership; brand targeting and positioning and so on.	• **Competition**: the extent of competition in the market; whether there is non-price competition; competitor pricing and promotions.
• **Marketing mix strategy**: factoring in the cost/price implications of quality, distribution, brand differentiation and so on.	• **Demand**: the sensitivity of customer demand for the product to change in price (elasticity of demand) in the given market.
• **Costs**: at least setting the lowest viable price at which the company can afford to sell the product.	• **Customer perceptions** of price and what it means for quality, value and so on, within a given market.
• **Price-setting methodologies**: negotiated by sales force; set by management etc.	• **Suppliers and intermediaries**: impacting on costs; reacting to price decisions to protect their own margins.
• **Product portfolio strategies**: launch/new-product incentive pricing; 'loss leaders' to support the product range; and so on.	• **PEST factors**: economic factors determining affordability; government price watchdogs; social responsibility dictating affordability; changing perceptions of 'value'; technology lowering production costs.

Exam tip

Internal and external factors in pricing decisions (in the consumer electronics market) were worth 15 marks in the compulsory case study question in December 2005. Don't be tempted to 'skip' technical topics like this: the examiner has emphasised that *any* topic may be set as part of the compulsory question. The examiner was disappointed by answers that cited few factors – or confused 'internal' and 'external' factors: try and be systematic about approaching questions…. Factors in price setting were also set in June 2005 (in the household cleaning product market) and June 2006 (B2B microchips): the examiner is serious about testing this topic!

We will look at some of the key factors in more detail.

2.1 Business objectives

Pricing decisions are guided by one or other of two business objectives.

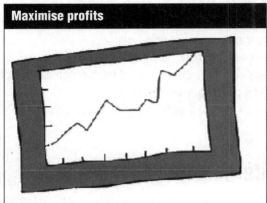

Maximise profits	**Maintain or increase market share**
Charge as **high** a price as possible. This depends on how good your product is and how much demand is affected by higher prices.	Charge a **lower** price than competitors, or the **same** price. You would do this if you want to hold on to existing customers and/or attract new ones.

Either approach may be used in specifying pricing objectives, and they may appear in combination. It is important that pricing objectives are consistent with overall **corporate objectives**: you might not want to raise prices, for example, if the corporate objective is to be an accessible, ethical low-cost provider of essential service.

 Marketing at Work

In recent years, a number of **low-cost no-frills** carriers have set up in business, for example easyJet. To compete, British Airways set up its own low cost no-frills airline. However, to include these services under the British Airways name would have resulted in consumer confusion. Customers do not expect a no-frills service from BA, which has a strong, reliable, upmarket image. Therefore, the no-frills services were run under the 'Go' banner.

Ironically, in May 2002, Go was bought out by its rival easyJet. BA's competitive strategy inadvertently led to easyJet overtaking Ryanair, the Irish no-frills operator, to become Europe's biggest low-cost carrier!

Exam tip

An unusual question on the December 2002 paper asked how an economist, an accountant and a marketer might view and contribute to pricing decisions. The examiner was looking for a consideration of economic issues (demand, elasticity, competition etc), accounting issues (such as costs and profitability) and marketing issues (price sensitivity, competition, promotion, product positioning). This chapter contains enough material on pricing policy to be able to answer such a question well.

2.2 Costs

FAST FORWARD

In practice, **cost** is the most important influence on price. In cost-based (full-cost or cost-plus) pricing, costs are estimated and then a profit margin is added to set the price.

A study by *R Lanzillotti* (1989) gave a number of reasons for the predominance of **cost-based pricing**.

- Planning and use of scarce capital resources are easier
- Easier assessment of divisional performance
- Emulation of successful large companies or benchmarks

- Belief by management in a 'fair return' policy
- Fear of government action against 'excessive' profits
- Tradition of production orientation rather than marketing orientation
- Tacit collusion in industry to avoid competition
- Adequate profits for shareholders are already made, giving no incentive to maximise profits
- Easier administration of cost-based pricing strategies based on internal data
- Stability of pricing, production and employment produced by cost-based pricing

There are two types of cost-based pricing: full cost pricing and cost-plus pricing.

2.2.1 Full cost pricing

Full cost pricing takes account of the full average cost of production of a brand, including an allocation for overheads. A profit margin is then added to determine the selling price. This method is often used for non-routine jobs which are difficult to cost in advance, such as the work of solicitors and accountants where the price is often determined after the work has been performed.

2.2.2 Cost-plus pricing

Under cost-plus pricing, only the more easily measurable direct cost components such as labour and raw material inputs are calculated in the unit cost, whilst an additional margin incorporates an overhead charge and a residual profit element. This method is used where overhead allocation to unit costs is too complex or too time consuming to be worthwhile.

A common example occurs with the use of **mark-up pricing**. This is used by retailers and involves a fixed margin being added to the buying-in price. In the UK, for example, fast moving items such as cigarettes carry a low 5-8% margin (also because of tax factors); fast moving but perishable items such as newspapers carry a 25% margin; while slow moving items which involve retailers in high stockholding costs, such as furniture or books, carry 33%, 50% or even higher mark up margins.

Action Programme 2

Look at the following advertisement for SWATCH.

FROM PLASTIC TO PLATINUM

WORLDWIDE

**INDIVIDUALLY NUMBERED LIMITED
EDITION OF 12,999**

£1,000 INC VAT

- **Most exclusive Swatch ever produced.**

- **950 Platinum case and crown.**

- **Stainless steel presentation case
  with acrylic glass inlay.**

- **Interchangeable royal blue leather
  and padded plastic straps.**

- **Limited availability in the UK.**

Suggest how Swatch might have chosen the price of £1,000.

Since the cost-plus approach leads to **price stability**, with price changing only to reflect cost changes, it can lead to a marketing strategy which is reactive rather then proactive.

2.2.3 Limitations of cost-based pricing

There is very limited consideration of **demand** in cost-based pricing strategies.

(a)   From a marketing perspective, cost-based pricing may reflect **missed opportunities**, as no account is taken of the price consumers are *willing* to pay for the brand, which may be higher than the cost-based price.

(b)   Particular problems may be caused for a **new brand**, as initial low production levels in the introduction stage may lead to a very high average unit cost and consequently a high price. A longer term perspective may be necessary, accepting short-term losses until full production levels are attained.

2.2.4 Techniques of cost analysis

While you probably won't need an in-depth knowledge about cost analysis for this exam (costing and budgeting are included in the **Marketing in Practice** syllabus), it is worth being aware of the key techniques and concepts.

- **Fixed costs** are costs which do not vary according to how many units are being produced or sold (eg salaries, advertising costs)

- **Variable costs** are costs which vary directly according to how many units are being produced or sold (eg materials costs, sales force commissions)

- **Contribution** is the amount that a product or project contributes to covering fixed costs. It is calculated as:

Selling price/revenue *minus* variable cost

If a product or marketing plan generates sufficient contribution to cover fixed costs, it may be worth pursuing in the short term.

- **Breakeven analysis** is used to calculate how much of a product/service must be output at a given price, in order for sales revenue to equal the total costs of producing/marketing it. The breakeven quantity (BEQ) equals:

$$\frac{\text{Fixed costs}}{\text{Contribution}}$$

This calculation enables marketers to calculate the effect of different prices on the breakeven point/quantity.

2.3 Competition

FAST FORWARD

Prices may be set on the basis of what **competitors** are charging rather than on the basis of cost or demand.

This sometimes results in '**going rate**' pricing. Some form of average level of price becomes the norm, including standard price differentials between brands.

2.3.1 Non-price competition

In some market structures, price competition may be avoided by tacit agreement, leading to concentration on **non-price competition**: the markets for cigarettes and petrol are examples of this. Price-setting here is influenced by the need to avoid retaliatory responses by competitors, which could result in a breakdown of the tacit agreement and profit-reducing price competition. Price changes based on real cost changes are led in many instances by a 'representative' firm in the industry, followed by other firms.

Whether agreements exist at all is hard to prove: competitors are exposed to the same market forces and so might be expected to set similar prices. This is a problem for government agencies, such as the Office of Fair Trading, when attempting to establish if unethical pricing agreements exist.

 Marketing at Work

There are three key constructs to consider when setting a price: the value of the offering to the **customer** (ie **demand**), the prices charged by **competitors** and the organisation's **costs** of production.

But then comes a more subtle cost: that of **changing prices** in the first place. In many instances firms incur greater losses by increasing their prices than leaving them at the same level. Because the physical, labour and communication costs associated with a price change often exceed the marginal increase in revenues.

Hope is at hand, however.

- NCR has just launched Electronic Shelf Labels in the US, thus ensuring that supermarkets can cut the incompetent marketer out of the pricing task altogether. Prices are displayed in the supermarket on small LCD panels. As goods are scanned, computers at head office make a calculation based on the remaining supply of goods and the predicted demand and alter the price in each store.

- Not to be outdone, Coca-Cola is testing a prototype vending machine that increases the price of each can as the temperature gradually rises. Pure, perfect, elastic pricing will soon be ours and economists will rule the world! You have been warned.

Adapted from *Marketing,* 27 June 2002

2.3.2 Competitive bidding

Competitive bidding is a special case of competition-based pricing. Many supply contracts, especially concerning local and national government purchases(where it is compulsory) involve would-be suppliers submitting a sealed bid **tender**.

The firm's submitted price needs to take account of expected competitor bid prices. Often the firms involved will not even know the identity of their rivals but successful past bids are often published by purchasers and it is possible to use this data to calculate a realistic bid.

2.4 Demand

 FAST FORWARD

Prices may be based on the **intensity of demand**: strong demand may lead to a high price, and weak demand to a low price. The concept of **price elasticity** illustrates how demand can be affected by price changes.

2.4.1 Price elasticity of demand

In classical economic theory, price is the major determinant of demand. More recently, emphasis has been placed on other factors. The significance of product quality, promotion, personal selling and distribution and brands has grown.

Key concept

> **Price elasticity** is measured as:
>
> $$\frac{\text{\% change in sales demand}}{\text{\% chage in sales price}}$$

As you might expect, 'elasticity' indicates how much demand will 'stretch' or how far a change in price will affect demand. The more elastic demand is, the more demand will *increase* if you *lower* the price slightly – and the more demand will *decrease* if you *raise* the price slightly. In other words, if demand is elastic, buyers are very sensitive to price and price changes: if it is inelastic, price is not a key factor in demand.

Economists would state our informal explanation as follows.

(a) When elasticity is greater than 1 (**elastic**), a change in price will lead to a change in total revenue so that, if the price is

(i) lowered, total sales revenue would rise, because of the large increase in demand.
(ii) raised, total sales revenue would fall, because of the large fall in demand.

(b) When elasticity is less than 1 (**inelastic**), if the price is

(i) lowered, total sales revenue would fall, because the increase in sales volume would be too small to compensate for the price reductions.
(ii) raised, total sales revenue would go up in spite of the small drop in sales quantities.

Marketing management needs to be able to estimate the **likely effects of price changes** on total revenue and profits.

> 'Price elasticity of demand gives precision to the question of whether the firm's price is too high or too low. From the point of view of maximising revenue, price is too high if demand is elastic and too low if demand is inelastic. Whether this is also true for maximising profits depends on the behaviour of costs.' (*Kotler et al*, 1999)

In some cases, however, other factors may influence price elasticity, so that previous responses to price changes no longer produce the same consumer responses. Products do not stay the same forever.

Action Programme 3

What are the limitations of price elasticity as a factor in determining prices?

Marketing at Work

British Gas, Britain's biggest energy supplier, cut its gas and electricity **prices** for the second time in April 2007, shaving 3% off gas and 6% off electricity prices.

British Gas announced its first price cut for six years in February. The group apparently signed up 678,000 customers since those original cuts were announced – having lost a million in 2006 after record-breaking price rises, which saw its share of the gas market fall below 50% for the first time ever.

The new round of cuts came just days after it emerged that complaints about British Gas had more than trebled in the past year, due to teething troubles with a new billing system.

Three competitors immediately followed with cuts of their own. The two competitors who kept their rates unchanged were 'slammed' by energy regulator Ofgem, which urged customers to switch to a cheaper supplier!

BPP
LEARNING MEDIA

2.4.2 Price discrimination

A firm might successfully charge higher prices for the same product to people who are willing to pay more. This is called **price discrimination**, or **differential pricing**.

By market segment	By product version	By time
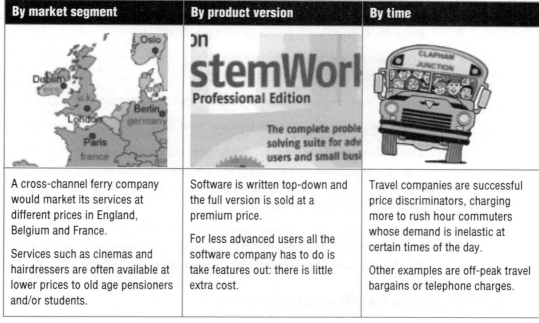		
A cross-channel ferry company would market its services at different prices in England, Belgium and France. Services such as cinemas and hairdressers are often available at lower prices to old age pensioners and/or students.	Software is written top-down and the full version is sold at a premium price. For less advanced users all the software company has to do is take features out: there is little extra cost.	Travel companies are successful price discriminators, charging more to rush hour commuters whose demand is inelastic at certain times of the day. Other examples are off-peak travel bargains or telephone charges.

Price discrimination will only be effective under certain conditions.

(a)   The market must be **segmentable** in price terms, and different sectors must show **different intensities of demand**. Each of the sectors must be identifiable, distinct and separate from the others, and be accessible to the firm's marketing communications.

(b)   There must be little or no chance of a **black market** developing, so that those in the lower priced segment can resell to those in the higher priced segment.

(c)   There must be little chance that competitors can/will **undercut** the firm's prices in the higher priced (and/or most profitable) market segments.

(d)   The **cost** of segmenting and administering the arrangements should not exceed the extra revenue derived from the price discrimination strategy.

2.5 Price sensitivity

FAST FORWARD

Subjective perception is important in the way customers react to price and price changes. **Price sensitivity** refers to the extent to which price changes affect customer demand.

Key concept

> **Price sensitivity** refers to the effect a change in price will have on customers.

Price sensitivity will vary amongst purchasers. Those who can pass on the cost of purchases will be least sensitive, and will respond more to other elements of the marketing mix.

(a)   Provided that the price fits the corporate budget, the business traveller will be more concerned about an hotel's level of service and quality of food. In contrast, a family on holiday are likely to be very price sensitive when choosing an overnight stay.

(b)   In industrial marketing, the purchasing manager is likely to be more price sensitive than the engineer who might be the actual user of new equipment. The engineer places product characteristics as first priority, the purchasing manager is more price oriented.

Research on price sensitivity of customers has shown that in general the following apply.

- Customers have a good concept of a **'just price'** – a feel for what is fair for the benefits offered.

- For **special purchases**, customers search for price information before buying, become price aware when wanting to buy, but forget soon afterwards

- Customers will buy at what they consider to be a **bargain price**, without full regard for their present needs and the level of the price itself

- **Down payment and instalment price** are more important than total price

- In times of rising prices, the **price image** tends to lag behind the current price

- If there are **substitute goods**, especially close substitutes, customers will be more sensitive to price. For example, in a greengrocer's shop, a rise in the price of one fruit such as apples or pears is likely to result in a switch of customer demand to other fruits, many fruits being fairly close substitutes for each other.

- Over **time**, consumers' demand patterns are likely to change. If the price of something is increased, the initial response might be a small change in demand. But as consumers adjust their buying habits in response to the price increase, demand might fall substantially.

2.5.1 Estimating the effects of price changes

The firm could use a **market test** to estimate the effect on demand of a price change. This might involve a change of price in one region, say, and a comparison of demand for the brand with past sales in that region *and* with sales in similar regions at the old prices. This is a high risk strategy: special circumstances (confounding factors) may affect the test area (such as a competitor's advertising campaign) which could affect the results. Also, customers may switch from the test brand if a price rise is being considered and become loyal to a competitive brand; they may not switch back even if the price is subsequently lowered.

Alternatively, a direct **attitude survey** (or similar) may be used. **Pricing research** is difficult. Respondents may try to appear rational to the interviewer while their buying behaviour would be more complex. The respondent is not in an actual 'choice' situation, faced with having to pay out hard earned income.

2.5.2 Price perception

Subjective **perception** is important in the ways customers react to prices. It is not always true that you will sell more of your product if you lower the price. Sometimes you might sell more if you charge a higher price! This could occur if buyers:

- Expect further price increases to follow (they are 'stocking up')

- Assume the quality has increased

- Feel that the product has 'snob appeal' because of the high price

- Associate the product with other benefits worth paying more for. ('If someone buys a coke at a five star hotel, they may pay $5 for it. Why don't they walk outside and buy it for $2? The answer is that they are not buying the bottle of coke. What they're buying is the experience of sitting in a five star hotel, and that's why they are willing to pay a premium.' *C Jasper*, 2005)

Examples of price strategies which exploit price perception include: hieroglyphics

(a) **Quantum price**. In retail selling the concept of a **'quantum point'** is often referred to. When the price of an item is increased from, say, £9.65 to £9.95, sales may not be affected because the consumers do not notice the price change. However, if the price is increased from £9.95 to £10.05 a fall in sales may occur, £10 acting as a quantum point which can be approached but not passed if the price is not to deter would be purchasers.

(b) **Odd number pricing**. Sometimes referred to as **'psychological pricing'**. This involves pricing at £1.99, £2.99 etc rather than £2, £3. The psychological effect of increasing from £1.99 to £2.05 can be significant.

(c) **One coin purchase**. Rather than change price to reflect cost changes, firms alter the quantity in the unit of the product and keep the same price. This is a case of **'price-minus'** pricing. The firm determines what the market will bear and works backwards.

(d) **Gift purchases**. Gift purchasing often relies on the idea of price reflecting quality. If a gift is to be purchased in an unfamiliar product category, an acceptable price level is often fixed by the buyer and a choice made from the brands available at that price. Cosmetics are often priced at £4.99 and £9.99 to appeal to gift purchasers at the £5 and £10 price level.

2.6 Other factors influencing pricing decisions

FAST FORWARD

Other internal and external factors in pricing include: quality and portfolio considerations; intermediaries; suppliers; government intervention; economic activity; and social responsibility.

Several factors influence the pricing decisions of an organisation.

(a) **Intermediaries' objectives**

If an organisation distributes products or services to the market through independent intermediaries, the objectives of these intermediaries have an effect on the pricing decision. Intermediaries aim to maximise their own profits rather than those of suppliers. Conflict over price can arise between suppliers and intermediaries which may be difficult to resolve.

Many industries have traditional margins for intermediaries. To deviate from these might well cause problems for suppliers. In some industries, notably grocery retailing, the power of intermediaries allows them to dictate terms to suppliers.

(b) **Competitors' actions and reactions**

An organisation, in setting prices, sends out signals to competitors and they are likely to react in some way. In some industries (such as petrol retailing) pricing moves in unison. In others, price changes by one provider may initiate a **price war**, with each provider attempting to undercut the others.

(c) **Suppliers**

An organisation's suppliers may attempt to increase prices on the basis that the buying organisation is able to pay a higher price. (This argument is sometimes used by trade unions negotiating the price for the supply of labour.)

(d) **Quality connotations**

In the absence of other information, customers tend to judge quality by price. A price change may send signals to customers concerning the quality of the product. A rise may be taken to indicate improvements, a reduction may signal reduced quality. Any change in price needs to take such factors into account.

(e)   **New product pricing**

Most pricing decisions for existing products concern price changes, which have a **reference point** from which to move (the existing price). A new product has no reference points. It may be possible to seek alternative reference points, such as the price in another market where the new product has already been launched, or the price set by a competitor.

(f)   **The economy**

In times of **rising incomes**, price may become a less important marketing variable. When income levels are falling and/or unemployment levels rising, price will become more important. In periods of **inflation** the organisation's prices may need to change in order to pass on increases in the prices of supplies, labour, rent and so on.

(g)   **Product range**

Most organisations market not just one product but a range of products. The management of the pricing function is likely to focus on the profit from the whole range, using low-cost products to attract customers, who can then be encouraged to buy related products with higher profit margins. (This is discussed in Section 3 below.)

(h)   **Social responsibility**

Ethical considerations are involved, such as whether to exploit short-term shortages (or life-and-death products such as some pharmaceuticals) through higher prices.

(i)   **Government**

Some organisations are compelled by government to charge certain prices. For instance, in the UK Oftel have a say in how much British Telecom is allowed to charge.

 Marketing at Work

The Iceland supermarket chain is to broaden its marketing away from a purely price promotions-led positioning to emphasise its service and product range, following its sales collapse last month.

The shift in ad strategy comes as the frozen food retailer moves toward an **everyday low pricing (EDLP)** strategy. It blamed its sales slump of 8% during the first three weeks of July on its moving too quickly toward EDLP.

Iceland, owned by The Big Food Group and cash-and-carry retailer Booker, has focused its marketing for the past couple of years on a combination of buy one get one free and meal-deal offers.

Its current TV ads emphasise the great value deals to be had at Iceland stores, with the strapline, 'Are we doing a deal or are we doing a deal?'

Although Iceland insists it is not abandoning promotions, the company claims it is moving toward an EDLP strategy that will allow it to offer consistent good value across consumers' core shopping baskets.

Iceland is working on a broader brand campaign, due to break in the autumn, that is likely to encompass other elements, such as the range and quality of products, its 'shopability', and its level of service.

In 2000 Iceland was judged a marketing success story, winning accolades for its focus on issues such as GM food and internet shopping. At the time, its decision to rebrand its stores as iceland.co.uk was hailed as an innovation in tune with the aspirations of consumers. However, its shift upmarket failed to convince its core customers and sales plummeted.

Extracts from *Marketing*, 1 August 2002

3 Price setting strategies

FAST FORWARD

Companies may undertake any of a variety of pricing strategies, depending on their objectives and the industry they operate in. **Product line** and **competitive pricing** have specific requirements.

Pricing strategies can be used to pursue a number of marketing objectives, as introduced at the beginning of Section 2.

3.1 Market penetration

The organisation sets a **relatively low price** for the product or service, to **stimulate growth** of the market and/or to **obtain a larger share** of it. This strategy was used by Japanese motor cycle manufacturers, for example, to enter the UK market. It worked! UK productive capacity was virtually eliminated and the imported Japanese machines could later be sold at a much higher price and *still* dominate the market.

Sales maximising objectives are favoured when the following apply.

- Unit costs will fall with increased output (economies of scale)
- The market is price sensitive and relatively low prices will attract more sales
- Low prices will discourage any new competitors

Marketing at Work

Ford has recently announced the launch of its first small sedan model **aimed at the Chinese mass market**.

Until now, Ford's strategy has been to enter the market with high-end imported vehicles. The new sedan, however, will be built in China in a 50:50 joint venture between the auto giant and Changan, a state-owned automobile maker.

With a price tag of about RMB100,000 (US$12,150), the sedan will be targeted at the mass market, compared with at least RMB300,000 for imported models.

Ford is focusing on the lower-end market because this segment is only now taking off.

Media Asia, 14 June 2002

3.2 Market skimming

The opposite objective to market penetration, skimming involves setting a **high initial price** for a new product (in order to take advantage of those buyers prepared to pay a high price for innovation) and then gradually to **reduce the price** (to attract more price sensitive segments of the market). This strategy is an example of **price discrimination over time**.

This strategy is favoured in the following situations.

- Insufficient market capacity and competitors cannot increase capacity
- Buyers are relatively insensitive to price increases
- High price perceived as high quality (interaction in marketing mix)

3.3 Early cash recovery

Here the pricing objective is to recover the investment in a new product or service as quickly as possible.

This objective would tend to be used in the following conditions.

- The business is high risk
- Rapid changes in fashion or technology are expected
- The innovator is short of cash

One approach to this would be **target pricing,** where the company tries to determine the price that gives a specified rate of return for a given output. This is widely used by large American manufacturers, such as General Motors and Boeing.

3.4 Product line pricing

When a firm sells a **range of related products**, or a product line, its pricing policy should aim to maximise the profitability of the line as a whole.

(a)   There may be a **brand name** which the manufacturer wishes to associate with high quality and high price, or reasonable quality and low price. All items in the line will be priced accordingly. For example, all major supermarket chains have an 'own brand' label which is used to sell goods at a slightly lower price than the major named brands.

(b)   If two or more products in the line are complementary, one may be priced as a **loss leader** (a low profit-margin item) in order to attract customers and demand for the related products.

(c)   If two or more products in the line share **joint production costs** (joint products), prices of the products will be considered as a single decision. For example, if a common production process makes one unit of joint product A for each unit of joint product B, a price for A which achieves a demand of, say, 17,000 units, will be inappropriate if associated with a price for product B which would only sell, say, 10,000 units. 7,000 units of B would be unsold and wasted.

Exam tip

A June 2004 question asked for factors that should be taken into account 'when setting the price of one of the products in your range'. The examiner expected you to notice that this referred to product line pricing – not just price-setting of a stand-alone product!

3.5 Competitive pricing

E Corey (1989) summarised the role of price in the competitive marketplace.

'The struggle for market share focuses critically on price. Pricing strategies of competing firms are highly interdependent. The price one competitor sets is a function not only of what the market will pay but also of what other firms charge. Prices set by individual firms respond to those of competitors; they also are intended often to influence competitors' pricing behaviour. Pricing is an art, a game played for high stakes; and for marketing strategists it is the "moment of truth". All of marketing comes to focus in the pricing decision.'

In established industries dominated by a few major firms, it is generally accepted that a **price initiative** by one firm will be countered by a **price reaction** by competitors. Consequently, in industries such as breakfast cereals (dominated in Britain by Kellogg's, Nabisco and Quaker) or canned soups (Heinz, Crosse & Blackwell and Campbell's) a certain **price stability** might be expected without too many competitive price initiatives.

A firm may respond to **competitor price cuts** in a number of ways.

(a)   **Maintain existing prices**, if the expectation is that only a small market share would be lost, so that it is more profitable to keep prices at their existing level. Eventually, the rival firm may drop out of the market or be forced to raise its prices.

(b)   **Maintain prices but respond with a non-price counter-attack**. This is a more positive response, because the firm will be securing or justifying its price differential with product quality, improved back-up services etc.

(c)   **Reduce prices**, to protect the firm's market share. The main beneficiary from the price reduction will be the consumer.

(d)   **Raise prices and respond with a non-price counter-attack**. The extra revenue from the higher prices might be used to finance the promotion of product improvements, which in turn would justify the price rise to customers.

3.6 Price leadership

A **price leader** will dominate price levels for a class of products: increases or decreases by the price leader provide a direction to market price patterns. The price-dominant firm may lead without moving at all. (This would be the case if other firms sought to raise prices and the leader did not follow: then the upward move in prices would be halted.)

The role of price leader is based on a track record of having initiated price moves that have been accepted by both competitors and customers. Often, this is associated with a mature, well established management group, efficient production and a reputation for technical competence. A price leader generally has a large, if not necessarily the largest, market share.

Any dramatic changes in industry competition (a new entrant, or changes in the boardroom) may endanger the price leadership role.

Exam tip

> To find an appropriate pricing strategy, you have to consider the nature of the product: is it exposed to competition or could a premium price strategy be justified by the niche nature of the product or the prospect of enthusiastic early adopters?

Action Programme 4

Collect some examples of prices for goods and services that appear to you (since you aren't privy to the price-setting decisions) to illustrate some of the strategies outlined in this chapter.

(This is an opportunity for you to gather exam-usable examples in industries of your choice, in your own local market and currency.)

Exam tip

> You may like to remember the key factors in pricing strategy as the 4Cs = Costs, Customer (demands), Competition and Company (objectives).

Chapter Roundup

- **Pricing decisions** are important to the firm, as they are the basis of profits. Pricing is also the only element of the marketing mix which generates revenue rather than creating costs.

- Pricing decisions are effected by a range of factors, both **internal** (to the organisation) and **external** (in the competitive environment).

- In practice **cost** is the most important influence on price. In cost-based (full-cost or cost-plus) pricing, costs are estimated and then a profit margin is added to set the price.

- Prices may be set on the basis of what **competitors** are charging rather than on the basis of cost or demand.

- Prices may be based on the intensity of **demand**: strong demand may lead to a high price, and weak demand to a low price. The concept of **price elasticity** illustrates how demand can be affected by price changes.

- Subjective perception is important in the way customers react to price and price changes. **Price sensitivity** refers to the extent to which price changes affect customer demand.

- Other internal and external factors in pricing include: quality and portfolio considerations; intermediaries; suppliers; government intervention; economic activity; and social responsibility.

- Companies may undertake any of a variety of pricing strategies, depending on their objectives and the industry they operate in. **Product line** and **competitive pricing** have specific requirements.

BPP
LEARNING MEDIA

Quick Quiz

1   Pricing decisions are guided by one or other of two business objectives. What are they?

1 ....

2 ....

2   Why might a cost-based approach to price setting be problematic from a marketing point of view?

3   If organisations set their prices for similar products at the going rate, there is effectively no competition in that market.

True   ☐

False   ☐

4   Which of the following statements is true?

A   Price discrimination invariably leads to the development of a black market

B   Strong demand will lead to a low price

C   People will know how much they would be prepared to pay for a new product if it is described to them by a market researcher

D   The danger of test marketing a price rise is that customers will switch to a competitor's brand and not return to you even if you abandon the price rise

5   Sales people are very sensitive to the cost of hotels when they are on a sales trip.

True   ☐

False   ☐

Give reasons for your answer.

6   List three factors that might influence a farmer's pricing policy.

7   Match the items in the first column with the appropriate strategies from the list below.

£99.99

High initial price

Worthwhile net contribution

Low initial price

| Early cash recovery | Product line promotion | Market skimming | Quantum price |
| Market penetration | Odd number pricing | Price discrimination | Going rate pricing |

8   List four ways of responding to a price cut by a competitor

Answers to Quick Quiz

1 Maximise profits; Maintain or increase market share.

2 Because it does not take proper account of the price consumers may be willing to pay and because in the case of a new product it does not take account of the typical pattern of the product life cycle, the diffusion of innovation and so on.

3 False. The organisations will compete on product features, availability and delivery and by means of different marketing communications (for example, Formula 1 sponsorship).

4 D

5 Your answer will depend on the type of organisations you have worked for, and how honest you are. In theory the statement is false because sales people can simply pass on the cost to their employer. Prudent organisations, however, set a budget for expenses and check that it is not being exceeded, so the salesperson's price sensitivity will depend how generous the allowance is, and their attitude towards the profitability of the organisation.

6 The main one will be intermediaries' objectives. Many farmers have gone out of business in recent years because, they claim, supermarkets drive down the prices they can obtain for their goods. Most of the other factor we mentioned in this chapter may play a part: for instance competition from cheap imported goods, the quality of their goods (eg organic vegetables), government subsidies or quotas and so on. Make sure you can explain the factors you chose.

7

£99.99	Odd number pricing
High initial price	Market skimming
Worthwhile net contribution	Product line promotion
Low initial price	Market penetration

8 Maintain existing prices; maintain prices but respond with extra advertising; reduce prices; raise prices and respond with extra features or higher quality.

Action Programme Review

1 You might have identified a number of different factors here. Perhaps the most important general point to make is that price is particularly important if the other elements in the marketing mix are relatively similar across a range of competing products. For example, there is a very wide variety of toothpastes on the market, most of them not much differentiated from the others. The price of a particular toothpaste may be a crucial factor in its sales success.

2 One possibility is that the cost of the product was established (to make sure of breaking even), VAT added since it makes a significant difference for the customer, and comparisons were made with items of similar quality and rarity on the market. A range of possible prices, based on this data, might then have been presented to potential customers to see how they reacted to them. Data may also have been collected about the results of similar exercises by other watchmakers (or the like) in the past.

3 The main problem is that, unless very detailed research has been carried out, the price elasticity of a particular product or service is unknown. As a theoretical concept, it is useful in gaining an understanding of the *effects* of price changes; but it is of little use as a practical tool in *determining* prices. When Kotler says that price elasticity of demand gives 'precision' this is only true after the event, when you can calculate exactly what effect a price change had on how many units you sold you sold.

4 Your own research.

Now try Questions 10 and 11 at the end of the Study Text

Place or distribution

7

Chapter topic list

1   The role of place in the marketing mix
2   Channels of distribution
3   Channel decisions
4   Logistics and supply chain management
5   Distribution and ICT

Syllabus content

- Describe the wide range of tools and techniques available to marketers to satisfy customer requirements and compete effectively (3.2)
- Define channels of distribution, intermediaries and logistics, and understand the contribution they make to the marketing effort (3.10)
- State and explain the factors that influence channel decisions and the selection of alternative distribution channel options, including the effects of new information and communications technology (3.11)

Introduction

In this chapter, we examine the various channels of distribution and approaches to logistics that an organisation might use to satisfy customer requirements most effectively – and profitably.

We explore key issues in channel decisions and supply chain management including:

(a)   the formulation of **distribution strategies**: direct or indirect;

(b)   the selection of **distribution channels** and intermediaries; and

(c)   the effect of **ICT developments** on product/service distribution and logistics management.

1 The role of place in the marketing mix

FAST FORWARD

Place is concerned with the selection of **distribution channels** used to deliver goods to the consumer.

A market is, in literal terms, a physical place. It has its own sights and sounds and smells and sunny spots and nooks and crannies. But even in the earliest days of exchange this must have caused problems. Once you'd handed over your three bags of corn for your sheep you had an instant problem. How could you get your sheep home?

If you were lucky the sheep farmer might have offered you a lift in his cart. Or perhaps some other bright spark might have seen this flaw in the exchange process – and had the initiative to buy his own cart and offer a **delivery service**.

That is why the 'place' element of the marketing mix is really concerned with the processes by which the product reaches the consumer in a convenient way. Other terms for 'place' include **distribution**, or **delivery** systems or channels.

The importance of place within the marketing mix should not be underestimated. If you get it right for your market it can be a crucial source of competitive advantage. Marketing effort will be futile if the product is not actually **in the right place at the right time** so that the customer has the choice of buying your product, not your competitors'.

The choice of a particular **distribution policy**, such as whether or not to use wholesalers or retailers, may result in the company delegating at least part of its marketing function to others.

Key concept

Place is concerned with the selection of **distribution channels** used to deliver goods to the consumer.

2 Channels of distribution

FAST FORWARD

The term **'channels of distribution'** refers to the methods by which goods or services are transferred from producers to consumers.

2.1 Distribution functions

FAST FORWARD

Distribution functions include transport, stock management, local knowledge, promotion and display.

BPP LEARNING MEDIA

A variety of functions are involved in distribution.

- **Transport**

  This function may be provided by the supplier, the distributor or may be sub-contracted to a specialist. For some products, such as perishable goods, transport planning is vital.

- **Stock holding and storage**

  For production planning purposes, an uninterrupted flow of production is often essential. A good stock or inventory control system is designed to avoid stockouts whilst keeping stockholding costs low.

- **Local knowledge**

  As production has tended to become centralised in pursuit of economies of scale, the need to understand and be 'close to' local markets has grown.

- **Promotion**

  Whilst major promotional campaigns for national products are likely to be carried out by the supplier, the translation of the campaign to local level is usually the responsibility of a distributor or retail outlet.

- **Display for sale**

  Presentation of the product at the local level is often the responsibility of the distributor. Specialist help from merchandisers can be bought in if required.

Action Programme 1

For many types of goods, producers invariably use retailers as middlemen in getting the product to the customer. Try to think of some of the disadvantages of doing this, from the producer's point of view.

2.2 Intermediaries

FAST FORWARD

Companies may distribute **direct to customers** or choose from a wide range of **intermediaries**: retailers, wholesalers, dealers, agents, franchisees and multiple stores.

An intermediary is someone who 'mediates' or brings about a settlement between two persons: in this case between the original supplier and the ultimate buyer. There are a variety of types of intermediary and several may intervene before a product gets from the original provider and the final buyer: Figure 7.1.

Figure 7.1: Intermediaries

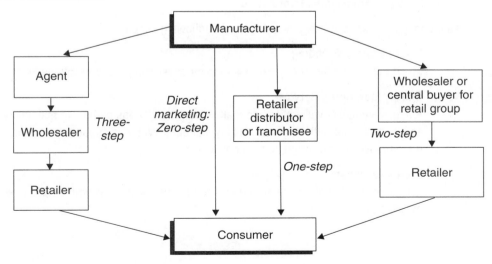

(a)   **Retailers** are traders operating outlets which sell directly to households. They may be classified by:

- Type of goods sold (eg hardware, furniture)
- Type of service (self-service, counter service)
- Size and/or ownership
- Location (rural, city-centre, suburban or out of town shopping mall)

(b)   **Wholesalers** stock a range of products from potentially competing manufacturers, to sell on to other organisations such as retailers. Many wholesalers specialise in particular products.

(c)   **Distributors and dealers** contract to buy a manufacturer's goods and sell them to customers. Their function is similar to that of wholesalers, but they usually offer a narrower product range, sometimes (as in the case of most car dealers) the products of a single manufacturer. In addition to selling on the manufacturer's product, distributors often promote the products and provide after-sales service.

(d)   **Agents** differ from distributors, in that they do not purchase and resell the goods, but sell goods on behalf of the supplier and earn a **commission** on their sales

(e)   **Franchisees** are independent organisations which in exchange for an initial fee and (usually) a share of sales revenue are allowed to trade under the name of a parent organisation. For example, few of the Kall Kwik chain of High Street print shops are actually owned by Kall Kwik – most are run by franchisees.

(f)   **Multiple stores** (eg supermarkets, department stores) buy goods for retailing direct from the producer, sometimes under their 'own label' brand name.

(g)   **Direct sales/distribution** methods include:

- Mail order
- Telephone selling
- Door-to-door selling
- Personal selling in the sale of industrial goods
- Sales through retail outlets owned by the supplier
- TV shopping channels
- E-commerce (Internet selling)

 Marketing at Work

Kodak Malaysia Franchising Information

As a Kodak Express member, you will enjoy the following benefits:

- **Kodak Express Branding**
  The rights to use the Kodak Express logo for advertising and promotions in the store.

- **Quality Monitoring Service**
  Kodak's engineers will advise and make recommendations on how to maintain your print quality according to international Kodak quality standard. With this support, your store will be able to provide quality color prints to the consumers.

- **Exclusive Rebates**
  Exclusive only to you, these discounts and rebates will provide your business with a leading edge over the rest.

- **Training**

  One of the best benefits in the franchise program. Each year, Kodak will organize at least four training sessions to help the franchisees to improve on their business performance.

- **Retail Shop Concept**

  A new store concept for the Kodak Express shops is specially designed to project Kodak Express as young, vibrant & a professional retail store to the consumers.

- **360° Checklist Program**

  Your Business Support Executive will conduct checks and monitoring exercises in your store regularly. The quality of the photos processed, the store layout, the visual displays and the quality of the staff services will be measured to ensure that your store meets the quality requirements to stay competitive in the market.

- **Mystery Shopper Concept**

  On top of the shop improvement program and the Quality Monitoring Service, Kodak has specially designed a Mystery Shopper program to help the franchisees understand the various areas in the shop that require further improvement.

- **Best Kodak Express Award**

  Designed to reward members who provide consistently good services and quality prints to the consumers. Every year, the top ten Kodak Express Award winners will receive cash prizes and public recognition in the local papers.

- **Uniform**

  Uniforms will be provided to project a professional image for the Kodak Express outlets.

- **Newsletter**

  One of the ways which you will be kept update on the latest products, services and trends in the photo-retailing industry.

- **Advertisements**

  You will benefit from the advertising plans and strategies initiated by Kodak.

- **Annual Conference**

  An annual event where members' will not only interact and discuss way to improve Kodak Express program, but also gain knowledge.

  www.my.Kodak.com/MY, 17th March 2004

3 Channel decisions

Choosing distribution channels is important for any organisation, because once a set of channels has been established, subsequent changes are likely to be costly and slow to implement. Distribution channels fall into one of two categories: *direct* and *indirect channels*.

Direct distribution means the product going directly from producer to consumer without the use of a specific intermediary. These methods are often described as **active**, since they typically involve the supplier making the first approach to a potential customer.

Indirect distribution means systems of distribution, common among manufactured goods, which use an intermediary; a wholesaler, retailer or perhaps both. In contrast to direct distribution, these methods are **passive**, in the sense that they rely on consumers to make the first approach by entering the relevant retail outlet.

Action Programme 2

One factor influencing the choice between direct and indirect methods is the average order size for a product. State what you think the relationship might be between average order size and the occurrence (or non-occurrence) of direct distribution.

Independently owned and operated distributors may well have their own objectives and these are likely to take precedence over those of the manufacturer or supplier with whom they are dealing. Suppliers may solve the problem by buying their own distribution route or by distributing direct to their customers. **Direct distribution** is common for many industrial and/or customised product suppliers. In some consumer markets direct distribution is also common, particularly with the advent of e-commerce via the Internet (as we will see in Section 5).

3.1 General principles

FAST FORWARD

> When **selecting a distribution channel** many factors come into play. How much support should be given to dealers? How far should marketing efforts be integrated up to the point of sale? What are the characteristics of the product or service? What do competitors do?

Distribution involves certain basic processes.

- Bringing buyers and sellers into contact
- Offering a sufficient choice of goods to meet the needs of buyers
- Persuading customers to develop a favourable opinion of a particular product
- Distributing goods from the manufacturing point to retail outlets
- Maintaining an adequate level of sales
- Providing appropriate services (eg credit, after-sales service)
- Maintaining an acceptable price

The choice of channels of distribution will depend on how far a manufacturing company wishes to carry out these processes itself, and how far it decides to **delegate** them to other organisations.

A number of other considerations will determine the choice of distribution strategy

(a) The number of **intermediate stages to be used**. There could be zero, one, two or three intermediate stages of selling (as shown in Figure 7.1). In addition, it will be necessary to decide how many dealers at each stage should be used – ie how many agents should be used, how many wholesalers should be asked to sell the manufacturer's products, and what the size of the direct sales force should be.

(b) **The support that the manufacturer should give to the dealers**. It may be necessary to provide an efficient after-sales and repair service, or to agree to an immediate exchange of faulty products returned by a retailer's customers, or to make weekly, bi-weekly or monthly stock-checking visits to retailers' stores. To help selling, the manufacturer might need to consider advertising or sales promotion support, including merchandising.

(c) **The extent to which the manufacturer wishes to dominate a channel of distribution**. A market leader, for example, might wish to ensure that its market share of sales is maintained, so that it might, for example, wish to offer exclusive distribution contracts to major retailers.

(d) **The extent to which the manufacturer wishes to integrate its marketing effort up to the point of sale with the consumer**. Combined promotions with retailers, for example, would only be possible if the manufacturer dealt directly with the retailer (and did not sell to the retailer through a wholesaler).

3.2 Factors in channel decisions

In setting up a channel of distribution, the supplier has to take into account.

- Customers
- Product characteristics
- Distributor characteristics
- The channel chosen by competitors
- The supplier's own characteristics

3.2.1 Customers

The **number** of potential customers, their **buying habits** and their **geographical locations** are key influences. The use of mail order and Internet purchases for those with limited time or mobility (rural location, illness) is an example of the influence of customers on channel design.

3.2.2 Product characteristics

Some product characteristics have an important effect on design of the channel of distribution.

Characteristic	Comment
Perishability	Fresh fruit and newspapers must be distributed very quickly or they become worthless. Speed of delivery is therefore a key factor in the design of the distribution system for such products.
Customisation	Customised products tend to be distributed direct. When a wide range of options is available, sales may be made using demonstration units, with customised delivery to follow.
After-sales service/ technical advice	Extent and cost must be carefully considered, staff training given and quality control systems set up. Suppliers often provide training programmes for distributors. Exclusive area franchises giving guaranteed custom can be allocated, to ensure distributor co-operation; the disadvantage of this is that a poor distributor may cost a supplier dearly in a particular area.
Franchising	Franchising has become an increasingly popular means. The supplier gains more outlets more quickly and exerts more control than is usual in distribution.

Action Programme 3

How might a *service* organisation choose channels of distribution?

3.2.3 Distributor characteristics

The location, customer base, performance, promotion and pricing policies of different types of distributor, and specific distribution outlets, will have to be evaluated. Selling to supermarket chains in the UK, for example, is now very difficult as the concentration of grocery retailing into a few large chains has increased the power of the buyers.

Marketing at Work

'Poland's traditional milk bars have almost disappeared off the gastronomic map, as people increasingly turn to fast food. Out have gone the old favourites, such as pancakes and dumplings, to be replaced by hamburgers, French fries, hot dogs and pizza.

'It is mainly younger diners, aged between 20 and 29, who are attracted to one of the seven thousand fast food outlets in the country, which now make up a sixth of all of Poland's restaurants.

'But there is still a long way to go before the market becomes saturated with fast food places. For all their desire to eat in trendy outlets, Poles are still very traditional in their dining habits, and 65% of the population customarily eat at home. ...

'Many fast food places try to catch customers' attention with special offers and promotions (particularly aimed at children). Major chains like McDonald's and KFC are also expanding services, so that customers can order by phone or Internet.

'Apart from extended chains some, such as McDonald's, are offering franchise opportunities. A fourth of the McDonald's outlets in the country are franchised, and within a few years the company is planning to develop this area of operation extensively. Although the franchises are quite expensive, there is no shortage of takers.

'One reason for the desirability of these **fast food franchises** is the fact that the brand names virtually ensure an upward profit line, although an inflexible labour market, ever higher fixed costs and strong competition keep the market from even more impressive growth.'

E Sledz (2004)

3.2.4 Competitors' channel choice

For many consumer goods, a supplier's brand will sit alongside its competitors' products. For other products, distributors may stock one name brand only (for example, in car distribution) and in return be given an exclusive area. In this case new suppliers may face difficulties in breaking into a market.

3.2.5 Supplier characteristics

A strong financial base gives the supplier the option of buying and operating their own distribution channel: Boots the Chemist is a good example in the UK. The market position of the supplier is also important: distributors are keen to be associated with the market leader, but other brands may experience distribution problems.

3.3 Making the channel decision

Producers have to decide the following.

    (a)   **What types of distributor** are to be used (wholesalers, retailers, agents)?

    (b)   **How many of each type will be used?** This depends on what degree of market exposure is required.

- Intensive, blanket coverage
- Exclusive, appointed agents for exclusive areas
- Selective, some but not all in each area

    (c)   **Who will carry out specific marketing tasks?**

- Credit provision
- Delivery

- After-sales service
- Training (sales and product)
- Display

(d) How will the **effectiveness** of distributors be evaluated?

- In terms of cost?
- In terms of sales levels?
- According to the degree of control achieved?
- By the amount of conflict that arises?

Action Programme 4

In the UK Premiership football used to be distributed on terrestrial television by the BBC. In 2001 the sole distributor became ITV. Why do you think the change was made?

To develop an **integrated system of distribution**, the supplier must consider all the factors influencing distribution, combined with a knowledge of the merits of the different types of channel.

3.4 Direct or indirect distribution?

Factors favouring the use of direct selling	Factors favouring the use of intermediaries
(a) The need for an expert sales force to demonstrate products, explain product characteristics and provide after-sales service. Publishers, for example, use sales reps to keep booksellers up-to-date with new titles, to arrange for the return of unsold books and so on.	(a) Insufficient resources to finance a large sales force.
	(b) A policy decision to invest in increased productive capacity, rather than extra marketing effort.
(b) Intermediaries may be unwilling or unable to sell the product.	(c) The supplier may have insufficient in-house marketing 'know-how' in selling to retail stores.
(c) Existing channels may be linked to other producers.	(d) The product line may be insufficiently wide or deep for a sales force to carry. A wholesaler can complement a limited range and make more efficient use of his sales force.
(d) The intermediaries willing to sell the product may be too costly, or they may not be maximising potential sales.	
(e) Where potential buyers are geographically concentrated, the supplier's own sales force can easily reach them (typically an industrial market).	(e) Intermediaries can market small lots as part of a range of goods. The supplier would incur a heavy sales overhead if its own sales force took 'small' individual orders.
(f) Where e-commerce is well established, potential buyers can be reached online.	(f) Large numbers of potential buyers spread over a wide geographical area (typically consumer markets).

3.4.1 Multi-channel decisions

A producer serving both industrial and consumer markets may decide to use:

- **Intermediaries** for his **consumer** division
- **Direct selling** for his **industrial** division.

For example, a detergent manufacturer might employ salesmen to sell to wholesalers and large retail groups in their consumer division. It would not be efficient for the sales force to approach small retailers directly.

Exam tip

Relatively easy marks were available in the June 2004, June 2005 and December 2006 exams for outlining alternative distribution channels for organisations in particular markets and explaining the factors to be taken into account in making the choice. You had to read the 2005 question carefully, though. You were asked about factors to take into account in choosing channels 'when entering a new international country market': this raises extra challenges for getting hold of information, using local knowledge, controlling the process and so on. (There are also specific means of entering foreign markets – which we will discuss in Chapter 10.) The word 'international' in any exam question should make you think carefully about the implications.

3.5 Industrial and consumer distribution channels

FAST FORWARD

Different distribution strategies may be adopted for **consumer** and **industrial** markets. Industrial channels tend to be more direct and shorter.

Industrial markets are generally characterised as having fewer, higher-value customers purchasing a complex total offering of products/services which fulfil detailed specifications. Industrial distribution channels therefore tend to be more direct and shorter, allowing partnership level relationships. There are specialist distributors in the industrial sector, which may be used as well as, or instead of, selling directly to industrial customers.

There have traditionally been fewer direct distribution channels, from the manufacturer to the consumer in the **consumer market**. Where there are numerous, lower-value sales, geographically dispersed, of more standardised offering. Examples were found in small 'cottage' industries or mail order companies. Even with the advent of e-commerce in some sectors, it is still more usual for companies in consumer markets to use wholesalers and retailers to move their product to the final consumer.

3.6 Distribution strategy

There are three main strategies.

(a) **Intensive distribution** involves blanket coverage of distributors in one segment of the total market, such as a local area.

(b) Using **selective distribution**, the producer selects a group of retail outlets from amongst all retail outlets. The choice of selected outlets may be based on reflecting brand image (eg 'quality' outlets), or the retailers' capacity to provide after-sales service ('specialist' outlets).

(c) **Exclusive distribution** is where selected outlets are granted exclusive rights to stock and sell the product within a prescribed market segment or geographical area. Sometimes exclusive distribution or franchise rights are coupled with making special financial arrangements for land, buildings or equipment, such as petrol station agreements.

Action Programme 5

One of the fastest growing forms of selling internationally has been the *factory outlet centre*. Discount factory shops, often situated on factory premises, from which manufacturers sell off overmakes, slight seconds, or retailers' returns were already well-established in the UK, but now developers have grouped such outlets together in purpose-built malls.

What would you suggest are the advantages of this method of distribution for customers and manufacturers?

4 Logistics and supply chain management

FAST FORWARD

Ever-increasing customer demands, together with developments in technology have made **logistics management** and **supply chain management** increasingly important.

Availability is a critical factor in managing the marketing mix. Increasingly, logistics management has been recognised for the advantages in terms of customer benefits which such an approach brings, along with saving in costs, and improved company image.

4.1 Logistics

Key concept

Logistics is that part of the supply chain process that plans, implements, and controls the efficient, effective forward and reverse flow and storage of goods, services, and related information between the point of origin and the point of consumption in order to meet customers' requirements.

Logistics management is a bigger concept than distribution because it also involves **materials management**, encompassing the inflow of raw materials and goods as well as the outflow of finished products.

4.1.1 Tasks in logistics management

Logistics managers organise inventories, warehouses, purchasing and packaging to produce an efficient and effective overall system. Typical tasks of logistics management include:

- Managing incoming materials/components
- Inventory/stock management
- Managing flow of outbound goods
- Packaging/transport management
- Quality assurance and control
- Information management
- Managing 'reverse' flow (eg for recycling) of returned products

4.1.2 Benefits of effective logistics management

The benefits of effective logistics management include the following.

(a) **Customer** channel value, through: more choice and customisation; better quality control; faster delivery; less likelihood of stockouts; service-driven supply planning; convenient, safe and undamaged handling, storage, transport and display of goods

(b) **Cost savings** that can be made when a logistics approach is undertaken, allowing long, steady production runs; Just-in-Time supply, to minimise inefficient stock holding; and so on.

(c) **Closer links between suppliers and manufacturers**, for example, using EDI (Electronic Data Interchange), e-commerce and relationship marketing at proactive or partnership levels (particularly in B2B markets)

Marketing at Work

DHL launches International Day Definite Service to the Baltics

'DHL has expanded its European overland transport network by launching a day definite service between Europe and the Baltics. The road-based Eurapid service is available for shipments up to 2,500 kgs to and from Estonia, Latvia and Lithuania. With the introduction of the three Baltic countries, DHL now offers the service across 21 countries in Western, Central and Eastern Europe. It offers transit times of three to five days plus daily line-haul departures. This provides an extra competitive edge to the new DHL service.

'The three Baltic countries offer considerable potential for future growth in the logistics market as accession to the European Union (EU), on May 1st 2004, has contributed to the emergence of a stable and dynamic economic environment. DHL's new service offering was developed with a view both to the firm trade relations between the Baltics and Europe, where DHL already has a strong market position, and in response to customers' demands for a reliable export and import services to and from the Baltics.

'Operations include the transport of general cargo shipments to and from the Tallinn gateway, the capital of Estonia. Tallinn serves as the entry point for the destination terminals of Riga and Vilnius. Customers of the Eurapid service benefit from the convenience of one of the largest self-operating networks on the continent.

'Further customer benefits of the Eurapid service include:

- Reliable day-definite service
- Money back guarantee
- 21 countries and 97 terminals connected by one network

- Unified service and quality standards
- More than 400 daily line-haul departures
- Included insurance up to 66,000 euros
- Customer links and track and trace of shipments

www.dhl.com'
Press release posted 10th March 2004

4.2 Supply chain management

Key concept

Supply Chain Management is the systemic, strategic co-ordination of business functions and tactics within a particular company *and* across businesses within the supply chain, for the purposes of improving the integration and performance along the whole length of the supply chain.

D Minkema (2002) describes the development of purchasing and supply in terms of phases of increasing integration.

(a) **Independence**: the purchasing department operates according to its own inventory-driven guidelines.

(b) **Dependence**: the purchasing department consults other departments, in order to dovetail purchasing policy with organisational needs.

(c) **Business integration**: the purchasing department attempts systematically to integrate its activities with other departments in the organisation, with the aim of fostering logistical efficiency.

(d) **Chain integration**: systematic co-operation and information sharing is emphasised throughout the supply chain, supported by ICT. Chain integration is focused on speed, service, decision support (through management information) and relationship management with supply chain partners. It may include collaboration on quality assurance, training of suppliers and distributors, collaborative promotions and joint ventures.

BPP LEARNING MEDIA

A variety of **ICT developments** have supported supply chain management, including:

(a)　The computerisation of purchase systems and record keeping, covering stock control, purchase requisitions, purchase orders, expediting/tracking of deliveries, goods receipts and the generation of reports.

(b)　Databased records, allowing interrogation and reporting in relation to supply performance, prices, requisitions by different functions, usage rates of stock categories, transaction summaries and so on.

(c)　Electronic Data Interchange (EDI), allowing direct transfer of queries, information, orders, invoices, payments (and so on) via cable or telecommunication link between supplier and purchaser.

(d)　Point-of-sale data capture systems, such as bar-coding and electronic point of sale (EPOS) systems, which allow stock and sale information to be databased and processed as management information for retailers and suppliers.

(e)　Warehousing data capture systems, using barcodes and portable (or robotic) scanners to carry out inventory checks, re-ordering and so on.

(f)　E-purchasing systems, including B2B marketplaces and 'private exchange' procurement sites (inviting supply bids) on the Internet.

5 Distribution and ICT

FAST FORWARD

ICT (especially in the form of Direct Response TV and the Internet) has brought new methods of displaying wares, new methods of paying for them, and for some goods, new methods of delivering them.

We have already outlined some of the ICT developments which have supported supply chain management (in Section 4.2 above). In Chapter 4 (Section 5.3) we also summarised some of the ways in which 'place' has been influenced by ICT.

Here, we will look in a little more detail at some of these impacts. Others will be looked at in the wider context of the 'virtual marketplace', in Chapter 10.

5.1 DRTV (Direct Response Television)

DRTV (home shopping) is presently conducted mainly through the use of television commercials or infomercials (which combine information with a commercial), which direct customers to a website or telephone order lines. In the UK, cable and satellite also provide a number of channels exclusively devoted to shopping.

The ability to shop from home and choose items directly is being integrated with direct advertising. **Infomercials** which the consumer has chosen from a databank will be relayed directly to the home down cable or telephone links. These may take the form of recipes, DIY hints, car repairs and so on. Consumers will also be able to purchase the necessary ingredients or parts simultaneously through the use of the television remote control.

Freemans, the catalogue company, which currently has 10% of the home shopping market, is keen to make inroads into this sector. Over 5,000 of its agents are equipped with the necessary hardware and software to make instant buying decisions. Customers are able to view a full motion picture and then order via a modem.

It is, however, difficult to predict how successful and how big the market for home shopping will become in different countries. It appeals to consumers within the United States because many people live in remote parts, some distance away from a main shopping centre. Within a country like the UK, however, the vast majority of people live within easy reach of a shopping centre or out-of-town complex. The speed of adoption will depend upon how readily the public accept the technology and find benefits in using it.

BSkyB is to launch a *retail marketing channel* called 'TV High Street' that will provide companies with half-hour direct-response infomercials to promote their products.

The channel will broadcast from September 2, offering a 'walled garden' of 12 companies including Argos and Kays, the UK's largest mail-order company.

Consumers will be able to choose which infomercials to view. As well as encouraging people to go out and shop, mail-order firms can publicise phone order numbers and web sites. It is thought retailers will devise exclusive offers for TV High Street.

As well as appearing on the BSkyB channel, Argos will broadcast its output in-store at its bigger branches.

Unlike BSkyB's interactive TV service, Sky Active, the channel will not offer e-commerce, but will act purely as a product and brand marketing vehicle. It will reach the 5.7 million UK households that subscribe to BSkyB. Further retailers will be invited to join, although it is understood BSkyB is keen to limit partners to around 20.

Marketing, 11 July 2002

5.2 Internet distribution

5.2.1 Display

Information gathering is still the most common Internet activity, whether it be information about a historical fact, a medical problem or, hopefully, about your product. At present the five most common online purchase categories are books, CDs, clothing, toys and games, and computer software, but many buyers for other types of product do their initial 'window shopping' online and then go to a more conventional distribution outlet to actually make their purchase.

The Internet is perfect for the display of many types of product – anything, in fact, that customers don't need to be able handle physically, but which can be adequately shown off in words, still and moving pictures and sound.

A website offers an effortless and impersonal way for customers to find out the details of the products and services that a company provides, and spend as long as they like doing so: much longer than they might feel comfortable with if they had a sales person hanging over them. The 'browser' is very aptly named.

For businesses, the advantage is that it is much cheaper to provide the information in electronic form than it would be to employ staff to man the phones on an enquiry desk or walk the shop floor, and much more effective than sending out mailshots that people would either throw away or forget about.

Electronic purchasing is still viewed nervously by many people, although it is steadily growing. Somewhat illogically, people are reluctant to supply their credit card details over the Internet, although they will do so over the telephone, and happily transcribe the details onto a bill that they are paying by post. Logical or not, customers need to be reassured about security before online purchasing really takes off.

In fact as long as it is used responsibly encryption software provides whatever reassurance is needed, and once people are used to this method of buying it is likely to become the norm for many transactions.

BPP LEARNING MEDIA

5.2.2 Local knowledge

Web servers (the computers that host websites) automatically log certain information about visitors, such as the time of their visit, their name and location of the service they are using to connect to the Internet, what pages they visited and what features they used.

If a visitor chooses to register with a website and provide a little further information such as their post code, sex and age, offerings can be closely tailored to the needs of the visitor. This is as good or possibly much better than any local knowledge a conventional distributor can offer.

The customisation is done by means of dynamically-generated pages: the page you see is only created when you request it and it is built up from elements that are of direct relevance to you: clothes in your favourite colour (if they are available in your size), your local weather forecast, your favourite background music, and so on. The information is a combination of your customer profile and information on products and services that are a direct part of the organisation's information system.

5.2.3 Transport

The Internet can be used to get certain products directly into people's homes. Anything that can be converted into digital form can simply be uploaded onto the seller's site and then downloaded onto the customer's PC (even some mobile phones). The Internet offers huge opportunities to producers of text, graphics/video, and sound-based products. Much computer software is now distributed in this way.

For products that cannot be delivered in this way, the issue of **fulfilment** is immensely important. In fact, a US survey by the Boston Consulting Group found a variety of problems.

• Had to contact customer service	20%
• Product took much longer than expected to arrive	15%
• Returned the product	10%
• Tried to contact customer service and failed	8%
• Ordered product that never arrived	4%
• Wrong product arrived and couldn't return it	4%

Source: www.bcg.com

 Marketing at Work

'The online grocery war continues. **Tesco.com's** pick-from-store business model took an early lead and is already profitable. Its pick-from-warehouse rivals lag way behind. Competitor **Sainsbury's to You**, whose costs for last year increased by a quarter to £50 million, does not foresee a profit for at least a year.

'Despite this, Waitrose, John Lewis and European investment bank UBS have invested more than £60m into **Ocado**, a pick-from-warehouse online grocer that is opening a 111,484 square metre warehouse in Hatfield, north of London.

'Picking in-store is fine in the short term, but warehouse fulfilment makes sense as online grocery orders increase, because warehouse space is cheaper than retail space, and offers more reliability and efficiency.

'Successful online ventures require a lot of scaleable storage space, but walk-in supermarkets are geared to keeping smaller stocks of a wide variety of items. The warehouse fulfilment model will get more cost-effective as order volumes grow, but the pick-from-store model will not.

'One of the main gripes of online shoppers is substitution. If an item in their order is not available, something similar (which they may or may not like) is put in to replace it. An online venture needs enough stock to keep substitutions to a minimum, and warehouse fulfilment can do this more reliably because the website is kept updated about exactly what it has to offer....

'Picking items for online order delivery is more efficient in warehouses, which are designed purely for picking speed, and not for luring customers or helping them navigate a store. And warehouse pickers aren't hampered by store customers, who could slow down in-store pickers.

'These advantages for warehouse fulfilment increase as order volumes grow.'

Revolution, 31 July 2002

Action Programme 6

Make notes for a presentation to marketing staff, showing how ICT developments impact on *each* of the key functions of distribution: direct marketing, local knowledge, stock/storage, transport, promotion and display for sale.

Chapter Roundup

- **Place** is concerned with the selection of **distribution channels** used to deliver goods to the consumer.

- **Distribution functions** include transport, stock management, local knowledge, promotion and display.

- Issues include **transport**, **stock management**, **local knowledge**, **promotion** and **display**.

- Companies may distribute **direct to customers** or choose from a wide range of **intermediaries**: retailers, wholesalers, dealers, agents, franchisees and multiple stores.

- When **selection a distribution channel** many factors come into play. How much support should be given to dealers? How far should marketing efforts be integrated up to the point of sale? What are the characteristics of the product or service? What do competitors do?

- Different distribution strategies may be adopted for **consumer** and **industrial** markets. Industrial channels tend to be more direct and shorter.

- Ever-increasing customer demands, together with developments in technology have made **logistics management** and **supply chain management** increasingly important.

- **ICT** (especially in the form of Direct Response TV and the Internet) has brought new methods of displaying wares, new methods of paying for them, and for some goods, new methods of delivering them.

BPP LEARNING MEDIA

Quick Quiz

1   A stock control system should keep (1)........................ .... low, but avoid (2).................... .
    Fill in the gaps.

2   A clothing manufacturer may try to control the display of its goods in retail outlets by employing the
    services of a .... What?

3   Draw a diagram illustrating possible intermediaries between a manufacturer and a consumer.

4   Which of the following statements is true?

    A   Producers may need to provide dealers with after-sales or support services
    B   There can never be more than three or less than one intermediary
    C   It is illegal to offer exclusive distribution contracts to specific retailers
    D   Wholesalers do not promote their services in case ordinary consumers find out about them

5   The ideas in the table below are jumbled. Rearrange them into the proper order.

Product characteristic	Issue
Perishability	Training required
After-sales service	More sales outlets
Franchising	Demonstration units are used
Customisation	Speedy delivery

6   An organisation has limited financial resources and a small assortment of products, but potentially a
    global market. Which type of distribution should it use?

    A   Direct
    B   Intermediary

7   Which of the following statements is true?

    A   Logistics is only concerned with materials flows, not customers' needs

    B   Supply Chain Management is only of interest to purchasing departments

    C   Good management of an organisation's supply chain is beneficial for the final consumer of its
         products

    D   Logistics managers need to understand logarithms

8   There is no such thing as direct response radio.

    True   ☐

    False   ☐

Answers to Quick Quiz

1   (1) Stockholding costs; (2) Stockouts.

2   If you said 'merchandiser' or 'window dresser', score full marks. If you said mannequin you had the right idea. If you said plastic dummy, that's less elegant, but hopefully you were still on the right lines! If this area of marketing interests you see (for example) www.fashionwindows.com.

3

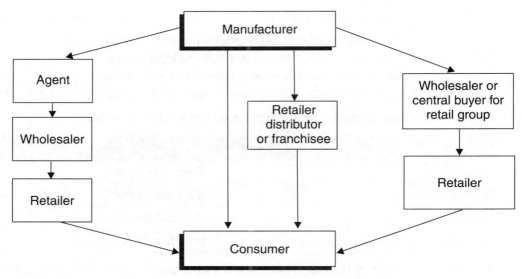

4   A

5

Product characteristic	Issue
Perishability	Speedy delivery
After-sales service	Training required
Franchising	More sales outlets
Customisation	Demonstration units are used

6   In theory the organisation should use an intermediary. However, effective Internet distribution may make direct selling possible, especially if the product can be distributed over the Internet.

7   C

8   False. Direct response radio is more limited than DRTV for products which need to be demonstrated visually, but it can be very effective for intangibles, such as financial services, and for information-rich tangibles such as newspapers. However, it is fair to say that the interactive and marketing possibilities of digital radio are largely unexploited at the time of writing.

BPP LEARNING MEDIA

Action Programme Review

1   Your answers might include some of the following points.

(a)   The middleman of course has to take his 'cut', reducing the revenue available to the producer.

(b)   The producer needs an infrastructure for looking after the retailers – keeping them informed, keeping them well stocked – which might not be necessary in, say, a mail order business.

(c)   The producer loses some part of his control over the marketing of his product. The power of some retailers (for example W H Smith in the world of UK book publishing) is so great that they are able to dictate marketing policy to their suppliers.

2   Other things being equal, if the order pattern is a small number of high-value orders, then direct distribution is more likely to occur. If there are numerous low-value orders, then the cost of fulfilling them promptly will be high and the use of intermediaries is likely.

3   It depends very much on the type of service.

- Hairdressers cannot deliver their own haircutting skills through an intermediary: the customer would get a different haircut and a different experience. (On the other hand, a self-employed hairdresser may rent a 'seat' in a number of different salons. This is not dissimilar to distributing via a retailer.)

- A train company has little option but to deliver transport services using the existing railway infrastructure. There are all manner of possible outlets for ticket sales.

- Insurance companies often deliver though agents who get paid commission, but they also use direct selling, for instance distributing via a mixture of the Internet, telesales or DRTV and conventional post.

Try to think of some more examples of your own.

4   It happened because ITV bid more money for the exclusive right to distribute Premiership football than the BBC. It is not uncommon for a producer to charge distributors for the right to distribute a product. A more straightforward example is the distribution of software: the software producer may ask potential resellers to pay an annual fee and require them to meet certain training requirements (eg accountancy software resellers).

5   Prices are up to 50% below conventional retail outlets and shoppers can choose from a wide range of branded goods, that they otherwise might not be able to afford. They can also turn a shopping trip into a day out, as factory outlet centres are designed as 'destination' shopping venues, offering facilities such as playgrounds and restaurants.

Manufacturers enjoy the ability to sell surplus stock at a profit in a controlled way that does not damage the brand image. They have also turned the shops into a powerful marketing tool for test-marketing products before their high street launch, and selling avant-garde designs that have not caught on in the main retail market.

6

- Managing income materials/components
- Inventory/stock management
- Managing flow of outbound goods
- Packaging/transport management
- Quality assurance and control
- Information management

- Long, steady production runs: cost saving
- Just-in-Time supply: minimise inefficient stock holding
- Timely supply of channel/customer demand: service-driven
- Goods undamaged, preserved, safe, convenient for handling, storage, transport, display
- Customer/channel value through reduced (or identified) defective products
- Partnership throughout value chain, feedback for planning and control

Now try Questions 12 and 13 at the end of the Study Text

BPP
LEARNING MEDIA

Promotion or marketing communications

Syllabus content

- Describe the wide range of tools and techniques available to marketers to satisfy customer requirements and compete effectively (3.2)
- Describe the extensive range of tools that comprise the marketing communications mix, and examine the factors that contribute to its development and implementation (3.12)
- Explain the importance of measuring the effectiveness of the selected marketing effort and instituting appropriate changes where necessary (3.16)

Introduction

Although the word **promotion** is still widely used, it implies that the seller is doing all the shouting. In a market-orientated business (following relationship marketing principles) there is a two-way dialogue, where the buyer's response is as important as the seller's message. Hence the growth of the term **'marketing communications'** – which you will most likely see in the exam.

It could be argued that all the other Ps are merely elements of the marketing communications mix: product and packaging have a quality and design that 'communicates' a great deal to the customer; price speaks volumes; and the choice of distribution outlet says something else again.

This is the longest chapter in this book, but it only scratches the surface of the area of marketing that the marketer has most control over: liaison with customers. You will cover the topic in much more detail in the *Customer Communications* module: we have reproduced some of the 'overview' level material from the BPP Study Text.

We outline some of the tools used in marketing communications and (in Section 9) suggest how the marketing communications mix for a given product can be determined.

1 Overview of the marketing communications mix

1.1 An integrated approach

Figure 8.1 indicates the extensive **range of tools** that can be used to communicate with a customer or potential customer.

Figure 8.1: The marketing communications mix

BPP LEARNING MEDIA

Exam tip

> Promotional mix decisions are frequently examined.
>
> In December 2003, you were asked to select marketing communication tools for FMCGs, and to give reasons for your choice: in December 2005, for a B2B computer hardware marketer – and how the effectiveness of the chosen tools could be measured: in June 2006, for a processed food manufacturer – and factors in the selection decisions: in December 2006, the same question in the context of a B2B market of your choice. Pay careful attention to the **uses** and **advantages/disadvantages** of each tool or approach, then look at the broader criteria covered in Section 9. And don't forget to read exam questions very carefully, for **context** (consumer/B2B, industry etc).

1.2 Above or below 'the line'?

Promotional activities are often classified as above-the-line and below-the-line.

Key concepts

> **Above-the-line promotion** is advertising placed in paid-for media, such as the press, radio, TV, cinema and outdoor/transport poster sites. The 'line' is one in an advertising agency's accounts, above which are shown its earnings on a commission basis, from the buying of media space for clients.
>
> **Below-the-line promotion** is a blanket term for a range of non-commissionable marketing communication activities. (Agency earnings on a fee basis are shown below the 'line' in their accounts.) More specifically, it refers to activities such as direct mail, sales promotions, sponsorship and exhibitions or trade shows.

We will discuss the nature and uses of each of these activities as we come to them.

2 Personal selling

FAST FORWARD

> **Personal selling** encompasses a wide variety of tasks including prospecting, information gathering and communicating as well as actually selling.

Key concept

> **Personal selling** is 'the presentation of products and associated persuasive communication to potential clients, employed by the supplying organisation. It is the most direct and longest established means of promotion within the promotional mix'.
>
> (*S Baron et al*, 1991)

Personal selling, or sales force activity, must be undertaken within the context of the organisation's overall marketing strategy. For example, if the organisation pursues a **'pull' strategy**, relying on massive consumer advertising to draw customers to ask for the brands, then the rôle of the sales force may primarily be servicing, ensuring that retailers carry sufficient stock, allocate adequate shelf space for display and co-operate in sales promotion programmes.

Conversely, with a **'push' strategy**, the organisation will rely primarily on the sales force to persuade marketing intermediaries to buy the product.

2.1 Sales roles

Kotler et al (1999) suggest that a salesperson might perform any of six different activities.

Activity	Salesperson's role
Prospecting	Gathering additional potential customers.
Communicating	Communicating information to existing and potential customers about the company's products and services can take up a major proportion of the salesperson's time.
Selling	Approaching the customer, presenting benefits, answering objections and closing the sale.
Servicing	Providing services to the customer, such as technical assistance, arranging finance and speeding delivery.
Information gathering	Feedback and marketing intelligence gathering.
Allocating	Allocating products to priority customers, in times of product shortages.

Action Programme 1

Describe your own job in Kotler's terms.

2.2 The selling process

FAST FORWARD

Personal selling is part of an **integrated promotional strategy**. It will be supported by a range of other activities such as advertising and PR, lead generation and sales support information.

Elements of the selling process can be depicted as follows: Figure 8.2.

Figure 8.2: Elements of personal selling

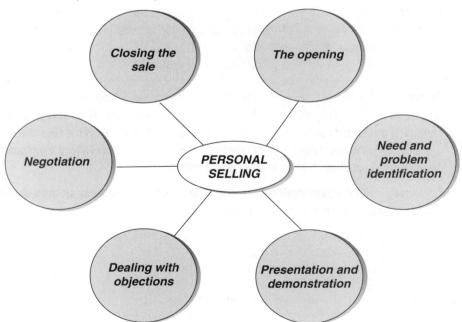

The stages need not occur in any particular order. Objections may occur during the presentation; negotiation may begin during problem identification; and if the process of selling is going well, the salesperson may try to close the sale.

BPP LEARNING MEDIA

Also, the salesperson's job begins *before* meeting the buyer. **Preparation** could include finding out about the buyer's personal characteristics, the history of the trading relationship, and the specific requirements of the buyer and how the product being sold meets those requirements. In this way, the salesperson can frame sales presentations and answers to objections.

At the other end, the selling process does not finish when the sale is made. Indeed, the sale itself may only be the start of a long-term **relationship** between buyer and seller.

Personal selling is part of the integrated promotional strategy of the organisation. Note that it will be **supported** by a range of other marketing communication activities.

(a) **Product advertising, public relations and sales promotion**, drawing consumer attention and interest to the product and its sources *and* motivating distributors/retailers to stock and sell the product

(b) **'Leads'** (interested prospective customers) generated by contacts and enquiries made through exhibitions, promotional competitions, enquiry coupons in advertising and other methods

(c) **Informational tools** such as brochures and presentation kits. These can add interest and variety to sales presentations, and leave customers with helpful reminders and information

(d) **Sales support information**: customer/segment profiling; competitor intelligence; access to customer contact/transaction histories and product availability and so on. (This is an important aspect of customer relationship management, enabling field sales teams to facilitate immediate response and transactions without time-lags to obtain information.)

2.3 The advantages and disadvantages of personal selling

FAST FORWARD

Personal selling is often appropriate in **B2B markets**, where there are fewer, higher-value customers who are looking for a more complex total offering tailored to a more specific set of requirements.

Shimp & Delozier (1998) identify a number of advantages that can accrue from using personal selling compared to other promotional tools.

(a) Personal selling contributes to a **relatively high level of customer attention** since, in face-to-face situations, it is difficult for a potential buyer to avoid a salesperson's message.

(b) Personal selling enables the salesperson to **customise the message** to the customer's specific interests and needs.

(c) The two-way communication nature of personal selling allows **immediate feedback** from the customer so that the effectiveness of the message can be ascertained.

(d) Personal selling communicates a larger amount of **technical and complex information** than would be possible using other promotional methods.

(e) In personal selling there is a greater ability to **demonstrate** a product's functioning and performance characteristics.

(f) Frequent interaction with the customer gives great scope for the **development of long-term relations** between buyer and seller, making the process of purchase more of a team effort.

The main disadvantage of personal selling is the **cost** inherent in maintaining a salesforce. In addition, a salesperson can only interact with **one buyer at a time**. However, the message is generally communicated more effectively in the one-to-one sales interview, so the organisation must make a value judgement between the effectiveness of getting the message across against the relative expense.

Personal selling is often appropriate in **B2B markets**, where there are fewer, higher-value customers who are looking for a more complex total offering tailored to a more specific set of requirements. Personal selling allows a partnership relationship to be established, which:

(a)   Allows customer needs to be more flexibly met

(b)   Allows salesforce effort to be targeted to high-return areas; and

(c)   Reinforces the 'inertia' of industrial markets, making it hard for buyers to switch suppliers.

3 Direct marketing

FAST FORWARD

Direct marketing involves use of a wide variety of media to communicate directly with the target market and to elicit a measurable response.

Key concept

Direct marketing creates and develops a direct relationship between the consumer and the company on an individual basis.

(a)   The Institute of Direct Marketing in the UK defines direct marketing as 'The planned recording, analysis and tracking of customer behaviour to develop relational marketing strategies'.

(b)   The Direct Marketing Association in the US defines direct marketing as 'An interactive system of marketing which uses one or more advertising media to effect a measurable response and/or transaction at any location'.

3.1 Features of direct marketing

It is worth studying these definitions and noting some key words and phases.

(a)   **Response**. Direct marketing is about getting people to respond by post, telephone, e-mail or web form to invitations and offers.

(b)   **Interactive**. The process is two-way, involving the supplier and the customer.

(c)   **Relationship**. Direct marketing is in many instances part of an on-going process of communicating with and selling to the same customer.

(d)   **Recording and analysis**. Response data are collected and analysed so that the most cost-effective procedures may be arrived at.

Direct marketing helps create and develop **direct one-to-one relationships** between the company and each of its prospects and customers. This is a form of **direct supply**, because it removes all channel intermediaries apart from the advertising medium and the delivery medium: there are no resellers. This allows the company to retain control over where and how its products are promoted, and to reach and develop business contacts efficiently.

Postma (1999) goes further and defines direct marketing as 'the execution of the marketing process, or parts thereof, using electronic and/or printed information carriers (media) **without human intervention!**' This has been made possible by e-commerce, database marketing and customer relationship management technologies.

3.2 Tools of direct marketing

FAST FORWARD

Direct marketing tools include: direct mail, e-mail, text message, DRTV advertising and telemarketing.

Direct marketing is the fastest growing sector of promotional activity. It now embraces a range of techniques, some traditional – and some new technology based.

(a) **Direct mail** (DM): a personally addressed 'written offering'(letter and/or sales literature) with some form of response mechanism, sent to existing customers from an in-house databased (or commercially obtained) mailing list.

(b) **E-mail**: messages sent via the Internet from an e-mail database of customers. E-mails can offer routine information, updates, information about new products and so on: e-mail addresses can be gathered together via enquiries and contact permissions at the company's website.

(c) **Mobile phone text messaging (SMS)**. 'SMS combines mobility, intimacy, immediacy and the ability to push a simple powerful message to a receptive audience. There is nothing else like it. For marketing purposes SMS allows customer services, alerts, CRM, communication – two-way direct response mechanism, brand bonding, event ticketing: the possibilities are still being explored.'(*R Mullin*, 2002)

(d) **Direct response advertising**. This may be traditional advertising in a newspaper or magazine with a cut out (or stuck on) response coupon; loose inserts with response coupons or reply cards; direct-response TV or radio advertisements, giving a call centre number or Web site address to contact. The ultra-modern equivalent is advertising on interactive (digital) TV when a 'pop up' button gives you the option to interact by transferring to a website.

(e) **Mail order**. Mail order brochures typically contain a selection of items also available in a shop or trade outlet, which can be ordered via an order form included with the brochure and delivered to the customer. Mail order extends the reach of a retail business to more (and more geographically dispersed) customers.

(f) **Catalogue marketing** is similar to mail order, but involves a complete catalogue of the products of the firm, which typically would not have retail outlets at all. Electronic catalogues can also be downloaded on the Internet, with the option of transferring to the website for transaction processing, and on CD-ROM.

(g) **Call centres and tele-marketing**. A call centre is a telephone service (in-house or out-sourced by the marketing organisation) responding to or making telephone calls. This is a cost-effective way of providing a professionally trained response to customer callers and enquirers, for the purposes of sales, customer service, customer care or contact point for direct response advertising.

Action Programme 2

Collect examples of the use of each of the above tools in your own culture. Which are the most highly regarded (by marketers and by customers and other recipients)?

Marketing at Work

A survey of recent (2005) **direct mail campaigns** (in *B&T*, 12 may 2006) includes the following creative ideas to overcome 'junk mail' resistance and marketing fatigue.

- **Great Ormond St Hospital, (UK)**

    How do you make it clear that a new ultrasound scanner would mean that surgeons could avoid unnecessary surgery when diagnosing children? Send a donation request in a clear package, that asks "If you could see inside every envelope, would you open every one?"

- **Oroverde, Tropical Rainforest Founding (Germany)**

  How do you remind potential donors of the precarious state of the world's rainforests? Send them a paint-by-numbers kit with only one colour included: black.

- **Genesis Energy (New Zealand)**

  How do you let customers know you're there to help them save on their energy bills? Print your energy-saving tips in fluorescent ink, so they can read them with the lights off.

- **First Direct bank (UK)**

  How do you show customers that you're still the most thoughtful bank? Send them a single sock that they can marry to the odd one we all have in our sock drawer.

4 Advertising

FAST FORWARD

Advertising is paid-for mass communication. The selection of media for a campaign depends on matching the target market and budget to the characteristics of the media themselves.

Key concept

Advertising is 'any **paid** form of **non-personal** presentation and promotion of ideas, goods or services by an **identifiable** sponsor.'(American Marketing Association)

Advertising is a means of reaching large audiences in a cost-effective manner. Personalised feedback from an advertising message is not usually obtained. It is normally undertaken by specialist agencies.

4.1 Advertising objectives

Advertising can be effective for a range of purposes.

(a) **To promote sales**

Advertising is particularly good at raising awareness, informing and persuading. It can be used to stimulate both primary demand for a product category (as in the introduction of a completely new product) and selective demand for a particular brand (as in brand competition). This works in industrial as well as consumer markets, effectively 'introducing' the product in advance of a sales call.

(b) **To create an image or to promote an organisation or idea**

Institutional advertising is used by companies to improve their public image, and by not-for-profit and public sector organisations to promote their programmes (to persuade people not to drink and drive, to support education, to give to a charitable cause and so on).

(c) **To support personal selling**

Advertising can support the sales force by raising consumer awareness of the product/service and motivating/facilitating consumers in contacting sales representatives. (It is also often used for the knock-on effect of motivating the sales force to maximise sales from the leads generated by advertising.)

(d) **To offset competitor advertising**

Companies often attempt to defend market share by responding aggressively to competing campaigns.

BPP LEARNING MEDIA

(e) **To remind and to reassure**

Advertising reinforces the purchase decision and repeat purchase by reminding consumers that the product continues to be available (and offer benefits) and reassuring them that they made the right choice. In industrial markets, advertising may add credibility to sales visits by demonstrating professionalism and expenditure.

Action Programme 3

Get a magazine and work through all of the ads classifying them under the above headings.

Marketing at Work

hp (Hewlett Packard)

A 2005 hp advertising campaign for colour printers targeted small and medium-sized businesses and inexperienced users in the B2B press with the following **proposition**.

'1   Take a free hp course on using color effectively
2   Buy an hp Color LaserJet printer for only $499
3   Print a customised brochure for your prospect
4   Get a brand-new client worth a lot more than $499

More advice before you buy and more support after. www.hp.com/smb/color.'

For reflection: What makes this effective B2B marketing?

4.2 Campaign planning

An advertising campaign is normally mounted through the services of an advertising agency. It will be necessary to provide clear guidance to the agency on how the campaign is to proceed by means of briefings, though the campaign will then probably be developed by the company and the agency working together.

A good **agency** brief should include, as a minimum, the following elements.

(a) The **background to the proposed campaign** including comments about the internal and external environment, how it has shaped the need for the current advertising, and how the advertising and communications strategy fit into the overall strategy for the brand.

(b) Advertising **objectives** should be stated, alongside the marketing objectives that they support. The objectives should be clear and stated in measurable terms

(c) **Target markets** should be specified. These are the people the advertising is intended to influence. As much detail as possible is required. For example, for a consumer product, basics such as social class, geographic dispersion, age, sex, income and ethnicity should be supplemented with information about such things as attitudes to the product and the competition.

(d) The client should provide as much detail as possible about the **product or service** to be featured. The agency should understand about the processes involved in product/service delivery, alongside features, benefits and how the product/service is differentiated from competitive offerings.

(e)   The **budget** must be clear.

(f)   The **timescale** must be specified. The advertising may need to be timed to coincide with a particular calendar date such as Easter, Christmas or Valentine's Day.

4.3 Advertising media

FAST FORWARD

Advertising media are selected according to audience size (reach) and relevance (targeting), suitability and cost.

Major advertising media include television, cinema, radio, newspapers, magazines and outdoor media (poster sites, bus stops, buildings etc). In addition, opportunities are emerging in interactive advertising through **new media** such as the Internet, Direct Response Television, mobile telephone text messaging, enhanced CD and CD-ROM, websites and so on.

Media are selected according to the following criteria.

(a)   **The size of the audience which regularly uses the medium**. Mass media (such as television, radio and national newspapers) have large exposure. Reader/viewer numbers (newspaper circulation, programme ratings) are closely monitored, helping the media planner to assess the reach of the advertisement.

(b)   **The type of people who form the audience of the medium**. There is a trade-off between the size and relevance of the available audience. Segmentation (for example placing an ad in special-interest section of a newspaper) or targeting (in local or regional media, specialist magazines and journals and so on) may be possible.

(c)   **The suitability of the medium for the message**. Print ads, for example, allow high volumes of information to be taken in and kept, with response mechanisms (for example coupons) if desired. Television and cinema have a high impact on awareness and retention because of the potential for creativity, and sound/moving image combinations. Radio has a highly personal quality, but as a sound-only medium has limited potential for information retention.

(d)   **The cost of the medium in relation to all the above**. Cinema and TV have very high space and production costs. Newspapers and magazines cost by circulation, which may or may not be relevant to the target audience of the advertiser.

Media planning, buying and scheduling, and the origination and production of highly designed and technically demanding advertising formats, are generally undertaken by specialist agencies, who form a multi-billion dollar global industry. The main tasks of the marketer in the client organisation will be to brief the agency and liaise with account executives to monitor, co-ordinate and approve plans at each stage of the process.

Action Programme 4

The posters medium is sometimes given the more general name of 'outdoor'. See if you can think of examples other than large poster sites. It may help if you go for a walk round your town and take a notepad.

Marketing at Work

Live demos in Singapore taxis

'Sony Ericsson has installed live demo units in taxis around Singapore, allowing users to test the sights and sounds of its new W810i Walkman Phone. In the installation, the W810i is mounted on the back of the passenger seat with a set of headphones for passengers to listen to the phone's sound quality. The campaign is supported by print and cinema campaigns.'

B&T, 19 May 2006

4.4 Advertising effectiveness

Advertising may be judged to have been effective if it has met the objectives or tasks previously set for it. The following table gives some examples.

Advertising task/objectives	Example	Measure of effectiveness
Support increase in sales	For example, a local plumber's advert in a regional newspaper	Orders; levels of enquiries
Inform consumers	An Amnesty International newspaper ad about political prisoners	Donations Number of new members clipping appeal coupon
Remind	A Yellow Pages television commercial	Awareness levels
Create/re-inforce image	Dulux 'You find the colour, we'll match it' ads	Awareness levels Image created Sales
Change attitude	Argos' moving upmarket (PA refurnishing designer flat for rock star TV ads)	Demographic profile of purchasers; type of goods purchased
Build relationships	Hyundai's 'I'm sticking with you' ads	Repeat purchase

5 Sales promotion

 FAST FORWARD

Sales promotion techniques add value to a product in order to achieve a specific marketing objective.

Key concept

The Institute of Sales Promotion (ISP) defines **sales promotion** as 'a range of tactical marketing techniques, designed within a strategic marketing framework, to add value to a product or service, in order to achieve a specific sales and marketing objective.'

Sales promotion activity is typically aimed at **increasing short-term sales volume,** by encouraging first time, repeat or multiple purchase within a stated time frame ('offer closes on such-and-such a date'). It seeks to do this by **adding value** to the product or service: consumers are offered something extra – or the chance to obtain something extra – if they purchase, purchase more or purchase again.

Exam tip

It is worth being aware of the potential for confusion between the terms 'promotion'(used as another way of saying 'marketing communications' in general) and 'sales promotion'(which is a specialist term reserved for the techniques described here). In an exam, especially if you are reading through questions fairly quickly, it is all too easy to answer the 'wrong' question.

5.1 Objectives of sales promotion

The following are examples of consumer sales promotion objectives stated in broad terms.

(a)   To increase awareness and interest amongst target audiences.
(b)   To achieve a switch in buying behaviour from competitor brands.
(c)   To smooth seasonal dips in demand.

5.2 Consumer sales promotion techniques

FAST FORWARD

Consumer promotion techniques include reduced price; coupons; gift with purchase; and competitions and prizes.

The range of consumer sales promotion techniques can be depicted as follows: Figure 8.3.

Figure 8.3: Consumer sales promotion techniques

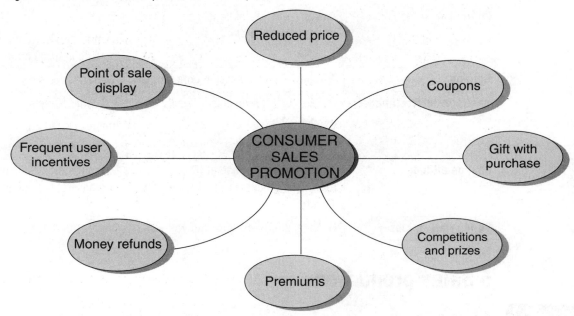

Consumer sales promotion techniques include:

- **Price promotions**: for example discounted selling price or additional product on *current* purchase, or coupons (on packs or advertisements) offering discounts on *next* purchase

- **'Gift with purchase'** or **'premium'** promotions: the consumer receives a bonus, gift or refund on purchase or repeat purchase, or on sending in tokens or proofs of multiple purchases

- **Competitions and prizes** for example, entry in prize draws or 'lucky purchase' prizes, often used both to stimulate purchase (more chances to win) and to capture customer data.

- **Frequent user (loyalty) incentives** for example, Air Miles programmes, points-for-prizes cards.

Marketing at Work

Coca-Cola is making glamour the theme of its biggest **sales promotion** so far for its Diet Coke brand. The on-pack promotion, 'silver spending spree', features an instant-win top prize of £100,000 and smaller cash prizes and trials with Cannons Health Clubs. All Diet Coke bottles will be silver during the campaign. Large outdoor teaser ads break next week, with straplines such as 'Money is the root of all evil? I'll take my chances'. These will be followed by 48-sheet outdoor executions and press ads highlighting the prizes, placed in fashion and style magazines such as Vogue and Glamour. The promotion is based on a similar campaign run earlier this year in Ireland.

Marketing, 22 August 2002

Action Programme 5

Over the next few weeks, identify and note the different forms of sales promotion you encounter as you shop.

5.2.1 Point-of-sale display

It is reckoned that two-thirds of purchases result from in-store decisions. Attractive and informative point-of-sale displays are therefore of great importance in sales promotion.

Point of sale materials include product housing or display casing (such as racks and carousels), posters, leaflet dispensers and so on. Their purpose is to:

- Attract the attention of buyers
- Stimulate purchase in preference to rival brands
- Increase available display and promotion space for the product
- Motivate retailers to stock the product (because they add to store appeal)

Marketing at Work

Creatable Media (Australia)

'Major advertisers have signed up to secure ad space on a **medium targeting consumers** at the point of purchase – food court table tops.

'Created by Sydney-based company Creatable, the tables will be located in the food courts of major shopping centres... Flight Centre's marketing director said table-top advertising was "an opportunity to drive sales into stores as well as an effective tool for brand building".

'[Creatable executive directors] said the medium was a way to reach a "captive audience for an average of 10-15 minutes" at a time. "We are targeting shoppers at the point of purchase when they are in buying mode with money in their pockets. About 75% of consumer decisions are made in the shopping environment, and 50% are made in the store itself." '

B & T Weekly, 5th July 2002

5.2.2 Product packaging

Product packaging is also a promotional aid.

- The design can be used to attract attention, convey brand identity and promote brand recognition. (Most people come to recognise their favourite brands on the shelf – even from a distance – by the packing colour and design.)

- Printable surfaces can be used for product labelling and information (some of which is required by law) and also promotional messages, sales promotions and coupons.

- Values integral to the packaging itself (size, environment-friendliness, convenience, attractiveness, protection of product quality) are part of the overall benefit and image bundle of the product

5.3 Trade promotions

FAST FORWARD **Trade promotion techniques** include baker's dozen, tailor made promotion and promotional support.

This category of promotion acts to encourage a distributor to stock or sell more of a product or service. Techniques (Figure 8.4) include:

- **Discounts**, **special terms** or occasional promotions such as 'baker's dozen' packs (13 items/packs for the price of 12)

- **Advertising/promotion** support: for example, dealer/stockist listing; financial contribution to stockist advertising that features the product; collaborative campaigns/ promotions benefiting the stockist and brand.

Figure 8.4: Trade promotion techniques

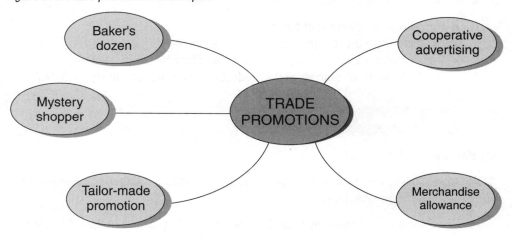

5.4 Measuring promotional effectiveness

The results of a promotion should always be measured against objectives. All sales promotions can be measured in terms of **promotional take-up**: for example, number of vouchers redeemed, or number of competition entries. The absolute redemption figure should be expressed as a percentage of all possible redemptions in order to give a benchmark for future promotions.

Ad hoc **research** can be undertaken into the effects of specific promotions. For example, Heinz have used research to monitor promotional effort. Five thousand reply-paid questionnaires are supplied to the handling house to be mailed off alongside purchase vouchers to a random selection of promotion applicants. Questionnaire content is tailored to the specific needs of the promotion, but core questions are retained for comparability.

The effect of a sales promotion campaign is often to bring **sales** forward in time. A short-term surge in sales will then be followed by a dip, with no lasting increase. It is possible that the sales promotion effort has zero overall effect other than to impose an extra cost. For this reason, it is usually necessary to combine sales promotion with advertising, so that sales may be built up over a longer period of time.

6 Public relations

FAST FORWARD

Public relations aims to enhance goodwill towards an organisation from its publics.

Key concept

The Institute of Public Relations has defined **public relations** as 'the planned and sustained effort to establish and maintain goodwill and mutual understanding between an organisation and its publics'.

This is an important discipline, because although it may not directly stimulate sales, the organisation's image is an important factor in whether it attracts and retains **employees**, whether **consumers** buy its products/services, whether the **community** supports or resists its presence and activities and whether the **media** reports positively on its operations.

An organisation can be either reactive or proactive in its management of relationships with the public.

- **Reactive** PR is primarily concerned with the communication of what has happened and responding to factors affecting the organisation. It is primarily defensive.

- In contrast, **proactive** public relations practitioners have a much wider rôle and thus have a far greater influence on overall organisational strategy. The scope of the PR function is much wider, encompassing communications activities in their entirety, counselling and strategic planning.

 Marketing at Work

'The next asbestos?'

American nutritionist Mary Enig (among others) released research in 2005 claiming that soy products are toxic and inhibit mineral absorption. Soy products were dubbed 'the next asbestos' in *B&T* magazine (4 March 2005). The Solae Company's marketing and communications manager 'hit back' immediately, contacting the magazine to affirm that:

- Soy products used by Solae and rival Sanitarium are free of the compounds said to cause gastric problems

- Studies by numerous other scientists have shown that soy can aid in protection against cancers, including breast and prostate cancer

- Contemporary research does not in fact support claims of mineral absorption inhibition

(*B&T*, 25 March 2005)

6.1 Public relations techniques

FAST FORWARD

Organisations will have to deal with more than one **public**, including consumers, business customers, employees, the media, financial markets and wider society.

The scope of PR is very broad. Some frequently used techniques are as follows.

(a) **Consumer marketing support**
- Consumer and trade press releases (to secure media coverage)
- Product/service literature (including video and CD-ROM)
- Special events (celebrity store openings, product launch events etc)
- Publicity 'stunts' (attention-grabbing events)

(b) **Business-to-business communication**

- Corporate identity design (logos, liveries, housestyle of communications)
- Corporate and product videos
- Direct mailings of product/service literature and corporate brochures
- Trade exhibitions and conferences

(c) **Internal/employee communications**

- In-house magazines and employee newsletters (or intranet pages)
- Recruitment exhibitions/conferences
- Employee communications: briefings, consultation, works councils and so on

(d) **Corporate, external and public affairs**

- Corporate literature

- Corporate social responsibility and community involvement programmes: liaison with pressure and interest groups

- Media relations: networking and image management through trade, local, national (and possibly international) press

- Lobbying of local/central government and influential bodies

- Crisis and issues management: minimising the negative impacts of problems and bad publicity by managing press/public relations

(e) **Financial public relations**

- Financial media relations
- Design of annual and interim financial reports
- Facility visits for analysts, brokers, fund managers etc
- Organising shareholder meetings and communications

Action Programme 6

Start collecting examples of:

(a) Editorial articles (or radio/TV news segments) which quote representatives of named commercial organisations): what impression is created by the attribution of the quoted statement?

(b) Named or visibly identifiable brands (watches, cars, soft drinks) in movies and TV programmes: this is called 'product placement': how noticeable are they, and what effect does their presence have?

(c) Letters, notices or statements from spokespersons apologising for mistakes or errors (in advertising or customer service, or on larger issues of public relations crisis such as a product recall or damaging revelations): how effectively do they minimise potential negative feelings on the part of customers/consumers?

6.2 Measuring PR effectiveness

Without adequate mechanisms for monitoring and control it is impossible to know whether the objectives of the PR activity have been met. The evaluation of PR activities often concentrates on the measurement of the effectiveness of the process of communications rather than on the impact of the communications programmes on the target publics. Typical measures of PR activity include:

- The monitoring of any **media coverage received**, which may include an assessment of the number of column inches/minutes of broadcast coverage, the position of articles, the accuracy of the content and the use of key words or phrases

- **Attendance at exhibitions** together with the **number of orders and enquiries** received

- **Replies to response coupons**, included in advertorials, articles and brochures

- **Telephone or web enquiries** following the appearance of an article or broadcast programme

However, such methods only provide a measure of the effectiveness of the implementation of the programme, not of its ultimate impact. In order to do this, it is necessary to carry out more detailed **research** into the attitudes and behaviour of the target publics.

7 Sponsorship

FAST FORWARD

Sponsorship entails providing money for an event or activity in return for publicity and prestige.

Key concept

Sponsorship involves supporting an event or activity by providing money (or something else of value, such as product prizes for a competition), usually in return for naming rights, advertising or acknowledgement at the event and in any publicity connected with the event. Sponsorship is often sought for sporting events, artistic events, educational initiatives and charity/community events and initiatives. A relatively new field in the UK is TV/radio programme sponsorship.

Sponsorship is often seen as part of a company's socially responsible and community-friendly public relations profile: it has the benefit of positive associations with the sponsored cause or event. The profile gained (for example in the case of television coverage of a sporting event) can be cost-effective compared to TV advertising, for example. However, it relies heavily on awareness and association: unless additional advertising space or 'air time' is part of the deal, not much information may be conveyed.

Marketers may sponsor local area or school groups and events – all the way up to national and international sporting and cultural events and organisations. Sponsorship has offered marketing avenues for organisations which are restricted in their advertising (such as alcohol and tobacco companies) or which wish to widen their awareness base among various target audiences.

- There is wide corporate involvement in mass-support sports such as football and cricket.

- Cultural sponsorship (of galleries, orchestras, theatrical productions and so on) tends be taken up by financial institutions and prestige marketing organisations.

- Community event sponsorship (supporting local environment 'clean-up' days, tree planting days, charity fun-runs, books for schools programmes and so on) is often used to associate companies with particular values (for example, environmental concern, education) or with socially responsible community involvement.

7.1 The purpose of sponsorship

The objective of the **organisation soliciting sponsorship** is most often financial support – or some other form of contribution, such as prizes for a competition, or a prestige name to be associated with the event. In return, it will need to offer potential sponsors satisfaction of *their* objectives.

The objectives of the **sponsor** may be:

- **Awareness creation** in the target audience of the sponsored event (where it coincides with the target audience of the sponsor)

- **Media coverage** generated by the sponsored event (especially if direct advertising is regulated, as for tobacco companies)

- Opportunities for **corporate hospitality** at sponsored events

- **Association** with prestigious or popular events or particular values

- Creation of a **positive image** among employees or the wider community by association with worthy causes or community events

- Securing **potential employees** (for example, by sponsoring vocational/tertiary education)

- **Cost-effective** achievement of the above (compared to, say, TV advertising)

Sponsorship as a promotional technique also has limitations.

- Sponsorship by itself can only communicate a restricted amount of information (unless integrated with advertising and other initiatives).

- Association with a group or event may also attach negative values (such as sports-related violence and alcohol abuse).

 Marketing at Work

South East Asia's Largest Outdoor Cinema Festival

Starlight Cinema, an outdoor movie venture, has signed four **sponsors** for its launch next month, which is expected to attract 20,000 people over 10 days.

The Catcha Group venture has signed up Standard Chartered Bank, Stella Artois, Smint and Evian for the June 13-22 screening of Hollywood blockbusters at the Fort Canning Park in Singapore. Sponsors will be provided with signage, exposure in collateral material and cinema commercials.

Apart from reaching young, single attendees, Pacific Beverages marketing manager, Mark Wilson, said the sponsorship fitted in with Stella Artois' global marketing strategy of developing an association with cinema.

Stella Artois is the presenting sponsor of the Cannes Film Festival and it also advertises in outdoor cinemas in Europe and the US.

Standard Chartered is using the event to reward its credit cardholders with a 20 per cent discount on movie tickets as well as drive credit card usage.

The bank's general manager for credit cards and personal loans, John Chang, expected the 10-day event to be a success because Singapore had "one of the highest ratios of annual cinema attendance in the world".

Media Asia, 31 May 2002

7.2 Developing a sponsorship programme

Smith (1993) suggests the following approach to developing and managing a sponsorship program.

(a) **Analyse the current situation**, looking especially at who else is a present or previous sponsor in the chosen field, and what else competitors are sponsoring.

(b) **Define sponsorship objectives**. There may be many of these, such as raising awareness; building an image; or getting round advertising bans (tobacco companies).

(c) **Clarify the strategy**: how does the sponsorship programme contribute to the overall corporate, marketing and communication objectives and how can it be integrated with other promotions?

(d) **Develop the tactical details** of the programme.

(e)   **Define target audiences**. Sport in particular may reach a number of very different audiences.

(f)   **Consider what resources are needed** to run the programme.

(g)   Establish a **method of measuring the effectiveness** of the sponsorship.

Action Programme 7

List some examples of sporting, artistic, educational and community sponsorships that you are aware of in your country (or internationally).

*   What image of the sponsoring company or brand does association with that particular event/group/cause create?

*   How much promotional coverage (advertising, publicity) does the sponsor get as a result of sponsorship: how much information about the organisation or brand is conveyed?

8 Branding

FAST FORWARD

Branding is used to differentiate products and so build consumer and distributor loyalty. It is most relevant in marketing mass market items in competition with very similar generic products.

Key concept

A **brand** is a name, term, sign, symbol or design intended to identify the product of a seller and to differentiate it from those of competitors.

Branding is now apparent in just about all markets. Not long ago – and this is still the case in many less developed countries – most products were sold unbranded. Today even salt, oranges, nuts and screws are often branded. There has been a limited return recently in some developed countries to 'generics': cheap products packaged plainly and not heavily advertised. This apparent lack of branding is in fact establishing a brand identity itself, as with 'No Frills' brands.

Branding is a very general term covering brand names, designs, trademarks, symbols, jingles and the like. A **brand name** refers strictly to letters, words or groups of words which can be spoken. A **brand image** distinguishes a company's product from competing products in the eyes of the user.

A brand identity may begin with a name, such as 'Kleenex', 'Ariel', but extends to a range of visual features which should assist in stimulating demand for the particular product. The additional features include typography, colour, package design and slogans.

In addition, of course, a brand shares the attributes of a *product*: it is a bundle of tangible and intangible benefits which deliver customer value.

Exam tip

Branding questions have been set in December 2003 (explain how branding has been used to build the case study business); December 2004 (explain the concept and importance of branding to an automobile manufacturer); June 2005 (explain the concept and how it could be used by an existing strong brand – Levis's jeans - to develop a new retail business); December 2005 (explain the concept and how the 4Ps can be used to position a fashion industry brand); and June 2006 (apply the principles of branding to the case study business, a global financial services provider). These should be relatively straightforward marks! The examiner has emphasised that branding will have higher priority in future exams, as it is 'key to modern marketing business'.

Marketing at Work

Jeansmaker, Lee, has launched a 'limbo rock' **rebranding campaign** to build up its image as a trendsetter among China's young elite.

The campaign involves outdoor, print and point-of-sale to spearhead the revitalisation of the Lee brand as it launches its hipster line, where the beltline sits three inches below the wearer's belly button. The campaign is running in Shanghai, Guangzhou and Beijing.

The driver of the campaign is a series of limbo rock contests at shopping malls, housing Lee outlets.

Media Asia, 17 May 2002

McDonald's

Global brand McDonalds was losing ground to competitors by 2001, due to poor service, boring food – and bad publicity arising from the obesity 'epidemic' associated with fast food. It launched a 'Plan to Win' **total rebranding campaign**, designed to woo back core customers: mothers, kids and 20-somethings. McDonald's recognised that the brand was losing relevance, because it had focused on opening new outlets – rather than maximising sales at existing outlets. The worldwide "I'm lovin' it" campaign, featuring celebrities like Justin Timberlake, Destiny's Child and Yao Ming, has **repositioned** McDonalds as an energetic lifestyle brand. Service and décor have been revamped. New health-conscious menus have been introduced – at a profit-raising price premium. The results? Same-store results up 7% worldwide. Complaints down 11%. Compliments up 18%.

(*Business*, Jan/Feb 2005)

Action Programme 8

What characteristics do the following brand names suggest to you?

Brillo (scouring pads)
Pampers (baby nappies)
Cussons Imperial Leather (soap)
Kerrygold (butter)
Hush Puppies (shoes)

8.1 Objectives of branding

The key **benefit of branding** is product differentiation and recognition.

Products may be branded for a number of reasons.

(a)   It aids **product differentiation**, conveying a lot of information very quickly and concisely. This helps customers readily to identify the goods or services and thereby helps to create a customer loyalty to the brand. It is therefore a means of increasing or maintaining sales.

(b)   It maximises the impact of **advertising** for product identification and recognition. The more similar a product (whether an industrial good or consumer good) is to competing goods, the more branding is necessary to create a separate product identity.

(c)   Branding leads to a **readier acceptance** of a manufacturer's goods by wholesalers and retailers.

(d)   It reduces the importance of **price differentials** between goods.

(e)   It supports **market segmentation**, since different brands of similar products may be developed to meet specific needs of categories of uses. (Think of all the cereal brands produced by Kellogg's, for example.)

(f)   It supports **brand extension** or **stretching**. Other products can be introduced into the brand range to 'piggy back' on the articles already known to the customer (but ill-will as well as goodwill for one product in a branded range will be transferred to all other products in the range).

(g)   It **eases the task of personal selling**, by enhancing product recognition.

The relevance of branding does not apply equally to all products. The cost of intensive brand advertising to project a brand image nationally may be prohibitively high. Goods which are sold in large numbers, on the other hand, promote a brand name by their existence and circulation.

The decision as to whether a brand name should be given to a **range of products** or whether products should be branded **individually** depends on quality factors.

(a)   If the brand name is associated with quality, all goods in the range must be of that standard. Examples of successful promotion of a brand name to a wide product range are the St Michael brand of Marks & Spencer, and Kellogg's.

(b)   If a company produces different quality (and price) goods for different market segments, it would be unwise to give the same brand name to the higher and the lower quality goods because this would deter buyers in the high quality/price market segment.

8.2 Branding strategies

Brand extension is the introduction of new flavours, sizes etc to a brand, to capitalise on existing brand loyalty. (Recent examples include the introduction of Persil washing up liquid and Mars ice cream.) New additions to the product range are beneficial for two main reasons.

(a)   They require a lower level of marketing investment (part of the 'image' already being known).

(b)   The extension of the brand presents less risk to consumers who might be worried about trying something new. (Particularly important in consumer durables with relatively large 'investment' in a car, stereo system or the like.)

Multi-branding is the introduction of a number of brands that all satisfy very similar product characteristics. This can be used where there is little or no brand loyalty, in order to pick up buyers who are constantly changing brands.

The best example is washing detergents. The two majors, Lever Brothers and Procter & Gamble, have created a barrier to fresh competition as a new company would have to launch several brands at once in order to compete.

Family branding uses the power of the brand name to assist all products in a range. This strategy is being used more and more by large companies, such as Heinz. In part it is a response to retailers' own-label (family branded) goods. It is also an attempt to consolidate expensive television advertising behind one message rather than fragmenting it across the promotion of individual items.

Lucozade Energy is extending its range of flavours with the addition of a berry variant supported by a £1.5 million outdoor campaign.

The GlaxoSmithKline (GSK) drink is launching what it describes as a "contemporary and engaging" new flavour, Wild Berry, with the aim of generating a further £6.5 million sales for the brand in its first year on the market.

The flavour sees Lucozade Energy entering "berry-based" flavours for the first time.

Customer marketing controller Henry Dummer said: "Lucozade Energy Wild Berry is set to create a buzz within the cold drinks market and drive penetration. Research shows that Wild Berry is not only very well received by current Lucozade Energy drinkers but will also bring new consumers in to the brand, researching as the number one flavour choice for new users."

The latest flavour **expands** the current Lucozade Energy range which includes original, orange, citrus clear, lemon and tropical. The launch of citrus clear spearheaded the "brain and body energy" **repositioning launch** in September last year.

GSK wants to revitalise Lucozade Energy and to introduce flavoured variants to capture the interest of a younger market, with rival Coca-Cola Great Britain already establishing its Fanta Zesty Berry brand. Lucozade Citrus Clear was the first variant for the brand since the launch of Lucozade NRG in 1996, which was ditched in 1999.

It is believed that limited edition variants under both brands may be unveiled later in this major Olympic and European Football Championship year, and would be permanently added to the range if successful.

www.mad.co.uk, 8 March 2004

9 Selecting the promotional mix

FAST FORWARD

The planning of an appropriate **promotional mix** depends on factors such as push-pull, the product life cycle, product/market type and buyer readiness – as well as strengths and weaknesses of the various promotional tools themselves.

Choosing the correct tools for a particular promotional task is not easy – although new technology is making it somewhat more scientific: computers can match databased consumer and media profiles to formulate an optimal mix, and promotional budgets can be modelled on spreadsheets for a variety of different mixes.

At a basic level, however, promotion planning can be seen as a typical decision sequence (Figure 8.5).

Figure 8.5: The promotion planning process

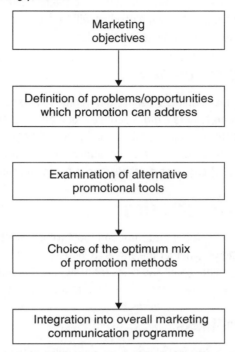

The relative emphasis placed on different promotion tools will differ according to:

- Push or pull strategy
- Type of product/market
- Product life cycle stage
- Buyer readiness stage

9.1 Push or pull?

'Push' and 'pull' are two basic promotion strategies, according to whether the target audience of promotional communication is primarily **channel members** (distributors, retail outlets and so on) or **consumers**: Figure 8.6.

Figure 8.6: Push and pull techniques

Key concepts

Push strategy involves 'pushing' the product into distribution channels. Marketing activities aim to encourage distribution and/or retail outlets to stock, promote and sell the product. Push techniques include personal selling, trade advertising and promotion, and trade exhibitions.

Pull strategy 'pulling' the product through distribution channels towards consumers. Marketing activities aim to arouse consumer awareness, interest and desire so that they approach distributors and/or retail outlets to make enquiries and purchases. Pull techniques include television and press advertising, sales promotions, customer loyalty programmes and point of sale display.

In practice, most marketers will use a combination of push and pull techniques. Distributors are more likely to stock a product if they can see that their own promotion/sale efforts will be supported by 'pull' promotions for the brand, sending consumers to them. Trade advertising and selling often involves demonstrating how aggressively the product will be promoted to consumers, and what benefits this will create for the distributor (as well as the supplier).

9.2 Type of product/market

Consumer and business markets behave differently. In most business markets, there are fewer, higher-value customers, who require a more complex total offering: as professional buyers, they are generally less susceptible to mass communications and prefer to negotiate and develop on-going business terms and relationships with suppliers. While **consumer markets** favour advertising (supported by sales promotion), **industrial/business markets** favour personal selling (supported by sales promotion).

9.3 Product life cycle stage

As we saw in Chapter 5, different promotion tools will be most effective at different stages of the product life cycle, depending on whether the aim is to increase awareness (at introduction stage: advertising is key), maximise branding, recall and sales (at growth and maturity: branding, PR, sales promotion), or secure last available sales at low cost (decline: reduce activity, except for sales promotion).

9.4 Buyer readiness

Buyers move through different stages from awareness of the product to knowledge about it, to liking, preference and conviction, and finally to readiness to buy. Different promotional tools will be effective at each stage.

- **Awareness/knowledge**: advertising, PR
- **Liking, preference, conviction**: sales promotion, sampling, exhibitions, demonstrations, personal selling, on-going advertising/PR
- **Readiness to purchase**: sales promotion, personal selling, POS display, direct marketing

Note that more labour intensive (and therefore costly) techniques such as personal selling will generally be brought into play where consumers are approaching readiness to buy, and used to 'close' the sale. (In business markets, the high value of orders makes them cost-effective for more general use.)

BPP
LEARNING MEDIA

Chapter Roundup

- **Personal selling** encompasses a wide variety of tasks including prospecting, information gathering and communicating as well as actually selling.

- Personal selling is part of an **integrated promotional strategy**. It will be supported by a range of other activities such as: advertising and PR, lead generation and sales support information.

- Personal selling is often appropriate in **B2B markets**, where there are fewer, higher-value customers who are looking for a more complex total offering tailored to a more specific set of requirements.

- **Direct marketing** involves use of a wide variety of media to communicate directly with the target market and to elicit a measurable response.

- Direct marketing tools include: direct mail, e-mail, text message, DRTV advertising and telemarketing.

- **Advertising** is paid-for mass communication. The selection of media for a campaign depends on matching the target market and budget to the characteristics of the media themselves.

- **Advertising media** are selected according to audience size (reach) and relevance (targeting), suitability and cost.

- **Sales promotion** techniques add value to a product in order to achieve a specific marketing objective.

- **Consumer promotion techniques** include reduced price; coupons; gift with purchase; and competitions and prizes.

- **Trade promotion techniques** include baker's dozen, tailor-made promotion and promotional support.

- **Public relations** aims to enhance goodwill towards an organisation from its publics.

- Organisations will have to deal with more than one **public**, including consumers, business customers, employees, the media, financial markets and wider society.

- **Sponsorship** entails providing money for an event or activity in return for publicity and prestige.

- **Branding** is used to differentiate products and so build consumer and distributor loyalty. It is most relevant in marketing mass market items in competition with very similar generic products.

- The key **benefit of branding** is product differentiation and recognition.

- The planning of an appropriate **promotional mix** depends on factors such as push-pull, the product life cycle, product/market type and buyer readiness – as well as strengths and weaknesses of the various promotional tools themselves.

Quick Quiz

1   Kotler identifies six tasks that a sales person may undertake. What are they?

P......................

C......................

S......................

S......................

I......................

A......................

2   Which of the following is an advantage of personal selling?

A   It is more cost-effective than other methods of promotion
B   It is useful when technical or complex information needs to be communicated
C   Customers pay less attention than they would to an advertisement
D   The message is the same for everybody

3   Which of the following is not true of direct mail?

A   It is easy to conduct initial tests
B   Competitors are less likely to know about it
C   It is cheaper than magazine advertising
D   It can be very precisely targeted

4   List five reasons why a company may use advertising.

5   Which of the following statements is not true?

A   The positioning of advertisements in their media context can make a difference to how they are perceived

B   The political stance of a newspaper may be a factor in whether it is a suitable advertising medium for certain products

C   A radio audience usually concentrates more than a newspaper audience

D   It may be necessary to plan a magazine ad several months in advance

6   Draw a diagram showing the various types of consumer sales promotions.

7   Put the term from the list below into the first column in the appropriate space.

PR technique	Example
	Shareholder meeting
	In-house magazine
	Celebrity store opening
	Trade exhibition
	Government lobbying

Consumer marketing support	Business-to-business	Internal communications	Public affairs	Financial relations

8   What are the limitations of sponsorship?

9   Which of the following is not true of branding?

A   Quality is less important if a product has a brand name
B   It creates customer loyalty
C   Once a brand is established other products can be added to the range
D   It makes it easier to segment markets

10   What promotional mix strategies are best suited to:

(a)   A 'push' strategy
(b)   A B2B market
(c)   A declining product?

BPP
LEARNING MEDIA

Answers to Quick Quiz

1 Prospecting, communicating, selling, servicing, information gathering, allocating

2 B

3 B

4 To promote sales
To create an image
To support sales staff
To offset competitor advertising
To remind and reassure

5 C

6

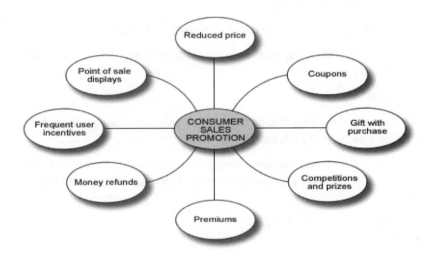

7

PR technique	Example
Financial relations	Shareholder meeting
Internal communications	In-house magazine
Consumer marketing support	Celebrity store opening
Business-to-business	Trade exhibition
Public affairs	Government lobbying

8 Limited information conveyed
Association with a group/event may be negative as well as positive

9 A

10 See Sections 9.1, 9.2 and 9.3 for a full answer.

Action Programme Review

1   Your approach to this activity depends upon your own job description.

2   Your own research.

3   You may find that some advertisements have several objectives.

4   Examples include: bus shelters, buses and trains themselves (inside and outside), commercial vehicles, noticeboards in many public places, skywriting, hot-air balloons, news-stands, kiosks (for example in post offices), and many others.

5   Here is a suggested approach to the activity:

   • Categorise the types of sales promotion into groups. Are certain types of promotion a characteristic of certain product categories?

   • Are all the promotions appropriate to the products? Why?

   • Try to distinguish objectives of the different promotions. What are they and, in your opinion, are they being achieved?

6   Your own research.

7   Your own research again. This is good practice for 'give examples' questions in the exam – and the only way for you to stay culturally relevant and up-to-date!

8   Possible answers include the following although you may have other valid interpretations. Have a wander round your kitchen and see if you can explain other brand names you see on the products in your larder and fridge.

Brillo: Practical, cleansing (brilliant).
Pampers: Soft, caring.
Imperial Leather: High quality, reputable.
Kerry Gold: Rural, natural.
Hush Puppies: Comfortable, friendly.

Now try Questions 14, 15 and 16 at the end of the Study Text

BPP LEARNING MEDIA

Part D
Marketing in context

Marketing in context

Syllabus content

- Explain the importance of contextual setting in influencing the selection of and emphasis given to marketing mix tools (4.1)
- Explain differences in the characteristics of various types of marketing context: FMCG, business-to-business (supply chain), large or capital project-based, services, voluntary and not-for-profit, sales support (eg SMEs), and their impact on marketing mix decisions (4.2)
- Compare and contrast the marketing activities of organisations that operate and compete in different contextual settings (4.3)

Introduction

We've mentioned the **marketing context** in passing on many occasions in this text. A cement mixer and a can of baked beans are both mature products but pricing issues, the choice of distribution methods and promotional tools used will be quite different.

In this chapter we are going to consider the differences in the characteristics of various types of marketing context and see what impact these differences may have on marketing mix decisions.

1 Consumer marketing

FAST FORWARD

The classic context for marketing is the **FMCG** market where most of the tools and techniques described in this book so far were originally developed. Other contexts require variations in the marketing mix.

There are two principal types of consumer marketing.

- **Fast moving consumer goods** are goods such as packaged food, beverages, toiletries, and tobacco.

- **Consumer durables** are items such as home appliances and cars.

Consumer marketing of such goods is the **classic marketing context**. It was in this context that the majority of marketing tools and techniques that we have described in this book so far were first developed, and are most fully developed.

For this reason it would be overkill to devote a section of this chapter specifically to the marketing of consumer goods. (If you want a 'section' on that, re-read Chapters 1 to 8!) Instead we will be describing how other contexts differ from consumer goods marketing.

 Marketing at Work

With the squeeze on from supermarket giants moving towards giving more shelf space to private label products, increasing competition and high TV advertising rates, the pressure has never been greater for the marketers of **fast moving consumer goods (FMCG)**.

Australian analysts at a 2005 FMCG marketing conference identified plans by supermarkets chains Cole and Woolworth's to step up their private label strategies as one of the key issues that will have a major impact on the marketers of FMCG brands.

The same analysts argue that far too many FMCG marketers 'did not have a real instinct for their market, did not really understand their consumers or their product, and don't understand the advertising process.'

(*C Ryan*, 'FMCG sector under pressure' *B&T*, March 25, 2005)

2 Business-to-business marketing

FAST FORWARD

Business-to-business (B2B) marketing is concerned with goods and services specifically designed for business use (as well as with ordinary consumer items used in business). Such goods may be of a different standard to consumer goods.

Business-to-business marketing (often abbreviated as **B2B**) is concerned with **industrial goods and services**, which are bought by manufacturers, distributors and other private and publicly owned institutions, such as schools and hospitals, to be used as part of their own activities.

In addition, of course, many of the products involved in business-to-business markets are the same as those bought within the ordinary consumer markets, for example, company cars, computers, mobile phones and so on. As we'll see in a moment, however, organisational **buying behaviour** may be quite different from that of an ordinary consumer.

B2B market categories (to recap) can be classified as follows.

(a) **Capital goods** include such items as buildings, machinery and motor vehicles.

(b) **Components and materials** include raw, partly and wholly processed materials or goods which are incorporated into the products sold by the company.

(c) **Supplies** are goods which assist production and distribution. This would include small but important items such as machine oil, computer disks and stationery, and cleaning products.

(d) **Business services** are services used by businesses, for instance employer's liability insurance.

2.1 Business products

When bought in a business-to-business context, products are distinct from consumer goods in several ways.

(a) **Conformity with standards**. Industrial products are often bound by legal or quality standards, and as a consequence, products within a particular group are often similar. Differentiation, which is such a key dimension of *consumer* goods, is more difficult here. At the same time, buyers lay down their own specifications to which manufacturers must adhere.

(b) **Technical sophistication**. Many products in this area require levels of complexity and sophistication which are unheard of in consumer products. Often the industry standard gradually influences the consumer equivalent as, for instance, in the case of power tools in the DIY market. After-sales and maintenance contracts have become essential in certain areas.

(c) **High order values**. As a consequence of (a) and (b), many business goods, particularly capital equipment, are very often extremely costly items. Even in the case of supplies, where the single unit value of components and materials may be comparatively low, the quantity required frequently means that orders have a very high value.

(d) **Irregularity of purchase**. Machinery used to produce consumer goods is not bought regularly. Materials used to produce the goods certainly are, but components and materials are often bought on a contract or preferred supplier basis, so that the opportunity to get new business may not arise very often.

2.2 Business buying behaviour

FAST FORWARD

Organisational buying decisions are usually made by groups (the DMU) not individuals and that makes it more difficult to decide what marketing efforts should be made. Other differences are that prices are often negotiated, personal selling is more common, and delivery tends to be direct.

One of the major differences between consumer and organisational buying behaviour is that organisational purchase decisions are rarely made by a single individual. Normally, purchasing decisions are made by a number of people from different functional areas, possibly with different statuses within the organisation, and almost certainly with different interests.

2.2.1 The decision making unit

The concept of the **Decision Making Unit (DMU)** (or **buying centre**) is a useful basic framework for considering these issues. (You will learn more this in the *Customer Communications* module.)

Key concept

> The **Decision Making Unit (DMU)** is all those individuals and groups who participate in the purchasing decision process, who share some common goals and the risks arising from the decision.

There are up to six groups within a typical Decision Making Unit.

(a)   **Users**, who may initiate the buying process and help define purchase specifications.

(b)   **Influencers**, who help define the specification and also provide an input into the process of evaluating the available alternatives.

(c)   **Deciders**, who have the responsibility for deciding on product requirements and suppliers.

(d)   **Approvers**, who authorise the proposals of deciders and buyers.

(e)   **Buyers**, who have the formal authority for selecting suppliers and negotiating terms.

(f)   **Gatekeepers** who control the flow of information to and through the group.

Action Programme 1

Identify the people or groups who play these roles in your own organisation. What procedure do you have to go through if you need someone or something to help you do your job?

This obviously complicates the process of marketing and selling the product. Here's an example.

- **Users** on the factory floor may want the very latest, high quality power drill, because they have been influenced by advertising or demonstrations, and they like new 'toys'.

- **Deciders** may accept that the holes the company is producing are not as good as they could be, but they may have been impressed by the marketing efforts of a completely different product.

- **Buyers** may want to stay loyal to their normal supplier of power tools, who only stocks yet another product.

- The **approver**, who is responsible for staying within budget, may be quite unwilling to sanction any expenditure on new equipment at all, without very good reason.

So where should the marketing effort be applied? There is no easy answer to this, but we make some suggestions on the following pages.

Marketing at Work

The long neglected area of accurately **targeted business-to-business direct marketing** has been given a boost with the news that a system that classifies businesses according to their location has been launched.

B2B direct marketing has long been thought to have lagged behind consumer marketing, because of the lack of technology that classifies businesses geographically.

The Geodemographic Industrial Classification system claims to be the UK's first such product and has been developed by database marketing services consultancy Information Arts.

Simon Lawrence, joint managing director of Information Arts, said: "B2B direct marketing is widely recognised for its poor levels of data accuracy and targeting and, to be fair, it is often because the availability of classification products is next to none, especially when compared with the business-to-consumer market."

The system is based on the same principle as the consumer classification technology and was developed in response to the lack of accuracy and knowledge available when targeting businesses.

Brand Republic, 23 July 2002

2.3 Marketing mix differences in B2B marketing

The B2B marketing mix differs from the marketing mix for consumer products. Often business products are not packaged for resale, prices tend to be negotiated with the buyer and distribution tends to be more direct. The promotional mix may also be different.

2.3.1 General principles

The following general observations can be made.

(a) A **marketing orientation** is just as valid within the business-to-business sector as it is in the consumer goods sector. Business customers seek answers to their problems. Business products must be full of customer benefits, providing answers to customers' problems rather than simply being 'good products'.

(b) **Business-to-business target markets** should in theory be easier to identify than consumer market segments, because more data is readily available on businesses than on individuals within the general public. Much information about business markets is published in government statistics, and there are companies that specialise in the provision of company data (eg the *Financial Times* Business Information Service, Reuters, LexisNexis). Collating the data has been a problem until very recently, however (see the case study above).

(c) In business-to-business marketing it is important that the marketer knows as much as possible about the composition of a potential customer's **buying group** and the relative importance to the purchase decision of the individuals within it.

 Marketing at Work

Business-to-business magazines are used regularly for work purposes by more decision-makers than any other medium. 87% of decision-makers are regular users. B2B magazines dominate all other media in terms of usefulness to business decision-makers.

When asked, for eleven types of information, which medium was most useful, B2B magazines not only achieved the highest score in every case but also did so by wide margins.

The typical pattern was that, for a given type of information, the proportion of decision-makers who declared that B2B magazines were the most useful medium was usually around four to six times larger than for the medium in second place. The remaining eight media then tailed away with few people thinking them the most useful source.

The eleven types of information for which B2B publications were so pre-eminent were:

- Providing thorough coverage of your sector
- Helping you to stay in touch with what's going on in your sector
- Helping you to understand how your sector is changing

- Helping you to learn from the successes and mistakes of others
- Keeping you up-to-date with news of product launches
- Providing you with information about new products and services
- Helping you select new suppliers
- Looking for jobs, or helping you to keep up-to-date with the job market
- Helping you to spot new business opportunities
- Containing advertising which is useful to you
- Helping you to do your job better

Source: <u>Periodical Publishers' Association survey</u>

Action Programme 2

Have a look through the trade magazines relevant to your own business and make a note of the business-to-business ads and advertorials.

2.3.2 Product

Most business-to-business marketing mixes will include **elements of service** as well as product. Pre-sales services may involve technical advice, quotations, opportunities to see products in action and free trials. After-sales service will include Just-in-Time delivery, service and maintenance and guarantees.

Products will also be **custom-built** to a much greater degree than for consumer marketing mixes. Frequently, products will have to be tested to customer-specified conditions. Packaging will be for protection rather than for self-service.

Efficiency features may be a powerful buying motive. Other product-unique features may be the ease of, or safety of, operation. If an operator can manage two machines rather than one, his potential output is doubled. (**Training** of operators is another service often provided by suppliers of business-to-business products.)

2.3.3 Price

Price is not normally fixed to the same degree as in consumer markets. Particularly where products or services are customised, price is a function of **buyer specification**. Price is **negotiable** to a much greater extent and may depend upon the quantity purchased, add-on services and features and sometimes the total business placed per year. Retrospective annual discounts act as loyalty incentives. Mark downs and special offers, as used in consumer markets, are also a feature of business-to-business market pricing.

2.3.4 Promotion

Figure 9.1 shows the relative importance of differing elements of the promotional mix between consumer and business-to-business markets. These differences are reflected when developing marketing communication strategies for business-to-business markets.

Exam tip

> The December 2004 exam asked for examples of marketing communications tools that can be used in a B2B market. These should be straightforward marks!

BPP LEARNING MEDIA

Figure 9.1: Relative importance of promotional elements

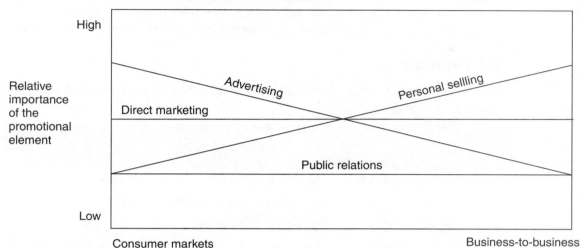

Advertising, though still important in business-to-business marketing, is less so than for consumer marketing. The types of **media** used for advertising differ greatly from those in consumer markets. Mass media are rarely used. Advertising is usually confined to **trade magazines**, which reach more precise targets. Direct mail is used to supplement personal selling. **Business-to-business exhibitions** are popular as a means of personal contact with particular target markets, and factory visits are used as a means of engendering confidence in the manufacturer's abilities and standards. More business-to-business marketers are using PR, through agencies, as a means of gaining favourable **publicity** in the trade media and to build up their corporate images.

The clearest difference, however, is the importance of **personal selling** in business-to-business markets.

- Some business products are complex and **need to be explained** in a flexible way to non-technical people involved in the buying process. Exhibitions and demonstrations are also used extensively for this reason.

- Buying in business-to-business marketing is often a group activity and, equally, selling can be a **team effort**. Salespeople are expected to follow-up to ensure that the products are working properly and that the business buyer is perfectly satisfied.

- Where a business equipment manufacturer markets through an industrial dealer, the manufacturer's salesforce may be required to **train** the dealer's salesforce in product knowledge.

- A **partnership** approach to relationship marketing is present to a much greater degree in business-to-business selling, where the buyer needs information and services and the seller is seeking repeat business in the long term.

2.3.5 Place (distribution)

Business-to-business marketers tend to **deliver direct** except where agents are used, as in international markets.

Sometimes, however, business-to-business distributors are employed, particularly for consumable and lower-value goods. **Business-to-business channels** are:

- Manufacturer   → Business buyer
- Manufacturer   → Agents → Business buyer
- Manufacturer   → Business distributor → Business buyer
- Manufacturer   → Agents → Business distributor → Business buyer

On-time delivery can be an extremely important requirement in business-to-business markets, especially where valuable contracts can be held up for want of a relatively small piece of equipment. In such circumstances, the premium on delivery is so great that penalty clauses for lateness are invoked.

2.3.6 Summary

To summarise, here is a chart showing a baker's dozen of differences between business-to-business and consumer marketing.

	Area	Business-to-business marketing	Consumer marketing
1	Purchase motivation	Multiple buying influences Support company operations	Individual or family need
2	Nature of demand	Derived or joint demand	Primary demand
3	Emphasis of seller	Economic needs	Immediate satisfaction
4	Customer needs	Each customer has different needs	Groups with similar needs
5	Nature of buyer	Group decisions	Purchase by individual or family unit
6	Time effects	Long term relationships	Short-term relationships
7	Product details	Technically sophisticated	Lower technical content
8	Promotion decisions	Emphasis on personal selling	Emphasis on mass media advertising
9	Price decisions	Price negotiated Terms are important	Price substantially fixed Discounts are important
10	Place decisions	Limited number of large buyers, short channels	Large number of small buyers Complex channels
11	Customer service	Critical to success	Less important
12	Legal factors	Contractual arrangements	Contracts only on major purchases
13	Environmental factors	Affect sales both directly and indirectly	Affect demand directly

T Powers, 1991

Exam tip

Twenty marks were available in the June 2004 exam for explaining the different characteristics of B2B and B2C markets – and explaining how these differences affect the choice and use of marketing communications (promotion) techniques. These should be straightforward marks – but bear in mind the need to cite examples!

3 Capital projects

FAST FORWARD

A **capital project** is a large-scale, very expensive project such as building an office block or a bridge. Public relations is highly important. Pricing is complex and the customer has the last word due to tendering processes. Marketing is relatively under-developed, but there is a strong impetus in the industry to address issues such as branding, project quality and delivery and eliminate cut-throat pricing.

3.1 What is a capital project?

To take an extreme example, a capital project is an undertaking such as building the Channel Tunnel.

A more common example is building an office block: clearly a very large, expensive and time-consuming undertaking, but not unique because you could build an identical office block on the next street.

Large-scale construction, civil engineering or equipment installation projects probably provide the best examples.

A capital project therefore has the following main features.

- It is on a very large-scale
- It is very expensive
- It takes a long time to complete
- Sometimes it is unique

If this is not a familiar area for you, you may wish to look at the websites of some of the major companies in the capital project sector. Here's a sample.

Arup	www.arup.com
Bovis Lend Lease Ltd	www.bovislendlease.co.uk
Costain Group Plc	www.costain.com
John Mowlem & Company Plc	www.johnmowlem.co.uk
Sir Robert McAlpine Ltd	www.sir-robert-mcalpine.com
Skanska Construction Group Ltd	www.skanska.co.uk
Taylor Woodrow Construction Ltd	www.twc.co.uk
Wates Group Ltd	www.wates.co.uk

3.2 Features of capital project marketing

Marketing in this context has some odd features. For instance, although there may be a hugely substantial physical product, perhaps visible for miles, it is generally not branded. Once they are completed, bridges, roads, tunnels, office buildings and so on do not proudly display the manufacturer's name so that everyone knows where they can get one.

Action Programme 3

The British Airways London Eye has been voted one of the Seven Wonders of Britain. Let's say you like the London Eye so much you want one in your back garden. Who would you approach to install it? Investigate on the Internet and see how long it takes you to find out.

Although the capital project firm may not get due credit for its work it may well have the additional 'after-sales' task of **maintaining** it. This is obviously an excellent source of continuing business, especially if the project uses some technology or equipment that is unique to the firm that constructed it. The downside is that maintenance work may well give rise to adverse publicity, especially if there are safety risks.

Given that a capital project will usually have a major impact on the environment, **public relations** is highly important. Not every project will damage a site of natural beauty, but if this is an issue public relations will be difficult to co-ordinate: objections will be directed against local or national government planners as much as against the organisation actually doing the job. And the 'public' that protests may not be the 'public' directly affected by the project. The case study below is a famous example from the mid 1990s that illustrates the issues involved.

 Marketing at Work

For the third day in a row, **demonstrators** yesterday prevented work being started on a new road around the British town of Newbury.

The protesters, who preach a philosophy of 'non-violent direct action' in defence of environmental causes, point out that the road scheme will damage important wildlife habitat surrounding the town.

However supporters of the bypass claim that building a new road will help solve Newbury's traffic problem. The town suffers from the pollution and congestion caused by thousands of cars and trucks on its streets every day - much of it traffic heading for England's south coast ports.

The nine mile bypass project, which is costing the Department of Transport £100 million, will mean the loss of 10,000 trees. The road will cut through Snelsmore Common (a 'Site of Special Scientific Interest'), the North Wessex Downs, and the site of the First Battle of Newbury (an English Civil War battlefield in 1643).

In what has become known as the 'Third Battle of Newbury', protesters are trying to prevent the British Government's road-building contractors from going ahead with bulldozing work. Meanwhile, **environmental groups** emphasised the wider implications of the dispute.

"Newbury is national," insisted Friends of the Earth. "We remain committed to the use of peaceful process to protect the cream of Britain's wildlife habitats from the Department of Transport's bulldozers," said FoE's Director, Charles Secrett.

Whilst local opinion seems to be in favour of the bypass, support for the protesters' actions is increasing across the country, where concerns over pollution-related respiratory diseases and the perceived under-funding of public transport has undermined the Government's traditionally pro-car transport policy.

Source: www.oneworld.org

Even if there are no trees, involved a capital project will still give rise to environmental concerns because of the **noise and mess** associated with building works. A building site may be a major opportunity to put up hoardings, displaying your company's name and logo, but people are more likely to notice the inconvenience.

3.3 The extended marketing mix for capital projects

Although a capital project appears to be a product, the best marketing response to environmental concerns is to use the service Ps. For instance, the **Considerate Constructors Scheme** is a voluntary Code of Practice, driven by the UK construction industry, which seeks to:

- Minimise any disturbance or negative impact (in terms of noise, dirt and inconvenience) sometimes caused by construction sites to the immediate neighbourhood (physical evidence).

- Eradicate offensive behaviour and language from construction sites (people).

- Recognise and reward the contractor's commitment to raise standards of site management, safety and environmental awareness beyond statutory duties (processes).

3.3.1 The place

The place of delivery for a capital project also has more in common with some types of service marketing than with product marketing, because the decision is made by the customer: if the customer wants a bridge over a river in Country A there is no point in offering to build one in Country B, even though the Country B 'channel' might be far more cost-effective and manageable for your organisation.

3.3.2 Pricing

Pricing in a capital project context has three aspects.

(a) There will have to be a **highly complex costing** exercise taking account of designer and architect fees, sub-contractors' costs (for example, for initial excavation), a huge variety materials and components costs (many items may have to be custom-built) and labour costs over an extended period.

(b) It is highly likely that the contract will include **penalty clauses** for late delivery. Obviously the organisation should do everything it can to anticipate and avoid delays but factors like bad weather or unexpected geological features are hard to control.

(c) Most importantly, the client may have the last word on price. Projects are usually put up to **tender** (government projects must be, by law), so it is not only necessary to cover your own costs and try to make a profit, there is also competition to beat. If **sealed bids** are required you will have little idea what profit margin your competitors are trying to achieve, even if you can estimate their costs.

3.3.3 Promotion

Promotion issues, apart from PR, are fairly straightforward, since there are (relatively) few customers who can afford large projects. The market consists of governments for infrastructure projects and large businesses that need physical assets (warehouses, oil rigs and so on). These can be reached directly by personal selling and by direct mail, or through specialised trade press. Client events like tours of the site combined with corporate hospitality are also likely to be important.

Mass market advertising is rare in most cases, although capital projects may provide excellent photo opportunities (huge pipelines, massive reservoirs, especially if they are in a glamorous setting) and some organisations have tried corporate image TV ads. An exception is housing developers who are likely to advertise in local press.

4 Services

FAST FORWARD

Service marketing is dependent on the distinctive features of services (intangibility, perishability and so on). People and processes are relatively more important compared with marketing of goods, as is personal selling.

Differences between selling goods and services are shown below.

Issue	Comment
Customer's purchase perception of services	• Customers view service as having less consistent quality • Service purchasers have higher risks • Service purchasing is less pleasant • When services are bought greater consideration is given to the particular salesperson • Perception of the service company is an important factor when deciding to buy a service
Customer's purchase behaviour with services	• Customers may do fewer price comparisons with services • Customers give greater consideration to the particular seller of services • Customers are less likely to be influenced by advertising and more by personal recommendations
Personal selling of services	• Customer involvement is greater • Customer satisfaction is influenced by the salesperson's personality and attitude • Salespeople may have to spend more time reducing customer uncertainty

Many service issues were dealt with in Chapters 4 and 5, and service marketing is mentioned at appropriate places elsewhere. However, we did not have much room in the chapter on promotion to deal with service issues, so we will address that now and also say a few words about online distribution of services.

Action Programme 4

Do a bit of revision before you go on.

(a)   What are the three service Ps?
(b)   What are the five characteristics of services that distinguish them from goods?
(c)   How could you charge different groups of people a different price for the same service?

4.1 Service promotion

Promotional objectives for services are not much different to those related to those for products.

- Build awareness and interest in the service and the service organisation
- Communicate and portray the benefits of the services available
- Build and maintain the overall image and reputation of the service organisation
- Advise customers of new channels
- Advise customers of special offers or modifications to the service
- Persuade customers to use or buy the service

However, in a service context there are four particular elements of the service that need to be taken into account: Figure 9.2.

- The **core service concept** and any auxiliary (augmented) service
- The **accessibility** of the service
- The **interactive communications** that take place in delivering the service
- The **influence of the consumer** and other consumers receiving the service

Figure 9.2: Model of service communications

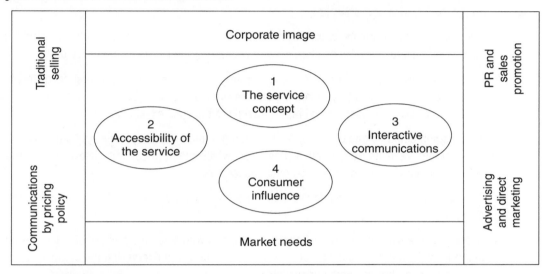

Four **promotional methods** are then generally used to influence the customer.

- Traditional selling
- Advertising and direct marketing
- Public relations and sales promotions
- The communication aspects of pricing policy

4.1.1 Developing a marketing orientation

Service organisations have been much slower to realise the need to adopt a marketing orientation and the marketing function is still relatively undeveloped in many organisations. The following table, adapted from *D Cowell* (1989), is still highly relevant.

Service characteristics	Consequences
Lack of market orientation	Managers are untrained, unskilled and unaware of the role of promotion.
Professional and ethical constraints	Places limitations on certain promotion methods. Sometimes legal restrictions.
Small scale of many service organisations	Limits size of promotion budgets.
Nature of capacity available	Capacity for delivering the service may be limited. Promotion may produce too much demand.
Attitude to promotion methods	Limited knowledge of and attitude to the wide range of promotion methods.
Nature of the service	Services may be very specific, which excludes mass advertising.

Service characteristics	Consequences
Consumer attitudes	Consumers may rely on subjective judgements made at the point of service delivery.
Buying process	The need to develop a professional relationship with the service provider makes customer care important.

 Marketing at Work

Connex, the train company loathed by commuters in the south east of England, is searching for its first head of marketing, who will be charged with **rebuilding** the company's tattered brand.

Connex is searching for a strategic marketing director to oversee its marketing department, as well as look after other areas such as ticket planning and 'revenue protection strategy' – or tackling fare dodging. The person who takes the position will report directly to the chief executive.

The position could be one of the more challenging in the marketing industry. Connex recently announced plans to remove seats from its busiest services, which run in to London Victoria and Charing Cross stations, to allow more room for standing passengers.

The salary offered for the position runs in to six figures, for someone who can turn "commuters into customers".

According to a spokesperson for Connex, the person who takes the role will also be looking at branding and price structures, attracting more off-peak customers and overseeing the company's agencies. Details of the marketing budget were not available.

Brand Republic, 5 August 2002

4.1.2 Guidelines for service promotion

These factors lead to a number of guidelines that must be considered when designing promotional campaigns for service markets.

(a)   Use **clear, unambiguous messages** to communicate the range, depth, quality and level of services.

(b)   **Emphasise the benefits of the services** rather than their technical details.

(c)   **Only promise what can be delivered**, to avoid disappointment.

(d)   **Advertise to employees**, as they are particularly important in many people-intensive services.

(e)   Obtain **maximum customer co-operation** in the service production process as the service is often an interactive system.

(f)   Build on **word-of-mouth communication** from one satisfied customer to another.

(g)   Provide **tangible evidence** to strengthen promotional messages. Use well known personalities to support the messages.

(h)   Develop **continuity in promotion** by the use of consistent and continuous symbols, themes, formats or images.

(i)   **Remove post purchase anxiety** by reassuring the buyer of the soundness of choice, especially where there is no tangible product.

(j)   **Personal selling** becomes more important in the promotion of services.

4.2 ICT and service marketing

Many services can be distributed online as effectively, or almost as effectively, as if they were digital products like videos or software. That is because, at heart, many services consist of processing information.

The most obvious example of this is **online banking**, now offered by all major high street banks. Online banking allows you to look at your balance ('physical evidence' that they still have your money, or at least, visible evidence), transfer money between accounts, make payments, set up direct debits and standing orders and so on. There's nothing that you can do online that you can't do by posting a letter, picking up the telephone and speaking, or visiting a branch, but it is less effort.

It is also less effort for the bank, of course, and less costly, because they are 'empowering' you to do things that a member of their staff would have done previously.

Much the same applies to any service where the outputs are **information**. Examples are accountancy, legal work, architectural plans, graphic design, education, entertainment/travel bookings – and many others.

Action Programme 5

Online distribution of services, where possible, is massively convenient. Can you see any drawbacks?

5 Not-for-profit marketing

FAST FORWARD

In **non-profit marketing communications** there is likely to be less money available, messages are likely to be subjected to greater scrutiny and the objectives of the communication will be quite different from those applying in consumer marketing. The major categories of non-profit communicators are political parties, social causes, the government, religious bodies and professional bodies.

The wide category of voluntary and not-for-profit (NFP) organisations might be defined as organisations which do not have increasing the wealth of the owners as a primary objective. Many voluntary NFP bodies undertake clearly **commercial ventures**, such as shops and concerts, in order to generate revenue. However, their first objective is to be **'non-loss' operations** in order to cover their costs. Profits are only made as a means to an end such as providing a service (eg the Scouting Association, local government), or accomplishing some socially or morally worthy objective (cancer charities, children's charities, Greenpeace).

S Dibb et al (2001) suggest that non-business marketing can conveniently be split into two sub-categories.

(a) **Non-profit organisation marketing,** for example by hospitals and colleges.

(b) **Social marketing**, which seeks to shape social attitudes: protecting the environment, saving scarce resources or contributing towards good causes, say.

If you view marketing as persuading people to part with money for things they don't really need (a selling orientation) then it is rather distasteful for a NFP organisation to use marketing practices. No doubt this is partly (another reason is lack of resources and professional marketing expertise) why marketing is *not* practised at all by many such organisations and only in a primitive way in others.

However, marketing in a modern sense is, in fact, *particularly* relevant to voluntary and NFP bodies, since its philosophy is to base processes on the customer's needs rather on what the producer would like to provide.

If marketing is defined in terms of delivering **mutually satisfying exchanges** between two or more parties, we get a more satisfactory view. Just as products are exchanged for cash in order to make profits, so advocacy, religious values, solace and services are 'exchanged' for contributions, support and acceptance of values. The principle of exchange can apply equally to the act of giving and receiving, as well as buying and selling.

Marketing management is now recognised as equally valuable to profit orientated or NFP organisations. The tasks of marketing audit, setting objectives, developing strategies and marketing mixes and controls for their implementation can all help in improving the performance of charities and NFP organisations.

5.1 Distinctive characteristics of NFP marketing

Whilst the basic principles are appropriate for this sector, Dibb *et al* (2001) suggest that four key differences exist relating to:

- Objectives
- Control of marketing activities
- Target markets
- Marketing mixes

5.1.1 Objectives

Objectives will not be based on profit achievement but rather on **achieving a particular response** from target markets. This has implications for reporting of results. The organisation will need to be open and honest in showing how it has managed its budget and allocated funds raised. Efficiency and effectiveness are particularly important in the use of donated funds.

5.1.2 Control of marketing activities

Controlling activities is complicated by the difficulty of judging whether **non-quantitative objectives** have been met. For example, assessing whether a charity has improved the situation of client publics is difficult to research. To control NFP marketing activities, managers must specify what factors need to be monitored and permissible variance levels. Statistics related to product mix, financial resources, size of budgets, number of employees, number of volunteers, number of customers serviced and number and location of facilities, may be useful.

5.1.3 Target markets

The concept of targeting is different in the not-for-profit sector. There are no buyers, but rather a number of different audiences. A **target public** is any group of individuals who have an interest in the activities of the organisation. Those benefiting from the organisation's activities are known as the **client public**. In addition, the voluntary sector depends heavily on relationships with donors and volunteers from the **general public**. There may also be a need to lobby local and national government and businesses for support.

Bruce (1997) has identified four types of 'customers' for charities, for example

(a) **Beneficiaries** include not only those who receive tangible support, but also those who benefit from lobbying and publicity.

(b) **Supporters** provide money, time and skill. Voluntary workers form an important group of supporters. Those who choose to buy from charities are supporters, as are those who advocate their causes.

(c) **Regulators** include both the more formal bodies, such as the Charities Commission and local authorities, and less formal groups such as residents' associations.

(d) **Stakeholders** have rights and responsibilities in connection with charities and include trustees, managers, staff and representatives of beneficiaries.

BPP LEARNING MEDIA

Action Programme 6

Do something for charity! Your organisation may have a payroll giving scheme, whereby a small amount is deducted from your salary and donated to a charity of your choice. Alternatively, many charities encourage you to give a small regular amount by setting up a direct debit. If you are selfish enough to wonder what the benefit to you will be, you will find that you get a regular newsletter from the charity from which you can extract examples of NFP marketing to use in your *Marketing Fundamentals* exam.

5.2 The NFP marketing mix

5.2.1 Product

A charity's products include **ideas** as well as goods and services. Ideas are very important in fund-raising, pressure-group activity and communicating with the public.

- When a supporter provides money to a charity, the idea of what the money will be used for is a kind of product, providing satisfaction to the supporter.

- Pressure groups work, in part, by promoting new ideas into the public consciousness, so that bodies with power can be persuaded to take a desired course of action.

- Ideas can also be promoted to the public with the aim of changing their behaviour. Governments often take this approach, as, for instance, with energy conservation and road safety campaigns.

Marketing at Work

Mother's Choice, a Hong Kong **charity** that provides support to pregnant teens, has launched a campaign to educate 12 to 20-year-olds about sex and relationships.

Bates, which developed the public service campaign, said the charity had altered its strategy in an effort to stem the growing number of unplanned pregnancies. In the past, Mother's Choice's efforts were directed at helping teens deal with unwanted pregnancies, but the new campaign targets the root cause, teaching teenagers how to deal with sex and relationship issues.

Bates' executive creative director, Iris Lo, said Mother's Choice aimed to provoke teenagers to think before they act.

Three executions were created – 'Seduction', 'Argument' and 'Pregnancy'.

In Seduction, a young girl is asked by her boyfriend to move their relationship to a more intimate level and she agrees, but the final shot shows the girl kissing her mirror image, underlining the message that teens should not be pressured into making the wrong choice in relationships.

Media Asia, 22 March 2002

5.2.2 Price

Pricing is probably the most different element in this sector. Financial price is often not a relevant concept. Rather, **opportunity cost**, where an individual is persuaded of the value of donating time or funds, is more relevant. However, price is very important to larger charities since sales of goods and services provide their largest single source of income.

5.2.3 Place

It is common for charities to have significant problems with the distribution of **physical goods** when they rely on volunteer labour. This is especially true of charities that operate internationally, unless they are well established. In particular, the type of charity fund that is set up to relieve a disaster overseas is likely to have great difficulty moving the necessary supplies to where they are needed.

On the other hand, charities that merely **disburse funds** within one country, to the deserving poor, for instance, or to pay for medical research, may have very short and easily managed distribution chains.

5.2.4 Promotion

The major principles of marketing communications for non-profit organisations are the same as for consumer and business-to-business marketing. There are, however, considerable differences of emphasis. Promotion is often dominated by personal **selling**, with street corner and door-to-door collections or awareness campaigns. The sum of money available for organised communication may be less. Public scrutiny of policies may be higher. Almost certainly there will be a different set of communication objectives.

- Making target customers **aware** of a product, service or social behaviour
- **Educating** consumers about the offer or changes in the offer
- **Changing beliefs** about negative and positive consequences of taking a particular action
- **Changing the relative importance** of particular consequences
- Enlisting the **support** of a variety of individuals
- Recruiting, motivating or rewarding **employees or volunteers**
- Changing **perceptions** about the sponsoring organisation
- Influencing **government bodies**
- Preventing the **discontinuity** of support
- **Proving benefits** over 'competitors'
- **Combating** injurious rumours
- **Influencing** funding agencies

Once the non-profit marketer has developed the broad objectives for the communications plan the next step is to decide specific messages. These messages may be developed within one of the three frameworks.

(a)   **Rational, emotional and moral framework**

   (i)   Rational messages pass on information and serve the audience's self interest. For example, messages about value, economy or benefits.

   (ii)   Emotional messages are designed to develop emotion to shape the desired behaviour. For example, with fear, guilt, shame appeals to stop doing things like smoking, drinking, taking drugs or overeating.

   (iii)   Moral messages directed at the audience's sense of right or wrong. For example, to support a cleaner environment or equal rights or help the under-privileged, or help stop others abusing their children or animals.

(b)   **Reward and situation framework**

   There may be four types of reward: rational, sensory, social or ego satisfaction rewards. Rewards may result directly from use, or indirectly from the products in use, or be incidental to use. The UK National Blood Service, for example, used the very powerful message: 'Do something amazing. Give Blood. Save a life.' and backs this up with very powerful TV advertising.

BPP LEARNING MEDIA

(c)   **Attitude change framework**

    (i)   Changes in the importance of one or more outcomes

    (ii)   Changes in the beliefs about one or more outcomes

    (iii)   Adding new positive outcomes

Marketers of non-profit organisations can reach target audiences in various ways.

Method	Comment
Paid advertising	Non-profit organisations may have limited funds but this can still be an effective route even on low budgets. Alternatively, the budget may be boosted by obtaining commercial sponsorship.
Unpaid (public service) advertising	Media owners may provide airtime or press space on a free of charge basis as a public service. However, there is little control over this and the times or spaces may occur at unpopular times or places.
Sales promotions	Short-term incentives to encourage purchases or donations. Market control is strong and promotions are often newsworthy (for example, Red Nose day or Poppy Day promotions).
Public relations	Many of the stories of non-profit organisations are of considerable interest. They may feature in the press or the broadcast media. Control over the message is good and feedback is possible.
Personal selling and communications	Staff at all levels of the non profit organisations should be trained in personal communications. They will often have the opportunity to 'sell' to their supporters and possible benefactors.

 Marketing at Work

Red Nose & Bandanna Day

'Quite aside from being great causes that we should all support, Red Nose Day (SIDs and Kids) and Bandanna Day (CanTeen: Kids with cancer) are top-shelf case studies on how to successfully win a **promotions and merchandising campaign**.

'Simple plastic red noses worth a cent or two, and some 60cm square pieces of cloth, have lifted two organisations into the mainstream consciousness of Australia …..

'In a fast-paced consumer world where even our family snapshots are digital, a real physical object delivers real value… Promotional products are **brand platforms**, a physical stage on which you present your brand to the world: a stage that persists for the life of the promotional product.

'CanTeen now believes it sells more bandannas each year than all the rest of the fashion market combined – although Bandanna Day is just one day, hundreds of thousands of consumers have collected these bandannas over the years and wear them out again and again…. Bandanna Day has a flow-on effect, helping to open other doors and fill venues.'

Branded (Vol 2: May 2006)

5.2.5 Direct marketing

This is a medium increasingly being used by non-profit organisations, particularly arts foundations and charities. It has important advantages for non-profit marketers.

    (a)   It can be very focused for maximum effect on the target market.

    (b)   It can be private and confidential. This is especially important when dealing with sensitive issues.

(c)   There is less direct regulation on direct mail promotions. In the past charitable advertising in the broadcast media has been limited.

(d)   Cost per contact and cost per response is low and controllable, which is important where funds have to be used wisely.

(e)   Results are clearly measurable and can make the programmers more accountable.

(f)   Small scale tests of proposed strategies are feasible.

(g)   The effectiveness of direct marketing can be assessed in terms of behaviour (ie orders, donations, requests for membership).

6 Sales support and SMEs

FAST FORWARD

SMEs' marketing efforts are constrained by limited resources (money, people). **Sales support**, however, can help to maximise the time the salesperson spends selling, target the best customers and enhance customer satisfaction.

An SME is a **small or medium-sized enterprise**. There are legal definitions of SMEs for various tax and accounting purposes that set out turnover limits and number of employees, but we do not need to be too precise. We use SME as a convenient term for segmenting businesses and other organisations that are somewhere above the 'small office-home office' operation but below large, household-name organisations.

SMEs have products or services and they have to set prices and distribute their wares: they simply do so on a smaller scale than larger organisations. The key marketing issue in such an organisation is one of **limited resources**. An SME will typically not be able to afford elaborate, high-profile advertising campaigns or other promotional techniques and not be able to justify the costs of running a full marketing department.

 Marketing at Work

'Some 39 per cent of **small businesses** do not plan any regular marketing activity for their business, according to Bibby Financial Services research, and more than a third of firms less than a year old have no marketing plan at all. Bibby's Greg Charlwood said the figures are alarming, "I am very surprised businesses are neglecting the marketing aspect of their business when this is an area that, if done well, can significantly drive sales, boost profits and protect market share," he said.

'Mr Charlwood says many business owners believe advertising and marketing are the same and this is why marketing activity has taken a back seat. "A lot of small businesses are unaware that advertising is just a component of marketing and that it is just one of many tools used by businesses to promote themselves."

Many businesses also believe marketing is an expensive activity, which is not necessarily the case. Simple actions such as getting businesses listed in the Yellow Pages and staying in regular contact with customers via a newsletter are ideal activities for the budget conscious, he said.'

Daily Telegraph, (Sydney, Australia) Small Business Section, 30 May 2006

That does not necessarily mean that an SME cannot have a marketing orientation, just that marketing activities typically focus on **supporting the personal selling function**. Often they will actually be carried out by members of the customer service team, in addition to their job of taking and processing orders.

Sales support activities have the following aims.

- To maximise the proportion of sales time spent in face-to-face or voice-to-voice client contact

- To provide direction, and to ensure sales resources are targeted at the market segments and leads offering the greatest potential
- To provide the necessary backup to help the salesperson ensure a continuing relationship with a satisfied customer

6.1 Sales research

Good information can both reduce sales costs and help to increase sales revenues.

(a) Profiling the 20% of customers who generate 80% of the business, provides **segmentation information**, which means more customers of the same type can be identified and targeted.

(b) Analysis of the **sales effort** reveals important management information.

- The most profitable balance of new to old calls
- The most effective call rate per day
- The best use of presentations and demonstrations etc in a sales visit
- The most effective frequency of sales calls

The average sales person often spends less than 10% of his or her time in direct customer contact. Any improvements either in the amount of **effective selling time** or the **effectiveness of the selling process** can generate significant improvement in performance. Information provides the clues which enable managers to make these improvements.

6.2 Customer and competitor intelligence

ICT provides the systems to store and rapidly retrieve information about customers and competitors. In a B2B setting, sales teams should be able to access an up-to-date record on a company immediately before a sales visit. This should record four main categories of information.

- Sales contacts made, including those made by other sales teams from the company

- Orders received, value, frequency and so on

- Current financial standing, including overdue accounts

- Any intelligence on changing personnel in the company, new business won, contracts signed or plans announced

Information should also be gathered on **competitors**. Providing the sales team with early information about proposed special offers, or new products being launched by competitors, helps the salesperson be better prepared when negotiating with a customer.

 Marketing at Work

'A new report, *CRM for small business* by Datamonitor shows small and medium enterprises are to become the next big growth engine for CRM vendors. The report highlights the huge potential of this previously untapped market.

'Datamonitor expects global CRM spend by SMEs to total close to $2bn by 2008 – more than double the value of today. In the Asia-Pacific region, the spend is estimated to exceed $500m in 2008.

'Technology analyst at Datamonitor Tom Pringle said smaller companies are faced with many of the same problems large companies have. These include difficulties in the field of sales, marketing and service. Availability, revenue generation and customer service are the primary reasons driving uptake of CRM.

' "A new **CRM market** is being created, one which encompasses those businesses which are not part of the initial CRM adoption phase – it is being pressed into the mass marketing," Pringle said.'

Professional Marketing, Feb 2005

6.3 Measuring sales potential

Both specific sales information about calls and sales actually made, and market intelligence about customers and competitors, provide managers with an insight into sales potential. In an SME, the sales force is a valuable and scarce resource, and it must be used with care. Maximising its value to the organisation means using it in areas where the sales potential is perceived to be greatest.

Sales potential can be affected by a number of issues.

(a)   **Competition**. It can be more profitable to concentrate activities on a part of the market with a lower total potential because there is less competition.

(b)   **Future forecasts**. Sales potential should not be judged only on a short-term basis, but should also be assessed on a forecast of the longer-term future. A company in a mature industry wishing to place a very large order now, may offer a lower potential in the long term than a smaller company operating in a growth market, which today only requires a small order.

(c)   **External factors**. All business is influenced by its external environment. Suppliers should assess both factors which affect their business and also those which affect their customers.

Whilst it is possible to identify factors likely to influence sales potential, it should be remembered that the greatest opportunities are not always the most obvious and the customer who seems to offer the least potential may in fact offer the greatest. If too narrow an approach is prescribed by managers, this may hinder the identification of new sales opportunities.

6.4 Providing leads

A role of sales support is to provide a flow of **qualified leads**. These should represent potential customers who are aware of the company and/or product, are already interested in it and who have, or have begun to have, a positive attitude to its purchase. The conversion rate of contacts already this far down the decision-making process is likely to be higher than if the buyer has to be approached cold by the salesperson. Leads may come from unsolicited enquiries, mail-in responses to advertising, the identification of cross-selling opportunities or database mining.

7 Marketing in micro enterprises

FAST FORWARD

Micro businesses are sometimes assumed to use watered down versions of the marketing tools available to large businesses, but this is only true to a limited extent. Many of the tools are too expensive or simply not relevant. **Word of mouth** marketing is the most important technique. **Websites** are important, but will achieve nothing on their own.

A micro enterprise is an organisation that measures its income in thousands of pounds rather than millions and employs 10 or fewer people. There are millions of such businesses because this context includes one-person companies and anyone who is self-employed.

The marketing problem is the same as that for SMEs – lack of financial resources and lack of people – but it is obviously more acute. In the case of a one-person company, any time spent on marketing is a lost opportunity to spend time doing 'real' work that brings in income.

A glance through the many books on small business management and especially those claiming to reveal the secrets of successful low budget marketing will show that readers are given watered down versions of the conventional principles. You could argue that this demonstrates that these principles are of uniform application. There may be truth in that, especially if the business involves products (and we'll give you some watered down ideas in a moment!), but it is too easy an answer.

7.1 Product or service

Most micro businesses are **service** businesses, almost by definition, because a very small business does not have the capital to invest in production machinery or production staff. Exceptions would include **craftspeople** – for instance a maker of very high quality custom-built furniture items. Part exceptions include businesses in the building trade (who resell physical items as, say, part of their plumbing or electrical service) and shop-keepers.

If the business is a service provider, the main service marketing issue is **differentiating** it from others. Exactly how this is done depends on the type of service offered, of course, but it usually comes down to quality, flexibility and reliability.

- A typing agency has limited scope because the client will often specify exactly how the job is to be done, what fonts to use and so on. Faultless accuracy and a round-the-clock service will help distinguish such a business from others.

- A management consultant, however, may be able to offer quite unique experience and knowledge of a particular type of business.

7.2 Distribution

There are relatively few distribution options for micro businesses that make products. It is extremely difficult to get shelf-space in major retailers, and in many cases that would not be appropriate in any case. **Specialist retailers** (such as gift shops for arts and crafts items, pottery and the like) are a possible option, but these are few and far between. Mail order and website ordering are more likely options. **E-commerce** is possible, but it is expensive for a very small business to set up and maintain, especially because of credit card processing costs and the need to operate (and pay for) a secure server.

For micro service businesses the place of delivery will often be the **client's premises** – obviously in the case of building work, and frequently in the case of consultancy services, which will involve frequent meetings (consultations!) with the client's staff. Information-based services can usually be run from home or a small office, with delivery by post, telephone or e-mail.

7.3 Price

If there is a product the price issues are much the same as for large businesses: the aim should be to cover costs first and then charge as high a premium as customers are willing to pay, probably finding out by trial and error unless there is a competing product as a pricing guide.

The micro service business is often in an unusually weak position regarding price, especially if its clients are much larger companies. It may be very difficult to find out how much micro competitors are charging: they are unlikely to show you their contracts, for fear that you will undercut them, and you will probably feel the same way. In some cases, the micro business may know what the **'going rate'** is and be able to charge more or less, accordingly. An accountant who strikes out alone, for instance, would know what rate her previous employers were charging clients for her time.

7.4 Promotion

Promotion is the most crucial part of the marketing mix for most micro businesses, and the most important technique is getting others to talk about you: **word of mouth**.

7.4.1 Word of mouth

Word of mouth or personal recommendation is important for businesses of all sizes, of course, but especially important for businesses that are not well-known through other promotional efforts. It is particularly suitable for a micro business because it is free.

Key concepts

> **Word-of-mouth** is 'the spreading of information through human interaction alone.'
>
> **Viral marketing** means 'spreading a brand message using word of mouth (or electronically – 'word of mouse') from a few points of dissemination. Typical techniques include using e-mail messages, jokes, web addresses, film clips and games that get forwarded on electronically by recipients.' The classic example is Hotmail, which attaches its marketing message to the foot of every e-mail its users send.
>
> *CIM Glossary:* www.cim.co.uk/cim/ser/html/infQuiGlo.cfm

So how do you get people to talk about you? Here are some suggestions.

(a) **Focus**. The most common mistake made by micro businesses is to leave it unclear to potential clients what it is they actually do. Often this is because the business owners cannot decide themselves what it is they do, so they can hardly expect strangers to remember.

(b) **Know the market**. Many micro business people rely a great deal on intuition and may be reluctant to conduct research, but it will repay many times the effort devoted to it. To reduce risks, improve targeting and to get to know customers' needs and the competition better it is important that the micro business's managers conduct marketing research themselves. Then when they talk about their market they will be taken seriously.

(c) **WATN**. This stands for Walk Around The Neighbourhood: in other words, get out and about, introduce yourself to potential clients, make sure they have your business card. Cheeky, perhaps, but it can be surprisingly effective, even if you only get to talk to the receptionist. If the potential clients are not local people a similar approach can be tried at trade fairs, exhibitions and conferences.

(d) **Personal selling**. Personal selling in the conventional sense depends on getting invited to visit the client, or offering to visit and being accepted. Whether attempts to do this will be successful depends on the nature of the product or service and how carefully the target client's needs have been identified. The owner manager of a micro business will also usually be the company's main salesperson.

7.4.2 Websites

In the initial furore you would often read (in very respectable publications) that the Internet was going to 'level the playing field' between large and small businesses: 'Luigi's Deli' in Clapham High Street could have an online store right next to Harrods, and compete on equal terms ... so it was thought. This is clearly not the case.

A website is an absolute necessity, but not, as many recent start-ups have thought, because the world will instantly come knocking at their door offering vast riches. It is very difficult to achieve high rankings on the major search engines unless you pay them quite substantial sums of money for preferential treatment, probably beyond the pocket of a micro business.

Micro businesses should generally think of their website as the **second point of contact** with potential customers, *after* initial contact has been made by some other promotional means such as a letter (showing the website address in its letterhead) directly to the potential client, or an 'expert article' written in a trade magazine, giving the web address in the credits.

Website design does not need to be state of the art for a micro business (unless the business is web design, of course). The site needs to set out in a focused way exactly what it is that the business does. It should give brief well-informed answers to the sort of questions that a potential customer might ask at an initial meeting, include product descriptions and photos and prices if appropriate, or key information about the skills and qualifications of the staff and their previous experience. Above all it should give **contact information** and make it clear what the potential customer needs to do next if they want to buy. It is a **shop window**, not the entire business, so it should make visitors want to know more.

7.4.3 Conventional promotion for micro businesses

Other promotional possibilities are summarised in the table below.

Technique	Comment
Direct marketing	Direct marketing techniques, either **telemarketing** or **direct mail**, can be done cost effectively. The volume of direct marketing activity can be regulated by the amount of time there is available and by the number of customers the business is trying to reach. Unsolicited **e-mail** (SPAM) is extremely unlikely to generate a response, unless it is an angry or rude one.
Door drops	An alternative method of getting to households is to arrange for **door-to-door leaflet distribution** in your chosen target area. This can be considerably cheaper than incurring postal charges. It is also accurate in that particular districts and types of houses can be targeted.
Public relations	**Press releases** can be issued to the appropriate press (local press, trade magazines). If the business manager is an expert in the field, magazines may welcome **articles** on topics of interest and be willing to display the business name in the credits. Limited **local sponsorship** can be done for relatively little expenditure, for instance a business might consider buying football shirts for a local children's team.
Advertising	**Local media** including free newspapers and local commercial radio stations may be options. Yellow Pages may get good responses if the business does something that people are likely to look up in the phone book and there are not too many competitors. Relevant **trade magazines** are probably the best choice of medium for many micro businesses. Designing advertising and buying media space or airtime, however, can become quite expensive, especially for frequently repeated advertisements.
Sales promotions	It is possible for a business of any size to devise sales promotions. A free or low price introductory consultation is common with many micro consultancy businesses.

Chapter Roundup

- The classic context for marketing is the **FMCG** market where most of the tools and techniques described in this book so far were originally developed. Other contexts require variations in the marketing mix.

- **Business-to-business (B2B) marketing** is concerned with goods and services specifically designed for business use (as well as with ordinary consumer items used in business). Such goods may be of a different standard to consumer goods.

- **Organisational buying decisions** are usually made by groups (the DMU) not individuals and that makes it more difficult to decide what marketing efforts should be made. Other differences are that prices are often negotiated, personal selling is more common, and delivery tends to be direct.

- A **capital project** is a large-scale, very expensive project such as building an office block or a bridge. Public relations is highly important. Pricing is complex and the customer has the last word due to tendering processes. Marketing is relatively under-developed, but there is a strong impetus in the industry to address issues such as branding, project quality and delivery and eliminate cut-throat pricing.

- **Service marketing** is dependent on the distinctive features of services (intangibility, perishability and so on). People and processes are relatively more important compared with marketing of goods, as is personal selling. Important communications issues include providing some tangible evidence and reassuring the customer. Information-based services such as banking can now easily be delivered online.

- In **non profit marketing** communications there is likely to be less money available, messages are likely to be subjected to greater scrutiny and the objectives of the communication will be quite different from those applying in consumer marketing. The major categories of non profit communicators are political parties, social causes, the government, religious bodies and professional bodies.

- **SMEs'** marketing efforts are constrained by limited resources (money, people). Sales support, however, can help to maximise the time the salesperson spends selling, target the best customers and enhance customer satisfaction.

- **Micro businesses** are sometimes assumed to use watered down versions of the marketing tools available to large businesses, but this is only true to a limited extent. Many of the tools are too expensive or simply not relevant. **Word of mouth** marketing is the most important technique. **Websites** are important, but will achieve nothing on their own.

BPP
LEARNING MEDIA

Quick Quiz

1   You are trying to make a list of ways in which products, when bought in a B2B context, are distinct from consumer goods, and you have written the following. What should you have written?

- Irregularity of standards
- Technical values
- High sophistication
- Conformity of purchase

2   I DAB GU is a mnemonic for the members of the DMU (and it also rhymes with DMU!). What does I DAB GU stand for?

3   Draw a diagram showing the relative importance of promotional elements in consumer marketing and B2B marketing.

4   Which of the following is not true?

A   Capital projects are not clearly branded

B   Several of the Ps in the capital project marketing mix may be controlled by the customer

C   Project customers care about the way capital projects contractors treat their staff

D   Companies can ignore public relations issues if a capital project is being carried out for the government

5   What three issues have an impact on capital project pricing?

6   Which of the following is not true of service marketing?

A   The salesperson's attitude to the service may influence the customer

B   Customers are less likely to compare one organisation's price for a service with a competing organisation's price than they would be if they were buying a product

C   Customers perceive service purchases as less risky than product purchases

D   Customers may be influenced by what their friends tell them about an organisation's services

7   What are the charity equivalents of buying and selling?

Buy   ....

Sell   ....

8   Which of the following is not likely to be an objective for a NFP promotion?

A   Persuading givers not to give to competing charities
B   Recruiting volunteers
C   Obtaining funds from large organisations
D   Rewarding employees

9   Sales support aims to maximise (1) m.................. e...................... when (2) r .... are (3) l.............. . Fill in the gaps.

10   If a micro business invests in an impressive website there is no need for other forms of promotion.

True   ☐

False   ☐

Answers to Quick Quiz

1   Irregularity of purchase, Technical sophistication, High order values, Conformity with standards

2   Influencers, Deciders, Approvers, Buyers, Gatekeepers, Users

3

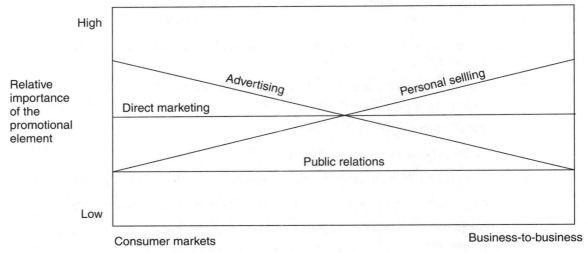

Relative importance of promotional elements

4   D

5   Highly complex costing, penalty clauses, competitive tendering (the client may set the price)

6   C

7   Buy   Give
      Sell   Receive

8   Option A is the only invalid one. An NFP promotion may tempt you to give money to a good cause rather than spend it on something utterly frivolous or harmful to you (eg cigarettes), but it would be quite unethical to try to persuade you to give to one good cause rather than another.

9   Sales support aims to maximise (1) **marketing effectiveness** when (2) **resources** are (3) **limited**.

      If you said marketing **efficiency**, lose a mark! You can be highly efficient and yet completely ineffective. Ideally, be both.

10   False. Micro businesses can spend silly money on impressive web design, but nobody will visit the site, or take it seriously, unless the business engages in other forms of promotion, too.

      Word-of-mouth recommendations are the Holy Grail of marketing for micro businesses. A website is just a convenient shop window.

BPP LEARNING MEDIA

Action Programme Review

1   Your approach to this activity will depend both upon your job and your organisation's structure and processes.

2   This will be a useful source of examples if there is a question in the exam on business-to-business marketing

3   If you researched this really well you should have come up with the following information. These companies worked together to make one of the Seven Wonders of Britain and yet the finished item is called the **British Airways** London Eye. It seems a little unfair!

Checking engineer: Babtie, Allott & Lomax
Architect: Marks Barfield Architects
Construction manager: MACE
Steel design & construction: Hollandia
Capsule design/construction: Poma
Foundation design: Tony Gee & Partners
Foundation construction: Tilbury Douglas
Boarding platform & pier design contractors: Littlehampton Welding
Marine engineer: Beckett Rankine Partnership
Environmental design: Loren Butt Consultancies
Scheme design engineer: Ove Arup & Partners

4   (a)   These were mentioned earlier in this chapter: People, Processes and Physical Evidence. Have a skim read of Chapter 4 if you can't remember.

(b)   Look back at Chapter 5 if you had trouble remembering, and skim read it to check that you could explain the marketing implications if asked.

- **Intangibility**: services cannot be touched or tasted
- **Inseparability**: services cannot be separated from the provider
- **Heterogeneity** (or 'sameness'): the standard of service will vary with each delivery
- **Perishability**: services cannot be stored
- **Ownership**: service purchase does not transfer ownership of property

(c)   Differential pricing or price discrimination is possible in some markets, for example in transport customers are charged more if they travel during the rush hour, and hotels and holiday companies charge more at peak times of year.

5   Security is the major risk. Sensitive accounting or legal data could be intercepted or go to the wrong person in the organisation if sent by e-mail. Some legal documents still need to be original paper documents, physically signed and witnessed by the relevant parties. Some customers simply don't like doing business this way: they value the personal contact and find it reassuring. All customers will get highly frustrated if your website is down when they want to use your service. You, in turn, are at the mercy of your customers' telephone connection.

6   Your own research.

Now try Questions 17, 18 and 19 at the end of the Study Text

10

The global context

Syllabus content

- Explain the global dimension in affecting the nature of marketing undertaken by organisations in an international environmental context (4.4)
- Explain the existing and potential impacts of the virtual marketplace on the pattern of marketing activities in given contexts (4.5)

Introduction

You may remember that we began this Text in a primitive market, where bags of corn were exchanged for sheep. Markets have come a long way since then.

This chapter takes a look at the **international context** of marketing (a topic you will learn much more about in your later studies), and at the **ICT developments** that have done so much to make the 'global marketplace' a reality: the virtual or e-marketplace.

1 The international context

FAST FORWARD

When developing an **international marketing mix**, an organisation will need to decide which aspects can be **standardised** globally, and which must be **adapted** to local conditions.

1.1 A global dimension

Markets are becoming increasingly global, due to facts such as:

(a)   Developments in media and travel which allow people to experience each other's cultures (and brands)

(b)   Trade agreements and de-regulation to facilitate cross-border trading (eg within the EU, between North and South America)

(c)   Developments in ICT (notably the Internet) enabling communication and transactions between widely dispersed parties, enabling e-commerce, strategic alliances and 'virtual' organisations (with workers and call centres all over the globe)

(d)   Political changes creating new markets (eg the opening of Eastern Europe and China)

(e)   The power of multi-national organisations and global brands, lobbying governments and working through the World Trade Organisation to foster conditions conductive to international trade.

On the other hand, international markets have different languages, different cultures, different legal systems, different geo-demographic profiles and so on. And they are further away, of course! Marketers who want to do business with other countries must expect to make minor (or sometimes major) variations in the marketing mix.

 Marketing at Work

For an idea of the issues, you might like to check out sites such as:

www.euromonitor.com   Euromonitor market/country fact files

www.export.gov/exportamerica/MarketBrief   US export briefings on overseas marketing opportunities, by countries

All of the considerations discussed previously in this book may be relevant in the practice of international marketing. There are some factors, however, which have a special significance.

Exam tip

The December 2004 compulsory question asked for five factors in the international environment – and how they would impact on the marketing mix.

In developing an international marketing mix, an organisation will need to decide which aspects can be standardised globally, and which must be adapted to local conditions.

1.2 Product

Products can often be standardised as long as they are not language-sensitive or subject to other foreign constraints (for instance, left- and right-hand drive cars).

International product strategy involves the following possible approaches.

(a) Marketing the same product to all countries (a **global product**) is possible when the products are not culture-sensitive and when economies of scale are significant. It assumes that consumer needs are very similar everywhere or that low prices will prove attractive enough to overcome differences.

(b) **Adapting** the product to local conditions. Keeping the physical form essentially the same in local conditions is very attractive, for obvious reasons, but faces certain dangers.

(c) Developing a **country-specific** product. The physical form of the product is specifically altered for one of a number of different reasons.

Marketing at Work

'ArtMagic E-marketing Consulting Group is a professional **search engine optimizing (SEO)** firm from St.Petersburg, Russia. International customers can consider us as offshore developers so they can benefit from high professional service by inexpensive rates. We provide website positioning services for improving search engine rankings and drive prospects and sales to your company site.

For international customers interested to present their products and services to Russian-speaking audience, we provide web localisation service. This is turnkey service, so you will get a Russian mirror of your corporate web online with no hassle to hire localisers in-house. Your site will be hosted in Russian backbone traffic exchange centre with 10Mbit channels so your Russian visitors will be delighted with the speed of webpage loading. To keep customers up to date with your latest products and services we can provide you with e-mail marketing solutions including writing texts, e-mail engine hosting and management of the mail-list.

Our service is built on the principles of not only putting your business online but bringing you more traffic, leads and of course, sales. This is why long after your website has been designed we continue to work with you providing services such as search engine marketing and web promotion. The way we see it, your success is our success.'

www.e-marketing.spb.ru, 2005

A product developed and successfully marketed within one country cannot necessarily be moved 'as is' into another market without problems. A product is composed of physical qualities and also symbolic and psychological aspects. Cultural, religious, economic, social and political factors must be taken into account in preferences in both areas.

1.2.1 Think global?

Arguments in favour of **product standardisation** include the following.

(a) **Economies of scale**

    (i) *Production*

- Plant is probably confined to one country rather than duplicated
- Plant expansion may attract 'home' government's grants or other support
- Plant used to maximum capacity offers best return on its costs
- Exporting is easier than arranging licensing deals

    (ii) *Research and development*

    Product modification to tailor products to specific foreign markets is costly and time consuming.

    (iii) *Marketing*

    Promotion which can use the same images and themes in advertising is clearly more cost effective. If distribution systems, salesforce training, after-sales provision and other aspects of the product mix can be standardised, this also saves a great deal of money.

(b) **Consumer mobility**. People travel the world more than ever, but it is reassuring to come across familiar products in different countries.

(c) **Technological complexity**. It may not be easy to modify some products to suit the special requirements or conditions found in the foreign marketplace. For example, it may be impossible to create a Chinese language version of an accounting software package without completely redesigning all the screen layouts.

Action Programme 1

Can you name any global brands – products that are the same the world over? Try to think of at least ten.

1.2.2 Think local?

Arguments in favour of **product adaptation** include the following.

(a) **Greater sales** and greater profitability, through meeting customer needs more effectively.

(b) **Differences in local conditions**. These may include:

- Climatic variations (eg corrosion in cars produced for drier climates)

- Literacy or skill levels of potential users

- Cultural, social or religious factors (eg Halal New Zealand lamb for Middle Eastern markets, or dolphin-friendly tuna for Europe and the USA)

(c) **Political factors** may force a company to produce a local product.

- Taxation
- Legislation
- Pressure of public opinion
- Requirement to work through joint ventures with local producers

(d) **Local producers** may already be producing an adapted product that meets the needs of local markets. A new entrant would have to either adapt to compete with this supplier, or undercut the local supplier on price.

1.3 Place

FAST FORWARD

Distribution channels are a key issue. The commonest method is by export, but there are also options to enter into a contract with a foreign organisation or invest in your own facilities in the country in question.

Distribution channels are a key issue for entrants to global markets. Getting the product to the consumer is a major hurdle and presents problems quite different in range and scale from those faced by marketers within a local setting. Here are the options.

- Export goods manufactured locally to the target country

- Transfer the technology and skills necessary to produce and market the goods to an organisation in the foreign country and make licensing/contractual arrangements

- Transfer manufacturing and marketing resources through direct investment in the foreign country

Major **entry modes** are as follows.

Export entry	Indirect
	Direct agent/distributor
Contractual entry	Licensing
	Franchising
Investment entry	Sole venture
	Joint venture

(*F Root*, 1987)

We will look at each in turn.

1.3.1 Export entry

This is the commonest form of export activity, with minimal financial risk involved. It may involve an intermediary (a company 'selling on', after purchasing from the manufacturer), and may be direct or indirect.

Indirect exporting means the firm makes no investment in production or an overseas sales force and relies on the expertise of domestic international middlemen such as export merchants, export agents and co-operative organisations.

Direct exporting involves using foreign-based distributors/agents or setting up operating units in the foreign country in the shape of branches or subsidiaries.

Exporting is suited to:

- SMEs with limited resources
- Markets where there is political risk (eg of civil war, nationalisation)
- Overseas markets that are small
- Overseas markets where there is no pressure for local manufacture

1.3.2 Contractual entry

Licensing involves a firm offering the right to use its technology, know-how, patents, company name or trade marks in exchange for payment.

This is less flexible and harder to control than exporting. A smaller capital outlay is required, however, and it is particularly appropriate when the market is unstable.

Franchising is similar to licensing, in that it grants the right to use the company's name, trademarks and technology. Typically the franchisee receives help in setting up. Service firms are particularly appropriate franchisees (for example, fast food businesses). This is a low cost option which combines local knowledge with entrepreneurial spirit.

1.3.3 Investment entry

Investment entry can take one of two forms

- Joint ventures
- Sole ownership

 Marketing at Work

'Prospective marketing and licensing deals with the Olympics and other sporting and cultural events are attracting Australian companies to China. Elite Sports Properties (ESP), a Melbourne sports management firm, is investigating expansion there through a **partnership** with a big Chinese sports company, China Sports Industry Group (CSI).

'The Chinese sports market is moving from government control to more of a corporate structure. Until recently, all facets of sport, from stadium ownership and team selection to marketing and sponsorship, have been handled by China's Ministry of Sport. Now, many of these functions and assets are being outsourced or privatised.

'ESP plans to break into the Chinese market by securing marketing deals for the 2008 Games and other events, such as the East Asian Games in 2007. It also wants to broker **sponsorship** deals with Chinese companies for the Olympics, and **endorsement** opportunities for Chinese athletes. ESP is also bidding for licensing opportunities for Olympics **merchandise**. The deal would be similar to the one ESP had for the Sydney Games in 2000, when it produced a series of commemorative coins and collectable items.

'Scott Davidson, a director of ESP, says that although the Beijing Games are still years away, negotiations with Chinese businesses can take time. "I started visiting China more than two years ago to start investigating what the market was, like there. In China, business is more relationship-based and the courtship process is extensive."

'ESP also signed a **joint-venture** deal with CSI to co-ordinate the charity Great Wall of China Walkathon in 2005, which begin near Beijing and finished in Shanghai. ESP sought sponsorships from international companies that had recently moved to China or were considering doing so. Davidson said: 'If you are going to be a successful business in China you have to be seen to be contributing to society in some way. So we have decided to try this **charity model** where corporates get to be seen as good corporate citizens.'

J Stensholt, 2004

Joint ventures involve working with one or more foreign firms to produce and market goods in the foreign market. The degree of ownership for the 'home' partner can vary. This approach is increasing in popularity: it avoids quotas and import taxes and satisfies government demands for local production. The outstanding examples are Japanese companies such as Nissan, Mitsubishi and Toyota, which have established joint venture motor manufacturing in the UK and the USA.

Joint ventures have often been used to overcome barriers to entry in international markets. Western companies operating in Eastern Europe and China, for example, often form joint ventures with local partners. One provides technical and managerial expertise and investment, while the local partner provides access to labour and local markets.

Sole ownership involves establishing a manufacturing facility in a host country which then makes its own operating decisions. The parent company provides finance, research and development, product specifications and product technology and retains complete control: there is no shared management.

(a) *Advantages*

- Lower labour costs
- Avoidance of import taxes
- Lower transport costs

(b) *Disadvantages*

- Significant commitment
- Higher involvement levels
- Higher levels of risk

1.4 Promotion

FAST FORWARD

For **promotion**, language is the most important consideration, but there may also be laws or customs that need to be taken into account. The availability or otherwise of different kinds of media will have an impact on advertising.

Marketing communications may need to be adapted in overseas markets.

(a) **Cultural factors** may be an issue. Values, attitudes and behavioural norms vary widely on a range of issues – including significant ones like gender roles, communication styles and humour.

(b) **Language** may be a significant barrier. There is a (possibly mythical) story of Vauxhall cars advertising its Nova brand in South America – where 'no va' (in Spanish) means 'doesn't go/work'.

(c) **Geographical remoteness** should be considered. Can the media actually penetrate to the areas in question?

International marketers would wish to use the same advertising in as many different countries as possible to keep costs down. However there are many factors that favour local adaptation.

- Very localised tastes (eg food and drink)
- Differences in the availability of media
- Problems in translating advertising messages

The general response is to use broadly the same approach but given a 'twist' which customises the campaign for specific audiences.

1.4.1 Media problems

Media problems are likely to relate specifically to the following.

(a) **Availability**. Media may be more important and effective in some countries than in others (for instance, cinema in India, radio in the USA) while there may be a lack of specific media in others.

(b) **Costs** may be very difficult to estimate in many countries, since negotiation and the influence of intermediaries is likely to be much greater. There may also be expectations of gift giving in the negotiation process.

(c) **Coverage of media** (or 'reach' of advertising message). Inaccessible areas may rule out the use of direct mail or posters, scarcity of telephones may rule out this form of advertising promotion. It may also be difficult to monitor advertising effectiveness.

(d)   **Lack of information on the characteristics of the target markets**. Often there is little information on the differences between groups within the population towards which advertising and promotion is being targeted. This is, of course, critical for decisions about the mix to be employed and decisions such as standardisation/ adaptation.

Action Programme 2

There are several TV programmes that show award-winning TV ads from across the world. Try to catch a programme of that type next time you get the chance, and watch out for differences in culture and customs, as captured in advertising.

An alternative would be to buy a foreign language magazine containing lots of advertisements.

1.5 Price

FAST FORWARD

Price is set internationally following the normal criteria (eg costs), but exchange rates and economic conditions are additional factors, especially the level of average income.

The factors outlined in Chapter 6 still apply when making international pricing decisions but there are added complications of **exchange rates**, and different **economic environments**.

For instance, average income in the exporting country may be much higher than in the target country so a straight conversion of the home currency price into the local currency at the prevailing exchange rate might not achieve the marketing objectives. It might turn what is a basic commodity at home into a luxury product in the foreign market.

In each country the factors influencing pricing will differ, so a different pricing policy in each country may be appropriate.

2 The virtual marketplace

FAST FORWARD

Both business-to-business (B2B) marketing and business-to-consumer (B2C) marketing on the **Internet** have progressed beyond the stage where a website is just a shop window or a place of delivery. It is now fairly common to use the Internet for transactions, or e-commerce.

We use the heading 'the virtual marketplace' solely because that is the term used in the syllabus: it is rarely used in practice.

Action Programme 3

The word 'virtual' was widely used in Internet contexts a few years ago, but it is much less used now. Why do you think that has happened?

Internet technology means that you can have a one-to-one conversation with a complete stranger who happens to visit your market stall. You can show off your wares, do a deal, agree terms, take payment, arrange delivery, give after-sales support, encourage repeat purchasing. Well ...so what? Bags of corn and sheep exchanges were like that, weren't they?

BPP
LEARNING MEDIA

The difference is that now you can do this, in real time, with anyone and everyone in the entire world. You can do it 24 hours a day, 7 days a week.

It is a marketing dream, but for many businesses it is becoming more and more of a reality.

- Up until two or three years ago the web was largely **information-orientated**, with business sites simply offering information to help customers choose products or services they might buy over the phone or by visiting a shop.

- Since then many businesses have made moves towards **online transactions**.

Key concepts

> **E-commerce** is typically, the online version of a business process or commercial activity that is already available offline, for instance buying from a supermarket over the Internet instead of physically going to the supermarket.
>
> This is as opposed to **E-business**, which is an entirely new business model that could not exist without the capabilities of the Internet.

This is pretty much the Web as we have described it at various points already in this book, especially in Chapters 4, 7 and 8. At present, in most cases, online transactions are not always integrated with the organisation's 'back-office' systems: this has been seen as difficult, and commercially risky. However, if your customers could do all your order entry and processing for you, then there would clearly be real returns to be made.

Let's describe the 'virtual markets' that can currently be recognised and think about the developments that are likely to come. We are going to look at:

- **B2B**
- **B2C**
- **B2E**
- **G2C**
- **C2C**

2.1 Business-to-business (B2B) on the web

FAST FORWARD

> For most businesses at present the Internet is no more than another payment mechanism – a glorified card-swipe machine – but as technology develops there are more and more opportunities to **integrate online systems** (web servers) with 'back office' systems and get real productivity gains.

A typical business-to-business process is purchasing supplies. In ICT terms this has led to **e-procurement** becoming the initial 'killer application' for 'e' business.

2.1.1 Business exchanges

Key concept

> A **business exchange** is a web-based marketplace where buyers and sellers can meet, communicate their needs and establish business relationships. On most such sites at present commerce is limited to product listings or online auctions in which the transaction is completed offline. The possibilities of what can be done on-line are likely to expand considerably in the future.

The standard model for a business exchange is to gather together the major organisations in a given market sector – let's say, aerospace – and create a market-place of sufficient volume to attract increased numbers of suppliers.

All the participants in the formation of the exchange will ask their existing suppliers to join in, thus creating a supplier pool. If each participant adds their own existing suppliers then all participants will immediately be able to enjoy the benefits of increased choice and competition.

Marketing at Work

Here is a small sample of aerospace exchanges and descriptions of what they do. You may wish to glance at some of the websites.

Airparts.com (Aviation On-Line Network)

Over 35 million **aircraft parts**, and searchable inventory database from leading manufacturers and suppliers worldwide; locates turbine aircraft for sale/lease; also includes a broad array of airline information and links. (www.airparts.com/index.shtml)

e-gatematrix

An B2B marketplace designed to manage all **catering and related services** for the airline and travel-related industries; services include menu design, sourcing and procurement, transportation and distribution, equipment ownership, inventory and distribution, and transaction management. (www.e-gatematrix.com)

eMaintenanceSolutions

A marketplace which links buyers with sellers of aircraft **maintenance** and related services through an online maintenance community. Part of GE Capital Aviation Services. (www.gecas.com/emaintenance.asp)

Enigma, Aerospace

Provider of content-driven, transaction-based B2B e-commerce solutions for the aerospace industry; includes service bulletins, illustrated parts catalogues, engine manuals, and the ability to locate, order, and track parts. (www.enigma.com/industries/aerospace.htm)

FreeMarkets

Creates business-to-business **online auctions** for buyers of industrial parts, raw materials, commodities and services such as injection moulded plastic parts, commercial machinings, metal, chemicals, circuit boards, corrugated packaging and coal. (www.freemarkets.com)

As a start this can work well, but it is unlikely that every business will find all their individual requirements for all aspects of their complex and differentiated businesses within just one exchange.

Our aerospace company may need to buy high-grade aviation fuel and lubricants from another exchange, and employee travel and transport from another. In other words, some areas of an organisation may need access to different, more highly specialised exchanges.

- **Tactical B2B**: items are bought (repeatedly and regularly) from the optimal source for that transaction

- **Strategic B2B**, however, is concerned with specialised, unlikely-to-be-around items, that provide differentiation and competitive advantage and must therefore be obtained in a 'closed' transaction. An example might be a new highly fuel-efficient engine, specially commissioned by British Airways

This suggests that a fully-developed business exchange model will require participation in many open exchanges in the search for the best tactical supply of everyday requirements, and in the creation of a closed exchange for strategic B2B suppliers to cater for items that require in-depth collaboration with the customer.

2.1.2 A fully-developed exchange model

Let's take the motor vehicle industry as a further example, because Covisint is probably the nearest thing yet to a fully developed exchange model. Covisint (www.covisint.com) is a co-operative venture set up in 2000 that now includes many of the major competing car manufacturers (Ford, General Motors, Nissan, Peugeot and so on). The purpose is to create a central marketplace for suppliers of car components.

The motor vehicle industry needs to build what has been sold, not sell what has been built. This may be a familiar theme. But how can an exchange help?

Well, think of the exchange in terms of a **meeting** (arranged and chaired by the car manufacturer) attended by representatives of the car manufacturer and all the suppliers. They sit round a table with the end customer and offer advice and help on the options they could provide.

The various people who have to deliver decide amongst themselves what the individual **business consequences** would be if the customer chooses different options and if they promise to deliver a car in, say, three days.

This particular customer (but also any other customers) can take pleasure in choosing the exact car that meets his or her personal 'value' criteria. And the global motor vehicle industry avoids the consequences of guessing wrongly what customers will want to buy in six month's time.

The latest technological developments mean that what we have described doesn't have to be a physical meeting. It can be an **automated exchange of information** between manufacturers' and suppliers' and customers' computers.

2.1.3 Making complex decisions simple

The mature exchange allows **all members of the supply chain to participate** in the process of satisfying the ultimate end customer, because they will provide, online and interactively, the information that will enable the customer to choose their preferred specifications.

- Although you can already design a car online, after a fashion (try www.ford.co.uk and click on 'want to buy' ... 'build your own'), the information you provide only goes as far as the car manufacturer before further human intervention is required.

- But the latest technology means that the information obtained from the customer is also fed to all members of the supply chain, so that they can immediately get on with fulfilling their part of the transaction.

This open, transparent structure allows buyers and sellers right through the supply chain to understand the totality of what is on offer. It makes complex decisions simple because all the participants have enough information to understand the consequences of choices and the interaction of the whole market.

We need not worry about the details of the underlying technologies that allow this to happen. Suffice to say the technologies have very recently become sufficiently advanced and secure to allow Company A's computer systems and databases to exchange whatever information is needed with Company B's (completely different) computer systems and databases, and with Company C's and Company D's, and so on, whatever type of software or hardware they might use.

Action Programme 4

Can you think of any reasons why allowing customers to design their own products (cars, clothes, etc) online might not be a success?

2.2 Business-to-consumer (B2C) developments

FAST FORWARD

B2C developments are likely to centre around the increasing number of consumer devices that can be used to connect to the web and 'portability' (whether you remain connected when you switch from one device to another).

It is quite a challenge for an organisation to consider offering its IT systems and services on line to other businesses, but at least those other businesses can be held responsible for their employees' behaviour and provide them with any support they need.

It is frightening to consider making the same offer to ordinary consumers, where there is no reassurance at all! Welcoming unknown users directly onto your valuable computer systems in large numbers is a challenge that is only just being addressed.

And security issues aside, how likely is it, in general, that consumers will be sitting at a PC when they decide to purchase something that you sell? They may want to use their mobile phones or interactive TV (iTV), or their Internet Toaster, for that matter.

Why not watch interactive television over breakfast, and then make contact from your mobile on the way to the office, and be able to pick up the thread started on the iTV – whether you were half-way through a news story, or half-way through a mortgage application when you left home?

Exam tip

The December 2002 paper contained a question on how new technology is being used in marketing communications for consumer products and services. Interactive TV, e-mail, SMS and the Internet could all be mentioned – as discussed throughout this Text. Remember, too, that ICT developments have implications for other elements of the marketing mix as well.

Competitive advantage demands that once the consumer logs in, your organisation is constantly available on all the devices. It is unlikely that consumers will enjoy being forced to repeat an identity check process and having to rekey all the mortgage application data, just because they have changed device. This 'portability', too, has become possible through 'cookies' and computer-telephony integration, for example.

 Marketing at Work

'The migration of advertising **from print to online** is an accelerating trend in the US. Now, the same thing seems to be happening in China's fast-growing ad market. With 111 million Internet users on the mainland – typically trend-conscious, young and relatively wealthy – few marketers can resist the lure of the Chinese web. On April 26, Tiffany & Co launched a 557-page site in Chinese to woo the mainland's *nouveaux riches*. Procter & Gamble set up a site pitching its beauty brands Olay, SK-11, and Hugo Boss during the last fall's Shanghai Fashion Week. Last winter General Motors Corp held an online contest to choose the Chinese name of a new Chevrolet compact, giving one of the cars, the Lova, to the winner. Online ad spending has been growing by more than 75% annually for the past three years. Its expected to reach $812m this year and top $1bn in 2007, according to Shanghai-based IResearch.'

B&T, 19 May 2006

2.3 New concepts: B2E, G2C, C2C

FAST FORWARD

The principles of B2B and B2C are being applied to other business models. As developments in technology continue, an increasing number of **e-business models** will appear and the variety in the way the pieces are organised, and the customers and communities addressed will continue to grow.

2.3.1 Business-to-employee (B2E)

Business-to-employee, or B2E, entails developing an organisation's internal (content-based) intranet into a platform for interactive internal work processes. The aim is to create a business model that is structured around internal **value chains** rather than traditional functional activities.

Key concept

> The **value chain** *(M Porter)* models a business as series of inter-linked activities. Some activities are identified as primary activities and others as secondary or support activities.
>
> The primary activities (also called core activities) are related directly to the production/creation of the business's product or service.
>
> The secondary activities (also called non-core, or context activities) provide support to the primary activities.
>
> Traditionally, primary activities are identified by means of functional labels: marketing, operations, in-bound logistics, and so on. Secondary activities typically involve procurement, research and development, management systems, etc.

The technology will also be used to support the **outsourcing** of non-core activities such as car fleet operation, use of corporate credit cards, and so on.

In organisations such as service businesses, where much of the value lies within employees, B2E can be used to offer increased **employee benefits**, for example by linking a request for holiday time to a provider of travel who will offer a special pre-negotiated discount to the employee. This creates a bigger pool of end customers for the travel supplier, therefore justifying a bigger discount to the bulk purchaser (the employer), and it adds benefits for the employees at no extra cost.

2.3.2 Government to citizen (G2C)

G2C offers the promise of 'virtual' services for numerous government-related activities such as voting, benefit payments, car road tax renewals, lodging tax returns and so on.

The challenge is for the Government to be able to make use of the Internet as a communication medium, whilst adding the unique ability to be able to recognise and transact with each individual citizen securely.

The scale of this task is huge. It is likely to have to embrace at least iTV, and mobile phones (possibly more so than PCs) and will probably require the use of the skills and facilities of commercial organisations.

 Marketing at Work

'The Australian Government's website www.business.gov.au has won the United Nations Public Service Award for **e-government**, the only Australian winner of these awards. Established in 1998, www.business.gov.au is a one-stop-shop for business information and advice, providing practical information ranging from starting up to growing business. It also provides business tools such as ABN (Australian Business Number) Lookup and Transaction Manager, which cuts red tape and speeds up transactions. In 2005, www.business.gov.au received 2.1 million visits, an increase of 12 per cent on the previous year.'

Daily Telegraph (Sydney, Australia) 30 May 2006

2.3.3 Consumer to consumer (C2C)

Early examples of C2C include the very successful **e-Bay** site, which allows consumers to sell and buy articles directly to and from other consumers by means of **online auctions**.

Other examples include a variety of **on-line communities** (such as www.bookcrossing.com) and discussion groups, and 'virtual' clubs and meetings (including online study groups) and web logs ('blogs') or web diaries.

Consumer to consumer dealings, such as auctions, are highly popular and could undermine the marketers control of pricing issues and (via word of mouth) create some promotional issues.

Chapter Roundup

- When developing an **international marketing mix**, an organisation will need to decide which aspects can be **standardised** globally, and which must be **adapted** to local conditions.

- Products can often be **standardised** as long as they are not language-sensitive or subject to other foreign constraints (for instance, left- and right-hand drive cars).

- **Distribution channels** are a key issue. The commonest method is by export, but there are also options to enter into a contract with a foreign organisation or invest in your own facilities in the country in question.

- For **promotion language** is the most important consideration, but there may also be **laws** or **customs** that need to be taken into account. The availability or otherwise of different kinds of media will have an impact on advertising.

- **Price** is set internationally following the normal criteria (eg costs), but exchange rates and economic conditions are additional factors, especially the level of average income.

- Both business-to-business (B2B) marketing and business-to-consumer (B2C) marketing on the **Internet** have progressed beyond the stage where a website is just a shop window or a place of delivery. It s now fairly common to use the Internet for transactions.

- For most businesses at present the Internet is no more than another payment mechanism – a glorified card-swipe machine – but as technology develops there are more and more opportunities to **integrate online systems** (web servers) with 'back office' systems and get real productivity gains.

- **B2C** developments are likely to centre around the increasing number of consumer devices that can be used to connect to the web and 'portability' (whether you remain connected when you switch from one device to another).

- The principles of B2B and B2C are being applied to other business models. As developments in technology continue, an increasing number of **e-business models** will appear and the variety in the way the pieces are organised, and the customers and communities addressed will continue to grow.

BPP
LEARNING MEDIA

Quick Quiz

1 What are three arguments in favour of product standardisation?

E...

C...

T...

2 Which is the following is a suitable scenario for exporting?

A   The target country is politically stable
B   The target overseas market is very large
C   When you are a SME with limited resources
D   The target market is highly competitive

3 What is the single most important factor when considering whether a marketing message should be adapted for audiences in target countries?

4 Why does an e-commerce transaction not update an organisation's back office systems, in normal circumstances?

5 Business-to-employee developments may help to improve many internal aspects of an organisation including:

W..................... P.....................

E.....................B.....................

6 Consumer-to-consumer developments may have an impact on the marketer's control of:

P...................

W.......... O........... M...............

Answers to Quick Quiz

1 Economies of scale
Consumer mobility
Technological complexity

2 C

3 We didn't actually spell this out in the body of this chapter, but hopefully you realised the answer is whether the target audience will understand the language that the message is spoken in or written in.

4 The practical answer is because (as of today, at least), it would be highly insecure to allow this to happen. A malicious or careless user could do untold damage to your computer systems if this were allowed. (A techy answer is that the transaction is between the user's computer at home and the organisation's public web server –.organisations are most unlikely to run their precious accounting and marketing systems on a public web server.)

5 Work Processes; Employee Benefits

6 Price (because of auctions); Word-of-Mouth (because they may talk about your organisation behind your back).

Action Programme Review

1   Here is the top 20 according to some recent research. Were any of these on your list?

1	COCA-COLA	11	FORD
2	MICROSOFT	12	TOYOTA
3	IBM	13	CITIBANK
4	GE	14	HEWLETT-PACKARD
5	INTEL	15	AMERICAN EXPRESS
6	NOKIA	16	CISCO
7	DISNEY	17	AT&T
8	MCDONALD'S	18	HONDA
9	MARLBORO	19	GILLETTE
10	MERCEDES	20	BMW

2   This may seem like a frivolous task, but watching such programmes will highlight cultural variations such as language, social systems, and maybe even religious differences.

3   Probably because 'virtual' has connotations of not being real. That may be fine for unashamed fantasy 'virtual reality' products (experience a space trip to Alpha Centauri; get intimate with your favourite movie star, etc).

However, if your online guarantee is that you can deliver a box of two dozen widgets by lunchtime tomorrow the last thing you want your potential customers to believe is that it is only a 'virtual' guarantee.

4   The real issue is whether customers actually want to do it online. Many people that buy cars or clothes still don't like computers, and perhaps don't trust online dealings. (Confidence is gradually rising, but a critical mass is not going to be reached in most countries for some time yet.) Many car-buyers would not even consider buying a car unless they could sit in it and test drive it: are they supposed to part with their money before the custom assembly has even been started? As for clothes, although buying from catalogues has been common for years, the item supplied is not custom made, so it does not much matter to the manufacturer if it is returned. If a clothes item has been cut to the precise measurements of an individual it is unlikely to fit other individuals, so what if a customer wants to return a clothing item they designed themselves?

Now try Questions 20 and 21 at the end of the Study Text

BPP)))
LEARNING MEDIA

Question and Answer Bank

1 Marketing orientation

How does marketing orientation differ from product orientation?

2 Objectives, strategies and control

Using a product of your choice, distinguish between objectives, strategies and control as key elements in the annual marketing plan.

3 Marketing planning process

(a) What is a SWOT analysis and how does it lead to an understanding of realistic market opportunities?   **(8 marks)**

(b) Explain the importance of marketing planning for a new consumer product to be launched in your country.   **(4 marks)**

(c) Using examples, identify the main steps involved in the marketing planning process.   **(8 marks)**

(20 marks)

4 Segmentation

Using a consumer *and* an industrial product or service by way of comparison, list and justify sets of segmentation bases for each of these.

5 Marketing research

(a) Explain what is meant by secondary research and why it is often important to conduct secondary research before primary research is undertaken   **(12 marks)**

(b) Identify how the use of information technology could assist in the marketing research process for a product or service of your choice.   **(8 marks)**

(20 marks)

6 Marketing planning process

What do you understand by the following concepts which are used in the marketing planning process?

(a) Market segmentation
(b) Targeting
(c) Positioning

7 The marketing mix

What are the elements of the marketing mix? Outline some of the factors to be considered for a company to arrive at an appropriate marketing mix.

8 Services marketing

What are the distinctive features of services marketing? Why are they becoming more important for marketing in general?

9 Life cycle concept

You work for a company which manufactures prestigious luxury cars. There is a range of models currently in production - some models have been in production since 1981 and one which has just been launched. The marketing planning manager is reconsidering the use of product life cycle analysis when making strategic decisions about each model.

You have been invited to submit a memo to the marketing planning manager covering the following.

(a)   The application and usefulness of the product life cycle concept for decision-making.   **(10 marks)**

(b)   The limitations of product life cycle analysis.   **(10 marks)**

(20 marks)

10 Pricing

Write brief notes on the following.

(a)   Cost plus pricing
(b)   Market skimming pricing
(c)   Marginal cost pricing
(d)   Market penetration pricing

11 Pricing policy

Construct a report to marketing management that explains the factors that should be taken into consideration when pricing for a product line.

12 Distribution

Distinguish between selective, intensive and exclusive methods of distribution.

13 Physical distribution and marketing

The company in which you work is considering the idea that physical distribution should become a component part of marketing, rather than being the final delivery part of the production process. Your Line Manager has asked you to prepare a report for the board of directors outlining how such an arrangement might improve service to customers.

14 Promotional campaign

(a)   Using a consumer product or service of your choice, identify and comment upon each stage involved in planning a promotional campaign.

(b)   Why might the selection of promotional tools differ for a campaign for an industrial product?

BPP
LEARNING MEDIA

15 Sales promotion

As promotions manager of a well established UK manufacturer of women's beauty products, explain how you would use sales promotion to support the national launch of 'Chico'. This is a new fragrance targeted at B, C1, 18-45, experimentally-minded women who are prepared to try a new perfume.

16 Pull techniques

Prepare notes for presentation to general management that describe a range of typical promotional 'pull' techniques that can be employed in order to reach a target audience.

17 Relevant marketing mix

Indicate the main characteristics of marketing mixes which would be appropriate for any **two** of the following.

(a)   A large banking group
(b)   A company that manufactures electronic components for computer manufacturers
(c)   A car manufacturer
(d)   A road haulage company

Include in your answer the relevant justification.

18 Marketing concept

(a)   Explain and identify both:

    (i)   A business-to-business organisation

    (ii)   A non-profit organisation

    which, in your opinion, have been successful in the adoption of the marketing concept. Give specific reasons to justify your choices.   **(12 marks)**

(b)   Explain how the use of Information Technology could assist in the management of a customer oriented culture within one of the above organisations.   **(8 marks)**

                                                                                (20 marks)

19 Relationship marketing

You are working for a car dealership and are considering the current database of people who have purchased new cars during the last two years.

(a)   Explain how this database could be used to help to build relationships with past customers.
                                                                                (10 marks)

(b)   Explain why it is important to consider relationship marketing management for the retention of customers.   **(10 marks)**

                                                                                (20 marks)

20 E-commerce

What is e-commerce? Why is it becoming increasingly important for businesses?

21 Interflora worldwide flower deliveries

Interflora is a non-profit making Trade Association owned by its members who are independent floristry businesses located throughout the world. These members are able to vote on issues at regional meetings and an Annual General Meeting. The aims of the Interflora organisation are encompassed in the mission statement:

'Our mission is to ensure that Interflora will always be the consumer's first choice for flowers and appropriate gifts. This means: recognising and responding to our customers' changing needs; providing a seamless service to our customers; leading our industry in innovation and design; continual improvement in quality, service, processes and costs and enabling our employees and associates to give their best.'

The Interflora organisation consists of 58,000 florists worldwide delivering flowers to 146 countries – each and every one maintaining the stringent standards that Interflora demands. From China to Russia, the USA to Europe, Interflora is able to deliver 'an expression of your thoughts through the most beautiful flowers imaginable.'

Starting with a fresh and original idea, Interflora grew into the world's largest and most popular flower delivery network. Today, the organisation boasts that no one can compete with its combination of creativity, experience and guaranteed quality.

The wide product range includes bouquets, hand-tied flowers, planted arrangements, floral arrangements, cut flowers, and unusual tailor-made floral gifts. Customers purchase their products for a variety of special occasions such as tokens of love, sympathy tributes, birthdays, new births, anniversaries and many others.

A customer selects and pays for a flower order in one of the participating florists who are members of Interflora. The order is then communicated electronically to the nearest convenient Interflora member who makes it up and delivers it to the destination required by the customer (which may be to any place in the world). Interflora uses only floristry businesses that meet stringent criteria such as good shop image, qualified staff, good variety and quality of stocks.

Interflora's trademark depicting the Roman God Mercury, is one of the most recognised trademarks and symbols of quality and service in the world, and which forms a common bond between the worldwide network of florists. The Interflora service is known by different trading names in some parts of the world, such as 'Fleurop' in parts of Europe and 'FTD' in America, Canada and Japan. The name 'Interflora' is used in the UK, Ireland and some other countries.

<u>Source: Adapted from the Interflora website</u>

The Directors of Interflora have approached your marketing agency and require specific advice for improving levels of customer service. They realise that customer retention and sound customer care are crucial in today's marketplace and that a more targeted promotional campaign may help to achieve increased awareness throughout the world.

Therefore, you are to write a report which:

(a) Explains the practical approaches which the organisation should consider to improve the standards of customer care and customer satisfaction across the participating florists. **(15 marks)**

(b) Comments on how the three elements of the extended marketing mix, relating specifically to people, process and physical evidence, could be developed for this service. **(15 marks)**

(c) Identify and briefly describe the major promotional methods that could be included within a campaign to raise the awareness of Interflora's products and service within your own country.

(10 marks)

(40 marks)

1 Marketing orientation

Product orientation as a business philosophy can take two forms, **product orientation** and **sales orientation**.

Product orientation

In the last half of the nineteenth and the beginning of the twentieth century business was mainly production oriented. Demand for new products was high, due to the mass production methods that reduced prices and increased output. The products that were produced and the prices paid for them depended on the production methods and raw materials that were available. Typical of this ethos is Henry Ford's statement 'you can have any car you like as long as it is black'.

A production orientation looks at **what the company can produce**, rather than what the customer wishes to purchase. Promotion is not considered to be of great importance. Good quality products are supposed to 'sell themselves', and if they do not this is usually blamed on the sales staff or on the customers themselves! Improvements are concentrated on the productive efficiency of the company. Senior management in this type of company often have production backgrounds. If **demand is buoyant** this approach can be reasonably successful, but can be difficult to sustain in the long run. Some firms still are production oriented, for example some **high technology** industries.

Sales orientation

Sales oriented companies are also basically product oriented. In the 1920s and 1930s the downturn in economic activities made firms realise they did not face an insatiable demand for their products and products do not simply sell themselves. Promotional activities came to be of more importance than under a production orientation but the main focus in a sales oriented business is selling the products that have been produced. Again the products and sales figures are important rather than any aspect of customer satisfaction.

Companies which are sales oriented are often typified by 'hard sell' tactics. Examples still occur of sales oriented companies, especially in home improvements or insurance sectors. It should be remembered that selling is an important function of the marketing mix. The basic assumption of a selling orientation is that customers will not seek out your products and they actually have to be sold to them, which is closer to a market orientation than a production orientation. However, a selling orientation does not build brand loyalty and is a rather short-term vision of the market place.

Marketing orientation

Marketing orientation is often called **customer orientation**. Instead of products and the selling of products being of central importance, the consumer is the focus of the marketing oriented firm. This takes a longer term view of business and profitability. A marketing oriented company sets out to **define what the customer actually wants,** and then produces goods that fill those wants. Companies then make what customers want to buy, rather than produce what they are good at or have traditionally supplied.

To be truly marketing oriented the firm should practice consumer orientation at all levels and within all functions of the organisation. This means that from Managing Director to shop floor workers all staff should have the customer in mind. Marketing should not simply be a functional department that organises the promotional aspects of the firm, rather it should be practised as a philosophy by all departments whether they be finance, production or marketing. This will change the objectives of all departments: for example, if the production department is customer oriented it may only produce short runs of certain products, whereas from a purely production point of view, it might prefer longer runs.

Change to marketing orientation

The organisational changes necessary for a company to move from being product oriented to marketing oriented are difficult for companies to make because they are not simply bureaucratic but require retraining and reorganisation at all levels. Usually a would-be marketing oriented firm has a marketing director high up in the organisation's hierarchy, but this must be more than a token gesture if a true marketing orientation is to be achieved.

Within a customer oriented firm there is a great need for **marketing research,** as this is the main way in which customer needs are identified. These needs may not simply be the obvious need that the product fills, but the less obvious needs that encompass the total product offering. For example, a car fulfils the need for transportation but there are many more personal and social needs that are filled by the particular model of car.

Markets are dynamic. Customer orientation means that these changes can be monitored and perhaps acted upon before the competition. Customer orientation also fosters the idea of **brand loyalty**. If you are satisfying customer needs, and are monitoring those needs for changes, then customers are less likely to go elsewhere for products. A marketing orientation takes a much longer-term view of business than a product orientation.

Societal marketing

Recently there has been an interest in what has been termed societal marketing. What the customer wants may not be in his best interest in the long run (eg smoking) or in society's best interest. Societal marketing aims to move from a simple marketing orientation to one that assesses the **environmental and long-term consumer interest**. In practice, of course, this is unlikely to make much headway unless backed by government legislation, but in the UK the Body Shop is one example of a company whose marketing orientation has a strong societal bias.

Conclusion

A product orientation makes the needs of the producer central, but marketing orientation makes the consumer central. For a company to be truly marketing oriented it should adopt a marketing orientation throughout the whole organisation and not simply treat it as a divisional role.

2 Objectives, strategies and control

The product chosen to illustrate the annual marketing plan is washing powder.

The annual marketing plan is the operational plan that is based on the longer-term strategic marketing plan. Annual plans explain the way in which the company is aiming for the objectives of the strategic marketing plan. There are a number of reasons **why it is important to formulate annual marketing plans**.

(a)   They explain what the **present situation** is and **what is expected** in the year ahead

(b)   They indicate the **resources that are necessary** to fulfil the objectives

(c)   They **specify expectations** so that the company can anticipate where it will be in a year's time

(d)   They describe the **course of action** over the next year

(e)   They allow performance to be monitored

The basic marketing planning process can be shown in diagrammatic form.

The annual marketing plan

BPP
LEARNING MEDIA

Here, we will concentrate on three areas of the planning process using washing powder as an example.

Objectives

Objectives in the annual plan concentrate on product rather than strategic applications. The **SWOT** (strengths and weaknesses/opportunities and threats) analysis would indicate a number of implications for the washing powder manufacturer. There may be a new competitor in the market, or new product attributes sought by the consumer, for example more environmentally 'friendly' powders.

The objectives for the brand of washing powder over the next year can now be defined. One could be to improve **market share** by a certain percentage, but with a new competitor the company might be pleased if it maintains market share for this year. A certain **sales volume** may be specified depending, of course, on the company's assessment of opportunities in the market. **Profits** will be another objective of the company and are often stated in terms of return on investment (net profits divided by total investment). The company may have to decide whether the **return on investment** is substantial enough, or whether it could do better investing elsewhere. The annual marketing plan should also set objectives for the **marketing mix variables**. These objectives are necessary in order to satisfy the broader objectives of market share etc. For example, if the washing powder manufacturer wishes to increase market share by 5% over the year, then this will have implications for the marketing mix objectives. Promotional effort will probably have to be increased in order to take market share from other companies, as there would be few new users to target.

Strategy

There are many levels in the organisation where strategies can be developed. **Corporate strategy** deals with the overall development of an organisation's business activities whilst **marketing strategy** looks at the organisation's activities in the markets served. This can be long term or short term as in the case of annual marketing planning. Going back to the above model, when product objectives have been formulated then the marketing strategy that should allow these objectives to be met can be developed. There may be refinements to be made as to the target market the company is aiming for.

Perhaps the washing powder brand has slipped downmarket over time. A decision has to be made whether to fully address this target market or to reposition the powder. Marketing mix variables can then be developed to accomplish these objectives. If the objective is to increase sales by a certain percentage then a promotion of a money off coupon may be used to increase sales. If the objective is to build brand awareness then an extensive advertising campaign can be used. Different objectives will have different implications for the marketing mix strategy that is most appropriate.

Control

The purpose of control of the annual marketing plan is to examine **whether the objectives have been achieved**. Control of marketing planning should not simply be left to the end of the year evaluation of the success of the product, but be reviewed throughout the year. The results of evaluation and control should be included in the formulation of the annual plan in the following year.

If sales of the washing powder are below those that were indicated in the objectives then reasons for this should be analysed. It may be that during the year the introduction of liquid detergents for washing clothes and heavy promotion of these products detracted from the company's brand. In this case a decision should be made whether to sit back and see if this was just a short-term phenomenon or whether to promote the powder aggressively. One way in which control can be managed by a company is through '**management by objectives**'. Management set short-term goals (monthly or quarterly), performance against these goals is analysed, and if these are not met then the reasons are analysed and corrective action taken. Usually sales analysis, market share analysis, marketing expenses to sales analysis, financial analysis and customer attitudes are used to control the annual marketing plan. The main responsibility for annual marketing plan control is with top or middle management.

3 Marketing planning process

(a)   A **SWOT analysis** identifies the strengths and weaknesses of the organisation relative to the opportunities and threats it faces in its marketing environment. The SWOT analysis leads to an understanding of **realistic market opportunities** through the process of a detailed **marketing audit**, covering market and environment analysis, competitor and supplier analysis, customer analysis and internal analysis.

This analysis will highlight potential market gaps, new customer needs, marketing channel developments, competitor strategies and their strengths and weaknesses. The organisation can evaluate market opportunities against its strengths and weaknesses and identified threats and determine what actions to take to exploit the opportunity.

(b)   To successfully launch a new customer product into the UK market the organisation needs to have clear and realistic **objectives**, and identification and understanding of its **target market segment**. Its channel of distribution, branding, packaging and communications activity need to be in place to support the launch. Forecasts of future demand, and return on investment need to be assessed and projected.

A formalised **marketing planning system** that involves all departments, customers, agents and suppliers, the complexity and timing of activities is required to support the launch to prevent lack of coordination, resource and ultimate failure. A **monitoring system** is also required to evaluate the effectiveness of the launch and take actions as required. A successful launch requires a planning process that pulls all the people and activities together, co-ordinates what is done, by who, when and with what resource.

(c)   Marketing planning involves the following stages.

Market analysis

Objective setting

Strategy development

Implementation

Evaluation and control

(i)   **Market analysis**. This phase involves establishing an audit process that assesses the macro and micro market environment, market segment analysis, customers, competitors and development strategy. Without a clear understanding of these issues it is difficult to set objectives and develop strategy.

(ii)   **Objective setting**. Once the issues arising from market analysis have been understood, objectives can be set. Objectives should be consistent with the overall mission of the organisation and goals, and they must be realistic.

(iii)   **Strategy development**. This phase can begin once the objectives have been agreed. In this process alternative strategic options will be evaluated to determine the best way forward for the organisation. Strategy evaluation should consider the organisation's current strengths and weaknesses, market attractiveness, resource requirements, and profitability.

(iv) **Implementation**. This is frequently the hardest part of the marketing planning process. Effective implementation requires co-ordination between different organisations, people and departments. An organisation structure and culture that supports this co-ordination, good communication and access to information and appropriate levels of resources. In reality, many issues, conflicts and trade offs occur within organisations that act as barriers to effective implementation.

(v) **Evaluation and control**. The final phase of the process involves setting an effective system of monitoring and control to measure and evaluate performance.

4 Segmentation

Firstly, you need to identify the objectives of using segmentation as a prelude to suggesting the basis of segmentation of a consumer product.

The role of segmentation in marketing strategy is as follows.

(a) To divide the total market into targetable, profitable groupings to whom promotional mixes can be addressed.

(b) To position the firm's product against clearly identified market segments.

There are two approaches to identifying customer groupings.

(a) Market segmentation through an analysis of the **characteristics of the customer**.

(b) Market segmentation through an analysis of the **response of the customer**.

Whether the firm is offering a consumer or industrial product to the market, for a strategy of market segmentation to be successful a number of requirements need to be met.

(a) For a segment to be viable, it must be **distinguishable** from other segments. At the same time the customers within each segment must have a high degree of similarity on the criteria adopted for segmentation. It follows that on the aggregate level customers must be different in some other dimensions, thus allowing segments to be isolated within the overall market.

(b) The criteria used to differentiate between customer groupings (market segments) must be **relevant to the purchase situation**. These criteria should be related to differences in market demand.

(c) The segment must be of sufficient potential **size** to ensure that any marketing investment made within it will result in an adequate return.

(d) An identified market segment can only be exploited if it can be **reached**. It must be possible to direct a separate marketing strategy to each segment. This means that the customers within each segment will respond to differing promotional tools and will have differing buying behavioural attributes (true within consumer markets and across the industrial/consumer market divisions). They will also respond differently to pricing strategies, to personal selling and will have different expectations of the product, and different product benefit needs.

Bases for segmentation of a consumer product

(a) **Age**: people buy different products at different times during their own life cycle.

(b) **Sex**: some products are particularly required by females, others by males.

(c) **Family size**: some products, eg large cars and caravans, are more suited to the needs of large families than to couples or individuals.

(d) **Family life cycles**: the stage of development of the family will influence what families want and what families do. Products are developed to satisfy these needs.

(e) **Social class**: one's place in the 'social strata' will determine in part product needs, eg type of holiday taken, hobbies and interests followed.

(f) **Geo-demographic factors** (eg ACORN classification): how much earning potential people have, and where they live can influence the types of products and services they are willing to pay for. Firms should only therefore segment against effective demand.

(g) **Education**: the complexity of the consumer in terms of his mindset, thinking and educational background will influence purchase decisions, the newspapers he reads and his responsiveness to promotional effort.

(h) **Benefit/lifestyle segmentation**: consumers can be segmented against the kinds of benefits they seek (how they will use them and what they wish products and services to provide) from the products and services they are willing to pay for. For example, financial services: some people want security, others return on investment, others insurance against life threatening illness, theft or fire.

(i) **Loyalty status**: consumers can be segmented against their acceptability to branding and the degree to which they are likely to stay loyal to the brand or the firm once committed. For example, those people who will 'always buy Nescafé' or those who will always 'buy Ford cars' or 'shop at Marks & Spencer'.

Bases for segmentation of an industrial product or service

(a) **Size of firms**. Some products or services may only be useful to firms of a specific size (eg specific manufacturing plant).

(b) **Type of industry**. Some products or services may be industry specific and not used outside that industry.

(c) **Geographical region**. Some firms may find their markets being highly concentrated into specific areas where there are a large number of similarly characterised firms, all of whom are likely to want similar products and services.

(d) **Type of buying organisation**. Some firms may want to focus their selling activities towards centralised buyers – units which buy for the whole firm, thus larger sales become possible, rather than towards decentralised buyers who must be approached individually.

(e) **The use of the end product being marketed**. Where products have a multi-use, some firms may prefer to target such buyers in the hope of gaining sales of related products.

5 Marketing research

INTERNAL MEMORANDUM

To: Mr R Hudson-Davies, Marketing Manager
From: R H Roper, Marketing Executive
Date: 7th December 20XX

Subject: Marketing Research- The Importance of Secondary Research and the Role of IT in the Marketing Research Process

(a) As you are aware we are currently planning our next phase of research for our newly developed casual shoe which we plan to bring to the market within the next year. Therefore, I feel it is important that we look at the role of secondary research and more specifically the use of information technology in the process of collecting, analysing and presenting the data collected.

However, before we can consider the primary phase of the research it will be necessary to consider the role of secondary research and why we should conduct this type of research before we embark on the more expensive primary phase.

Secondary research

This is the collection of information which has been already gathered for a particular purpose and has been previously published.

There are two types of **secondary research** sources – internal and external to the organisation.

Internal sources of data could be used to consider the current market place. Internal databases can be used to assess the current sales figures for our existing casual shoe sales from our intermediaries. Information about market needs and trends is usually held within our organisation's marketing intelligence system supported by our sales teams.

External sources relates to collection of information from outside the organisation. Information which has been gathered by the Government such as social trends gives information about lifestyles and leisure activities. The state of the economy can be gathered from the Office of National Statistics which will be important for us to consider in relation to disposable income etc. The Census and population figures will allow us to identify the demographics of the country and identify the size of the potential market.

Market reports which have been researched by agencies, such as Mintel and Keynote, usually provide excellent market intelligence and are now available on the Internet. Journals and newspapers also offer a good range of information about certain issues at the industry and company level.

Secondary research is important to complete prior to devising the primary stage of the research. This is due to that fact that it may provide all the answers required and therefore negate the need to undertake primary research. Secondary research can be more economical than primary research due to the ease of collection and analysis. It also helps in the design of the research instrument and may identify areas which need to be presented by field research.

(b) **Use of information technology in marketing research**

The use of developed information technology can now be considered for collecting Secondary data because most governments publish their reports on the Internet, business reports are also available online and often via CD Roms. Competitors' websites can be interrogated with the use of search engines to collate information in a format determined by the user.

Primary data can be collected via observational scanning equipment at the retail outlet and home for panel members of a marketing research agency. Interactive digital television will also allow the researcher to gather additional information directly from respondents. These types of data collection methods are known at **quantitative** as they usually be statistically analysed.

However, IT can also be employed in collecting **qualitative** information. Examples of this approach could involve the use of chat rooms and online focus groups with webcams etc. There are now also a number of computer packages which can analyse qualitative data.

Analysis of information is another important area where IT can help the researcher. The use of computer software to analyse data with such packages as Windows packages (ie SPSS, Excel), can be used to statistically evaluate quantitative data. Indeed, online questionnaires are often set up with a database for responses which can be immediately analysed as soon as the respondents reply.

The **presentation of data** can be vastly enhanced with the use of quite sophisticated IT packages that are linked to the databases used for analysis

Therefore, it can be seen that IT is able to vastly assist in the market research process, from the collection of data, analysis of data to the presentation of data. The use of IT can ensure a high degree of accuracy and credibility of the completed market research report.

6 Marketing planning process

(a) Market segmentation is the subdividing of a market into distinct subsets of customers, where any subset may conceivably be selected as a target market to be reached with a distinct marketing mix.

(Kotler)

The primary reason for market segmentation is to identify within markets distinct groups of people with similar needs, characteristics or behaviours that can be targeted with an appropriate marketing mix. Customers benefit because they are supplied with products and services that more closely relate to their requirements and organisations benefit in terms of improved competitiveness, more efficient use of marketing resource and the potential to identify new market opportunities.

Consumer segment variables	Industrial segment variables
Demographic	Organisational characteristics
Socio- economic	Regional
Lifestyle	Product/service application
Attitudes/motives	Benefits sought
Geodemographic	Complexity of DMU/purchasing policy
Benefits sought	Nature of business relationship

(b) Targeting is the evaluation and selection of market segments that offer the best potential and ideally best fit the capabilities of the organisation. Marketing activity can be tailored to the target segments selected.

There are three broad approaches to targeting which demonstrate the extent to which markets can be broken down and strategies for reaching them.

(i) **Undifferentiated strategy**

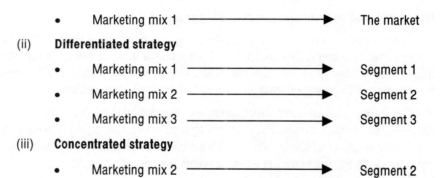

- Marketing mix 1 ⟶ The market

(ii) **Differentiated strategy**

- Marketing mix 1 ⟶ Segment 1
- Marketing mix 2 ⟶ Segment 2
- Marketing mix 3 ⟶ Segment 3

(iii) **Concentrated strategy**

- Marketing mix 2 ⟶ Segment 2

Undifferentiated strategies assume that the market is one homogeneous mass with no significant differences. The marketing of the Lottery is to some extent based upon this targeting strategy.

Differentiated strategies assume that the market can be broken down into segments each with distinct characteristics and needs. Products and marketing activity are developed that target these distinct segments. Organisations such as Procter and Gamble use such multi segment/multi product strategies to compete in the FMCG market.

Concentrated strategies is the most focused approach of the three and involves specialising in serving one specific segment. An example of a concentrated strategy is The Travel Lodge hotel chain who focus upon the company representative who uses his car as a primary form of transport and needs comfortable low cost accommodation close to main motorway and A road networks.

BPP
LEARNING MEDIA

Targeting also involves evaluation and selection of segments. Many potential segments may be identified but only certain segments may be worth exploiting. The common criteria given for evaluating market segments include:

- Segment size
- Segment profitability
- Competitor activity
- Growth potential
- Access to segment

The most attractive segments can then be evaluated in terms of the organisation's capability to serve the segment.

(c) Positioning is the perceived attributes, feelings and emotions that a customer attaches to a product or service in their mind. Positioning of products and services can be managed by marketers through their marketing activity.

Positioning is the way the product is defined by consumers on important attributes. It is the place the product occupies in the consumers' mind relative to competing products. Consumers position products with or without help from marketers. It is the role of marketing to ensure that the product is strongly and clearly positioned to give them the best advantage in a crowded and competitive marketplace.

Marketers can position products using several alternative dimensions.

- Product attributes
- Usage occasions
- Types of users
- By activity
- Emotional criteria

These criteria are often used to develop positioning maps.

Positioning map for newspapers

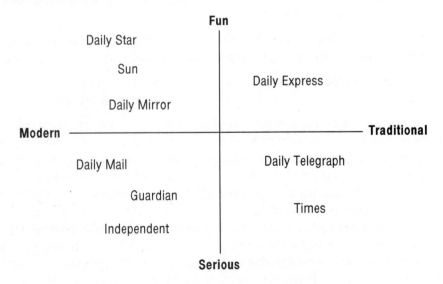

Positioning is a critical part of the market segmentation process. Brands that have been successfully positioned include Renault Clio, Mercedes, Heinz and Lucozade. Brands that have not managed the positioning as well in recent years include Levis, Marks & Spencers and Cross & Blackwell. Attention must therefore be paid to identifying exactly what these brands stand for and promise to deliver. This must be clearly communicated via strong advertising and promotions to ensure a strong positioning in the consumers' mind.

7 The marketing mix

A company's marketing mix includes all the tools that come under the organisation's control to affect the way products and services are offered to the market. Borden coined the phrase 'the marketing mix' from the idea that business executives were mixers of ingredients. From observing industries and individual firms it can be seen that there are wide ranging applications of the tools of marketing. The elements of the marketing mix are often described as the 'four Ps', Product, Price, Place and Promotion. It includes all the policies and procedures involved in each of these elements. This can be on a strategic level: for instance, whether to adopt a penetration or skimming pricing policy for a new product. It can also be on a more tactical level, for instance special price discounts. Each element is looked into in more detail below.

Product

Decisions to be made regarding products include the product lines that are produced, product improvements, new product development and which market(s) to sell them in, including whether to adopt a market segmentation approach.

Pricing

Decisions include the appropriate price level to adopt, the specific prices, price strategy for new products and price variations.

Place

The 'place' aspect of the four Ps is often also called 'channels of distribution'. This includes the way in which goods are passed from the manufacturer to the final consumer.

Promotion

Promotional aspects include personal selling, advertising, publicity and sales promotions. Each of these must be looked into to give an overall consistent message to the public. For example, it is not good to stress service quality in advertising if the actual personal selling of the organisation is not of high calibre. Decisions have to be made on the amount of time and money spent, media selection, desired image and length of campaign.

This is obviously not an exhaustive list. Some elements of the marketing mix do not easily fall exclusively into one category. Packaging, for example, has promotional aspects and product aspects.

There are many factors that come into play when the organisation is considering the most appropriate marketing mix. Some of these are market forces and some are product specific.

Many product areas are dominated by players that excel in one area of the marketing mix. A market may be typified by price competition for example, whereas in another branding may be of importance. This dominance of one aspect of the marketing mix will have an influence on competitors in the industry. This does not mean to say that all firms within the industry successfully differentiate themselves from the competition by focusing on neglected areas of the marketing mix. The stage in the product life cycle also has an influence on the appropriate marketing mix. In the introductory stage any design problems with the actual product should be solved. Price will depend on the costs of developing the product and the strategy regarding required market share. Promotion may concentrate on creating awareness and distribution may be selective. Throughout the other stages in the product life cycle the objectives of the marketing mix may change and the growth and maturity stage product differentiation, image building and quality may be concentrated on; whilst in the decline stage rationalisations may occur.

Other factors that should be taken into account when designing a marketing mix include the following.

Buyer behaviour

The behaviour of consumers and the behaviour of intermediaries should be taken into account. The actual number of buyers in a market is important as is the motivation for purchase and their buying processes. It is of no use to provide products by mail order, for example, if there is a strong resistance from buyers to purchasing products in this way. Whether the firm is providing goods or services will have an influence on buyer behaviour, as will whether the purchaser is in the consumer or industrial market. All these aspects will have an influence on marketing mix decisions.

Competitors

To a certain degree this has been dealt with above. However, the influence of competitors on marketing mix decisions is far reaching. Companies must analyse competitor strengths and weaknesses and their likely response to any marketing tools used.

Government

The Government imposes some controls on marketing that would affect decisions made regarding the marketing mix. These include regulations on advertising (eg cigarette ban), product specifications, pricing and competitive practices.

Company specific

All the above factors have to be taken into account when designing an appropriate marketing mix. However, it is easy to overlook one important consideration, that is company resources. The amount of money and staffing resources that marketing is allocated will determine to a large extent the elements of the marketing mix that are viable. The efficiency and effectiveness of marketing programmes need to be constantly monitored and built into the marketing planning process for the future.

All these factors, including the size and resources of the organisation, should be taken into account when marketers are designing marketing mix programmes.

8 Services marketing

Services are more important today because of the growth of service sectors in advanced industrial societies and increasingly market-orientated trends within service-providing organisations (eg 'internal markets', 'market testing' and so on). The extension of the service sector and the application of 'market principles' across what were previously publicly-owned utilities has made a large number of service providers much more marketing conscious.

The definitions offered of services are:

'... those separately identifiable but intangible activities that provide want-satisfaction, and that are not, of necessity, tied to, or inextricable from, the sale of a product or another service. To produce a service may or may not require the use of tangible goods or assets. However, where such use is required, there is no transfer of title (permanent ownership) to these tangible goods'. (Donald Cowell, *The Marketing of Services)*

'... any activity of benefit that one party can offer to another that is essentially intangible and does not result in the ownership of anything. Its production may or may not be tied to a physical product'. (P Kotler, *Social Marketing)*

Services marketing differs from the marketing of other goods but it is difficult to make a judgement which encompasses the wide variety within service types and situations. Broadly, however, the **marketing characteristics of services** which make them distinctive from the marketing of goods involves five major differences.

- Intangibility
- Inseparability
- Heterogeneity
- Perishability
- Ownership

Intangibility

Refers to the lack of substance which is involved with service delivery. Unlike a good, there is no substantial material or physical aspects of a service: no taste, feel, visible presence and so on. Clearly this creates difficulties and can inhibit the propensity to consume a service, since customers are not sure what they have.

In fact it would be incorrect to make this a 'black or white' phenomenon. Shostack has suggested viewing insubstantiality not as an 'either/or' issue but rather as a continuum.

Marketers and consumers need to try to overcome this problem and typically seek to do so in a number of different ways, and of course for different reasons. The consumer needs information to avoid making a mistake, to form some grounds for judgement and to cut down risk. The marketer wishes to make the choice of the product 'safer' and make the consumer feel more comfortable about paying for something they do not then own and which has no physical form.

Inseparability

Service often cannot be separated off from the provider. The creation, or the performance, of a service often occurs at the same instant a full or partial consumption of it occurs. Goods in the vast majority of cases have to be produced, then sold, then consumed, in that order. Services are only a promise at the time they are sold: most services are sold and then they are produced and consumed simultaneously. Think of having dental treatment or a journey. Neither exists until they are actually being experienced/consumed by the person who has bought them.

Creation of many services is coterminous with consumption. Services may have to be, at the same time

(a)   made available
(b)   sold
(c)   produced
(d)   consumed

Heterogeneity

Many services face a problem of maintaining consistency in the standard of output. Variability of quality in delivery is inevitable, because of the number of factors which may influence it. This may create problems of operation management, for example, it may be difficult or impossible to attain precise standardisation of the service offered or influence or control over perceptions of what is good or bad customer service.

This points up the need to constantly monitor customer reactions. A common way addressing this problem involves applying a system to deliver a service which may be franchised to operators. The problem remains, however, and almost the only way to address it is by constant monitoring and response to problems.

Perishability

Services cannot be stored, of course. They are innately perishable. Seats on a bus or the services of a chiropodist consist in their availability for periods of time, and if they are not occupied, the service they offer cannot be used 'later'.

This presents specific marketing problems. Meeting customer needs in these operations depends on staff being available as and when they are needed. This must be balanced against the need for a firm to minimise unnecessary expenditure on staff wages. Anticipating and responding to levels of demand is, therefore, a key planning priority.

Ownership

Services suffer from a fundamental difference compared to consumer goods. They do not result in the transfer of property. The purchase of a service only confers on the customer access to or right to use a facility, not ownership. Payment is for the use of, access to or the hire of particular items. Often there are tight constraints on the length of time involved in such usage. In the case of purchasing a product there is transfer of title and control over the use of an item.

This may well lessen the perceived customer value of a service and consequently make for unfavourable comparisons with tangible alternatives.

The importance of service

The service dimension has become the focus of a new approach for organisations providing products as well as services. Most of the ideas in this approach are well-established from the marketing approach, the 'quality movement' or 'TQM'. Tom Peters argues for a radical review of managerial approaches, insisting that the delivery of extra 'added value' through the service dimension is a critical competitive factor in marketplaces which are becoming more crowded and more competitive by the day. Theodore Levitt's **total product concept** is used to analyse systematically the value process through the service dimension.

Levitt proposes that we see products as composed of a number of different layers. This runs from an inner core to an outer ring of layers.

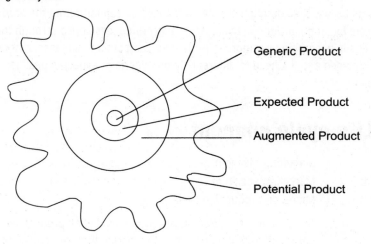

Generic Product

Expected Product

Augmented Product

Potential Product

Levitt's total product concept is explained as follows.

(a)   The **generic product** (eg washing powder or bread or clothes) is at the centre.

(b)   The **expected product** (eg the format used, the functions it fulfils, the fact that it does what it is supposed to do) comes next. How white does it wash? How well does it fit? Clearly some products will do what they are expected to do better than others.

(c)   The **augmented product** refers to the extra elements which aim to provide additional customer satisfaction, such as helpful and well-trained salespeople, range of products provided, guarantees of delivery and responsiveness to customer needs; having 'just the right' flavour, colour, price and so on.

(d)   The **potential product** refers to the extra service dimensions of customer care which companies develop, for instance, no quibble refund, return-anything policies, extra high quality decor or extra value provided in service encounters by, for example, music, flowers, entertainment in the service environment; sensitivity to customer needs and empowerment of staff to deal with them without referring to higher levels of management. These are all aspects of 'potential product'.

Peters argues that companies pursuing a customer care strategy are creating totally new products by concentrating on the two outer rings of the Levitt TPC.

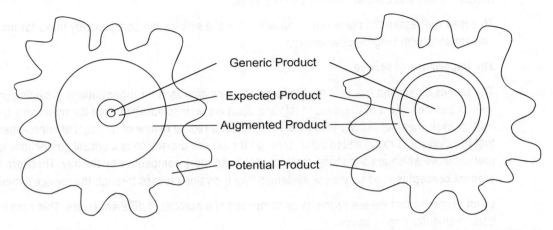

The customer care product   *Traditional thinking on the product*

Generic Product

Expected Product

Augmented Product

Potential Product

Peters believes that attention should be focused on **repositioning** the product in order to create whole new markets by emphasising the two outer (Levitt) rings, developed through the service dimension. He argues that this is becoming ever more important as competition increases, marketplaces become heavily overcrowded and the need to differentiate on generic or expected qualities becomes ever more problematic.

9 Life cycle concept

To: Marketing Manager
From: Marketing Assistant
Re: Memo on product life cycle

(a)   (i)   The product life cycle concept proposes that all products will go through a life cycle from introduction of the product to the market through to decline. The standard shape of the product life cycle is shown below. In reality the shape of each individual product life cycle will vary in terms of time and rates of growth maturity and decline.

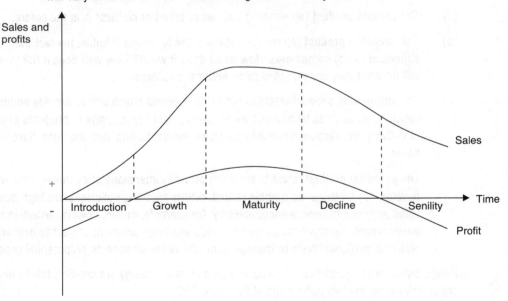

The above graph provides a useful illustration for a luxury car manufacturer to understand the current market situation of its product portfolio. Models which have been in production since 1981 are likely to be in the mature or potentially the decline phase of the PLC. It is

BPP LEARNING MEDIA

likely that over the years marketing activity has been implemented and modifications have been made to the models to sustain the life cycle. The **new** product launch, on the other hand, will be shown at the introduction phase of its life cycle.

Prior to the launch of the new model, product development activity will have taken place. The timescale of pre-launch activity should be indicated as pre-launch on the product life cycle to ensure that new product launches can be planned on time.

(ii)　Each stage of the product life cycle has implications for marketing activity.

(1)　**Introduction**

The aim at the launch phase is that the model generates a high awareness and impact upon the market place particularly within the target market and key media/influencers of purchase activity. The launch of the new model will require heavy advertising and promotional support with relevant information and incentives provided to distributors. The product will require careful planning in terms of price, branding, targeting and positioning to give the launch every chance of success.

Jaguar, at the moment, is launching a new model.

(2)　**Growth**

The primary aim at this stage is to stimulate increased interest, desire and purchase for the new model. To ensure that growth rates are sustained promotional activity in terms of advertising, sales promotional support and sales force activity should be maintained/increased. At this stage in the PLC some minor product modifications might be necessary, and the product range expanded. Stock levels for the new product should be available on time which will require accurate forecasting of expected demand levels and close monitoring of distribution outlets and logistics. However, it is not always possible to predict demand and customers might have to wait for their cars to be made.

(3)　**Maturity**

At the mature phase of the PLC, market saturation will mean limited future growth potential for the model. Marketing activity will be refocused upon defending the model's position in the market place and increasing promotional activity focused upon encouraging previous customers to repurchase newer models. Emphasis of promotional activity will be upon brand differentiation and the brand's values. The range of models available is likely to be increased to encourage upgrades and constantly refresh the brand. Special price promotions might be offered to stimulate purchase activity and defend against competitor activity. For a luxury car manufacturer, we could consider sports versions, open-top versions or other branded offerings.

(4)　**Decline stage**

Careful analysis of the nature and extent of the decline phase should be made and actions taken to either reposition the model, or enter a phase of planned divestment with a reduction in sales and promotional activity. If the decline phase is critical, a decision should be made to immediately withdraw the model. This is similar to the recent relaunch of Jaguar, under Ford.

(b)　**Limitations of the PLC concept**

The primary limitations of the product life cycle are that as a concept its stages are not easily definable or identifiable and that there is a lack of an agreed formula for calculating and predicting its shape.

(i) The **stages are not easily identifiable** because it is not clear **when** a product moves through them, yet the model suggests that marketing activity be adapted at each stage. Marketers will rely on market and customer information rather than a conceptual model to make decisions on appropriate timings of marketing activity.

(ii) All products do not go through the same life cycle. A complex range of market and market environment factors will influence each stage and the overall lifespan of the product. This lack of predictability and variance limits the life cycle concept as a planning tool. Whilst we can plot and see product life cycles in a historical context, this has limited value in future.

(iii) An organisation's own marketing activity can influence the shape of the life cycle and can sustain a product's life through modification and repositioning. The life cycle concept does not in itself recognise or explain how a product's life can be sustained or weakened through the marketing actions of the organisation. Similarly, competitive activity can weaken the chances of a product being sustained on the market.

(iv) The brand can outlive a product. Rolls Royce is a good example of this in that the brand is targeted at the luxury market, although the models have changed over time.

The product life cycle concept whilst intuitively attractive does not provide the marketer with any agreed methodology for predicting each stage and whilst modelling techniques can be developed for each industry it is applied in, this will potentially require a complexity of different predictors, variables and rankings and little predictive validity.

Overall the PLC model has value as an academic concept but limited validity and application when

10 Pricing

(a) **Cost plus pricing**

Costs are the most important influence on pricing decisions. Many firms base their pricing policy on simple cost plus rules. This means that costs are estimated and then a profit margin is added to arrive at the price. This method of pricing is relatively easy for management to implement and affords some degree of stability over pricing. There are two main types of cost-based pricing.

The first is **full cost**. Although it is not appropriate to go into this in detail here it is worthwhile pointing out the differences between full and cost plus pricing. Full cost pricing takes account of the full average costs of production including an allocation for overheads. The profit margin is then added to determine the price. The problem with full cost pricing is that if the company produces many brands the allocation of overheads costs can be difficult to determine.

Cost plus pricing on the other hand only uses the direct cost components; for example, labour and raw materials are used to calculate unit costs. An additional margin is then added that includes profit and an overhead charge. Cost plus pricing is used extensively in the UK retailing sector, where the mark up price includes a fixed margin that varies between product classes. The percentage margin may also vary according to demand factors. The problems of cost plus pricing arise out of the difficulties in calculating direct costs and the allocation of overhead costs. The cost plus approach leads to price stability because in the main prices change due to cost changes.

(b) **Market skimming pricing**

Market skimming involves setting a high initial price for a new product. If a new product has a high value to consumers then a high price can be charged. The strategy is initially to command a premium price and then gradually to reduce the price to penetrate the more price sensitive segments of the market. One advantage of this method of pricing is that it is easier to reduce prices if a mistake has been made than it is to increase prices. A high price also creates an image of a quality product, especially if other aspects of the marketing mix reflect this. In order for this

BPP LEARNING MEDIA

strategy to be successful there must be enough consumers who are not price sensitive. The costs of producing the small volumes of premium price products should not be greater than the advantage gained by charging the higher price. The strategy will only work if the higher price does not stimulate competition, so is suitable for markets that have high entry barriers, for example, high development costs or high promotional costs.

(c) **Marginal cost pricing**

Marginal cost pricing is the setting of the price of one unit at the cost of producing an extra unit (marginal cost). From an economics viewpoint marginal cost pricing is the most efficient pricing method. This is because when price is equal to marginal cost it is allocatively efficient. In a perfectly competitive market the market mechanism ensures that price does equal marginal cost if profits are maximised. However, perfect competition never occurs in the real world. Profits are maximised instead when price is greater than the marginal cost of producing the good. If this is the case it is allocatively inefficient; that is, too little of a good is being produced to keep the price high, so consumption is below the optimum level. In theory nationalised industries were supposed to set their price equal to marginal costs but have recently been under instruction to price in a more commercial manner. In practice, marginal cost pricing is difficult because of problems in calculation. Again, there will be problems in the allocation of overheads and the additional problem of whether to set prices equal to long-run or short-run marginal costs.

(d) **Market penetration pricing**

In a market penetration pricing strategy the company sets a low price for the product in order to stimulate growth in the market or to obtain a larger market share. This strategy is only successful if demand is price sensitive and economies of scale can be achieved. That is, unit costs of production and distribution fall with increased output. So companies set a low price in the belief that consumers will value this and their market share can then increase. The low price strategy should also deter competitors from entering the market. The low price approach is often used with heavy promotional effort to penetrate mass markets and take market share. If the firm needs to recoup high development costs in a short time this may not be the most appropriate pricing strategy. If there are high barriers to entry, including a high degree of branding, the market may not be suitable for penetration pricing. Low prices, however, are not likely to be effective if the product is in the decline stage of the PLC, as customers are usually changing to substitute products.

11 Pricing policy

Report

To: The management
From: A Marketer
Re: Pricing policy of a product line

A product line can be defined in terms of a 'broad group of products whose uses and characteristics are basically similar'. Such products can be differentiated by

- Price
- Packaging
- Targeted customer
- Distribution channel used

A firm may have a line of products because it wishes to target a number of segments of the market, all of whom require different benefits. The following are the considerations you might make when detailing the influences on pricing of a product line.

(a) **Product quality**. If the firm is seeking a niche upper market segment and a reputation for quality then it may decide a high price is necessary (for example, the Caribbean cruise holiday market). This price may hold for all products in the line, yet there may be special offers for block bookings or during certain times in the year when demand falls.

(b) **Company image**. The firm may be seeking an exclusive image in the market place and may use pricing strategy in conjunction with public relations to achieve this, for example Marks & Spencer.

(c) **Costs of production**. The firm will want to meet the full costs of production and make sustainable profits so pricing must reflect this. The bigger the operation, the bigger the scale economies available from production and marketing, particularly where products are very similar (thus permitting bulk manufacture/purchase of parts). This situation would help secure lower prices and increased competitiveness in a mass market.

(d) **Degree of standardisation of products**. An extension of (c) above, this implies that where products in a line are quite different in order to meet consumer needs, then the costs of the product and, therefore, the price, will have to be higher.

(e) **Desired level of profit**. A firm may willingly take losses on one line of product as long as the range of products meets the forecast profits target. It may price, therefore, to achieve this goal.

(f) **Desired level of market share**. A firm may set or alter prices as a promotional tool to realise market share goals.

(g) **To manage the portfolio effectively**. The firm may have a number of product lines in the market (or different markets) at the same times. Portfolio analysis may indicate that price changes to specific products in specific lines at specific times may realise more revenue from life cycles; the firm is thus able to use pricing to manage profitability.

(h) **To market diversify**. The firm may be able, through lowering or increasing the price, to take its product line into a different market (upper or lower in income grouping). Some changes to the line (apart from price) would also probably be necessary in order to do this.

(i) **As a promotional tool**. A firm may use its pricing structure as a promotional tool to bring 'value for money' to the customer's attention. In order to increase added value it may additionally offer 'free servicing' as an added incentive.

(j) **To capitalise on novelty**. If the product line is new, and the market largely untapped, a firm may be able to 'harvest' significant profits from the market over the short term by pricing up the whole line. Innovative products will command this competitive advantage until other, like products enter the market when the firm will need to reduce its profits to stay competitive. Such 'pricing up' over the short term will additionally help cover the heavy research and development costs of innovation.

Please raise any queries regarding this report with me.

A Marketer

12 Distribution

A major element in distribution strategy is the degree of market coverage that is desired for a product. Linked to this question is the required support the distribution strategy needs from the producer. In order to serve existing and future customers to the required standard the company must decide how many outlets should be established in an area and what services channel members can offer. Market coverage is often termed 'distribution intensity' and refers to the number and size of outlets in a particular area. There are three basic choices in the method of distribution: selective, intensive and exclusive.

Exclusive distribution

Exclusive distribution means appointing outlets for an area to distribute your goods exclusively. Exclusive distribution **restricts the number of outlets** where the goods are available. This exclusivity can be in the overall type of channel chosen, for example selecting department stores rather than supermarkets. It is used in a number of circumstances. If customers are willing to exert some effort in searching for the product or service then exclusive distribution is possible. There may be an aim to restrict outlets providing your product to encourage a high quality image (the perfume industry offers a good example). This can be beneficial for the supplier and the store which sells the product. The producers may adopt exclusive distribution if there is a high degree of service or after-sales support required from the product. Exclusive distribution allows the producer more control of the marketing mix at the point of sale and minimises channel conflict. There is necessarily a close relationship between channel members in an exclusive distribution system.

Intensive distribution

Intensive distribution is the opposite of exclusive distribution. Here the aim is to **cover the market as intensively as possible**. Many intermediaries are used to bring the products to as many people as possible, both within one geographical area and throughout many areas. This coverage method is often used for goods and services that either consumers or organisational buyers purchase frequently. It can be typified by convenience goods that the buyer will not want to put any effort into purchasing. Examples include food, washing powder, tobacco and in organisational markets, office supplies. Outlets for these goods have to be easily accessible and to have a choice of readily available brands.

Selective distribution

Selective distribution is somewhere between exclusive and intensive distribution. It is suitable for products that consumers are willing to put some effort into purchasing. This method is chosen when brands are important to consumers or the outlets are important to consumers (for example Harrods). The reasons for adopting this type of channel strategy are similar to those outlined in our discussion of exclusive distribution.

Choice of strategy: factors

There are four main factors that determine the choice of distribution strategy.

(a)   **Customers**

Target customer groups have a major impact on market coverage decisions. Social class, income and geographic area are important market segmentation variables that have an influence on channel decisions. Consumer behaviour also plays an important part in market coverage decisions. How consumers view stores and products will influence the most appropriate distribution strategy to undertake.

(b)   **Products**

The actual product characteristics are important in determining appropriate market coverage. A relatively cheap, frequently bought product will be better suited to intensive distribution. An expensive product that is purchased infrequently may be better distributed exclusively or selectively.

(c)   **Outlets**

Too few or too many outlets in an area may affect the choice of distribution strategy. If an organisation has too few outlets in an area then sales targets will be difficult to achieve. If the organisation has too many outlets, this may not be efficient. When a reseller is unable to perform some marketing functions, for example after-sales service when an intensive strategy has been adopted, then this will determine the future of the distribution strategy.

(d)   **Control**

The level of desired control over how the product is presented to the public is a major determining factor in formulating a distribution strategy. If an intensive distribution strategy is adopted, then the supplier usually gives up some of its control over the marketing of the product. For instance, if the product is sold in nationwide supermarket chains then display and final pricing is usually determined by the supermarket. If an exclusive distribution strategy is adopted then control is less likely to be relinquished.

13 Physical distribution and marketing

REPORT

To: Board of Directors
From: A Candidate
Date: 4 December 20XX

Introduction

The process of **physical distribution** is a key element of our marketing strategy in that we must ensure that our products reach the customer in the right quantity, at the right time and in perfect condition. In marketing text books it is described as the 4th P along with promotion, price and product. This report outlines the reasons why physical distribution should become a **component of marketing and not as the final delivery part of the production process.**

The customer's perspective

It is important to consider the extent to which our organisation has adopted a customer orientation. Customers of our products are not concerned with **how** the product reaches the point of sale, only that it is available in the quantity and at the quality they require. If we see distribution as the final delivery part of the production process then we are in danger of adopting a production orientation The focus of our attention will be on the efficiency and effectiveness of our production and distribution systems and not on market factors and customer needs.

Competitive advantage

By focusing our attention on the market it is possible for the organisation to identify and assess new/innovative distribution opportunities that will achieve a competitive advantage. Such opportunities will range from transforming the channel structure through to tactical activities with our distribution channel. Distribution has until recent years had the least attention of the marketing mix elements but with increasing levels of competition and commoditising of products, its importance as both a strategic and tactical weapon are now being recognised.

Service and added value

The matching of the distribution process to our organisation's service marketing activities is an important consideration. Management of the distribution channel can provide many opportunities for improved service delivery ranging from stock management, order processing to guaranteed delivery. It is also important for us to identify our customers distribution problems and provide solutions that add value to our overall product offer.

Supply chain management

Our major customers require increasingly sophisticated channel management techniques to ensure our products maintain their shelf presence. Examples of these are the increasing importance of trade marketing activities and category management techniques as opposed to traditional product management activity. We also need to establish closer and stronger relationships with other distribution channel members to ensure that we maximise the efficiency and effectiveness of the **total supply chain** not just

BPP)))
LEARNING MEDIA

our final part in the chain. Many retailers are now adopting the concept of efficient consumer response (ECR) in trying to ensure that the distribution system works in a co-ordinated manner. Similarly, information technology is playing an increasingly important role in our customers' stock handling and purchasing functions.

14 Promotional campaign

(a)   Planning a promotional campaign for a consumer product.

Consumer product: Boddingtons Beer

Boddingtons Beer was a declining regional bitter brand that was taken over by Whitbread PLC. The majority of the brand's sales were made in the North West of England. The brand at the time of the take-over was heavily discounted to maintain its position against competitive brands. At this time its credibility and appeal to its traditional target audience were weak.

A promotional campaign was launched to strengthen Boddingtons appeal in the North West but also to broaden its appeal to the rest of the UK. The key success factors were to establish a strong brand, that reflected a 'truth' about the product.

Objectives of the promotional campaign

- To strengthen Boddingtons appeal in the North West
- To grow Boddingtons Bitter outside its heartland region.

Target audience

Boddingtons Bitter was targeted initially at members of CAMRA and bitter connoisseurs to build the credentials of the brand as a **quality** bitter. Once acceptance was gained from these drinkers, the campaign was moved to appeal to a wider audience of quality beer drinkers and then the mass market bitter drinkers.

Promotional strategy

Advertising was the primary promotional tool used in this campaign. The campaign focused upon the smoothness, creaminess and colour of the product with its thick white head of beer but also emphasising its Mancunian character.

Media selection

The media strategy adopted linked with Whitbread's desire to establish the brand gradually. A tightly targeted press campaign was used to launch the brand. Outside back covers of magazines were used in a unique manner that supported the brand's positioning and gained high visibility. National television was not used until two years after the launch.

Results

The Boddingtons campaign achieved spectacular results and within three years became the UK's fourth largest bitter brand. Consumer awareness of the brand meant that 93% of people had heard of it. Its brand image and appeal also improved substantially as a result of the campaign. The brand was able to be priced at a premium to competitive brands thus reflecting its new added values.

(b)   The selection of promotional tools for a campaign for an industrial product might differ for the following reasons.

(i)   **The size and nature of the customer base** will differ substantially in industrial markets compared to consumer markets, therefore different promotional techniques will be adopted. Literature, exhibitions, selling/key account management and sales promotions are likely to be used more extensively than advertising.

(ii) **Promotional activity** will function more at the product level and appeal to a more rational buying decision process. Promotional activity targeted at consumers tends to be more brand oriented and emotional.

(iii) The **business buying process** for industrial products is likely to be more formal than the consumer buying process. Customers are likely to demand detailed product specifications, and require policy manuals. It is likely that the customer will carry out a more detailed supplier search.

(iv) The decision making process in an industrial purchase is likely to be fairly complex with different members of the decision making unit involved.

(v) **Relationships between manufacturer and supplier** form an integral part of industrial marketing. Organisations deal direct and the strength of relationship can significantly influence purchase decisions. Interpersonal communication is an important part of this process.

15 Sales promotion

Recommendations on appropriate sales promotions

To support the launch of Chico it will be necessary to use some form of sales promotion to support our above-the-line advertising campaign. The main objective of the sales promotions recommended is to stimulate trial of Chico by our target consumers.

Free sample

The first sales promotion recommended is a free sample of Chico attached to a monthly magazine. The use of impregnated paper in the pages of the magazine could be considered but this is usually the approach of the higher priced perfumes in glossy magazines. It is recommended that a phial of Chico be attached as a free gift to the full circulation of a monthly woman's magazine that is read by our target market. The magazine 'Essentials' has been chosen because the readership is from our target group social class and age bracket. The magazine has also run this type of promotion before and would be willing to co-operate.

The aim of this promotion is to enable potential customers to try our product without having to ask to test it in a store. This can also be combined with advertising copy within the magazine describing the type of woman that wears Chico.

Competition

In addition to the free phial of Chico on the outside of the magazine it is recommended that we include a competition inside the magazine. The first 200 postcards to be drawn on a certain date win a full-sized bottle of Chico.

Timing

The timing of this sales promotion will be crucial. Stores must already have adequate stocks of Chico so that as sales have been stimulated consumers are actually able to buy the product. It should also coincide with the above-the-line advertising campaign. This method of promotion should only be used once, preferably in the November issue of the magazine as this might encourage purchases for Christmas. A special Christmas promotional offer could be run in the stores at this time. This could be a special gift pack of perfume, talcum powder and body lotion in Chico.

Image

This sales promotion method will stimulate trial of Chico without any adverse effects on the image. Care has to be taken that the image we present during sales promotion does not conflict with the image from our media advertising. The image we want to build for Chico is elegant, sophisticated yet at the same time fun-loving and young. Any direct price promotions would 'cheapen' the image of Chico and should be avoided. The promotion method chosen for the launch should get over the buying inertia many women feel towards buying perfume and take the risk out of purchasing the product. As perfume can only really be tested on an individual's skin and then should be allowed to develop for a while before testing this method would be ideal in the circumstances.

After the initial launch further sales can be stimulated using another method of sales promotion. This could take the form of a competition, the details on a leaflet given with purchase, backed up of course with advertising. An appropriate prize would be an exotic holiday.

Evaluation

To evaluate the sales promotion effectiveness a number of methods can be used. Firstly the number of responses to the free draw for Chico should be analysed. Sales data before the promotion should be noted and compared with sales data during and after the promotion. As perfume is not purchased frequently there may be a drop in sales after the sales promotion. The market share Chico has gained needs to be monitored. It may also be necessary to hold consumer panels to see if people responded to the promotion and in what way. A survey could be carried out to evaluate the impact of the promotion on consumer purchase behaviour.

16 Pull techniques

A 'pull effect' is when the intended target audience is very familiar with a product and asks for the brand by its name, thus acting as an attraction for retailers and wholesalers to stock it. In effect, the **consumers' demand 'pulls' the product through the chain of distribution**. There are various 'pull techniques' used to encourage such a reaction in consumers.

(a) **Price reductions**. Made by the manufacturer, retailer or wholesaler, these 'offers' are usually 'timescaled' to encourage intention to buy. Examples are kitchen and household furnishings products.

(b) **Coupons**. These usually have to be collected by consumers so the tactic acts as an encouragement to re-buy and to engender loyalty. A gift, entry to a competition with a major price at stake or 'free product' is usually the outcome of saving the coupons.

(c) **Loss leaders**. Where some products (perhaps the least successful performances) are sold off deliberately at a loss to elicit interest in other products in the range (eg the 'star performers'). A good example here is holidays.

(d) **Competitions**. The incentive to compete, and the desire for materialism, is always strong within human nature. Firms realise this and often offer luxury products such as exclusive foreign holidays or new cars as prizes in competitions, entry to which is possible by purchasing the product.

(e) **Testimonials**. Well known and well liked show business or sporting personalities are used to endorse the product. Consumers are sub-consciously made to associate their lifestyle and successes with those of the personality through using the product.

(f) **Free samples**. These are often used as part of in-store demonstrations (for example, foods and wines) where the consumer is invited to try the product free and may be given special discounts if the product is purchased that day.

(g) **Merchandising and point of sale displays**. Usually consisting of large posters, cardboard displays with lots of colour and major promotional incentives, these are used in stores to inform and persuade the customer to try the product.

(h) **Packaging**. Through uniqueness of design, use of colour or logos, and through placing effectively on in-store shelving, packaging can be used to build brand image and as a product differentiator.

(i)   **Corporate sponsorship** (for example, sporting events). This can be used to elicit interest in products (but more commonly services) and if made accessible to television exposure can be very useful in eliciting interest in a company's range of products or indeed in promoting the image of the company itself.

(j)   **Trade-in facilities**. Often associated with 'white' or kitchen goods, and also cars, these can be used to persuade the customer to 'buy new' when in fact there may still be a long life in their existing purchase. Trade-in facilities usually offer a fairly attractive cash reduction on the new product.

(k)   **Credit facilities**. Used widely nowadays (particularly with cars and electrical goods), credit facilities allow customers to extend the payment period over many months or even years. The firm is able to offer these deals through agreements with banks and finance houses. Increasingly 'zero interest' or 'free finance' adaptations to these offers have made them very attractive as incentives to purchase.

(l)   **Guarantees**. These are additions to statutory rights made by firms to add value through differentiating themselves from competitors. Examples are where the firm offers to extend the statutory 'guarantee period' or guarantees to refund the cost of the product if the customer can buy it cheaper elsewhere.

17 Relevant marketing mix

(a)   **A large banking group**

A large banking group, such as Barclays has to focus on four key sectors.

*   The consumer market
*   The corporate market
*   The small/medium business market
*   The financial markets

In all these sectors both international and domestic considerations are necessary.

The bank, whilst essentially a service, offers its customers a range of products. Although some of these products are intangible, they are nevertheless perceived by customers as offering specific benefits and meeting specific needs. It is important for a large banking group to engage all the elements of the marketing mix for these sectors.

In the consumer market distribution has become a major issue, particularly with the advent of direct banking. Service is an important element of the bank's response to an increasingly competitive marketplace. New products are being launched as the bank's marketing environment poses new opportunities and threats. Communication is critical both in terms of customer acquisition and retention. The heavy use of advertising and direct marketing are evidence of the importance attached to these components of promotion.

Within the corporate market a different range of tools will be utilised. In particular, relationship marketing and sponsorship become important elements of the mix. A range of financial services is offered to corporate clients particularly with investments. The product mix, communication and distribution structure will vary from the consumer market, with the sales function becoming more dominant.

For the small/medium business the role of the business adviser is important, along with the various services the bank provides to assist the business in managing its financial affairs more effectively. It is not uncommon to see TV advertising targeted at entrepreneurs. Each element has an important part to play in the bank's competitive position.

BPP
LEARNING MEDIA

(b)   **Electric component manufacturer**

A company that manufacturers electronic components for computer manufacturers will focus its marketing activities on a relatively few number of customers in the business sector. The need for consumer marketing activity will therefore generally be unnecessary although organisations such as Intel have gained a strong market position in the supply of computer chips by building a strong brand reputation with consumers. The assumption in this case is that this manufacturer is focused upon its business customers.

The predominant marketing mix activities will focus upon product quality and delivery with strong salesforce and technical support. It is likely that corporate entertainment and the building up of relationships throughout the customer's organisation will be important aspects of the company's marketing programme. The role of distribution is important particularly in terms of product availability and speed of delivery. There is a danger that this market can become price-driven as technological change means new products are copied or become obsolete very quickly. A strong commitment must therefore be made to research and new product development.

Packaging and branding are less critical components as tools of communication, although they can play a role in supporting the manufacturer's overall positioning. Publicity, particularly in the trade press, can be an important tool of communication. The supply of support literature and price structure alongside easy-to-access order processes will enhance the competitive position of this company. With a focus on fewer customers, direct marketing techniques should predominate. The relationship that the manufacturer has with distributors in the supply chain will also be important to ensure wide availability of component parts.

As can be seen from the above, whilst all the elements of the marketing mix are evident in both examples, the nature of the mix varies considerably depending upon the nature of the market and sector in which the organisation operates. The marketing mix seen simply as the 7Ps does not divulge the diversity and choice that marketers have in managing and implementing their marketing activities. The above examples also demonstrate that some organisations gain competitive advantage by 'breaking the rules' through innovative use of the marketing mix.

18 Marketing concept

(a)   **Successful adoption of the marketing concept**

(i)   **A business-to-business organisation**

Trend Heating and Lighting, a division of Trend plc, faced a period of increasing competition and declining demand in several of its traditional core markets. It held a position as market leader selling heating and lighting systems to construction companies, architects, electrical installers and through specialised distributors.

Profitability was in decline and the company had reached a crisis point in terms of its future viability. Cost cutting had taken place in an attempt to maintain margins but frequently this was in areas such as marketing research and development and training. Limited research and development activity was taking place and reliance placed on an established salesforce who were increasingly being forced to sell systems at lower prices.

The company took actions to re-orientate itself. Extensive research of the market highlighted two significant trends. The first involved the increasing use of information technology in both the design and installation of systems. The second trend identified changing customer needs. A segment of the market was identified that required complex heating and lighting systems integration and solutions rather than just systems application and installation.

Trend proposed to its top design and installation engineers that it would support them in setting up their own independent distribution companies to service this segment. The company worked in partnership to identify markets and provide full service back up to these new distributors in return for exclusivity. As a result of this innovative market-led strategy, Trend established itself once again as market leader in a growing and profitable market segment.

(ii) **A non-profit organisation**

The Inland Revenue has undergone a significant internal and external reorientation in an attempt to reposition itself from an 'enemy to be feared' to a 'friend to be trusted'. Traditionally the Inland Revenue provided limited services other than to send out tax demands, administer tax collection and prosecute late payers and tax evaders. None of these processes were customer orientated, the Inland Revenue primarily being seen as answerable to the Government. Evidence of this lack of customer orientation fed down to the contact that was available between the consumer and the revenue with no contact name being provided just a district and reference number.

As a result of the introduction of self assessment the Revenue acquired a new identity and position to support its tax collecting and administration duties. A new openness was introduced that enabled direct contact to named revenue employees providing support and advice particularly on the completion of self assessment tax returns.

A more flexible and friendly face of the Revenue was introduced that was more supportive to the consumer. Employees were trained in the new work practices and the change was supported by an internal communications plan. Consumers were informed through an extensive advertising campaign to communicate this repositioning.

As a result of this reorientation the Revenue has succeeded in changing people's perceptions of its role and services. It is a good example of a non profit making organisation successfully adopting the marketing concept.

(b) **How the use of information technology could assist in the management of a customer-oriented culture in Trend Heating and Lighting**

Information technology can assist in the management of a customer oriented culture through the following ways.

(i) **Marketing information systems**

Gathering market and customer information and analysing and disseminating it, enable management to make speedier decisions and adopt a proactive rather than reactive approach to their market place and customers. These improvements feed into understanding the behaviour of customers and identification of potential market segments. The MKIS can also provide improved monitoring and control of marketing activities.

(ii) **Communication systems**

Internal and external communications systems can be developed enabling better communication between internal and external customers. The use of e-mail and the Internet are offering significant improvements in both speed of communication, targeting and response. Customer Relationship Management activity is enhanced through using such systems. These developments should result in improved service performance, improved efficiency and responsiveness to customer demands.

(iii) **Logistics management**

Management and planning of logistics systems including transport, materials handling and stockholding can all be improved through the adoption of information technology. Networks can be established along the total supply chain offering management information and order

BPP
LEARNING MEDIA

and payment capabilities. Information technology is now being used by organisations to control their European logistics systems.

(iv) **Marketing strategy and planning**

The marketing and strategy development process can be improved through investment in applications software, decision support systems and the application of knowledge management. Strategic Planning software is available to support company adoption of planning techniques and processes.

(v) **New product development**

Information technology can support the NPD development process through enabling marketers and researchers to work closely together on market-led technological innovations. Developments such as Quality Function Deployment, which bring the voice of the customer to the engineers and designers are being enhanced through investment in information technology systems.

19 Relationship marketing

(a)

MEMORANDUM

To: Mr N Shani, Managing Director, Signature Cars
From: Stuart Ford, Marketing Assistant
Date: 7th December 20XX

Subject: Database and Relationship Management

I should like to draw your attention to a number of issues which I believe we should be considering in building loyalty and customer relations from our current database.

Database marketing

As a car dealership for Fords motorcars, we have developed a database of customers who have purchased cars from this dealership in the last two years. This includes information relating to:

- Age, name, address,
- Date of purchase,
- Finance requirements,
- Type of car, colour, model, accessories,
- Customer service requirements, after-sales requirements
- Employee who dealt with the customers

This information allows us to have a clearer understanding of the needs of the customer and underpins the relationship with them. It also allows us to monitor lapsed customers and understand the contributing factors to their defection to the competition.

We will need to consider how we can use this database for analysing customer behaviour and decision making. Therefore, we will need to consider the use of mail shots specifically targeted for our special events. We will also be able to consider specific targeted sales promotions, such as free valeting for the first 12 months after purchase. We need to consider the introduction of loyalty schemes such as 'VIP' scheme for customers who purchase a new car from us, where the customer can receive 10% off all servicing.

We can use the data in a predicitive manner to anticipate future customer requirements and respond in an appropriate way, for example, a customer who has a history of purchasing a vehicle every two years should be contacted after 20 months to initiate the relationship during this complex decision process.

The data from this database will allow us to contact our customer directly and reassure them that they have made the right decision when buying a Ford car from us, creating loyalty through customer magazines, competition . This should help to reduce post purchase dissonance which customers often face after buying a new car which is a high involvement decision.

Databases will make it easier to contact customer for feedback therefore allowing us to discover satisfaction levels and set about delighting customers. Whenever a past customer contacts their dealership their records will be to hand, speeding up the processes and avoiding more paperwork.

(b) **Relationship marketing**

For any organisation it saves on resources to keep customers rather than finding new ones, thus relationship marketing is important in developing beneficial longer-term relationships. Therefore, RM focuses on servicing repeat purchasers rather than delivering short-term profit.

Under a relationship marketing approach, all the activities of an organisation are used to build, maintain and develop customer relationships, the objective being to build customer loyalty, thereby leading the customer retention. Relationship management is concerned with getting and keeping customers by ensuring that an appropriate combination of marketing, customer service and quality is provided. In order for relationship marketing to work, it is important to recognise that both parties must feel that they can benefit from long-term relationships rather than one-off transactions. A key element of relationship marketing is that development of such mutually beneficial long-term relationships between customers and suppliers. Relationship marketing also widens the concept of exchange to consider all of the parties involved. To ensure successful relationship marketing there needs to be an appropriate supportive organisational culture and everyone in the business must be concerned with generating customer satisfaction.

It is important to recognise that consumers have become more sophisticated and therefore, the purchasing buying behaviour has become more complex. Customers require a more customised offering and therefore require individual treatment. Customers are becoming more susceptible to switching behaviour between suppliers and competition has increase in the marketplace. Focus on trust and loyalty have become key elements of the marketing activity.

For the car dealership, relationship marketing can be applied through such service encounters as test drives, delivery of the purchase, subsequent servicing of the car and financing issues related to the purchase.

Conclusion

Relationship marketing is a technique that accommodates the broader perspective of building loyal customers in an ever increasingly competitive market place dominated by mobile customers with a wide variety of needs.

20 E-commerce

E-commerce means electronic commerce and refers to transactions carried out online via the Internet.

The role of e-commerce can be **strategic** (planning) and **tactical** (how to carry out the plan). For example, a business website can be used to monitor the number of times someone accesses the pages on the website ('hits'). The hit rate for each page can be analysed and used to determine the popularity of various products, eg by having each product on a new page. This information can be utilised to plan a promotion of a product. If the website is then used to promote the product, the hit rate will monitor the success (or failure) of the promotion.

BPP LEARNING MEDIA

Strategic marketing planning can use e-commerce in the following ways.

- Facilitating market research by means of Internet questionnaires/feedback
- Identifying segmentation bases by obtaining customer information using a registration form on the Internet site
- In direct distribution via the Internet
- For new promotional methods eg journalists' section of the website
- In media decision
- More effective evaluation methods

21 Interflora worldwide flower deliveries

(a)   **Report**

To: Directors of Interflora
From: A Student
Date: 15 June 20XX

Practical approaches that Interflora should consider to improve the standard of customer care and satisfaction across the participating florists include:

Customer research

Interflora should invest time and money into researching current levels of customer satisfaction. This can be done on a national basis providing a useful information resource and identifying best practice. Mystery shoppers can be utilised to contact and visit Interflora outlets and assess the quality of service and customer care.

Staff training and development

Interflora should identify training needs of Interflora staff and organise training and personal development programmes. It is essential that staff be given the appropriate levels of skills and knowledge to deliver high levels of customer care. This should include customer handling skills, management skills, and technical skills.

Internal communications

Interflora should ensure that clear channels of communication exist to all its outlets. Staff within outlets should be kept informed of plans and developments. Internal recognition and awards for performance should be recognised and communicated. A series of meetings can be arranged to ensure regular and open dialogue.

External communications

A national campaign to support the Interflora brand and local outlets should communicate the levels of service that a customer can expect from Interflora. This external communication will form an important part of the staff's identification with the Interflora brand name. Staff must feel they are an important asset to Interflora and critical to the service offered. This importance should be communicated as a fundamental part of the brand's value.

Standardised systems and processes

Interflora should support its outlets with the introduction of standardised systems and processes to ensure that customers receive the same level of service quality whichever Interflora outlet they contact. These systems and processes should be designed for the customer's benefit above all else.

Establishing performance standards and monitoring systems

Evaluation performance is an essential activity through which good and poor performance can be identified. Prompt actions can then be taken where problems occur. We should adopt a policy of prevention rather than cure to ensure high levels of customer satisfaction. Benchmarking performance can form part of this process to explore best practice.

(b) **How people, process and physical evidence could be developed for this service**

People

Employees and staff associated with Interflora are a key asset that must be invested in to ensure that customer service goals are achieved. The ability of staff to cope with customers, to deliver service reliably to the required standard and to present an image consistent with that which the organisation would want is a vital concern. A staff development and training programme should be introduced to ensure that each employee has the required levels of skill and knowledge. Many service failures stem from staffing problems.

Remuneration schemes should be introduced that reward development and performance. Particular attention should be paid to how staff interact with customers and their responsiveness to customer demands. Through the introduction of improved recruitment and selection processes management should try to influence the type of individual that outlets employ. This will also serve to improve the longer-term profile of Interflora staff.

Process

Interflora needs smooth, efficient, customer-friendly procedures. This includes both front office and back office procedures. The design of the service process and introduction of more advanced technology can both help to improve service level performance. The introduction of automated call handling, where orders can be made without interacting with staff is a good example of both improved process and introduction of advanced technology. Data software and data processing systems are now offering applications that enable organisations to provide better forecasting, measurement and control and keeping track of customers via the database. Well designed processes also ensure that the customer can place an order without any unnecessary delay. Interflora should also develop and expand its online ordering service via the Internet.

Physical evidence

Interflora should establish clear guidelines as to the design, ambience and atmosphere of its outlets. This can be achieved through co-ordinated colour schemes, shop layout, use of logos, staff uniforms and signage. Investment support should be given to outlets to enable this to happen. At all points where the customer contacts Interflora, physical evidence should reinforce these images as it can have a strong influence on brand image and perception of their experience of the service. Physical evidence can also provide a point of differentiation between Interflora and competitors. If this can be shared across all outlets then Interflora will reinforce its identity in the marketplace.

(c) **Major promotional methods for inclusion in a campaign to raise awareness of Interflora's products and service**

A range of professional methods can be considered to raise customer awareness of Interflora's products and service. These include advertising, direct marketing, public relations, sales promotion, selling and production of literature. The utilisation of new technology in particular the Internet and digital interactive media should also be considered as a high proportion of the target audience are now 'online'.

Advertising is defined as any paid form of non-personal presentation and promotion of ideas, goods or services through mass media by an identified sponsor. Advertising is delivered through media channels such as television, newspapers and radio but also includes posters and banner advertising on the Internet.

BPP
LEARNING MEDIA

Direct marketing is defined as an interactive system of marketing which uses one or more advertising media to effect a measurable response at any location, forming a basis for creating and further developing an ongoing direct relationship between an organisation and its customers. Direct marketing enables personal communication through channels such as the telephone, catalogues and direct mail but also utilises direct response advertising (such as freephone numbers) and sales promotions (such as coupons and competitions) to generate awareness, interest and action. Data is captured on a database which enables targeted communications to named individuals.

Sales promotion is defined as short-term incentives to encourage purchase or sale of a product or service. This includes gifts, coupons, special offers, loyalty cards, promotional price discounts and competitions. Sales promotions can be utilised to stimulate trial, encourage more frequent repeat purchase or simply as a reward for loyalty.

Public relations is defined as the deliberate, planned and sustained effort to institute and maintain mutual understanding between an organisation and its publics. Public relations activity includes media relations, publicity, community programmes, internal communications, corporate identity programmes and sponsorship.

It is recommended that Interflora invests in a communications campaign utilising the above promotional methods and technologies. The following plan of action should be followed.

Conduct a national advertising campaign within selected mainstream media supported with a direct marketing campaign. Advertising should contain strong brand imagery in visual media alongside detailed product and service information within press adverts. This advertising campaign can be supported with direct mail campaigns to targeted households. All adverts and mail shots should have a response mechanism enabling the customer to contact Interflora to place an order or ask for further information. Literature should be prepared and sent to all enquiries.

The Internet should be utilised with banner adverts supporting the Interflora web page. Adverts should be placed on sites where flowers might be a primary purchase such as weddings, funerals and birthdays. Information gleaned from visitors to the site can be held on database and passed onto outlets.

Public relations activity should be running in conjunction with the above campaigns to maximise publicity and gain high media coverage.

ANSWER BANK

298

Index of references

Index of references

Ace, C (2001), *Successful Marketing Communications*, Butterworth-Heinemann, Oxford.

Allen, C; Kania, D & Yaeckel, B (2001), *One to One Web Marketing* (2nd edition), Wiley, New York.

Baron, S (ed) (1991), *Macmillan Dictionary of Retailing*, Palgrave Macmillan.

Brassington, F & Pettitt, S (2002), *Principles of Marketing,* FT Prentice Hall, Essex.

Bruce, I (1997), *Successful Charity Marketing: Meeting Need,* ICSA Publishing, London.

Cannon, T (1998), *Basic Marketing: Principles & Practice*, Thomson Learning.

Commson, J (2003), 'CHACEM still market leader', *Ghanaian Chronicle* (Accra), March 9.

Corey, E R; Raymond, F; Cespedes, V & Kasturi Rangan, V (1989), *Going to Market*, Harvard Business School Press, Boston, MA.

Cowell, D W (1995), *The Marketing of Services*, Butterworth-Heinemann, Oxford.

Dibb, S; Simkin, L P; Pride, W M & Ferell, O C (2001), *Marketing Concepts and Strategies,* Houghton Mifflin.

Drucker, P (1955), *The Practice of Management*, Heinemann, London.

Gronroos, C (1990), 'Marketing Redefined', *Management Decision.*

Honey, P & Mumford, A (1992), *A Manual of Learning Styles* (3rd edition), Peter Honey, Maidenhead.

Jasper, C (2005), 'Pricing for more profit', *Business Essentials Quarterly,* (Feb-Apr).

Kotler, P(1965), 'Diagnosing the marketing takeover', *Harvard Business Review*, Nov-Dec.

Kotler, P (2002), *Marketing Management* (11th edition), US Imports and PHIPES.

Kotler, P; Armstrong, G; Meggs, D; Bradbury, E & Grech, J (1999), *Marketing: an Introduction*, Prentice Hall, Sydney.

Kotler, P; Gregor, W T & Rodgers, W H (1989), 'The Marketing Audit Comes of Age', *Sloan Management Review.*

Kotler, P; Roberto, E L & Lee, N (ed) (2002), *Social Marketing: Improving the Quality of Life (2nd edition),* Sage Publication.

Lancaster, G; Witney, F & Ashford, R (2001), *Marketing Fundamentals,* Butterworth-Heinemann, Oxford.

Lancaster, G & Witney, F (2005), *Marketing Fundamentals*, Elsevier Butterworth-Heinemann, Oxford.

Lanzillotti, R F (1989), *Phase II in Review: Price Commission Experience,* Brooking Inst.

Levitt, T (1986), *The Marketing Imagination,* Simon & Schuster Inc, New York.

Lloyd, S (2004), 'HP's Big Bank Theory, *BRW,* March 4-10 (26/8).

McDonald, H B (2002), *Marketing Plans: How to prepare them, how to use them*, Butterworth-Heinemann, Oxford.

Minkema, D (2002), 'Information Systems for Purchasing', in *Gower Handbook of Purchasing Management* (ed Frmer) (3rd edition), Gowe.

Mintzberg, H (1983), *Power In and Around Organisations*, Prentice Hall, Englewood Cliffs, NJ.

Morden, A T (1993), *Elements of Marketing*, Continuum International

Mullin, R (2002), *Direct Marketing*, Kogan Page, London.

Nordström, J & Ridderstråle, K (2001), *Funky Business,* FT Prentice Hall, Essex.

Overton, R (2002), *Customer Service*, Business Basics, Sydney.

Peppers, D & Rogers, M (1993), *The One-to-One Future: Building business relationships one customer at a time*, Piatkus

Peters, T J (1994), *Liberation Management*, Pan, New York.

Plummer, J (1974,) 'The Concept and Application of Lifestyle Segmentation', *Journal of Marketing*, January.

Porter, M (1998), *On Competition*, Harvard Business School Press, Boston, MA.

Postma, P (1999), *The New Marketing Era*, McGraw Hill, New York.

Powers, T L (1991), *Modern Business Marketing: A strategic planning approach to business and industrial markets,* West

Root, F R (1994), *Entry Strategies for International Markets*, Wiley

Ryan, C (2005), 'FMCG sector under pressure', *B&T,* 25 March 2005

Shimp, T A & Delozier (1998), *Promotion Management, Thomson Learning.*

Sledz, E (2004), 'Fast food on the menu in Poland', posted at www.tdctrade.com.mne on 09/03/04.

Stensholt, J (2004), 'Fast track to China', *BRW,* March 4-10 (26/8).

Sternberg, E (2000), *Just Business: Business Ethics in Action*, OUP, Oxford.

Wind, Y (1981), *Product Policy: Concepts, Methods & Strategies*, Addison Wesley

BPP LEARNING MEDIA

List of key concepts and Index

BPP
LEARNING MEDIA

BPP LEARNING MEDIA

REVIEW FORM & FREE PRIZE DRAW

All original review forms from the entire BPP range, completed with genuine comments, will be entered into one of two draws on 31 January 2008 and 31 July 2008. The names on the first four forms picked out on each occasion will be sent a cheque for £50.

Name: _____ Address: _____

_____

_____

How have you used this Text?
(Tick one box only)

☐ Self study (book only)

☐ On a course: college_____

☐ With BPP Home Study package

☐ Other _____

Why did you decide to purchase this Text?
(Tick one box only)

☐ Have used companion Kit

☐ Have used BPP Texts in the past

☐ Recommendation by friend/colleague

☐ Recommendation by a lecturer at college

☐ Saw advertising in journals

☐ Saw website

☐ Other _____

During the past six months do you recall seeing/receiving any of the following?
(Tick as many boxes as are relevant)

☐ Our advertisement in *Marketing Success*

☐ Our advertisement in *Marketing Business*

☐ Our brochure with a letter through the post

☐ Our brochure with *Marketing Business*

☐ Saw website

Which (if any) aspects of our advertising do you find useful?
(Tick as many boxes as are relevant)

☐ Prices and publication dates of new editions

☐ Information on product content

☐ Facility to order books off-the-page

☐ None of the above

Have you used the companion Practice & Revision Kit for this subject?   ☐ Yes   ☐ No

Your ratings, comments and suggestions would be appreciated on the following areas.

	Very useful	Useful	Not useful
Introductory section (How to use this text, study checklist, etc)	☐	☐	☐
Introduction	☐	☐	☐
Syllabus coverage	☐	☐	☐
Action Programmes and Marketing at Work examples	☐	☐	☐
Chapter roundups	☐	☐	☐
Quick quizzes	☐	☐	☐
Illustrative questions	☐	☐	☐
Content of suggested answers	☐	☐	☐
Index	☐	☐	☐
Structure and presentation	☐	☐	☐

	Excellent	Good	Adequate	Poor
Overall opinion of this Text	☐	☐	☐	☐

Do you intend to continue using BPP Study Texts/Kits/Passcards?   ☐ Yes   ☐ No

Please note any further comments and suggestions/errors on the reverse of this page.

Please return to: Jaitinder Gill, BPP Learning Media Ltd, FREEPOST, London, W12 8BR

REVIEW FORM & FREE PRIZE DRAW (continued)

Please note any further comments and suggestions/errors below.

FREE PRIZE DRAW RULES

1   Closing date for 31 January 2008 draw is 31 December 2007. Closing date for 31 July 2008 draw is 30 June 2008.

2   Restricted to entries with UK and Eire addresses only. BPP employees, their families and business associates are excluded.

3   No purchase necessary. Entry forms are available upon request from BPP Learning Media Ltd. No more than one entry per title, per person. Draw restricted to persons aged 16 and over.

4   Winners will be notified by post and receive their cheques not later than 6 weeks after the relevant draw date. List of winners will be supplied on request.

5   The decision of the promoter in all matters is final and binding. No correspondence will be entered into.